Cervantes' *Don Quixote*

THE OPEN YALE COURSES SERIES is designed to bring the depth and breadth of a Yale education to a wide variety of readers. Based on Yale's Open Yale Courses program (http://oyc.yale.edu), these books bring outstanding lectures by Yale faculty to the curious reader, whether student or adult. Covering a wide variety of topics across disciplines in the social sciences, physical sciences, and humanities, Open Yale Courses books offer accessible introductions at affordable prices.

The production of Open Yale Courses for the Internet was made possible by a grant from the William and Flora Hewlett Foundation.

RECENT TITLES
Paul H. Fry, *Theory of Literature*
Roberto González Echevarría, *Cervantes' "Don Quixote"*
Christine Hayes, *Introduction to the Bible*
Shelly Kagan, *Death*
Dale B. Martin, *New Testament History and Literature*
Giuseppe Mazzotta, *Reading Dante*
R. Shankar, *Fundamentals of Physics:*
    Mechanics, Relativity, and Thermodynamics
Ian Shapiro, *The Moral Foundations of Politics*
Steven B. Smith, *Political Philosophy*

Cervantes'
Don Quixote

ROBERTO GONZÁLEZ ECHEVARRÍA

Yale

UNIVERSITY PRESS

New Haven and London

Yale University Press books may be purchased in quantity for
educational, business, or promotional use. For information, please e-mail
sales.press@yale.edu (U.S. office) or sales@yaleup.co.uk (U.K. office).

Set in Minion Pro type by Newgen North America, Austin, Texas.
Printed and bound by CPI Group (UK) Ltd, Croydon, CR0 4YY

Library of Congress Cataloging-in-Publication Data
González Echevarría, Roberto.
Cervantes' Don Quixote / Roberto González Echevarría.
pages cm. — (Open Yale courses series)
Includes bibliographical references and index.
ISBN 978-0-300-19864-5 (pbk. : alk. paper)   1. Cervantes
Saavedra, Miguel de, 1547–1616. Don Quixote.   I. Title.
PQ6352.G65 2015
863'.3—dc23
2014031674

A catalogue record for this book is available from the British Library.

10 9 8 7 6 5 4 3 2 1

To my Yale College students,
for and with whom this course was created

Contents

Preface

This book was originally a lecture course for Yale undergraduates, which I have offered for many years through the Literature Major (Comparative Literature) and the Department of Spanish and Portuguese. This accounts for its containing some information that Hispanists in particular will find to be of an introductory nature. It also explains its occasional avuncular tone, which I tried to eliminate in the revision but traces of which inevitably remain. In my commentaries on Cervantes, however, I have endeavored to offer original insights; new slants on his life and works and even daring fresh interpretations. Yale undergraduates are sharp and willing to experiment, and I try to find ways of making accessible even the most complicated approaches, in the classroom and in my critical and scholarly work. Obscure critical jargon is not my style. I hope the general reader, to whom this book is aimed, finds my commentaries and arguments informative, illuminating, and compelling. I trust there is enough innovation in the book that I should not be embarrassed by specialists reading it.

Cervantes scholars will soon discover that I often summarize and even quote verbatim some of my earlier work on the *Quixote* and *The Exemplary Novels,* particularly from my *Love and Law in Cervantes* but also from my *Cervantes' Don Quixote: A Casebook.* I could not do otherwise; my teaching and scholarship are intimately intertwined, feeding off one another. Besides, I feel that in glossing my own work I am not just repeating it but refining it.

I have used John Rutherford's translation in the Penguin Classics edition with some resignation. It is good enough and it is prefaced by my introduction, which I naturally prefer to those of others. There is no exceptional translation of the *Quixote.* My favorite is Tobias Smollett's because he was a writer, not a former or current literature professor. But Smollett's somewhat archaic tone may put off some contemporary readers. Much is lost in the translations, anyway; first and foremost the contrasts between the speech of Sancho and other lower-class characters and that of Don Quixote. Cervantes is a virtuoso of dialectal forms. In any case, I am not a reader of translations, except when there is no alternative, as with the Greek classics and the Russian novelists. I have devoted a lifetime of work to be able to read with ease all the major works in the Romance languages, particularly French and

Italian but also Portuguese and others, in the original. I am not a believer in Jorge Luis Borges's quip about translations sometimes being better than the original texts. I do not think he believed in it either. He labored hard to read the Icelandic sagas in their language, and he was quite proficient in (at least) English, French, Italian, and German.

My native and dominant language is Spanish, and I consider myself part of the critical and prose tradition of that language, in which I have published not a small amount of scholarly work, essays, and some journalism. I am Cuban, therefore a Latin American, and since my childhood as a faculty brat I have been surrounded by Spanish and Latin American literature. The reader of this book may find traces of this determining linguistic foundation in my American English. I am not a Spaniard, however, though Spain has become for me like a second motherland, and I have often taught, lectured, and lived in Spain, for the most part in Madrid and Salamanca. What this means is that I have a perspective on Cervantes that is from within his language but not from inside the nationalist obsessions that have beset criticism of his works since the eighteenth century. I am happy to report that this trend has abated in the recent past, but also unhappy to report that Cervantes is not read much in Spain anymore, particularly in the schools and by young people.

I have read and corrected the transcriptions of the lectures that make up this book, trying to prune as much of the personal inflections as possible. I have cut out anecdotes, a few jokes, asides, and other matters that the reader will not enjoy, although I hope my students did in the classroom. A course, I realize now more than ever, is very much influenced by the personality of the professor, who with his rhetoric and body language establishes communication with the students in a way that cannot be captured on the printed page or even in a videotape. This is why I believe there is no substitute for the classroom when it comes to education, particularly in the humanities. But the Open Yale Courses and other projects at various institutions are valuable approximations that have the virtue of reaching many people all over the world. I receive countless e-mails from individuals in faraway places who have followed my course.

Acknowledgments

Matthew Tanico, a graduate student in the Department of Spanish and Portuguese at Yale, helped me in every conceivable way to transform the transcripts of the lectures that make up my course on Cervantes' *Quixote* into the manuscript of this book. He also very ably took care of permissions for the illustrations. I have no way of properly thanking Matthew for his diligence, efficiency, and complicity in the preparation of the book. Lawrence Kenney, copyeditor extraordinaire, did his usual wonderful job of shaping up my English prose. Professor Diana E. E. Kleiner of our Department of the History of Art, the organizer of Yale Open Courses, selected my "Cervantes' *Don Quixote*" to be included in that program. Diana was also an enthusiastic supporter of the course as it was being videotaped and often had some of her assistants attend my lectures. She is the source of this book, and I want to thank her for it.

My colleague Rolena Adorno, of the Department of Spanish and Portuguese, which she chairs, was, as always, willing to listen to my ideas with a critical ear and a cheerful disposition. Professor Giuseppe Mazzotta, of the Department of Italian and one of my closest friends and collaborators, was also very helpful. I watched every class of his Open Yale Course on Dante for inspiration and consulted him at every step. Undergraduate students have over the years made valuable suggestions and criticisms that I have, consciously or not, incorporated, and I want to express my gratitude for their acumen and enthusiasm in making their observations. The teaching assistants in the course also made their contributions, not infrequently with useful reflections and criticisms and also by reporting the feedback from students in their discussion sections. At the risk of omitting one of them, here are their names in alphabetical order: Anke Birkenmaier, Antonio Carreño-Rodríguez, Jennifer Darrell, Isabel Jaen Portillo, Heather Klemman, Dina Odnopozova, Elena Pellús, Charlotte Rogers, Meg Weisberg, and María Wilsted. Dina and Elena were the teaching assistants during the semester that the course was recorded but refused steadfastly to appear on camera.

I must also mention the many individuals from around the world who have followed my online course and written to me with comments and suggestions; I could not possibly list their names here, but their interest has been a continuing source of satisfaction and inspiration.

A Note on the Texts

Four texts were required for students enrolled in my course on Cervantes'
Don Quixote:

> Miguel de Cervantes. *Exemplary Stories.* Translated by Lesley
> Lipton. Oxford: Oxford University Press, 1998.
> Miguel de Cervantes Saavedra. *The Ingenious Hidalgo Don
> Quixote de la Mancha.* Translated by John Rutherford. Introduc-
> tion by Roberto González Echevarría. New York: Penguin, 2001.
> J. H. Elliott. *Imperial Spain: 1469–1716.* New York: Penguin,
> 1990.
> Roberto González Echevarría, ed. *Cervantes' Don Quixote: A
> Casebook.* New York: Oxford University Press, 2005.

The assigned readings from each of these texts are listed at the beginning
of each chapter. For the readings from the *Quixote,* the part and chapter
numbers are given along with the page numbers to assist readers who may
be using another edition.

CHAPTER 1

Introduction

Why Read the *Quixote*?

In this course we are going to read one of the unquestioned masterpieces of world literature, a work translated into dozens of languages. Cervantes' book has given pleasure to generations of readers and is in the curriculum of many schools and universities. In addition, I anticipate that the *Quixote* will affect your lives, not just your understanding and enjoyment of fiction. Cervantes' book is the first modern novel, one which already contains, according to Gabriel García Márquez, the Nobel Prize–winning Colombian novelist, everything that novelists would attempt to do in the future. Cervantes' fans have been many and very illustrious. The young Sigmund Freud formed a Cervantes club with his friends, and the *Quixote* was Jorge Luis Borges's obsession. Borges, as you may know, was the great Argentine writer, the author of *Ficciones* (1944). Ian Watt, the late British scholar, considered *Don Quixote* "one of four myths of modern individualism," the others being Faust, Don Juan, and Robinson Crusoe in works by, respectively, Goethe, Tirso de Molina, and Daniel Defoe.[1] But this is not the most important thing about the book.

The *Quixote* has been and continues to be read by millions of readers all around the world, and we will be asking ourselves why that is so. What is it that this book has that is so appealing to so many? I myself have answered the question in this fashion in the introduction to the Penguin Classics edition we will be using:

Miguel de Cervantes Saavedra's masterpiece has endured because it focuses on literature's foremost appeal: to become another, to leave a typically embattled self for another closer to one's desires and aspirations. This is why *Don Quixote* has often been read as a children's book and continues to be read by or to children. Experience and life's blows teach us our limits and erode the hope of living up to our dreams, but our hope never vanishes. It is the soul's pith, the flickering light of being, the spiritual counterpart to our DNA's master code. When the hero regains his sanity at the end of Part II, he dies. As the last chances of living an imaginary life disappear, so must life itself. Don Quixote's serene passing reflects this understanding; he knows that the dream of life is over, and as a Neoplatonist and Christian, his only hope now is to find the true life after death.[2]

For you, reading the *Quixote* will be an event you will always remember, and Don Quixote and Sancho, his squire, will become lifelong friends about whom you will think often. I can predict that safely—I think. In addition, the depth and enduring fame and currency of Cervantes' masterpiece are partly due to the rare combination of contrasting features that make up its protagonist. Rabelais's and Molière's grand comic characters are ultimately serious or funny. Shakespeare's tragic heroes Macbeth, Lear, and above all Hamlet are more complicated, and they awe us still with their dramatic dilemmas and the drastic solutions they take. But there is rarely anything comic, much less ridiculous, about them. Shakespeare saves his humor for his comical characters, like Falstaff. Cervantes, on the other hand, endows Don Quixote with both seriousness of the highest order and comicalness of the lowest. Sancho possesses both qualities, too, though in different doses. Cervantes offered modern readers a potential image of themselves that included the ridiculous as well as the sublime, a poignant, modern sense of self that did not appear again until Franz Kafka's *Metamorphosis*. We are all Don Quixote when we look into the mirror.

So, what is, after all, the *Quixote*? A novel, you will say. Well, first of all, the *Quixote*, if it is a novel at all, is two novels: one published in 1605, and the other in 1615. Together, they are known as the *Quixote*—much more about the title in a minute—and knowledgeable people refer to them as Part I and Part II, or the 1605 *Quixote* and the 1615 *Quixote*. So the first thing to learn—I like first things because I like to build on them from the ground up—is that the *Quixote* consists of two parts originally published separately ten years apart. But what Cervantes wrote, though considered the first modern novel, was not a novel as we know them today because novels did not exist as such yet. Novels developed in the wake of the *Quixote,* so Cervantes could not have set out to write a novel.

In Cervantes' time there were chivalric romances, stories about knights-errant—a lot more about that in the very near future—pastoral romances, stories about fake shepherds, picaresque lives—what we call today confusedly picaresque novels—and brief *nouvelle* or *novelle,* that is, long short stories, of which Cervantes wrote quite a few and very good ones. We will read some in this course. The modern novel would evolve from translations and imitations of the *Quixote,* particularly in France and England, and would attain its current form in the eighteenth century. I am very much a historian, and I would like for you to have a clear historical, chronological idea of the development of the novel and of Cervantes' own career, so take note of these chronological clarifications that I give you.

Now, what might you know about the *Quixote*? Many of you, I suppose, come to this course intrigued by the name of an author and the title of a book that you may have heard about but that, like most classics, you have not actually read in its entirety, much less studied. As is true of most classics, you have probably heard so much about the *Quixote* that it feels as if you had already read it. Many have heard the songs from *Man of La Mancha.* "The Impossible Dream" and so forth; perhaps you have even seen the show. It is quite a good show, by the way. I do not look down on it. It is a version of the *Quixote* in an American mode, very much an American mode, but a good one. So, many of you have seen *Man of La Mancha,* have heard the songs, and maybe you have even read a comic book based on the novel. Others may have read parts of it in high school; some of you may have read it in a course like Directed Studies, in conjunction with other Western classics, such as the *Odyssey,* the *Aeneid,* and the *Divine Comedy.* Whatever the case may be, most of you are probably puzzled by the spelling and pronunciation of the protagonist's name and the title of the book. Let me clarify those as a modest beginning, the first step having been to tell you that the *Quixote* is two novels. Now, the second step is to tell you about the name of the protagonist and how to pronounce it and how we pronounce it in Spanish and how it is spelled and why.

The way to pronounce it in modern Spanish is Quihote, *kee-ho-te.* No gliding to the *o.* No *kee-hoe-tay.* In Spanish we do not glide the vowels; they are short and crisp. Why, then, that vexing *x* in English? The reason is that when the book was written in the last years of the sixteenth century and the first of the seventeenth, the sound of the *j* in Spanish was still in the process of moving from the *sh* sound that it had thanks to the influence of Arabic—more about that later—toward the aspirated *h* of modern Spanish. That *sh* sound was then written with an *x* in the still-to-be-codified spelling of the language. The spelling of modern European languages was not codified until the eighteenth century. For instance, the modern word for soap, in Spanish—many of you who know some Spanish know it—*jabón*, was written then with an *x* and it was pronounced *shabón*. *México* was pronounced *Méshico* and was spelled with an *x*, and that *x* is still retained, though in Spanish it is pronounced *Mé-hi-co*, never *Mé-shi-co*. The book was translated into English very early. It was published in 1605, and the first translation appeared in 1612; seven years is very fast in the seventeenth century. So the English, seeing that *x*, in the middle of the title, mispronounced it *quic-sote*, giving it a sound it never had in Spanish. That is why you have the *x* in English and the mispronunciation *Quixote*. The French, meanwhile, hearing that *sh*, rendered it *qui-sho-t*, which is still the way they mispronounce it. The French call it Don Quishot. I will always say "Quijote" and hope you will learn to do the same from now on, at the risk of sounding a little snobbish to English speakers.

Let me give you a few more basic facts about the title of the book. The title of a book or a painting is like the first interpretation by its author. It is what we would call today in literary criticism a metatext, a text above the text. Sometimes titles can be misleading, but they are always interesting and should be examined carefully, making sure that you gain access to the full title of the first edition, not one that has been tampered with by editors or the reading public later. For instance, *Pickwick Papers*, the novel by Dickens, was really called *The Posthumous Papers of the Pickwick Club*, and it is interesting why it is called that. Now, be careful also with the translations of titles because sometimes they are very misleading. A novel by Alejo Carpentier called *El Siglo de las Luces* was translated as *Explosion in the Cathedral* because the editors thought that a true translation, *The Age of Enlightenment*, would sound like the title of a textbook. You have to be careful; if you are going to really read the title carefully you should go to the original title.

The full title of the first part of *Don Quixote*—remember, published in 1605; I want to engrave that date on your mind—is as follows: *El ingenioso hidalgo don Qvixote de la Mancha*. You know that the *u* was rendered then as a *v*. So, *El ingenioso hidalgo don Qvixote de la Mancha*. Here is a reproduction of the actual title page of the first *Quixote* (fig. 1). We are fortunate to have a copy of that first edition at the Beinecke Library here at Yale.

Figure 1. Title page of the 1605 edition of Miguel de Cervantes,
El ingenioso hidalgo don Qvixote de la Mancha. General Collection,
Beinecke Rare Book and Manuscript Library, Yale University.

Let us go over those words one by one. I can assure you we are not going to go over every word in the book one by one as I am going to do with
the title, or it would take the rest of our lives to finish reading the *Quixote*
together! *Ingenioso* here does not mean exactly what it means in Spanish today. Today *ingenioso* means something like 'sharp,' 'witty,' 'cute,' or 'inventive.'
In 1611 Covarrubias writes—now, Covarrubias is a name you are going to be
hearing throughout the semester. His name was Sebastián de Covarrubias y
Horozco. He was a lexicographer who in 1611 published the first dictionary
of the Spanish language, called *Tesoro de la lengua castellana o española,*
or "Thesaurus of the Castilian or Spanish Language." It is very convenient
that Covarrubias published that dictionary in 1611, right between the two
parts of the *Quixote*, 1605 and 1615; Covarrubias gives us Cervantes' Spanish. This is why it is such an important book for the reading of Cervantes'
Don Quixote. The title itself is interesting because it shows that Castilian and
Spanish are one and the same thing. I will talk about that a little more later.

Covarrubias writes the following about *ingenio:* "We commonly call *ingenio* a natural force of the mind that inquires that which through reason and intelligence can be found through all sorts of sciences, disciplines, liberal and mechanical arts, subtle inventions and deceit. Hence, we call engineer [*ingeniero*] he who builds machines to fight off the enemy and to attack him. *Ingenioso* is he who has a subtle and sharp wit."[3] So, *ingenioso* in the title of the *Quixote* means a heightened kind of wit or understanding, one that verges on madness, recalling what Plato said in the *Republic* about poets being slightly mad. In 1575, a few years before the publication of the *Quixote* (and within Cervantes' lifetime), Juan Huarte de San Juan, a medical doctor, published an important book called *Examen de ingenios para las ciencias.* "Wits Examined" would be the translation of that title, in which he studies different kinds of madness. *Examen de ingenios* meant an examination of various kinds of madness of the kind that Covarrubias mentioned. This gives you the context of the word *ingenioso* in the title *El ingenioso hidalgo don Qvixote de la Mancha.*

Now, *hidalgo* is a contraction of *hijo de algo,* which in Spanish means 'son of something.' We are all sons or daughters of something. But what that meant was if you are an hidalgo you are the son of someone of some distinction, of a worthy lineage, and Covarrubias, again, says it means "the same as noble, with an ancient pure lineage."[4]

In other words, pure of cast, of origin, of ilk, of tradition. An hidalgo, as you will discover in reading the first chapter of the book, is a petty nobleman, someone belonging to the lower nobility or aristocracy. Here, Cervantes does not call Don Quixote a *caballero,* a knight. The novel is, at its most basic level, the story of a petty nobleman who becomes, by dint of his own self-invention, a knight worthy of using the *Don* that is given in the title. In 1615, however, in the second part of the *Quixote*—we will look at that title page when we come to it—Don Quixote is called a *caballero* for a variety of reasons I will explain at the proper time.

Now, *don* is a form of address, like 'sir' or 'sire,' that not everyone had a right to expect. Don Quixote, that is, Alonso Quixano, the man who became Don Quixote, did not, by virtue of his modest station in life, but he takes on the *don* as part of his self-invention. Hidalgos, in other words, did not have the right to the *don; Don* derives from the Latin *dominus,* 'sir,' 'lord,' 'master.' Your readings in Elliott, *Imperial Spain,* one of the books for the course, will give you much further background on this.

Quijote, as you will learn in reading the first chapters of the book, is said to be a derivation of *quijada,* 'jaw,' or *quesada,* something having to do with cheese, or *quejana,* something having to do with complaint. It is said that *Quijano* or *quijana* could be the last name of Alonso Quixano, the hidalgo who turns himself into Don Quixote. These names echo those words mentioned before, *quijada, quesada,* and so forth. They are not high-sounding or ennobling words. Quite the contrary.

The *–ote* ending is a suffix that in Spanish always refers to something base or grotesque and sounds it: *gordote,* from *gordo,* is a fatso; *grandote,* from *grande,* is a hulking big guy, a lummox; *feote,* from *feo,* is an ugly cuss; so *Quijote,* then, was meant to sound abasing and ridiculous, particularly when paired with don, with which it forms a kind of oxymoronic pair, Don Quijote. *Don* is high sounding, and *Quixote* has all of these negative connotations. It also has echoes of *Lanzarote,* one of the knights-errant Don Quixote reads about, and it has also been discovered that *quijote* is the name of a part of the armor covering the leg. But the important background is what I gave before.

La Mancha is a region in central Spain, in Castile, that encompasses parts of the provinces of Toledo, Ciudad Real, Cuenca, and Albacete. Geography is very important in the *Quixote,* particularly in Part II. This is a novel that is deeply rooted in a given landscape. La Mancha is flat, arid, and monotonous. Its main products used to be cereals and wine, but the important thing here is that it is not—at least it was not until Cervantes' work—a particularly desirable place to be from. *Mancha* also means 'stain' in Spanish. It sounds like a put down. Being from La Mancha was like being from Bridgeport or Buffalo or Brooklyn or Podunk. This has all changed in light of the book, and now the name and the region have a poetic air, and there are theme parks in La Mancha with windmills and all. But that was not what Cervantes intended when he had Don Quixote be from La Mancha. His hidalgo was to be in contrast to knights who came from more distinguished places, Amadís de Gaula, from Gaul, or Palmerín de Inglaterra, from England, and then, Don Quixote de la Mancha. You see, this is what is supposed to be meant by the title. You would not have suspected this if I had not told you because you are still under the influence of *Man of La Mancha.*

The issue of Don Quixote's spurious *don* is significant in a broader historical sense. By the sixteenth century the glory days of the nobility were long gone. Noblemen were no longer much engaged in the military, except at the highest ranks, which never saw actual combat. Wars were fought by professional armies. There was little chance for the nobility to exercise martial-like activities, which were now played out in jousts and in hunting. War became sports for the aristocracy. The nobility was, on the whole, in a downturn in Spain because of policies initiated by the Catholic Kings, Ferdinand and Isabella, to curtail the power of the aristocracy. Certain groups at the highest level that clustered around the courts of the descendants of the Catholic Kings had a lot of power, but on the whole the nobility was on the decline, more noticeably so in La Mancha, which had a sparse population of hidalgos as opposed to northern regions of the peninsula. So, for Don Quixote to practice *caballería,* knight-errantry, was a way of reviving the past, of reliving a past of splendor and glory, now only really available through reading the chivalric romances, which portrayed a medieval world in which the aristocracy was truly involved in warfare, or through sports like hunting—of which Don Quixote was fond, as you will learn in the early chapters of the book. We will have much more on chivalric romances, as I promised, in the future.

What about the language of the *Quixote*? In what language did Cervantes write? You say, in Spanish; yes, but we are in the sixteenth, seventeenth century. In the sixteenth century Spanish was undergoing its last significant linguistic revolution, its last significant change. At the time the *Quixote* was written and published, pronoun and verb forms were still in relative flux. But Cervantes' Spanish does not sound as archaic and arcane to the modern Spanish ear as Shakespearean English does to modern English readers. I sometimes have a difficult time understanding Shakespeare on the stage with my American English. The Spanish of Cervantes does sound quaint, and the book's fame gives Cervantes' Spanish a formal sound today that it did not have to its contemporaries, for whom the book was not yet, of course, a classic.

If read out loud, the *Quixote* is more comprehensible to current speakers of Spanish from Spain and Latin America than *Hamlet* is to a modern British or American audience. But what language was it that Cervantes used? Well, he wrote in Castilian, or Spanish, which are the same, as we learn in Covarrubias's title. Americans have the mistaken notion that people speak Castilian in Spain, and they do not know what in Latin America. But it is the same language. Castilian was the language of Castile, land of castles, because as the Reconquest—you will learn what the Reconquest is, that is, the reconquest of Spain from the Moors—advanced in central Spain, as this Reconquest advanced, castles were built to secure the territories; hence, Castile. And then Castile became, as you will read in Elliott, the most influential political and military region in the entire peninsula, and with the unification of the peninsula under the Catholic Kings it tried to impose its language on the rest of Spain. Do you know what the difference between a language and a dialect is? A language is a dialect with an army, so a language is the language of a region with enough power to impose it on other people. There were—and are—other languages in Spain: Catalan, Galician, Basque, Valencian. But the Catholic Kings and their descendants imposed Castilian on the peninsula as much as they could and also on the vast territories of the New World, what is today Latin America, because the discovery and conquest were mainly Castilian projects. As a result of these policies Spanish is more uniform today than English is. What is spoken in the Bronx, Mexico City, and Madrid? Castilian, which is Spanish, is spoken in those places. You can erase that American prejudice from your mind if you ever had it.

If Spanish was undergoing its last major transformation in the sixteenth century, this was also a turbulent century for Spain in political, religious, social, and artistic terms. Consider that in the sixteenth century Spain settled the New World and beyond, the Philippines, and organized a vast imperial bureaucracy to rule it. Spain also controlled parts of Italy and the Low Countries and was itself adjusting to the unification brought about by the marriage of Ferdinand and Isabella, she from Castile, he from Aragon. They created the first modern state—by the way, you will find in the *Quixote* characters that come from various regions of Spain, most memorably, at the very beginning, a Basque who speaks broken Spanish because, even today, there are regions in Spain (as you know if you have been to Spain), where Spanish is really not the language spoken; in Galicia, the Basque countries, and Catalonia, and so on.

In the religious sphere, Spain became the defender of the Catholic Church, which was breaking up in the rest of Europe as a result of the Reformation. Remember, the Reformation is a sixteenth-century event, Spain was the bastion of orthodox Catholicism, and this tremendously affected its political, social, and literary life. In 1492 the Catholic Kings expelled the Jews from Spain and then, by 1614, the Moriscos, the descendants of the Arabs who were still left in the peninsula. There are distinct echoes of all of these processes and political events in the novel.

One could say that the *Quixote* is not only the first modern novel but also the first political novel in that it reflects very clearly the political controversies of its time. In the social domain there was a major population drain to the New World and social mobility caused by the deliberate erosion of the aristocracy by a Crown bent on centralization and control. You will find as you read the book that the characters move through areas that are depopulated, and this reflects the demographic reality. The new bureaucracy provided ways to attain wealth and power that threatened the status of the old, powerful aristocratic families as well as the traditional independence of provinces and fiefdoms that dated back to the Middle Ages.

In the literary world, Spain's greatest splendor came at this moment, in the waning of the Renaissance, with the emergence of new, modern forms and genres. The sixteenth century actually opened just before the sixteenth century, in 1499, with the publication of *Celestina,* and this was followed by the emergence of the picaresque in *El Lazarillo de Tormes. Lazarillo de Tormes* was the first picaresque novel, published in 1554. There also emerged what came to be known as the Spanish *comedia* in the theater. These were not all comedies, but they were called *comedias.* They were written first and foremost by Lope de Vega, a name you might want to keep in mind because he was a prolific writer who was also Cervantes' rival. He may have written several hundred plays. How many did Shakespeare write? Thirty-some? Lope was an amazing writer, and Cervantes had a tense relationship with him.

In poetry, the sixteenth century saw Garcilaso de la Vega, a name you will see in the *Quixote* many times, and his many followers, the late, great blossoming of the Petrarchan tradition, and the development from that Petrarchan tradition of a powerful strain of mystical poetry, particularly in the verse of Saint John of the Cross. So the sixteenth and seventeenth centuries are what are called in Spanish literary history the Golden Age. It was also a golden age in painting. If you have been to the Prado Museum in Madrid, you will see what I mean, and we will be talking a great deal about Spanish painting here, particularly about Diego Velázquez.

Our brief philological excursion into the title of the book reveals a number of things about the *Quixote* and about Spain. You may wonder, Arabic? What do the Arabs have to do with Spain? Well, the Arabs occupied Spain for eight centuries, from 711—these are good dates to remember—to 1492, when Granada, the last bastion of Arab power in Spain, fell to Ferdinand and Isabella. The Arabs left an indelible mark on Spanish history, culture, and language. It was not an occupation in the sense that we envision occupations in the modern period. Historians speak of a *convivencia,* that is, a living together of these Christian and Muslim cultures, which involved fighting with each other but also fighting among the Christians, and Muslims allied with Christians and living alongside each other for eight centuries. One could say that the Arabic component in the broader sense is the main difference between Spain and the rest of Europe. The title of the *Quixote* alludes to that difference by means of that *x,* but you will see it in many other ways as you read.

You can also glean from what I have said that the *Quixote* was translated very early into other European languages: 1612 for English, and it went on to be translated later into French and so forth. The *Quixote*, that first edition of 1605, rapidly became a European best seller, turning Cervantes, who was a minor figure, as you will read in the assigned readings from my Oxford *Casebook*, suddenly into a great success. It never brought him the financial rewards he desperately needed, but it turned him into a literary celebrity of sorts.

They say that in the beginning the *Quixote* was read almost universally as a funny book. This is obviously a misreading; it is much more than just a funny book. Now, let us return to basics about the title and to the protagonist's name in English. All of you, no doubt, have read or heard the word *quixotic* and surely have a general notion of its meaning. Someone who is a Quixote, says the *Oxford English Dictionary*, is "an enthusiastic visionary person like Don Quijote or Don Quixote, inspired by lofty and chivalrous but also unrealizable ideas." Hence, to be quixotic is to strive with lofty enthusiasm for visionary ideas. How many authors or books or characters have entered common usage in this way? Actions or people can be Dantesque, Kafkaesque, Rabelaisian, but are any of these as common as quixotic? *Dantesque* always refers to the *Inferno* and conveys a sense of gloom, of fire burning sinners—all of that is Dantesque. *Kafkaesque* describes the situation in which a labyrinth of forces appears to control your life, and it is applied mostly to bureaucracies. Yale's bureaucracy is becoming Kafkaesque, I can assure you of that. *Rabelaisian*, less common, means uncontrollable appetites, most of the time referring to gluttony: He had a Rabelaisian dinner. But you risk really sounding snobbish if you say you had a Rabelaisian dinner, but not when saying quixotic; *quixotic* is really part of the common usage.

I bet any one of you, if pressed, could give a *TV Guide* abstract of the book, even those who have not read a word of it. It would go something like this—I made this up: "Middle-aged man believes he can become a knight-errant like those he has read about in chivalric romances and takes to the road with Sancho, a peasant, as his squire to set the world aright, suffers many defeats but remains unbowed." That is the whole novel, right there, encapsulated. I have the fantasy that you can do that with any book, no matter how complicated. Try it with the Bible or the *Odyssey* or something like that. But I think with the *Quixote* it works, and that is what people have in their imaginations about the *Quixote*. General knowledge of this kind is the aura that surrounds most classics. Hence it can be a temptation not to read them. As a result, this sort of vague knowledge also has an undeniable influence on those who eventually read them. It is nearly impossible to read a classic innocently, unless you are a complete illiterate. Besides, you have read the *Quixote* if you have read *The Adventures of Huckleberry Finn* or if you have read *Madame Bovary* or if you have read Kafka's *Metamorphosis* because the influence of the *Quixote* in all of those works is so great that, in a sense, you have read it through them. Very few literary characters have this aura. I wonder which: Hamlet, of course, Faust, remembering what Ian Watt said, King Lear, Don Juan, Oedipus come to mind. Can you think of any others? There are few in each literary tradition. For instance, Huckleberry Finn in the American context and Jean Valjean, perhaps, in France.

Why is it that *Don Quixote* has such currency as a kind of literary myth? I think there is hardly another secular book to which we come with more preconceived notions and expectations. It is also one of the very few great works of world literature that is also a children's book. I read it first, it was read to me, as a children's book the first time. Is it akin to a modern secular Bible? Miguel de Unamuno, the Spanish philosopher, read the *Quixote* as if it were a kind of secular Bible. It is a kind of new gospel, a gospel for the modern age. Why not? You have to get something out of the *Quixote* that is relevant to your own lives, I think, or you are going to be wasting your time here, believe me. I cannot tell you what that is; you will have to find out for yourself. Can it not suggest something relevant to you? Why has it for so many over so many years?

I gave my own explanation in that first paragraph to my introduction to the Penguin Classics that I quoted before, but let me give a more detailed one here. Whatever other, more subtle and specialized answers we give to this question throughout the semester, the only way to respond to it is to say that the *Quixote* embodies the most modern of predicaments: the individual's dissatisfaction with the world in which he lives, and his struggle to make the world and his desires mesh. I mean *this* world, not a world yet to come, a promised heaven.

Why is this a modern predicament or crisis? Because the world is no longer a given by the time Cervantes writes. The Western conception of the universe, which up to about the sixteenth century was largely based on a combination of Aristotle and the Bible, that is to say, scholasticism and the work of Thomas Aquinas, has been proven faulty. Think of one major change: the first part of the *Quixote* is published in 1605, barely over a hundred years after the discovery of America—one hundred and thirteen, to be exact—and the confirmation that the world is round, which proved beyond argument or doubt that much of the legacy of the ancient world in the Middle Ages was open to question. Think of a second major change: the Reformation had challenged the authority of the Catholic Church and made political gains in many important European nations. Don Quixote is not a struggle between the individual and the gods, a fight against cosmic abstract forces, as in Greek tragedy; it is not, as in Dante, human desire transformed into the yearning for a sublime, transcendental vision cast in a universe of perfect coherence. It is, instead, the struggle of an individual against the intractability of a world in which he lives, a world redolent with the imperfections of the material, caught in a temporal flow that carries it further and further away from ideals that seem to exist only in the individual's mind. As Hamlet says, "The time is out of joint; o cursèd spite, / That ever I was born to set it right!"

This is what Don Quixote says, too. "The novel," says György Lukács, the Hungarian critic, "is the epic of a world that has been abandoned by God." He goes on: "The novel's hero's psychology is demonic. The objectivity of the novel is the mature man's knowledge, that meaning can never quite penetrate reality, but that without meaning reality would disintegrate into the inessential, into the nothingness of inessentiality."[5] This is the very abstract language of Lukács, who was a neo-Kantian, but I think the important thing to remember from this is that it is a world abandoned by God. It is not a God-centered world anymore, as in Dante, that the *Quixote* moves through.

There are other, less abstract definitions of the *Quixote*, global definitions I am fond of. One by Lowry Nelson reads as follows: "In crudest terms, the formula [of *Don Quixote*] may be expressed as the pairing of a tall thin idealist with a short fat realist and setting them off on a series of hazards. In previous fiction pairs of characters had almost always been young friends or lovers, at least normal, but most often exemplary. . . . This new, however simple, arrangement, together with the motif of bad literature influencing life, constitutes a primal and influential glory for Cervantes."[6]

A corollary issue to the question of the individual's maladjustment to the world is another crucial modern concern: the perception of reality and the organization of that perception into something that can be considered the truth. Modern criticism has labeled this in the *Quixote* as perspectivism. The interpretation of reality depends on the perspective of the individual, meaning, in gross terms, that one's interpretation of the world is colored by one's background, station in life, readings, desires, and experience in general. There is a hilarious series of episodes in which Don Quixote takes a basin from a barber, puts it on his head, and says that it is Mambrino's helmet, a famous helmet from the epic tradition. And in one of the episodes at the inn there ensues a scholastic-like discussion about whether this thing is a basin or a helmet, which is a funny reenactment of the issue of perspectivism: what for Don Quixote is a helmet to others is a barber's basin. This idea of the various perspectives is at the core of much of the humor in the book. Don Quixote sees giants, and Sancho sees windmills, and this clash repeats itself throughout the book. But this points to a highly important issue at the beginning of modern philosophy, one having to do precisely with the perspective of the individual on reality, and not a perspective that has to be determined by received ideas.

CHAPTER 2

Chivalric Romances and Picaresque Novels

Antecedents of the *Quixote*

Required Readings

Cervantes, *Don Quixote*, Part I, Prologue, chaps. 1–10, pp. 11–82.
Elliott, *Imperial Spain*, 15–44.

I want to begin by taking up some general questions concerning the *Quixote*, matters such as the difference between romance and novel and others such as what is a chivalric romance? Because you hear a lot about it, I am sure, but few people know what a chivalric romance was. I also want to consider who the Spanish precursors of Cervantes were because I want to, as much as possible, although in English, give you a Cervantes in his own sauce, in his own *salsa,* as it were, that is, within the Spanish tradition as well as a European one. But I will begin by elaborating on the issue of why the *Quixote* has continued to be read, why it has had such common currency. I just learned yesterday that the detainees at Guantánamo, Cuba, asked first for the *Quixote,* of all the books they wanted to read.

I have offered the most common of answers about why the *Quixote* is so current, the least specialized one. But *Don Quixote* is notoriously about literature, covering the entire range of *about.* First and foremost, it is about the effect that literature has on its readers. Don Quixote goes mad because he reads too much literature. Literature, fiction, allows us to rehearse in private our most secret desires, affecting our lives as if these desires had become true. It is like dreams. Dreams have the same effect. This is the allure of literature and also its danger. We can live lives other than ours full of adventures, untrammeled by society's constraints and by our own limitations. Does doing that purge us of those desires? or does it induce more desires and inflame the desire to close the gap between desire and reality? But the *Quixote* is, in addition, about the creation of literature, the relationship each text has with previous texts, as well as about questions of literary genre.

The *Quixote* appears at the end of the Renaissance, when improvements to the printing press had created mass readership—nothing compared to what we have today, but mass readership for the first time in history—and when the discovery, analysis, and imitation of classical treatises on poetics had brought to the fore questions about content and form as well as about ethics, public and private. The Renaissance humanists were interested in the classics, in reading the classics in the original, in translating and editing the classics to make them available to more readers.

What is secular literature good for? What is good literature? How do new ideas about reading and writing affect the interpretation of scripture? Is secular literature in the vernacular a danger to religious faith? The *Quixote* is full of writers and readers—you will meet them as you read the book—of books, stories, poems and also of people young and old affected by literature. You will meet two of them, Marcela and Grisóstomo, very early.

In this question about the *Quixote* and the issue of literature is lodged the originality of the book. The fact is that Cervantes' masterpiece does not belong to any known tradition or cycle, be it the pastoral or the chivalric, not to mention popular narratives or even mythology. The *Quixote* is not based on a classical myth or a traditional story handed down orally; it is a new story. Indeed, Cervantes boasts that it is new. It is no small accomplishment to set out to write a narrative without precedence, to make individual invention a fundamental factor of a literary work. The *Divine Comedy* tells an original story, yet it is based on received popular and cultural traditions, the descent to hell, ascent to heaven, and it recalls and incorporates many stories from biblical and classical traditions. The *Decameron* by Boccaccio retells tales drawn from many popular and cultural sources, too. The same goes for the pastoral and the chivalric romances, about which I will be speaking soon. But the story of a man who goes mad because he reads too much has only one known source, and it is so trifling as to be easily dismissed, although the fact that it exists is of some importance. The very act of invention on Cervantes' part is an important modern component of the work. Invention is the hallmark of modern literature.

How could such a revolutionary work appear in Spain? I am sorry to make this assumption, but your conception of Spain cannot be but the result of the Black Legend. What is the Black Legend? The Black Legend is the bad press that Spain's enemies disseminated beginning in the sixteenth century about the mistreatment of the Indians and about Spain's backwardness and brutality: the Inquisition, religious intolerance, a certain primitiveness and backwardness. This is all embedded in the English language; you cannot escape it. It is full of what we call factoids, things that are almost true but not quite. We call these factoids derisively, of course. Yet during the sixteenth and seventeenth centuries Spain produced Cervantes, Velázquez, the character of Don Juan, the picaresque, all figures, authors, and kinds of writing that are at the core of the modern Western tradition. How could that be? The *Quixote,* aided by Elliott's *Imperial Spain,* which you are, I hope, dutifully reading, as well as my comments here will help dispel these misperceptions about the Black Legend.

Let me first clarify as much as possible the confusion about terms like *novel* and *romance,* a confusion that is augmented by the fact that they do not quite coincide with their cognates in Spanish. Cognates are words in two languages that sound the same but do not have the same meaning. *Romance* is a term derived from the name Rome, meaning that originally these were works written in the languages derived from Latin, that is, French, Spanish, Italian, Portuguese, and so forth. Let us begin with Webster's definition of *romance.* It says, "Originally, a long narrative in verse or prose written in one of the romantic dialects." Remember what I said about language and dialect? A language is a dialect with an army, meaning that people who speak a certain dialect become powerful enough to impose it on the rest of the population. So, ". . . originally written in one of the romance dialects about the adventures of knights and other chivalric heroes, to a fictitious tale dealing not so much with everyday life as with extraordinary adventures or mysterious events." A popular dictionary of literary terms gives the following for *romance*: "Romance, a fictional story in verse or prose that relates improbable adventures of idealized characters in some remote or enchanted setting; or, more generally, a tendency in fiction opposite to that of realism."[1]

Etymologies are fun, but they do not always clarify what a word means in the present, and, in fact, sometimes etymologies work against such a clarification. How many know or how useful is it to know that the word *candid,* for example, derives from the Latin word *candidus,* meaning 'white'? It does not help you in the present to know that at all. It only helps you be pedantic if you tell somebody or if you bring it up at a party. In this case, knowing that the term *romance* derives from Rome and that it indicates that these stories were written in the romance languages does provide a historical insight. Romances emerged after the breakup of the Roman Empire during the Middle Ages, and the various national languages acquired individual identities. So, we have now a historical period that the etymology of *romance* gives us.

In English, romance means a story with a linear plot and unchanging characters. One episode follows another, and the heroes and heroines remain the same. This is the reason romances of chivalry are called romances. The romance form is preferred by popular fiction and by works with an ideological and doctrinaire purpose. They are easy to follow, and their moral is clear. Many cartoons, for instance, have the form of a romance—cartoons and comic books. Novels, on the other hand, are works in which there is a clash between the protagonists and the settings in which they move—remember the quotation from Lukács in my earlier lecture—and in which the characters evolve as a result of the actions in which they are involved. Characters in romances do not change; they are always heroic or evil. Characters in novels, on the other hand, do change; they evolve because of their adventures. Now, the *Quixote* is the first case of such a clash between the protagonist and his setting, though an argument can be made in favor of the picaresque and a work I will be mentioning today, *Celestina,* in which there is a clash between protagonist and setting and there is change in the characters. But the *Quixote* is the first full-fledged case.

I think and I hope that we now have a clear terminological distinction between novel and romance and that you will understand it when I speak about them. Matters get confused when we learn that in English, picaresque stories are often called romances—this is particularly so in English departments—while in Spanish we call them *novelas,* 'novels.' I will always refer to picaresque tales as novels because they are, according to the definitions I have given above. If you know Spanish, you may be further confused by the fact that *romance* in Spanish is a ballad, a narrative, originally popular poem, like the English ballads. So you must keep this distinction clear in mind. If you happen to read something in Spanish and you read *romance,* it is not a romance in the sense that I have been explaining, it is a poem.

Let's turn now to what it was that Don Quixote so avidly wanted to become. Let me clarify, too, what the chivalric romances were because this is something generally taken for granted. I like to clarify things and to start from the ground up. What is it that Don Quixote wanted to become? What is this whole business of the romances of chivalry? First, as I did with the term *romance* let me clarify the background of the word *chivalric. Chivalric* comes from the French word *cheval,* 'horse,' and it reflects the fact that the knight's form of transportation was the horse. What does French have to do with English? Well, William the Conqueror, the Battle of Hastings, the invasion of England by the French, and all of that which you learned in elementary school or high school, and the fact that French is one of the sources of modern English. But the horse was more than just a form of transportation. It was an instrument of warfare, a prized possession, with each having a sonorous name, if at all possible. The horse was part of the knight's identity; hence, the whole business about Don Quixote naming his horse at the beginning of the novel. Part of the culture of horses was a kind of courtesy, so we have in English also *chivalrous,* for instance. Horses have always created a whole culture of their own and have left a large imprint on languages because they were the principal mode of transportation until the beginning of the twentieth century. So technically, etymologically chivalric romance is a horse romance or, more appropriately, romances about horsemen. In Spanish the etymology is clearer, as the romances of chivalry are simply called *novelas de caballerías,* and *caballo* is the word for horse in Spanish.

Chivalric romances or, in Spanish, *novelas de caballerías* were the popular literature of the late Middle Ages and early Renaissance whose dissemination was greatly aided by the development of print. I am talking about the fourteenth and fifteenth centuries. The printing press, as you no doubt know, was developed in the fifteenth century, making available to many readers books to which only a select few had access before, including the Bible. A copy of the Gutenberg Bible—the first printed book—is in the Beinecke Library at Yale. The development of the printing press had a decisive impact on literature because it increased its dissemination; the *Quixote* and the novel in general owe their existence to this invention. We can see the impact the romances of chivalry had on our hero by the large number of them he had in his library (fig. 2). The romances of chivalry were the first best sellers. They are entertaining, and I encourage you to read one or two.

The chivalric romances originated in France and were derived from the *roman courtois,* or courtly romance. In French, *roman* eventually became the name for novel, but roman courtois, or courtly romance, was a narrative in verse which was a favorite of feudal lords no longer engaged in military exploits who looked back with nostalgia to a heroic age, as Don Quixote did. The roman courtois took its themes from classical legends like the Trojan War and the exploits of Alexander the Great and even oriental tales, but it preferred themes derived from Breton legends, legends from Brittany, such as that of Tristan and Isolde, the knights in pursuit of the Holy

Figure 2. Gustave Doré, *Don Quixote in His Library*. General Collection, Beinecke Rare Book and Manuscript Library, Yale University.

Grail, Percival and Merlin and Lancelot, or Arthurian tales about Arthur, the real or imaginary king of Britain, and the Knights of the Round Table. These adventures take place in a fantastic atmosphere, shrouded in a kind of lyrical and poetic air. When these roman courtois were turned into prose narratives, the chivalric romances appeared.

Each of these books had as a hero a knight-errant who incarnated heroism and amorous fidelity and was the defender of justice and the oppressed. The knight was involved in the most extraordinary adventures against fantastic and frightening wrongdoers. His passionate love for an idealized lady dominated his thoughts. Love was a fundamental component of these narratives. The knight would offer his lady the glory of his feats. This love for a lady is the same as courtly love, which, as you may know, inspired the medieval lyric as a fashion involving all sorts of rituals in the courts of elegant ladies. It is too long a story to be told here, but think of the romances of chivalry as being shot through, as it were, with the idea of courtly love. The knights were not just military heroes but also great lovers.

In Spain there were two notable antecedents to the romances of chivalry in the fourteenth century: *La gran conquista de ultramar* and *El caballero Zifar*. But these should not concern you. During the fourteenth century all European books of chivalry were disseminated throughout Spain in adaptations and translations, particularly those of the Breton cycle. The most significant chivalric romance in terms of circulation and influence as well as impact on the *Quixote* was *Amadís de Gaula*, about which you will hear and read a lot throughout this semester because he is Don Quixote's chief model. The *Amadís* was written around 1492, that miraculous year when so many things happened, but was not published until 1508 in Saragossa.

It is known that there were stories about Amadís circulating as far back as the early fourteenth century, and Garci Rodríguez de Montalvo, its author, states in the prologue that he took the story, which was written by several authors, divided it into four books, and recast it, adding a few touches and a fifth book about Esplandián, Amadís's son. These chivalric romances could and did have many sequels, much like today's soap operas on television, and responded to the same kind of demand from the public. This cannot end here, we want more Amadís adventures, we want Amadís's son's adventures, and so forth. In fact, all popular fiction from Sherlock Holmes to James Bond is sequential in this fashion, which is why soap operas are derisively called *culebrones* in Spanish, from *culebra*, 'snake,' because it is a snake that goes on, and on, and on.

The *Amadís* is a very free adaptation of novels from the Breton cycle. It is a complex network of the most varied and marvelous adventures. It tells the story of the hero's birth virtually in a river because he is thrown into a river as a baby to hide his mother's sin because she was not married. His parents were a king and a queen, and he is rescued and trained as a knight. When he grows up, he falls in love with Oriana, and she becomes his beloved; so Amadís and Oriana are one of the great couples of literary history. He is put through all kinds of trials, he is enchanted and disenchanted, and he is the most loyal and faithful of lovers against all temptations from various ladies. In fact, he is forced to go through the arch of faithful lovers, which could be crossed only by lovers who had been absolutely faithful. How many people could go through it today?

This is what is in Don Quixote's imagination and desires: this figure of an invincible hero who is noble and a great lover. The *Amadís* was so important in the sixteenth century that it acquired a didactic value. I mean it was used as a model for deportment and for courtesy; it surpassed the model for courtly behavior written by a great Italian writer named Baldassare Castiglione. His book is called *The Courtesan,* and it was published in 1528. It was a very important book. But the *Amadís* was much more fun to read, and therefore it bested Castiglione's book for providing a model of behavior for people in the courts.

For all of these reasons the *Amadís* achieved great success, among the greatest in Spanish literature; many expressed their admiration for it, including great political and intellectual figures. For readers of the time it was the only possibility for evasion, the only food for their fantasies. The romances of chivalry were, in the sixteenth century, what movies and television shows are for us today. But the romances, and *Amadís* in particular, had their detractors—spoilsports are everywhere, all of the time—who saw in such books a threat to public morals. They became a topic of debate, and this is behind the role *Amadís* plays in the *Quixote* and the reason Cervantes says he is writing his book against them so that people would not read them anymore. He is supposedly entering the debate about the value or lack thereof of the romances of chivalry.

I hope you have a clearer idea now of what it was that Don Quixote wanted to become. It is clear and concrete. I suppose a modern-day Don Quixote would like to be James Bond because we have to assume a modern Alonso Quixano to be middle-aged and to have grown up with James Bond as the image of heroism. I read that President Kennedy watched Bond movies for entertainment. Obviously, to a man of his age Bond was the acme of heroism: debonair, good-looking, all the women after him, and that sort of thing.

Amadís was the most obvious and avowed precursor of the *Quixote* in Spanish, but what were Cervantes' predecessors among more "serious" Spanish literary works? What Spanish works had Cervantes read, absorbed, and incorporated into his own literary project? I have mentioned some of these, but I want to mention them again because I want to lay the groundwork in the most thorough way possible.

The first was *Celestina,* which I mentioned above. It is from 1499 and was written by Fernando de Rojas. It is of indeterminate genre; the closest description would be a dramatic dialogue. *Celestina* is the most significant precursor to Cervantes. It is the tragic story of two young lovers, Calixto and Melibea, who consummate their love under the guidance of a go-between, the protagonist Celestina. Celestina is an old whore, the madam of a whorehouse, and a witch. But in spite of these unsavory characteristics she is the heroine of the work. This is the most original aspect of *Celestina*: that the protagonist is an old whore, go-between, and witch. Still, she is the heroine in the sense that she is willful and struggles against fate.[2]

Celestina controls the whole city (believed to be Salamanca) because she controls people's erotic adventures. There are two worlds: that of Celestina, the servants, and whores and that of the lovers, Calixto and Melibea, and Melibea's parents, who are of the gentry. So there is also a class clash here. Calixto is a Quixote in the making because he wants to playact the role of the courtly lover. He is killed when he falls off the wall of Melibea's garden, where he has been making love to her. Melibea commits suicide, and Celestina is murdered by the servants because she has swindled them too. *Celestina* is a pitiless book with what can already be called a realistic quality. I will talk about realism in a minute.

The second important work is *La vida del Lazarillo de Tormes. Lazarillo de Tormes* is the first picaresque novel, published in 1554. The author is unknown. It is a life story told to a judge, as in a deposition, by a petty criminal to justify his current status. He is married to the archpriest's mistress. So he acts as a front; he is a cuckolded husband who is compliant with society's hypocrisies. Lazarillo tells his life story from birth to the present in which he is writing. This is life as seen from the perspective of a low-class individual, a criminal who learned his tricks from his first master, who was, ironically, a blind man, a beggar.

Guzmán de Alfarache—I will not give you the whole title, which is long—is the second most important picaresque novel, published in 1599. It is a four-part, prolix tale of a criminal told in the first person, following the formula of *Lazarillo,* but the difference here is that the life is told after a religious conversion to the good. So the story of Guzmán's life is laced with sermons about where he went wrong and ways to improve his behavior, but this retrospective moralizing is always tempered by the appeal of the stories about sin—sin is more interesting, always. *Guzmán de Alfarache* became the model picaresque in Cervantes' time, and there are clear allusions to it in the *Quixote.*

What these works show is the emergence and development of realism as we know it, which would be continued in the work of Cervantes, particularly the *Quixote.* They lead all the way through to the seventeenth-, eighteenth-, and nineteenth-century novels. This is the beginning of realism in fiction. Its emergence, in my view, has a great deal to do with the Catholic Kings, about whom you are reading in Elliott, and their formation of a new, modern state with a large bureaucracy and penal institutions to punish criminals. In the nineteenth century a Spanish criminologist named Rafael Salillas (1854–1923) linked the picaresque with the birth of the social sciences. He believed that in the picaresque lay the beginnings of the study of society, as criminology and sociology would study it in later years.

In the picaresque there is a search for truth about human nature in the social commerce of people of the lowest possible levels, where civilization, as it were, has barely reached. There is an emphasis on the material and the sordid against Neoplatonic conceptions of humankind that are more typical of the Renaissance. The sordid, the ugly, the dirty become esthetically valuable and appealing in these realistic works, in the behavior of the characters, their actions, and also their attitudes. The point is that this sort of probe into the social is an attempt to uncover a truth about the human that is not available in the ancient classical literature or its imitators in the Renaissance. The picaresque goes against that kind of version of the human. It is a rejection parallel to that of Descartes as he formulates the philosophy of the self when he erases received tradition.

In realism, common objects—you will see common objects in the *Quixote*—appear frequently. This begins with *Celestina,* but it is mostly via the world of the picaresque that it passes to the *Quixote.* The characters' accessories are what endow the description of Don Quixote's world with an aura of reality: Sancho's wineskin, for instance. Look for such common objects. As you read the *Quixote* you will see there is a focus on them.

This depiction of objects is parallel to a development in painting which began with the work of Leon Battista Alberti (1404–72). He wrote a treatise called *De Pictura.* In simplistic terms, what Alberti nearly invented was the sense of perspective. That is, that objects appear in different sizes depending on where they are in reference to a *point de fuite, punto de fuga,* vanishing point in English. Objects, according to Alberti, are not to appear in painting as being flat, as in medieval paintings, but in relation to how they appear to the observer and how they are arranged according to perspective. Hence objects are now represented in all of their fullness, in all of their roundness, in all of their weight and measure. This is a form of realism that begins in painting. *De Pictura* is from 1435, the fifteenth century. Alberti had an enormous influence not just on the history of painting but on philosophy too. This was also a way of conceiving the perception of objects subject to time, because perspective in space involves also a sense of time. If something is back there and something else is here, closer, I can get to it faster than I can get to that other thing, if you understand what I mean. Now, if you have seen any of Velázquez's paintings, you will remember how those objects that are just common, everyday objects suddenly have fullness. This is what will appear in the picaresque and the novel, in the *Quixote*, and this is part of the development of realism.

It is a cliché about Spanish literature of the Golden Age, in the sixteenth century and the seventeenth, that there is a clash in it between this realistic conception or vision of the world and the idealistic conception that comes through the Neoplatonic tradition and that is, let us say, embodied in Don Quixote. Don Quixote's is an idealistic perspective, and Sancho's a realistic perspective. Sancho is close to the material, to the material world that he wants to eat if he possibly can, while Don Quixote does not eat. He does not need to eat; he lives in the world of ideas. But, of course, they influence each other. As you will see, this is one of the great things about this novel: that these characters influence each other. But keep in mind above all what I said about realism because realism will be one of the triumphs of Cervantes' work.

Let us finally turn to the *Quixote*. I assume and I hope you have read at least the first few chapters and that by the next lecture you will have read the first ten chapters as well as the assigned readings in the *Casebook,* which will give you a background on Cervantes' life that I am not giving you here, as well as other materials and the first chapter in Elliott.

The prologue. This 1605 prologue is one of the most important and famous texts in Spanish literature. Prologues are always very important in Cervantes. Why? Because of his concern about the relationship between the creator and his creation and his concern about the nature of the self, his own self, which is a very Renaissance preoccupation. Cervantes' prologues are much like Michel de Montaigne's *Essays.* I have mentioned Castiglione, now I mention Montaigne. These are great Renaissance figures that are part of the context within which Cervantes wrote. It is here in this prologue that Cervantes introduces one of his favorite tropes, one that runs through the whole of the *Quixote:* irony. This is an exceedingly ironic prologue, irony that is conveyed through a seductive kind of self-deprecation in Cervantes.

"Desocupado lector," it begins. "Idle reader." Cervantes assumes a reader who comes to his book for entertainment, not instruction, and who reads for pleasure, not for work. This is a novelty and a kind of challenge in a period when the function of literature was very much an issue discussed by secular and religious moralists. But we soon see that what Cervantes means by entertainment does not preclude consideration of thorny ethical issues that involve reading and literature in general; these issues emerge

immediately in the prologue. It is typical of Cervantes—you can expect to
see this throughout the work—to deal lightly and humorously with weighty
issues. This is one of his constants. He is able to deal with very grave issues
in a light and humorous way. That is his perspective. It is part of his ironic
perspective.

The prologue, although it comes first, is a kind of epilogue. It was obviously written after he finished the book. You cannot take for granted the sequential order of things as you read them in a book; they are sequential in a
conventional way. Cervantes did not sit down, write the prologue, and then
write the novel. He wrote the novel and then wrote the prologue to ponder
what he had just finished. There is in the prologue a tone, a prevailing theme
of self-doubt which is, again, an echo of Montaigne. Perhaps this explains
the self-deprecating statements about his own creation and inventive powers. It is very much like Montaigne because Montaigne's stance is very modern. Montaigne writes with the resignation of knowing he will never outdo
the classics.

By the way, there is an instructive piece on Montaigne in a recent issue of the *New Yorker*.[3] I mean Montaigne is still relevant and speaks to the
modern mind. He writes with the resignation of knowing that he will never
really know the truth, even about himself, and that received knowledge is of
dubious value. For instance, in his famous essay called "On Cannibals" he
asks what business Europeans had imposing their religious doctrines on na-
tives of the New World, who had been getting along just fine with their own
beliefs. And he says that it is worse to roast people alive, as Europeans do to
torture them, than to roast them once they are dead and eat them: of course,
he is right about that. He is a relativist in a post-Copernican world—I am
still talking about Montaigne—in which we know that the earth is not the
center of the universe, and hence humankind is not at the center either in
the way that it was believed to be before.

In his prologue, Cervantes sounds very much like Montaigne, who, if
he was not a source, was clearly a kindred spirit. They were both Hamlet-
like in their display of doubt. Shakespeare had read Montaigne. Now, who is
this friend who suddenly appears in the prologue? Of course, it is a made-up
friend; it is an imaginary friend whom Cervantes invents to turn the prologue into a story in which he is going to discuss how to write a prologue
while writing the prologue, and that is the whole joke behind this. It is a big
joke. Cervantes was fond both of telling stories and of using dialogue rather
than expounding on doctrine. He loved dialogue. He loved having a topic
discussed from various points of view. This is so throughout the whole of the
Quixote, and we have it already in the prologue. He has a dialogue with this

imaginary friend. He has created this friend, as we do occasionally, creating an imaginary friend or someone with whom we speak who is just another version of ourselves. Cervantes likes things that are being discussed from different points of view, even if made up, as you will see.

The main topic of the prologue is the genesis and intention of the book, a common topic for prologues only here it is told as the issue of how to write a prologue is discussed. There is an apparent contradiction here at the beginning. Cervantes says this book could not be other than himself because he is its father. Then he says, "No, I am the stepfather," by which he means that he is merely the transcriber of this book by Cide Hamete Benengeli, this fictitious Moorish author about whom you will hear a lot in the book. This is the first of many disclaimers of authorship in the *Quixote*. What Cervantes is probing here is the genesis of literature, the genealogy of invention, which can no longer be taken for granted by following the rules of Renaissance poetics.

In what way does a book belong to its author? This is why Cervantes mocks the usual front matter of other books in which authors boast of their erudition and ask others to attest to the quality of their productions. The whole business he is talking about of all of these sonnets that he could have asked other people to write for him. The front matter in a book is everything from the title all the way to the beginning of the book; prologue, preface, acknowledgments. This is called the front matter, *los preliminares* in Spanish, if you want to learn that in Spanish. These sonnets about the book, in praise of the book, are like today's blurbs. You pick up a book and you find that there are blurbs. "Roberto González Echevarría says . . . blah, blah," and there is praise, and what has happened is that the person blurbing the book has been one of the readers of the press to vet the book, and then they ask you to excerpt something from your report and put it on the back. Other times they just send you the book and say, "Please, would you write a blurb for this book?" I know many people who do it without reading the book. This is what Cervantes is mocking, but what he does instead of going outside for legitimation is that he has literary characters write the sonnets in praise of his book. It is as if I wrote a book and I had a blurb from James Bond, to continue with our fictional characters. What Cervantes is doing is showing that literature is self-legitimating. He is not going outside of fiction and outside of literature for legitimation. It is another game, another joke he is playing on the reader.

So what does the fictional friend tell him to do? The friend tells him to make up his own sonnets and also to make up a false bibliography, as it were, and put in the margins all of the sources he never consulted—as if you created a false bibliography for a paper you have written. It is a very amusing joke, but it is also quite serious. What the friend is telling Cervantes is this: forget about tradition, forget about Aristotle; Aristotle never wrote anything about romances of chivalry. You are doing something new, you can just make it all up. This is why the prologue is a kind of manifesto for the type of book the *Quixote* is, the kind of original, new book that it is that can break with tradition. The friend says, Make it all up!

There are also digs at Lope de Vega—remember I mentioned him earlier. Lope was a very successful playwright. He was rich, famous, and vain, and Cervantes is taking a shot at him. Apparently, Lope would get himself some thesaurus, a compendium of familiar quotations, and use them in his works to make it seem like he was erudite and learned. Lope also added the "de," Lope de Vega, to his last name to make it seem as if he were an aristocrat. You know the *de* in French and Spanish and German *von* indicate aristocracy. So Cervantes is mocking Lope de Vega. Lope was extremely successful and had also said a few disparaging things about Cervantes. But all of that is contingent. The important thing in the prologue is that Cervantes is saying, Away with tradition, I'm beginning here anew, I can make it up. That is the whole point.

I am going to end by simply alluding to the beginning of the book. The birth of *Don Quixote* is an act of self-invention by a man of fifty. At the time, fifty was a very advanced age. Age expectancy did not go beyond the late thirties or early forties at the time, so this is also commensurate with Cervantes' own age. He is in his late fifties when he publishes his book, as he says in the prologue. Don Quixote's is an act of self-invention by a man of fifty. He feels free to create himself beyond family ties. We do not learn anything about Don Quixote's family, only about his niece, but, do we learn anything about his parents? No. About his birth? No. About his needs? No. Cervantes has created a hero who is beyond Freud's family romance.

In Freud's theories the family romance is mommy, daddy, and the child; the boy is in love with mommy, and all of that. That is the family romance, and you go through life with the resentment of daddy or your secret love for mommy. That is the family romance. This is my mock version of Freud. But Cervantes' character is born beyond Freud. When you are fifty, who cares about who your parents were? You are who you are. And not only is he who he is, but he wills himself to be something else at the age of fifty. It is important that Don Quixote be that old. Can you think of another literary hero who is that old? Celestina, but she had the two young lovers as coprotagonists. But no, protagonists were men in their full strength, like Ulysses,

Aeneas, and the pilgrim in the *Divine Comedy* (I think he is thirty-three, not an old man). Why, then? Because his self-invention is an act of will based on nothing. He is beyond all of the pressures of family and of need, and this is why he can invent himself. Don Quixote's true family and genealogy are the books he reads.

CHAPTER 3

Don Quixote and Sancho on the Road

Books and Windmills

Required Readings

Cervantes, *Don Quixote,* Prologue; Part I, chaps. 1–10, pp. 11–82.
Durán, Manuel. "Cervantes' Harassed and Vagabond Life." In
Casebook, 23–33.
Elliott, *Imperial Spain,* 15–44.
González Echevarría, Roberto. "Introduction." In *Casebook,*
3–22.

Let me begin by repeating the last point I made in the previous lecture.
The birth of Don Quixote is an act of self-invention by a man of fifty, and
remember that in 1605 fifty is a very advanced age. He feels free to create
himself beyond family and need. In this, the novel is directly opposed to
most previous literature, particularly the romances of chivalry, where there
were miraculous births. And to the picaresque, very much in particular the
picaresque, in which family background and need determined the life of the
protagonist and his poverty, and the family background weighs heavily on
the rest of his life, as in the case of Lazarillo.

Don Quixote is beyond family and social determinisms. In most previous stories, young people leave home in search of adventures that will give
substance, meaning, and individuality to their lives. Can you think of another old protagonist before Don Quixote? How old was the pilgrim in the
Divine Comedy? How old was Odysseus in the *Odyssey*? How old was Ae-

neas in the *Aeneid*? Celestina, it is true, was old, but she shares the limelight with young lovers. Don Quixote, as I said in the last class, is beyond Freud, beyond the family romance. In fact, though we learn a great deal about him in the first chapter, we learn nothing of his parents. His genealogy is literary, the books he has read.

The most innovative aspect of Don Quixote is the character's self-fashioning, as Stephen Greenblatt would put it in a book called *Renaissance Self-Fashioning*.[1] The reader witnesses this self-transformation at all its levels, from the mental to the physical, from what Don Quixote thinks to what he wears. He, not an author, names himself, his horse, and his lady. His is a life that will be shaped like a work of art. Life will imitate art. But what is the significance of this self-invention, of this resurrection, as it were? Renaissance humanism emphasized the power of human agency. It is the beginning of a liberation from a God-centered conception of the world and of humankind. Remember the Lukács quotation about the *Quixote* being the first story of a world that has been abandoned by God. So in this world abandoned by God man creates himself, Don Quixote creates himself.

"En un lugar de la Mancha de cuyo nombre no quiero acordarme . . ." (In a certain village of La Mancha, the name of which I do not choose to remember . . .) (my translation). This is the first sentence of the book. This is a sentence, by the way, that most literate native speakers of Spanish know by heart even if they have not read the rest of the *Quixote*. It is known as well as English speakers know, "It was the best of times, it was the worst of times" from *A Tale of Two Cities* or "Call me Ishmael," the beginning of *Moby-Dick*.

In the *Quixote*, literature appears, as I have been saying, as a realm of self-legitimation and for the display of wit and capacity for invention, which is what Cervantes appears to be affirming in that first sentence of the book. As a narrator, Cervantes does not wish to remember the place in La Mancha where Don Quixote lived. It is a display of authorial will. The sentence is full of other implications, for example, there is the echo of the opening of traditional stories as well as that of official documents that attest to one's being by stating where one is from. In the stories, "in such-and-such a country long ago," and the country is named. Or "my name is so-and-so and I live in such-and-such a place, and was born in such-and-such a place," a legal document. To make such a statement about place is one's strongest form of grounding, but here it is willfully omitted. A place-name that is erased by the creative will of the author: "No quiero acordarme," I choose not to remember, against the traditional or legal formulas in which it is usually given.

The origin, this corner of the world, this place, this village, this *lugar*, as it is called in the sixteenth-century Spanish, to which the protagonist returns several times and definitively at the end, is not named. It is as if the source were nondetermining, as Don Quixote's family background is nondetermining in his adventures. This is perhaps why the origin—which is also the destination because Don Quixote will return to die at home (giving away the plot here, I am sorry)—is left blank, deliberately effaced from the story. It is a nonplace, although many towns in Spain claim to be the one in which Don Quixote lived.

Don Quixote's real surname was Quixano, his full name was Alonso Quixano. This issue of naming is prevalent throughout the book: the fluctuations of language in reference to meaning and to truth. If language is so shifty, how can we express the truth in language? Leo Spitzer, a great German critic who worked in this country for many years and taught at Johns Hopkins University, in the piece "On Linguistic Perspectivism" (which you will read in your *Casebook*) makes much of this, applying the knowledge of the linguist and philologist that he was. Language and its vagaries also constitute Cervantes' point of view about what is commonly accepted as the truth and how the truth can be commonly accepted in a medium as shifty as language. But the blurry name, Quixote, *quijana, quesada*, is also a way of playing with the absence of determinisms, like his being from La Mancha, a nonplace, as it were. A place marked the characters in the epic, the romances of chivalry, and the picaresque novels: Amadís de Gaula, of Gaul; Lazarillo de Tormes—Tormes is the river that goes through Salamanca, by the way, in which the *pícaro* is supposed to have been born; Gúzman de Alfarache, a place that is named Alfarache. But not in the *Quixote*, significantly.

Don Quixote names his lady Dulcinea del Toboso and his horse Rocinante. In the case of the lady he follows literary convention. Her name rhymes with Melibea, as we have seen, one of the protagonists of *Celestina*, a beautiful young woman. And *dulce* means 'sweet' in Spanish, so you can see the origin and the intention behind naming Dulcinea. The horse's name reflects something of his physical reality, Rocinante, *rocín-ante*, meaning he was a *rocín*, a 'workhorse,' before; *antes* is 'before' in Spanish. Rocinante, the name, reflects in a very direct, comical way the horse because it reflects precisely the appearance of this nag. Don Quixote's capacity for naming, as we will see, is quite extraordinary; he is a man of words and of the word. But the crucial point here is that he is naming himself, his lady, and his horse as part of this process of self-invention, like Adam giving names to things in the Garden of Eden or God giving names to things in the universe. This is part and parcel of the process of self-invention.

Chapter 2 contains one of the most remarkable moments in all of literature. The protagonist has created himself, and he leaves at dawn, the beginning of a new day, a new life, and sets out on the Montiel Plain alone riding Rocinante. It is a beginning from zero, from a voluntary severing of ties with any possible determining force except chivalry and literature. It is a moment of freedom, of freedom achieved, freedom from the past. But as he goes along Don Quixote anticipates the literary text that will be written about the exploits he is in the process of accomplishing or thinks he is in the process of accomplishing. There is a gap between the high-flown rhetoric of the romances of chivalry he uses and the literal plain upon which he trots. But this is precisely the gap between literature and reality, between writing and experience, that will be at the core of Cervantes' exploration of the nature of writing. The present and the writing of the text hang somewhere in between reality and this high-flown rhetoric, which are parallel and simultaneous in their appearance in the book. This is quite remarkable, and it may pass unnoticed, but I want you to take notice of it. It is on pages 30–31 of the translation we are using. As he goes forward on the Montiel Plain, Don Quixote says to himself, "Who can doubt but that in future times, when the true history of my famous deeds sees the light, the sage who chronicles them will, when he recounts this my first sally, so early in the morning, write in this manner: 'Scarce had ruddy Apollo spread over the face of the wide and spacious earth the golden tresses of his beauteous hair, and scarce had the speckled little birds with their harmonious tongues hailed in musical and mellifluous melody the approach of rosy Aurora who, rising from her jealous husband's soft couch . . .'" (I, 2, 30–31). He is using all of these references to classical mythology to refer to himself as he projects the text that will be written about him.

He arrives at an inn. We know—this is a fact to remember—from the episode in the inn that Don Quixote has left home on a hot Friday in July. How do we know this? We know it because Don Quixote is served fish at the inn, reflecting the fact that the eating of red meat was forbidden on Fridays by the Catholic Church, a restriction observed until the 1960s. So because it is a hot day and it is the month of July it is clear that this is a hot Friday in July. The specificity of time and place is a new feature of fiction, of this realist fiction. As we saw, the romances of chivalry took place in vague, fabulous countries and times. Not the *Quixote,* which derived from the picaresque a penchant for the particular in everything. It is the birth of what we know as realism, whose origins and intention I spoke about in the last lecture: interest in society at its lowest levels and the acquisition of aesthetic value by the sordid, the ugly, and the dirty.

The heat, by the way, would presumably (and it says so in the text) contribute to Don Quixote's madness according to theories of the time, which are probably not altogether wrong—if you were out in the desert in the heat, you might lose your senses too. But the weather is important for other reasons in the *Quixote,* specific weather, not the fabulous weather, mists and all of that, of the romances of chivalry. Both parts of the novel take place in a vaguely framed summer, because the heat contributes to Don Quixote's madness, as I said, but also because it makes it logical for everyone to be outdoors on the road. We will see a little bit more about why people are on the road as we go along. There is also the very important issue that begins in these early chapters of light and visibility—being able to discern objects and make them out—which leads to disputes among the characters about the nature of what they see. If you have been to Castile, you know that the air is clear. It is hot and dry, and the visibility is exceptionally good.

This first inn is crucial because it sets up one of the most important places where the action will develop. Inns, as you will soon discover, are way stations where all sorts of meetings take place and hilarious scenes develop. The *Quixote* follows the loose structure of the adventure book like the romances of chivalry that it parodies but also like the picaresque, so it needs these inns as stopovers where characters of various origins and classes meet. The inn can provide a kind of archaeology of society, a moveable home for characters away from home. What I mean by archaeology of society is that you see at the same time several social levels, as when you make a cut in the earth to study the various layers; here you see various layers of social classes all present at the same time in the inn. This is how the inn provides what I call an archaeology of society. It is at the inn that we encounter for the first time Don Quixote's ability to transform crass reality into literary illusion—although he has done some of that already in naming his horse—a process that is highlighted by the fact that in Rocinante he is confronted by the extreme of crassness. No ordinary women does he turn into damsels, but whores; no ordinary travelers does he encounter, but swineherds: the lowest of the low, people who dealt with pigs, which are the foulest and the most repulsive. There is a grotesque contrast between the innkeeper, the whores, and the knighting ceremony, for instance. It is a clash of extremes.

Is there an element of ennoblement in Don Quixote's dogged perception of the ugly as beautiful? Is this one of the reasons the book has endured, one's desire to ennoble reality through one's will? Do we begin to glimpse here in the madness a mission to force onto reality his perception of it? Also notice that because he treats the whores with deference they are kind to him, as is the innkeeper. It is a constant in Cervantes' work that lower-class people, even criminals, can be kind in given situations. There is no class determinism in Cervantes, making criminals evil; quite the contrary. Cervantes' overall vision of humankind is a positive one; no one is completely evil in his work. In this, he is quite different from Shakespeare and his somber conception of the human. Cervantes' view of humanity is not as negative; you will discover this as you read the book.

It is also at the inn where Don Quixote is turned for the first time into an object of amusement. The innkeeper plays along to have something to laugh at that night. Are not the innkeeper and the other guests in need of amusement like the "idle reader" that Cervantes addresses? Here is another level at which the *Quixote* is going to provide amusement. The ceremony of the knighting of Don Quixote is a parody of those in the romances of chivalry, but do we not begin to notice in this scene a certain degree of cruelty toward Don Quixote on the part of other characters and of Cervantes himself? This is something that Borges has remarked upon. There is a certain cruelness at times in the way Cervantes portrays his characters. There is a hint that trying to do good can be ridiculous and that no good deed goes unpunished, as it were. But this is so chiefly because Don Quixote is a living anachronism; he has conceptions of justice that are outmoded.

In the original, the contrast between Don Quixote and the other characters is achieved by means of the manners of speech and dialectal contrasts. We will see that in a minute in his fight with the Basque. Don Quixote's speech turns to the archaic—already archaic in Cervantes' time. When he speaks about matters of chivalry he uses archaic words drawn from the romances of chivalry. This is a very important part of Cervantes' achievement that is lost in the translation but that the English reader can gauge, that is, the differentiation between the characters or among the characters by the way they speak. You can understand it by thinking of a novel that was greatly influenced by Cervantes, *The Adventures of Huckleberry Finn*. Speech marks the characters by revealing their social station and even their region of origin. I read *The Adventures of Huckleberry Finn* as a child in Spanish, and, of course, they did not translate into the Spanish the differences in dialect between Jim and Huck. I still liked the novel, but when I read it in college once I had learned English I was astonished by the southern dialects. It was like another book; I had a great deal of difficulty understanding Jim's speech. This contrast in the speech of characters is prevalent in the *Quixote.* It is the first novel in which this is accomplished.

The innkeeper is himself like a literary character and a kind of Quixote in that he tells of his youth, a youth misspent as a pícaro as if it had been a romance of chivalry. He uses the rhetoric of the romance of chivalry to tell of his life of petty crime. He is a minor Don Juan who seduces widows and other women, he says with great pride, and he mentions the places he had been to as if they were great places, when they were really the most notorious emporia where pícaros gathered in Spain. So he too can play Don Quixote's rhetorical game; he is kind of an inverted mirror image of Don Quixote. You have to read carefully. Cervantes is very subtle in creating these characters, and here we have this character mocking but at the same time using Don Quixote's rhetoric to transform his life into something important. There is a certain synthesis in this character between the rhetoric of the romances of chivalry and that of the picaresque. This is what Cervantes achieves through this intriguing innkeeper.

The knighting is obviously a kind of baptism. It is a parody of similar ceremonies in the romances of chivalry, as I have said. It is true that it is a parody, but in the fictitious world that Don Quixote is creating it has a certain aura of sacredness, nevertheless. The act completes the process of self-invention that began in the first chapter; it legitimizes it within that world through the ceremony of his being knighted. He is being knighted by a ridiculous retired pícaro in this dingy inn surrounded by whores, but nevertheless the knighting has an air of sacredness, and he does finally achieve knighthood.

The two episodes on the road after the knighting underscore moral issues that Don Quixote's madness brings up. Why does his madness bring up these moral issues? Because in his madness he refuses to abide by, to recognize, and to accept social conventions. And in that way he highlights the arbitrariness of such conventions. Madmen and children do this by asking why, why, why, why? Or by acting as if they do not care why and then demonstrating that social conventions are, indeed, conventional. This is why Don Quixote will, again and again, provoke moral crises.

Such is the case with Juan Haldudo. Juan Haldudo is the fellow who is flogging Andrés, his servant, for having, according to him, stolen some of his animals. With regard to Juan Haldudo, Don Quixote puts his trust in a kind of honesty that does not exist anymore or perhaps never existed except in the romances of chivalry. His intervention makes matters worse, obviously. This is the first of several episodes in which the reader seems to be invited to judge. Who is right? There are hints that Andrés may well be a rogue, a pícaro, and that he may have indeed stolen from his master, in which case, according to the laws of the land, Haldudo had every right to flog him. In fact, when Andrés appears later on—and he will reappear—he is on his way to Seville, a telltale sign because Seville was the center of picaresque life. Now, think of Seville as being a very, very important port in Spain because it was through Seville—read your Elliott—that Spain communicated with its overseas empire. Everything came in through Seville, which is up the Guadalquivir River, so it is protected. Seville was a teeming port, and ports are always rife with corruption because of the intense exchange of goods and the variety of people who live in them. So, Seville was known for being the center of picaresque life. This detail that Cervantes throws in, when Andrés appears later and is going to Seville, leads you to believe he is a pícaro, so he may have been guilty when Haldudo whipped him. Don Quixote is applying a kind of justice that is anachronistic because by this time Spain had a well-developed, thorough criminal justice system. All of these matters found their way into it; it was a litigious society, almost as litigious as the United States is nowadays. So the way in which Don Quixote intervenes is totally anachronistic.

With the Toledo merchants, the conflict takes on a more philosophical, perhaps doctrinaire cast, even though it is a very funny episode. This is where Don Quixote appears before the merchants on the road and says they have to declare that Dulcinea del Toboso is the most beautiful lady in the world. One of them, who is a bit of a jester, Cervantes interjects, says something like, "Well, wait a minute, couldn't you at least show some kind of a picture or something that we can gauge this by? Because she may have some stuff pouring out of her eyes." Don Quixote angrily replies, "Nothing pours out of her eye!" and then he charges at them, but Rocinante falls. This is a totally hilarious scene, but the issue is, can one believe what one cannot see? Do you get what is behind this episode? What is the role of sensorial experience in questions of belief? Is there not also potentially a socioreligious subtext here? Is it not likely that these merchants from Toledo are Jews or converted Jews? That is, Jews who have been forced to convert. Then is the test to which they are being subjected not playing with the issue of conversion, of forced conversion? It also seems to allude to fierce debates in the sixteenth century about religious images, which the Protestants did not allow and the Catholics did. The stakes are getting higher. And as I explained in an earlier lecture, Cervantes always presents his higher stakes in a light vein and in very humorous episodes. But these serious issues are still there.

In the end Don Quixote is beaten to a pulp by one of the servants. This is the ultimate insult and humiliation: to be beaten by a commoner after having been let down by Rocinante. Rocinante simply cannot move from a trot to a gallop without falling—you will see similar accidents in the future. So, Don Quixote is picked up by Pedro Alonso—notice the common name. Cervantes gives very common names to very common people. Pedro Alonso is like Peter Johnson or something like that. This Pedro Alonso is one of his neighbors. He picks him up—and notice his kindness not only in picking up poor Alonso Quixano, his neighbor, but also in waiting until dark before going into the village so that people will not see him in such a sorry condition. Again, here is an act of kindness on the part of a low-class character. This is what I was saying before about characters in Cervantes: no matter what their social class they are able to perform acts of kindness. There are echoes here of the Good Samaritan, if you want to look for biblical echoes in the *Quixote.*

Now Don Quixote is madder than ever because of the beating he has been administered and because he is back home. Returns home are always problematic. Presumably one is returning to the familiar, to the canny, but now Don Quixote's house is going to turn into a very uncanny place. It is the house, one must remember, that is also the abode of the books; it houses the books that are the source of Don Quixote's madness. So it is the familiar, the home, but also the place where the source of his madness is lodged. It is also the place of his first battles, as we learn, when he would get up in the middle of the night and begin slashing with his sword. As we will see, it is a highly malleable place. This house changes as if the canny were also the uncanny. The background of my commentary here is the great essay by Freud on the uncanny, the *unheimliche.* His theory is that the uncanny is the canny, the familiar, becoming suddenly unfamiliar; not something totally unfamiliar, but the familiar becoming suddenly unfamiliar, and this is what is happening here with Don Quixote's house. Houses and shelters, inns, palaces, and all are very important in the *Quixote,* and I urge you to take notice of them.

Now, it was either here or after the scrutiny of the library where the *Quixote* was going to end, according to one of the theories contained in your *Casebook,* the essay by Ramón Menéndez Pidal. In any case, this return home brings up the issue of repetition, which leads to the philosophical question of whether there can be repetition and also to the aesthetic problem of representation because representing is also always a form of repetition: repeating something and the issue of representation is at the core of the questions about literature that Cervantes brings up throughout the book. The topic also dovetails with Don Quixote's project to revive the heroic age. Can something be revived? Can it be repeated? The return home also allows for a fuller analysis of Don Quixote's madness. The housekeeper and the niece relate Don Quixote's adventures prior to his first sally. The niece recounts how he would read for two days and nights straight, without rest, whereupon he would draw his sword and flail away as in a battle until exhausted. That is, the return allows us to learn more about the etiology, the source of Don Quixote's madness.

The literary madness is not sufficient for Cervantes, so he gives us more about his mental condition. Remember that I mentioned Huarte de San Juan's book, the doctor who wrote *Examen de ingenios*. Cervantes gives us some details about Don Quixote's physical qualities that make him prone to madness. For instance, his thinness, the dryness of his skin, a dry constitution on the whole. In the theory of humors of the time, this made him a candidate for the kind of madness that he had. Unlike Dante, whose *Divine Comedy* is thoroughly allegorical, Cervantes flirts with allegory but always seems to avoid it. What I mean is, this is not an allegorical madman; this is a particular madman with a specific illness, not an everyman who can easily be subsumed in the "we" at the beginning of the *Divine Comedy*: "Nel mezzo del cammin di nostra vita . . ." (in the middle of the journey of our lives). In the *Quixote* we have this particular madman. This is why all of these details about his life at home are given, his diet, for instance. These are details Cervantes has given to justify his madness. It is not just a literary madness.

The book burning and the walling off of the library will be attempts to cure Don Quixote, but both are also filled with all kinds of implications. Through both parts of the novel the characters will be searching for cures for Don Quixote. And here, obviously, the burning of the books and the walling off of the library are part of a cure: you eliminate the source and you eliminate the illness. Now, the inquisition of the library or the scrutiny of the library is one of the most famous episodes in the *Quixote* and one of the favorite ones among literary critics and historians because it deals with books. Again, it has been conjectured that the end of the library episode would have been the end of the novella of *Don Quixote*, if indeed what Cervantes proposed to write was a long short story about this man who goes mad from reading too much. This novella would end here, and that would have been it. Cervantes wrote many short novellas. He published twelve of them in 1613; he called them *Exemplary Novels*. It is conjecture—and you will read it in Menéndez Pidal's essay—that this was going to be the *Quixote* and that Cervantes took stock of the fact that the character and the situation had great possibilities and continued from then on with his novel. I will get back to that in a minute.

The inquiry of the library is clearly a satire of the Spanish Inquisition. The Spanish Inquisition also forbade books, collected and burned books; it is a mild satire. Here the Inquisition is represented by the niece, who is nineteen years old, the housekeeper, a village priest, and a barber; I mean, these are not exactly the high intellects that the Inquisition's officers were supposed to be. Satire in Cervantes, even against menacing institutions like the Inquisition, is always mild, never very bitter. Some details about the scrutiny of the library are significant; for instance, no book in it was published after 1591, which allows us to surmise that the *Quixote* was written after 1591.

This chapter is the bibliography that Cervantes refused to provide in the prologue. Remember when his friend says, "You can make it up"? Well, this is the bibliography. He could not have given his bibliography in the prologue because a bibliography made up of romances of chivalry is not an authoritative bibliography, as it were. It is not Aristotle, Plato, and Saint Thomas Aquinas, but Amadís de Gaula and others of that sort. So what Cervantes is giving here are the sources of Don Quixote's madness and his protagonist's literary genealogy. This is the family background he refuses to provide about Don Quixote's real family. Now, what has Don Quixote read? Well, chivalric romances, of course, but also Renaissance epics, pastoral romances, and some serious poetry. What is missing from this library? Classics and religious books. There are no devotional books in this library, as one will find in the library of Diego de Miranda, a character in the second part, who says he has many devotional books in his library. Most American readers are astonished that there is no Bible, but this is Catholic, not Protestant, Spain, and in Catholic countries we do not read the Bible much. We read devotional books or hear parts of the Bible in sermons during Mass. So if this were a library in New England or in Old England there would have been a Bible, but no Bible here at all and no devotional books either. What this means is that Alonso Quixano is a belated humanist, that is, a humanist that came at the end of humanism, like Cervantes himself, a Christian with a weakness for secular literature but not pious or devout. Although, Alonso Quixano being a humanist, there are no classics here either.

There is little poetry, although Don Quixote throughout the novel seems to know a great deal about poetry and even composes some poetry.

There is nothing by the great Garcilaso de la Vega, the important Petrarchan-style poet of the sixteenth century in Spain who was a model of poets and to whom Don Quixote alludes all the time. Somehow, he is missing. This library does not give the whole range of Cervantes' readings or even of Don Quixote's reading. What prevail are the romances of chivalry. To Don Quixote these represented a world of absolute values in a fictitious past and place, where there is no fissure, no break between the imagination, desire, and the real.

The fact is that few romances of chivalry appeared in Spain after 1565. Cervantes was born in 1547; the *Quixote* appears in 1605; the action supposedly takes place in the 1590s. So concerning the romances of chivalry, Don Quixote is also a bit out of fashion. These romances of chivalry seem to be already something of the past, but things move slowly, and many characters in the novel appear to have read them and to be conversant with them.

What else do we have in Don Quixote's library? Pastoral romances. Pastoral romances were stories of fake shepherds, people who play the role of shepherds from the eclogues of antiquity involved in amorous adventures in Neoplatonic fashion, going through beautiful bucolic settings that corresponded to the purity of their love. These stories could lead to tragic consequences, and this is the case, as you will see, in the Marcela and Grisóstomo episode that is coming up soon. These pastoral romances, I know, are the furthest thing possible from a modern sensibility. One can imagine a modern chivalric romance—I talked about James Bond and the Ian Fleming movies—but it is almost impossible to think of a modern pastoral. Perhaps not impossible but very improbable. A shepherd is one of the roles Don Quixote could have chosen to play, and, in fact, later on in the novel he will try to become one.

Whom does Cervantes surprisingly include among the authors in Don Quixote's library? Cervantes himself! The barber says, "That fellow Cervantes has been a good friend of mine for years, and I know he's more conversant with adversity than with verse. His book's ingenious enough [he is talking about Cervantes' pastoral romance *La Galatea*]; it sets out to achieve something but doesn't bring anything to a conclusion; we'll have to wait for the promised second part; maybe with correction it'll gain the full pardon denied it for the time being" (I, 6, 58). This is Cervantes winking at the reader and inviting us to fall into the same error as Don Quixote, blurring the line between literature and reality. This is what happens when Cervantes, the author whose name is printed on the cover of the book, appears within the fiction of the book; the distinction between fiction and reality is erased.

Cervantes is intimating that the reading of literature in general can lead to such confusion. All of these self-referential moments are very funny, but behind them are very serious ideas.

Notice also the irony that both the priest and the barber are steeped in the romances of chivalry; they too are readers of the romances of chivalry. They know them well, they defend some, and the priest speaks of having even begun to write one. We will find more readers of the romances of chivalry and more potential writers of romances of chivalry throughout the novel. Also notice the elaborate lie the niece comes up with to explain the disappearance of the library from the house. It is as astonishing a fantasy as Don Quixote's, so maybe it runs in the family: an old man riding a snake who leaves a trail of smoke. I hope you noticed this marvelous passage where the niece says,

> "No it wasn't the devil," replied the niece, "it was an enchanter who came one night on a cloud, after you'd gone away [she is addressing Don Quixote], and he climbed off a serpent he was riding and he went into the library and I don't know what he got up to in there, because a bit later he flew away over the roof and left the house full of smoke; and when we made up our minds to go and see what he'd done, we couldn't find any books or any library. All we remember is that as that wicked old man flew away he shouted that because of a secret grudge he bore the owner of the books and the library, he'd done the house the damage that we were about to discover. He also said that he was called the sage Munaton."
>
> "Frestón is what he must have said," said Don Quixote.
> (I, 7, 60)

Don Quixote does not question the reality of what the niece says; he just corrects the mispronunciation of the name of the enchanter. What does it mean that the niece should tell this lie? The physical disappearance of the library, walled off by the housekeeper and the niece, is an instance of the world of reality conspiring to increase Don Quixote's madness and of the canny, the familiar, the house, becoming unfamiliar. He began looking for the room and, running his hands along the walls, could not find the door. It has been said that there is a contradiction in this action of walling off the library when there are no longer any books in it, but Don Quixote does not know this, and also it would have been difficult to explain to him that the books had been burned or taken away. They were his property, so they have committed a punishable act. The barber, the priest, the niece, and the housekeeper are covering their actions with a fiction, a lie, embellished by the niece's wild imagination, which is contaminated by the romances of chivalry themselves. Notice that Cervantes does not tell us that she is a reader of romances of chivalry. We learn only through this speech of hers that she is a reader of romances of chivalry; it suggests that she too read the romances, probably sneaking into her uncle's library and reading them there secretly. You can see how much Cervantes can suggest without saying it directly.

A more significant contradiction is that while the library is walled off and the books burned the characters continue to speak to Don Quixote from within the fictions of chivalry. They both cure him and make him more insane, or they try to cure him because they realize he can be spoken to only from within his own mad world. This is because after this episode Don Quixote does not read another book; he does not even read the book about himself, as the characters in Part II do. One of the fun aspects of Part II is that the characters the protagonist encounters have read Part I, and they expect Don Quixote to act the way he acted in Part I; but Don Quixote has not read it. Alas, Sancho has not either, of course, because he cannot read. But Don Quixote does not read another book after leaving home.

Sancho now enters the scene. He represents European peasantry from time immemorial. Sancho, by the way, is a very common peasant type of name. The only comparable one I can come up with in English is Wilbur. I think a farmer in English would be called Wilbur. I mean, in Snuffy Smith, remember that comic strip? I would imagine someone being called Wilbur, I do not know why, but that is what I imagine. Sancho is a very, very common name; it gives us the last name Sánchez in Spanish, which many of you have heard, I am sure. Spanish surnames have that *-ez* that means 'belonging to the family of Sancho,' like Johnson, Davidson. Gonzalo becomes González, Rodrigo becomes Rodríguez, Martín becomes Martínez. You see? I told you you were going to learn tidbits about Spanish culture, and this is one. Panza means what? Belly, gut. It refers to his eating habits and to his being portly and in close touch with matter, with the earth.

Sancho represents common sense in contrast to Don Quixote's flights of fancy, and by *common sense* I mean the sense of the common people. Whereas Don Quixote is a voracious reader, Sancho is illiterate. He has in his head all of the traditional oral lore. He often expresses this through his *refranes,* or 'proverbs'—as you will see soon—proverbs that are the source of folk wisdom. Refranes fascinated humanists, by the way, because they

thought they were a form of common philosophy of the people and that that
philosophy could potentially contain as much wisdom as regular philosophy. There is the Book of Proverbs in the Bible, and philosophers have used
such snippets, like La Rochefoucauld in France in the seventeenth century,
who wrote *Maximes,* maxims. "La vertu n'est ce que le vice déguisé" (Virtue
is nothing but vice disguised), said La Rochefoucauld in his first maxim.
Nietzsche wrote such short snippets, too. But Sancho's are the common people's expressions of wisdom. Sancho will repeat them over and over again
until he makes Don Quixote angry for repeating them.

In terms of literary history, Sancho issues from the world of comedy,
of the theater, of the picaresque, and of *Celestina.* Some who have wanted to
do an allegorical reading of the *Quixote* see the pair as an allegory of mind
and body: Don Quixote the mind and Sancho the body (fig. 3). But the most
remarkable thing is that with his appearance the novel's world becomes one

Figure 3. Salvador Dalí, *Don Quixote and Sancho.* © Salvador Dalí, Fundació
Gala-Salvador Dalí, Artists Rights Society (ARS), New York 2013.

of constant dialogue, the dialogue between Sancho and Don Quixote. What is notable about Sancho—this will become even more evident in Part II—is that, even though he cannot read and is lacking in refinement, he is nevertheless endowed with sufficient wisdom to live and make valuable judgments. Common sense, the sense of the common people, is a sufficient quality of mind to have; this is a quite modern idea leading up to democratic and egalitarian notions that do not reach full development until the Enlightenment in the eighteenth century in philosophers like Jean-Jacques Rousseau. Sancho transcends his limitations and indeed influences his master in his attitudes and—you will see—he engages in dialogue with Don Quixote, and, although respectful, he holds his ground because he has enough wisdom to do so.

With Sancho the cast of the novel seems to be complete, and the second sally is set to begin. This second sally is where the *Quixote* as we know it really starts. If it was going to be a short story and Cervantes extended it to become the *Quixote,* it is here that the *Quixote* as we know it develops, with Sancho in place. So, in a sense, *Don Quixote* is its own source, again self-legitimation as proposed in the prologue.

The adventure of the windmills is a signature episode of the *Quixote,* as you know. You have seen it represented everywhere. At the Barajas Airport in Madrid you will find a thousand little trinkets you can buy with Don Quixote and the windmills. Why? It is the first adventure where the two characters disagree about the nature of what is being seen. It is tremendously funny; it has one of the funniest lines in the whole book. When Don Quixote tells Sancho to look at those giants, and he goes on and on about them, and, after a pause that a good comic would be able to exploit, Sancho says, "What giants?" (I, 8, 63). He does not see any giants. He sees windmills. So Don Quixote charges, with the catastrophic result that you know about.

There are other important things about this scene. It sets the four-part structure of most scenes that will follow. One, Don Quixote and Sancho see something; two, they argue about what it is; three, Don Quixote takes action; four, they discuss, in the aftermath of the adventure, what it was. There is that moment also when Don Quixote, in trying to explain how the giants became windmills, says something quite profound after this adventure. He says, " 'Not at all, friend Sancho,' replied Don Quixote. 'Affairs of war, even more than others, are subject to continual change' " (I, 8, 64). What Don Quixote is saying is that reality is in a state of flux. So things may appear to be something now and be something different a moment later. His interpretation is not foolish at all. Don Quixote also alludes to the disappearance of his library. I mean, these things can happen, he suggests. If my library can disappear, these giants can become windmills, and I could be unseated by them.

The next two episodes are very interesting. One is the fight with what Rutherford calls the Basque. These are people from the Basque country. The Basques occupy parts of Spain and France and are a proud people because they presumably were never occupied by others. First of all, they have been there since the beginning of time; their language cannot be traced back to Indo-European sources; they do not know where it came from. They are there, and the Romans could not take them over, the Arabs could not take them over, so they are very proud of that, and they take great pride as well in their aristocratic background. I know about this because my family, most of it, is Basque. Echevarría is a common Basque name. Even today they are a frightening people. There is this group called ETA in Spain that you may have heard about. It is a separatist terrorist group that blows things up and kills people, and both the Spanish and the French governments have been fighting them because the Basques, this group, want autonomy from Spain and France, they want their own country. This is the background of the episode. The Basque is the first of several characters you are going to meet in the book who are from regions other than Castile. Remember, Spain is made up of several regions, several cultures and languages, and the Basques are the furthest removed from the other cultures in the Spanish peninsula because they do not have a Roman background. Their language has nothing to do with Romance languages, and hence this character speaks funny. Part of the humor in this episode is that he speaks very broken Spanish and acts with a sense of self-assurance and haughtiness because he is a Basque.

I am going to stop here and read a couple of things from the background readings because I want to speak about the lost and found manuscript and all of that in relation to the self-reflexivity in the novel. I want you to consider—this is a way of encouraging you to read Elliott's *Imperial Spain*—the contrast that Elliott sets up here between Castile and Aragon:

> The medieval Crown of Aragon, therefore, with its rich and energetic urban patriciate, was deeply influenced by its overseas commercial interests [mostly in the Mediterranean]. It was imbued with a contractual concept of the relationship between king and subjects, which had been effectively realized in institutional form, and it was well experienced in the administration of empire. [They still are, as the Catalans are very good businessmen.] In all of these respects it contrasted strikingly with medieval Castile [where Isabella, the queen, came from]. Where, in the early four-

teenth century, the Crown of Aragon was cosmopolitan in out-
look and predominantly mercantile in its inclinations, contemporary Castile tended to look inwards, rather than outwards, and
was oriented less towards trade than war. Fundamentally, Castile
was a pastoral and nomadic society, whose habits and attitudes
had been shaped by constant warfare [against the Moors]—by
the protracted process of the *Reconquista,* still awaiting completion long after it was finished in the Crown of Aragon. (31)

The point I want to suggest here is that there is an echo of this nomadic,
warlike quality of Castile in the novel itself, where the characters are on the
move: Don Quixote and Sancho and all of the other characters who are on
the move. This is a reflection of this characteristic of Castilian society as Elliott describes it here. This is just to give you an idea of how productive the
reading of Elliott can be for this book.

The other text I want to read is from Manuel Durán's essay on the life
of Cervantes that is at the beginning of the *Casebook*. Now, this is just a brief
life of Cervantes. One cannot go much further because there are not many
documents. There are few documents to be found now. There are more,
many more documents than in Shakespeare's case, but nothing new has
been found lately. Two things are important in what Durán says here. One,
he suggests more than says, that Cervantes belongs to the first generation
of writers who are professional writers. Before, you had writers who were
aristocrats, and you had those who belonged to the clergy. They could write
because they had the leisure time to do it. They were idle readers and writers. Not Cervantes. Cervantes depends on aristocrats in the old style of the
patron, who gives you money, but he was unsuccessful that way. He was very
poor, and the publishers swindled him out of money. So he worked and was
put in jail. He was put in jail because his accounts were not too clear about
what he was doing as a tax collector (fig. 4).

And the second point, even more important, is about how Cervantes
was both inside and outside Spanish society. This is Durán:

If Cervantes' biography teaches us anything, it is that he was at
the same time *inside* and *outside* the mainstream of Spanish life.
As an insider, he took part in the battle of Lepanto and wrote at
least two successful books, *Don Quixote* and the *Exemplary Novels*. This is certainly much more than the level of achievement of
most middle-class hidalgos of his time. As an outsider, he was
always poor—almost to the point of being destitute—and not

Figure 4. Portrait of Cervantes by Gregorio Ferro (1742–1812). Engraved
by Fernando Selma. From the collection of Rolena Adorno.

infrequently in jail; he lacked influential friends in a society where
nothing could be done without them and without money; he was
often unable to protect adequately the female members of his family; the influential critics and writers of his time did not recognize
the quality of his work; his accomplishments as a soldier and as
a loyal member of the Administration were ignored—while his
every minor transgression was punished harshly. (31–32)

This is a good point about Cervantes, this figure who is both inside and outside society and hence can provide this deep probe into that society.

CHAPTER 4

Literature and Life

The *Quixote* and *Las Meninas*

Required Readings

Cervantes, *Don Quixote*, Part I, chaps. 11–20, pp. 83–165.
Dopico Black, Georgina. "Canons Afire: Libraries, Books, and Bodies in *Don Quixote*'s Spain." In *Casebook*, 95–123.
Elliott, *Imperial Spain*, 45–76.
Menéndez Pidal, Ramón. "The Genesis of *Don Quixote*." In *Casebook*, 63–94.

As I said in my last lecture and as you have already, I am sure, seen, the *Quixote* has two overarching plots. One is the story of the mad hidalgo and his squire, and the other is the story about the writing of the novel.

The one about the insane Don Quixote will acquire coherence after the fight with the Basque because he and his squire will now be pursued by the Holy Brotherhood—I will explain what the Holy Brotherhood was—and by the priest and the barber. His neighbors, the priest and the barber, want to return Alonso Quixano to his home in that unnamed village in La Mancha.

The episode about the lost manuscript and the search for the balance of the story, the found manuscript and its translation, follow themes mentioned in the prologue about the book's authorship. You will also have noticed how Cervantes plays with the divisions of the chapters; they seem to be arbitrary, they seem to be very whimsical. These are all winks at the reader, telling him that this is an artful, artificial, fictional work. Obviously, many of these divisions were made after the manuscript was finished; scholars have worked on this and come to that conclusion.

In the context of the business of finding the manuscript and the balance of the story one could ask, who is the second most important character in the *Quixote*? Is it Sancho? I think it is the narrator, the narrator and his various agents who appear throughout the novel. That would be, to my mind, the second most important character in the *Quixote*.

In this playing with the lost manuscript Cervantes is parodying the romances of chivalry, where such devices appear: the manuscript of this novel was found in a vault somewhere, it was written by some sage, and so forth. Cervantes is parodying that. Remember, a parody is a mocking imitation of a literary work or works ridiculing stylistic practices by exaggerated mimicry. In that sense, a parody is both a criticism and a homage because it is a copy of something; it is a distorted copy but still a copy.

So the business of the unfinished manuscript and its translation rekindles questions and issues that the narrator broached in the prologue. I will talk a little bit today about why all these games of authorship. But let us recapitulate how many texts or virtual texts of the novel we have so far.

We have the original text, which was supposedly written in Arabic by a lying Moorish historian called Cide Hamete Benengeli. The second is the text of the translation that the narrator pays for. Then, a further text is the one that this narrator presumably corrects and copies and rewrites and comments on in the margins, as you will see in several episodes in the future. But what about the manuscript up to chapter 8 and that initial narrator? We have no idea how that narrator came about that manuscript, so where the text of those first eight chapters came from is not explained. Now, this whole collection of manuscripts does not make a coherent whole; you cannot reduce it to a cogent system. Yes, we have the first one, the second one, the third one; it all remains vague and a mystery, and besides, we know the whole thing is a joke, beginning with the name Cide Hamete Benengeli, or *berenjena*. What is a *berenjena*? An eggplant. That is to say, his last name could be eggplant. So we are dealing with a joke.

Why are Cervantes and his narrator establishing this distance from their own text? How does this distancing mesh with the authorial willfulness we found in that first sentence, where the narrator says, "de cuyo nombre no quiero acordarme," "the name of which I purposefully omit," referring to the village in La Mancha where Don Quixote or Alonso Quixano lives? It is as if this modern author, Cervantes, could not posit his own existence without radical reservations, self-doubts about himself as creator. I have emphasized that this kind of ironic distancing has echoes of Montaigne's self-deprecatory irony and also echoes of Erasmus's irony—I have mentioned Erasmus only in passing, the great humanist Desiderius Erasmus of Rotterdam, who had many followers in Spain and who wrote a book that may be one of the sources of the *Quixote,* called *In Praise of Folly* (1511). It is an exceptionally ironic book; it is not praising folly, it is doing so in a mocking way, but it is that sort of mocking way you find in Cervantes.

It is as if Cervantes were removing the origin of the text, were leaving it in a sort of cloud of mystery, and this is part both of the irony and of the joke. Remember the quote from Lukács that I read in the first lecture about this first modern novel emerging at a time when the Christian God has abandoned the world? You do not have the centeredness you had in the *Divine Comedy.* In the *Divine Comedy* everything coheres because there is a cosmological system with the attendant symbolism provided by Catholic doctrine, and so the self of Dante, the pilgrim, is—even though he is like Don Quixote in some ways—traveling within a coherent universe, and, in fact, in the exact middle of the *Divine Comedy* the central verse of the *Divine Comedy* alludes to Dante. So Dante is at the center of this coherent universe.[1]

This is not the case in the *Quixote,* and these authorial games underscore that. Remember that Cervantes' world is a post-Copernican world, one in which the earth is no longer at the center; therefore, humankind is no longer at the center. So this is what is at stake, as it were, in all of these games. Again, these are quite serious issues, but Cervantes always presents them in a light, humorous tone, which is part of the irony itself, the humor, the laughing at oneself and laughing at others.

This is a highly important element of the *Quixote,* one that it has in common with a famous painting by Diego Velázquez, the great Velázquez about whom most of you must have heard. And that painting is *Las Meninas, The Maids of Honor* (fig. 5). First of all, as you look at the painting, think of what I mentioned before about Alberti's *De Pictura,* the treatise on perspective. Remember that I talked about Leon Battista Alberti (1404–72), an Italian who wrote a treatise on perspective? He was an architect and wrote on architecture, and I encourage you to read this little treatise; it is brief, but it is very influential because in it Alberti laid down the basis for perspective in painting. As you can see, we have perspective here because of the relative size of the figures as they move away from the front. So I want you to take that into account.

The relevance of *Las Meninas* to the *Quixote* is essentially because of this issue of self-reflexivity. In both works the creator has been given a

Figure 5. Diego Velázquez, *Las Meninas* (1656).
© Madrid, Museo Nacional del Prado.

prominent place within the work, and in both they appear in their function
as creators of the very work in question. That is Velázquez looking at us,
and he is, obviously, in the act of painting, as Cervantes appears within the
Quixote in the act of writing the novel. As we look at Velázquez, who looks
a little quizzical—I will speak a little bit more about his figure—you can recall the words of Cervantes in the prologue, when he wrote, "Many times I
picked up my pen to write it, and as many times I put it down again because
I didn't know what to say; and once when I was in this quandary, with the
paper in front of me, the pen behind my ear, my elbow on the desk and my
cheek in my hand, wondering what I could write" (12). And you can think
of Velázquez posed in a similar way, as if thinking about what to paint next
and also actually comparing his models—I will speak about who the models
are—to what he is painting. It is the same moment of doubt and hesitation

that we have in Cervantes. It is kind of a visual *aporia*—aporia is a rhetorical figure to express doubt. In *Las Meninas,* a visual aporia exists in that Velázquez appears to be hesitating over what the next brushstroke will be.

Las Meninas seems to capture a moment, and not a greatly significant moment, one that is significant in itself. How do we know it is not a very significant moment? Well, there are certain gestures, like the little girl on the right that just put her foot on the dog; the figures in the back, if we could see them more clearly you could see they are engaged in a trivial conversation. The princess is being offered, I think, a glass of water or something of the kind by a maid, and the man in the back is about to leave the room. So it is an insignificant moment, it is a moment like those in the *Quixote,* those many moments that are contingent, serendipitous, things that just happened, not in a sequence, but just caught, like a snapshot, and that is what is important about this moment in which Velázquez and all of these other people in the painting are caught up.

Of the canvas in the painting we see only the back, and we see the easel, the paints, the brush. That is, we see the instruments for creating the painting, and, in fact, we are in Velázquez's studio, his workshop, so Velázquez is painting the inside of the workshop within which the work of art is being created, as in the *Quixote* we read about the manuscript being copied and translated; we are given the details about the composition and the creation of the novel that we are reading. This studio of Velázquez would be akin to Don Quixote's library, where he keeps the books that have turned him mad and that are also Cervantes' sources.

The other important element, perhaps the most important, is that the line between reality and fiction, between life and art, has been abolished. How so? Well, who is the model of the painting? Well, presumably the king and queen, who are reflected in the back in the mirror, but in fact we are the real models as we position ourselves in front of the painting. In fact, the first time I saw this painting many years ago, in 1969 to be exact—now it is in a large room, and you can barely get to see the painting, there are so many tourists looking at it with guides talking about it—but when I saw it in 1969 at the Prado Museum it was in a room by itself, and the dimensions of the room and the way the painting was positioned were such that the moment you walked in, you walked into the painting, you became the model. It was really uncanny the sensation that you had, you really felt that you had walked into the painting and had become the painter's model, you had become that which he was in the process of painting. So here we are, becoming the model, and there is Velázquez within his own painting. He was a genius, vain, a little lazy, boastful.

All of the self-reflexive moves we have seen in the *Quixote* are present here. We see the painting, as it were, from behind, we see the preparation of the painting but not the painting itself. My late friend Severo Sarduy said that *Las Meninas* was within *Las Meninas* but backwards, the same way that in the Arabic manuscript of the *Quixote,* presumably the *Quixote* is backwards, because of course you write Arabic from right to left—it is a little bit too clever, perhaps, but you get the idea that the painting is within the painting, but you are seeing not the painting but how the painting comes about.

We also have the issue of the multiple perspectives, none of them complete. That is, Velázquez can see us and can see the model, but he cannot see the rest of his studio. The man in the back is the one with the most complete view because he can see the painting and he can see the model, if indeed the models are the king and queen. So, ironically, it is that man who is at that point leaving who has the most complete view. I say ironically because I detect a pun on Velázquez's part in that figure because, in terms of perspective, he is more or less at the *point de fuite,* in French, the vanishing point, the *punto de fuga* in Spanish, that is, the point at the center and the depth of the perspective, the vanishing point, and, ironically, in that *punto de fuga* is a man about to leave. There is, I think, a pun involved there, or perhaps I am just being too clever, like my friend Sarduy.

But the idea is that no one has a complete perspective; everything, everybody has a partial, incomplete perspective, including the artist. And this is fundamental because it makes for this ironic, incomplete view. Remember, the greatest part of the irony in Cervantes is that we only have a partial view of this infinite world, this post-Copernican, now-Galilean world—Galileo Galilei, who wrote around the same time as Cervantes and discovered the use of the telescope. He discovered the infinite spaces. So our perspective is always limited. In *Las Meninas* the perspectives are all limited and partial, and in that too the painting and the novel are alike. Now, Galileo said, "The more we know, the less we know," because he was discovering more stars, more space, and he knew then that it would be impossible to get to know all of space. We are still in that situation, although we have improved our capacity to explore space. By how much, we cannot tell.

So, what is the significance of what I have just said? I mean the limits of human knowledge, the limits of self-knowledge, and what else? We are the models of the painting, and Velázquez has given himself a prominent position in a painting that should be a painting of the king and queen, so he has usurped the place of the king and queen. He has given himself a more prominent position. He has, as it were, erased them to put himself in. This is the ambivalent position of the modern writer or author or painter or artist about his own creative powers. But Velázquez has put himself in the painting instead of those who should be the models, the king and queen.

Furthermore, Velázquez has opened the space of the model so that we, as we see the painting, actually occupy the position of the king and queen. This has all kinds of political implications; you see, the king and queen have been removed, and we, who are commoners, can occupy that position instead, so in that sense this is a very revolutionary painting. This painting is saying: anybody can be king and queen; by just stepping in front of my painting and becoming my model, you become king and queen for that moment. Remember, there was a show called "Queen for a Day," in which you became queen for a day or king for a day? You understand. So there has been a displacement of power here, in Velázquez's painting, by omitting the king and queen or by relegating them to the back, to a reflection, a blurry reflection of the king and queen.

Historically, if you read your Elliott, you will see that this reflects a real political situation in Spain, meaning that, in fact, the power of the monarchy had been diminished. This painting is from 1656. Remember, it is later than the *Quixote,* but history did not move that fast in the period, so 1605 first *Quixote,* 1656, fifty years give or take, but by the seventeenth century the Spanish monarchy has been weakened. It is in the hands of *validos,* noblemen who occupied positions of power, and the Hapsburgs were uninterested in governance and more interested in luxury and the frivolous life. Velázquez painted the Hapsburgs in some of those activities—hunting, for instance—but in this painting he has eliminated them from the position of power; he has placed himself at the center, and he has allowed us commoners to occupy the center. So this is the significance of what I have been noting about the painting. Now, the most important parallel to this will come in Part II of the *Quixote,* but I will anticipate it here, when Sancho Panza is made governor of a mock island, and Sancho, by the way, performs well as a ruler. So he, the commoner, has come to occupy the position of ruler, and this is something similar to what is happening here in *Las Meninas.* So this is why this painting is so important in relation to the *Quixote.*

But I also want you, in anticipation, to look at this figure, the woman behind the dog. The kings of Spain, like many others, including Aztec emperors, kept dwarfs and deformed people in their courts for entertainment and for amusement. This is, from our perspective, horrendous, but it was practiced all over, and Velázquez was fascinated by people who had peculiar features, irregular features. He painted dwarfs, and this is obviously a deformed woman. I think she is important because Cervantes too was very much interested in depicting strange individuals, individuals who are not beautiful but who have been scarred by time and by life and by bad luck.

So when you get to the chapter at the inn and read the descriptions of Maritornes, the wenchy prostitute who creates that whole fracas at night, think of the face of this figure—flat-faced, deformed—because it is another crucial correspondence between Velázquez's aesthetics and Cervantes' aesthetics. So much, for now, for *Las Meninas*. We will go back to Velázquez later—quite soon, as a matter of fact—to look at another one of his masterpieces, but for now, so much for *Las Meninas*.

The one thing I failed to mention is that, as you notice in looking at the painting, Velázquez has given himself an important position within the painting, but it is not really a central position; he is in an oblique position, as it were, a lateral one. This emphasizes his ambiguity about the power of creation of the modern author and, at the same time, the self-doubt, the self-doubt that the self-reflexivity expresses. So it is, I think, noteworthy that he is on the side, as it were, and he is looking obliquely at the model, in the same way that Cervantes says that he is father or stepfather of his book. Remember what he said in the 1605 prologue; the obliqueness of Velázquez's position within the painting is similar to that obliqueness of whether Cervantes is father or stepfather of the *Quixote*.

Now, to go back to the novel. After the episode with the Basque, when Don Quixote injures the man in a fight, Sancho is very apprehensive. He is sure they are now going to be pursued by the Holy Brotherhood. Don Quixote and Sancho move in a world of alienation, of madness, of unsociability, and how can society, real society, deal with Don Quixote's madness? This issue is highlighted by the presence of civil and criminal law in the book. Sancho knows they are being pursued by the *Santa Hermandad*. And who was the *Santa Hermandad*, or 'Holy Brotherhood'? This was a vigilante police force that the Catholic Kings, Ferdinand and Isabella, had created, if you remember your Elliott. Why? Remember that they invested a lot of effort in trying to unify the Spanish peninsula, but, as I have mentioned, Spain is divided into several regions with different cultures and languages and exemptions from the law, where royal authority, just like the federal law in this country, did not reach because of the exemptions these regions had.

Therefore, the Catholic Kings created a police force that could pass through those regional boundaries and apprehend fugitives.

The Holy Brotherhood was in charge of roads because the roads were under the purview of the Crown, and they were parallel to another institution the Catholic Kings created that could also police the entire peninsula: the Holy Inquisition. The Inquisition could police regions other than Castile; that is, Galicia, the Basque country, for instance, and so could the Holy Brotherhood. The Holy Brotherhood was feared because they could not only apprehend you but try you and execute you on the spot, and Sancho says he already hears their arrows buzzing around his ears. Why? Because Sancho is vulnerable to the Holy Brotherhood whereas Don Quixote, as an hidalgo, feels he is protected from the law. So Sancho is the one, if you will notice, who insists they are being pursued by the Holy Brotherhood and have to hide in the hills. The Holy Brotherhood—sorry to give away the plot—will eventually apprehend them but let them go at the end of Part I. The members of the Holy Brotherhood were just ordinary people who were engaged in this vigilante police force.

So we move now to the adventure with the goatherds and the speech on the Golden Age, one of the more famous episodes of Part I. This is an episode, like others, in which a contrast is established between what Don Quixote has in his head from having read so many books and the real world around him. He believes that these goatherds are like shepherds of the classical tradition, and this is what makes him think of the Golden Age, when there is no mine or thine, no private property, only goodness, and humans live at one with nature. So he delivers a beautiful speech filled with all kinds of clichés from the classical tradition to these goatherds, who do not understand at all what he is talking about.

What is the connecting thread between that idealized reality, that idealized world in Don Quixote's head, and the reality of these goatherds who are listening to the speech and not understanding a thing Don Quixote is saying? The one thing that connects the two—and it goes back to one of the points I made before—is the goatherds' kindness. That which has not changed from those classical idealized times to the present is the kindness of people. And remember that I said Cervantes likes to depict people from the lowest classes being kind to each other and to Don Quixote. The goatherds have not reacted to Don Quixote's appearance—it is striking, to say the least, that this man has suddenly shown up dressed in armor and started speaking this way—and they have allowed him to sit with them, to share their food and drink, and to be involved in their life. So there is a sharp contrast but also a commonality here: the goatherds are kind to Don Quixote and allow him to be what he wants, even if they do not understand what he is talking about.

This is the first of several postprandial speeches in the *Quixote*. This is another one of the words I am going to teach you in this class so you can be pedantic in the present and in the future; *postprandial* simply means an after-dinner speech. What is the import of these postprandial speeches? and what do they have to do with the theme of Don Quixote's speech? After-dinner speeches celebrate the defeat of the world, that is, of animals and plants, and the end of work as well as the plants' and animals' having been turned into food. Here they are eating some meat, they are drinking some wine, which is like the blood of the earth, they are passing the wine around, and they are enjoying the fruits of their labor at the end of the day; they are celebrating the end of work and rest. And there is a connection between the eating and the talking and the speech, oral activities, both pleasurable activities. So this is the connection between these postprandial speeches, between the food and the speaking. In others there will be much more merriment, a recurring theme in the *Quixote*.

There is a great deal about food in *Don Quixote*, and in some cases food and language actually coalesce, most memorably when Don Quixote and Sancho vomit on each other after the episode of the sheep. It is as if food and language have become one, and they have a dialogue between them: I vomit on you and you vomit on me, and that is a form of dialogue. I know this is not palatable to think about, especially if you just had lunch, but this is the significance here of speech and food. But the most important part is the contrast between Don Quixote's ideas and the clichés he draws from the classical tradition and the real, everyday life of these goatherds. The herders also serve as a transition to the Marcela and Grisóstomo episode, in which the whole theme of the pastoral will be taken up at, you could say, a higher literary and philosophical level.

The stakes are much higher in the Grisóstomo and Marcela episode because a death has occurred and there is a real conflict. So I think the transition here is smooth. The transition is made smoother by the figure of Vivaldo, the man with whom Don Quixote engages in conversation about the nature of knighthood. Don Quixote and Sancho have been told by the goatherds about the conflict involving the death of Grisóstomo.

So we move to that episode in which the main theme appears to be that of free will, but a very meaningful ancillary theme is, again, that of literature and its effects. Marcela and Grisóstomo are figures who are counterparts to

Don Quixote in their relationship to literature. Both Marcela and Grisósto-mo—but mostly Marcela—want to playact a literary role. She wants to be a shepherdess and take to the hills, and Grisóstomo dresses up as a shepherd in order to pursue her. But Grisóstomo is also a reader, and in this he is like Don Quixote; not only a reader but a graduate of the University of Sala-manca and a poet. So the stakes here, I repeat, are much higher. It is almost as if literature were on trial.

Grisóstomo has committed suicide. It is not said straightforwardly be-cause suicide is a mortal sin. Cervantes is writing within the context of a very Catholic Spain, so he cannot just write directly that Grisóstomo has committed suicide. But the word used in the text, *desesperado,* he became desperate, he was desperate, points to the fact that he committed suicide; he committed suicide because Marcela spurned him. In the sixteenth cen-tury, to *desesperarse,* to despair and become desperate, was a euphemism for committing suicide.

But what is amazing here is the highly detailed socioeconomic context of the episode. In this sense, Cervantes is anticipating Honoré de Balzac, the great nineteenth-century French novelist who gave exceedingly specific details about the economic situations of his characters. And here we have that because we learn that Marcela is filthy rich; she is the daughter of a rich man named Guillermo. Her mother died giving birth to her, and then Guillermo died and left Marcela entrusted to an uncle—to a brother of his, I guess—who is a priest and who will administer her estate until she gets mar-ried. Women could not hold property outright, and the moment a woman married, the estate would pass over to her husband.

Grisóstomo is no longer a youth, like those characters we will meet later in the book; he is thirty years old when he dies. When Don Quixote and the goatherds arrive at the funeral and see the body, the narrator describes him: "They saw the corpse, dressed as a shepherd, of a man who seemed to be about thirty" (I, 13, 101). Grisóstomo was rich also. He had inherited a great deal of property and lands and animals, and so it seems as if this couple would have been a perfect match. He is of noble lineage, she is not, but this would not be an impediment nor bring the line to a halt, as it were, because by Castilian law nobility was passed on through the male. So Cervantes has created a situation here for a perfect marriage in a small village: these two rich young people would marry and create an even larger estate. It could become a *mayorazgo*—a word you will learn more about later—an entailed state.

What intervenes to impede this perfect match? What intervenes is Marcela's desire to become a shepherdess, spurning all of her many suitors, and Grisóstomo's desperate pursuit of her. Grisóstomo is a poet. We learn that because his poem is read at the funeral, a typical Petrarchan *canzone.* He is also the one who writes the *autos sacramentales,* the allegorical plays performed on the day of Corpus Christi. These are religious plays that relate the story about the Eucharist. Grisóstomo is also a cosmographer; he can tell what the weather is going to be in the future. He is a kind of a budding Faust—Goethe's *Faust,* in the nineteenth century—in that he wants to fore-tell the future.

Grisóstomo is madly in love, he is a poet, and he has all of these de-monic qualities that lead him to desperation and to suicide. In fact, he wants to be so much in control that he has arranged for his burial in such a way that it is almost like a play. He wants to be buried where he met Marcela, not in consecrated ground, which raises the eyebrows of the church. His burial and funeral are going to be like an *auto sacramental,* like one of the plays he wrote; his body will be the main prop and protagonist. But Marcela appears at the funeral and delivers a spirited defense of herself in precise forensic rhetoric, that is, legal rhetoric and legal terms to defend herself, and the is-sue then becomes who is right in the end.

Female characters in Cervantes are quite active and want to take their destiny into their own hands. Marcela is a good example. So one could say Marcela is right, and this is what Don Quixote, acting as a judge, rules. When Marcela flees into the hills, some people want to pursue her, but he says, no, no, no, no; he says, I will defend her right to be free; she has proven beyond a doubt that she had no culpability whatsoever in the fate of Grisóstomo, and so she should be free. Is she right? or has Marcela also acted with some selfishness in wanting to become a literary shepherdess? to go around in the woods and play at being a shepherdess, not marrying? These two have squandered their estates, have squandered the possibility of forming a sta-ble, prosperous family. Who is right and who is wrong is not as clear as it would seem.

The question, I think, remains open. Grisóstomo has died, he has killed himself. Marcela has suffered a civil death in the sense that she has run into the woods, into the hills, into the thickest parts of the hills, the text says. We do not know what is going to become of her there, separated from society and playing this literary role. And so, I think, the end of the episode leaves us with a sense of ambiguity. We have to decide, as we did in the Andrés episode before, but, again, the answer is not as clear as it seems in the two cases.

It also seems that the episode is inviting us to consider the effects of lit-erature. That is, literature has given Marcela and also, in a sense, Grisóstomo the idea that absolute freedom is possible, that you can live your dreams and live out your desires. Obviously this is a dangerous proposition, one which can lead to the kind of conflict we have here. Remember, the one passing judgment in the end is a madman imbued in literature. Don Quixote's judgment is favorable to Marcela because, in a way, he is like her. He defends Marcela's right to be insane like him and to act out her madness.

This episode concludes on a hilarious note. In the next incident they go into the woods that Marcela has escaped to, and they find a *locus amoenus,* which is a commonplace in literary art and literature, a very pleasant place with grass, shade, water, a running brook making a pleasant sound, and so forth. And what happens there? We have here the translation of the previous amorous episode into animal love when poor Rocinante, who does not seem to be vigorous enough to harbor such desires, becomes interested in some mares that are being put out to graze and to be watered by some men from Yanguas—these are Galicians. And what happens? When poor Rocinante approaches the mares to, as the text says, communicate his desires to them, they respond with their hoofs; they kick him, and then their keepers come and beat the daylights out of poor Rocinante, and when Don Quixote and Sancho try to intervene, they too are beaten up by these people. This is the conclusion, in a way, of the Grisóstomo and Marcela episode, but in a humorous key. Cervantes likes to work with this kind of contrast and with this transposition of something that was deadly serious and even somber in the Grisóstomo and Marcela episode into this slapstick comedy episode of poor Rocinante trying to seduce the mares and being kicked viciously. So I think this is the end of the Marcela and Grisóstomo episode. The last comment on it, as it were.

The knight and his squire themselves are about to enter into the thick of the novel, which will be a counterpoint between the Sierra Morena—that is, the hills into which they go fleeing from the Holy Brotherhood—and Juan Palomeque's inn. That inn will become a temple and a courthouse where the complicated love stories in Part I will be resolved.

CHAPTER 5

Ugliness and Improvisation

Juan Palomeque's Inn

Required Readings

Cervantes, *Don Quixote,* Part I, chaps. 11–20, pp. 83–165.
Elliott, *Imperial Spain,* 45–76.
González Echevarría, Roberto. "Introduction." In *Don Quixote,* vii–xxii.

Let us begin today with some general issues that I think are pertinent to the reading of the *Quixote.* How significant is it that the *Quixote* is written in prose, not in verse? Prose, because it is the prose of the world, reflects everyday life. Everyday life is prosaic, and this is the life that is being depicted in the *Quixote.* It is devoid of the order and the rhythm of poetry. Hence the novel, from now on, will be written in prose, with few exceptions. Remember my allusion in the last lecture to the *Divine Comedy* and to the order of the *Divine Comedy* and that central line in the middle of the whole comedy alluding to Dante and the highly structured nature of that poem down to the tercets and to every line with its rhyme, with its meter. The same is true of the *Aeneid,* with its exquisite form and shape. In the *Quixote* what is represented is, I repeat, the prosaic. The prosaic is that which is common and ordinary and not apt to be expressed in verse, although there are, as you have seen, bits of verse in some episodes. Another general topic after the Marcela episode—when Don Quixote interferes and does not allow anyone to chase her into the woods—is that we have to ponder if Don Quixote is a hero. If he is, how does he differ from Ulysses, from Aeneas, from the Cid, from

Roland, and other heroes of the preceding Western literary tradition? Is he mostly a moral hero? This is something we should consider as we continue to read the novel.

The last general question I would like to bring up is, again, that of irony. Instead of saying what we think, with irony we feign to think what we say. Irony can become sarcastic, but not in Cervantes. Cervantes' irony is mild and humorous rather than cutting or sarcastic. The dialogue on which the book depends so much is essentially ironic because we can see the errors of both protagonists as they speak with each other, errors that they point out to each other. In the case of Don Quixote, as you will notice, time and again he points out the errors Sancho makes in speaking, but Sancho will also catch Don Quixote in a few mistakes himself.

We move now to one of my favorite parts of the book, the scenes in Juan Palomeque's inn. You have to remember the names of these characters. His name is Juan Palomeque. I am sure you did not quite retain it. He is the innkeeper, the most important innkeeper in the first part of the *Quixote*. Among the most famous and important episodes in *Don Quixote* are those at his inn. I have already spoken about the importance of inns in the plot of the *Quixote* when commenting on the first inn, in which Don Quixote was knighted. Karl Ludwig Selig, retired now, a professor at Columbia University, wrote, "Formally, structurally, thematically the inn is an important focal point, a place of configurations and conflations."[1]

Inns in the *Quixote*, in Cervantes, are derived from the picaresque tradition, where they figure prominently in books like *Lazarillo de Tormes* and *Guzmán de Alfarache*, which I have mentioned several times. In those books, the inns play a role similar to that in the *Quixote*. In fact, as I remarked, the first innkeeper was a retired pícaro, and he tells with relish his life of picaresque adventures, where he visited or stayed at the most notorious picaresque emporia throughout Spain. I also spoke of how inns provide a kind of archaeology of society, using that metaphor because characters from different social classes and professions meet in them. The inn run by Juan Palomeque is by far the most important building in Part I of the *Quixote*, even more important than Don Quixote's house. In Part II there will be other buildings, as you will discover. I emphasize, again, that it is good to remember the names of these secondary characters, like Juan Palomeque, who play major roles in the novel. They sometimes, as I have mentioned, have interesting names, and in some cases the names are interesting because they are so common, like Pedro Alonso, the neighbor who picks Don Quixote up, and Pero Pérez, the priest. In the case of Juan Palomeque, the last name has something to do with pigeons; *paloma* is Spanish for 'pigeon.' The -*eque* ending does not sound very good, like -*ote* in Quixote. Palomeque is mostly a funny last name.

We have arrived at the inn via a road which was, for the most part, a sunny and bright realm. But this will change now. The inn is in a kind of a *chiaroscuro,* which in Italian means 'bright dark'; it is a combination of darkness and light, and it is commonly associated with baroque art. I will be speaking about the baroque in later lectures because the cliché is that the first part of the *Quixote* is mostly Renaissance and the second part baroque. So the inn is a dark place. In Juan Palomeque's inn, people eat, fight, have sexual encounters, and live in very close proximity, as you have no doubt noticed, making for a great deal of friction, real and metaphoric, as the characters rub against each other in very confined quarters.

At the inns the humor is highly theatrical. It is like the characters are on a stage, and, in fact, in later episodes the inn really will become a theater, with characters coming in and out like actors on a stage. The inn is theatrical in the sense of slapstick comedy; slapstick because it is a comedy in which characters hit each other with that stick that has a flap and makes a sound like it is a hard blow. You hit somebody and pow! It comes from the *commedia dell'arte.* Commedia dell'arte was a kind of Italian theater of the fifteenth and sixteenth centuries in which there was no dialogue; the characters just pushed, slapped, and kicked each other. The word in Spanish for slapstick is a funny one: it is called *matapecados,* 'sin killer.' Comedy at the inn is slapstick.

This comedy involves physical violence, mistaken identities, and rowdy behavior. In episodes such as these Cervantes displays his talent for comedy, which he put to good use in writing his successful *entremeses,* or interludes for the theater. The *entremés* is a funny one-act play usually staged between the acts of a full-length play. Humor dominates in these episodes when Don Quixote's imaginings suddenly appear to mesh with what is happening in the tawdry world in which he finds himself. He takes the innkeeper for a nobleman in his castle, as he did at the first inn, and Maritornes as a damsel in love with him when she is really an ugly prostitute on her way to meet the muleteer, who happens to be lodging there too. The point seems to be that even the rather tangible reality of the inn can be transformed by the characters' needs, desires, and imaginings because this inn is as far removed as possible from a castle and the characters as far removed as possible from those in the romances of chivalry.

Don Quixote's erotic desires have been aroused by the innkeeper's daughter. The innkeeper has a young daughter who we imagine to be a mere teenager, and she is described in the text as "a very attractive girl" (I, 16, 122). This episode is the most explicit erotic display by Don Quixote in the entire book, erotic in a sense of explicit sexuality. More than anything, the episodes at the inn are an instance of the social being subverted by erotic desire, that of the muleteer and Maritornes as well as Don Quixote's. The ensuing violence involves even the law, as a representative of the Holy Brotherhood intervenes and brains Don Quixote with a candleholder in the darkness of the inn.

What does this show? Well, that the sublimated eros of literary tradition has its counterpart, perhaps its real driving force, in these unleashed erotic forces that propel the characters to violence. Cervantes is not moralizing here; he hardly ever does. All he seems to be doing is showing the real subconscious of literature, the counterpart, let us say, of the romances of chivalry and the pastoral; what lurks underneath the romances of chivalry and the pastoral. This is the reason for the darkness. It conceals and harbors all of these forces, as opposed to the pastoral. Pastoral literature always takes place in daylight, particularly in the eclogues—eclogues are long poems on a pastoral theme. The most famous were by Virgil. The duration of an eclogue is the time span of a day, but here it is the complete opposite, darkness revealing the real forces underneath those pastoral poems and the romances of chivalry.

Let me go over the cast of characters in Juan Palomeque's inn. As you, I am sure, have noticed already, Cervantes relishes in the presentation of characters drawn from the lower strata of society and tries to give a rounded view of them, meaning that along with their coarseness they often display kindness and human understanding. These characters, again, are drawn from the picaresque, but they are also derived from the numerous juridical documents of the period. The Spanish Crown created an extensive judicial system in the sixteenth century with hundreds and thousands of documents stored in archives testifying to the comings and goings of individuals, such as the ones we see at the inn. Cervantes, as I always emphasize, tries to give a rounded view of these characters drawn from the lowest classes and also from the criminal classes, showing that they can be kind, also. And they are not stereotypes; they are individualized by their moral and physical features. The best case is Maritornes. Maritornes, about whom I am going to speak now, is a name I hope you will retain. I have mentioned her a couple of times, and I want you to remember her name from now on.

The first character is the innkeeper Juan Palomeque, el Zurdo, the left-handed one, lefty—I will speak about that in a minute. Remember, I told you to look for details. This is a crucial detail, as you will see a little later. Look for details. His wife and the daughter—that is, the family—run the inn. Number two, Maritornes. She is an Asturian wench who in spite of her profession is kind to Don Quixote and Sancho. She gives Sancho a drink at the end when he is leaving. Notice that she is from Asturias.

We have already met the Basque, who is from the Basque countries. I spoke about the Basques. We met the Yanguesans, who were from Galicia, northwestern Spain, and here we have someone from Asturias (fig. 6). The Galicians are of Celtic origin and are somewhat like the Irish. They play bagpipes like the Irish; Galicians are known for their bagpipes. I will speak more about the Galicians as we go on, but Maritornes is from Asturias, also a northern region of Spain. They are very proud, the Asturians, because the Reconquest, the war against the Moors, began in Asturias, and they take great pride in that and in that it began right away, after the Moors occupied Spain. So the fact that she is Asturian might be a joke on the part of Cervantes; they are proud, but here we have an Asturian prostitute.

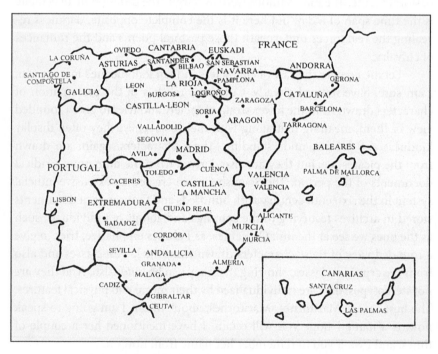

Figure 6. Map of Spain. Courtesy of Mark R. Williams.

And Cervantes was obviously a proud Castilian, but he has enough Castilians in the book who are not exactly individuals to be proud of; but he has a view, a particular view, of the people from various regions of Spain. So Maritornes is a wench from Asturias. She takes pride in being reliable in her professional dealings as a whore. She keeps her dates, in this case with catastrophic results. Though Maritornes is no princess, as Don Quixote imagines her to be, she is responsible within her profession and generous. Cervantes is not a moral relativist, but he has an understanding of human frailty and the tumbles of individual fate—if you read with care, you will have learned that Maritornes is a prostitute because a series of misfortunes has brought her down, not because she is inherently inclined to misconduct; and as I have said, she is ethical within the expectations of her trade. She delivers.

Cervantes also liked to show how morality can be a code that is coherent only within a given social context. You will see this better in Part II when there is a gang of outlaws and within that gang, within its rules, there are sets of ethical behavior. In his own case, as you have read in the essay by Durán in the *Casebook,* you will know that the women in Cervantes' family, because of financial pressures, were involved in questionable activities at certain points—and I do hope that you read that fine, succinct essay by Durán from which I quoted a little bit in the last class emphasizing the fact that Cervantes was an insider and outsider at the same time in Spain.

I am going down the list of characters at the inn: the carrier, a muleteer, who happens to be an acquaintance or even a relative of Cide Hamete Benengeli, the alleged author of this story. This is another instance of Cervantes' self-reflexivity. Here we have a character who is related to the "real" author. Now, it is true that Moriscos—fellows of Moorish origins—tended to be carriers like this one, but Cervantes is making, again, another hilarious connection between the fictional and the real worlds of his novel. Going down the list of these characters—and I am doing this as if this had been a play because, as I said, the inn is very much like a stage—there is an officer from the ancient Holy Brotherhood of Toledo, who represents the law, and he is the one who hits Don Quixote on the head with a candleholder. I explained in the last class what the Holy Brotherhood was at the time. It plays an important role in the *Quixote* because it is the police force that is pursuing Don Quixote and Sancho.

Finally, there are Pedro Martínez and Tenorio Hernández, who are among the rowdies who participate in Sancho's blanket tossing at the end of this episode (fig. 7). You remember when they go out and toss Sancho on

Figure 7. Salvador Dalí, *Blanket Toss of Sancho.* © Salvador Dalí, Fundació
Gala-Salvador Dalí, Artists Rights Society (ARS), New York 2013.

a blanket, a practice that was mostly reserved for animals during carnival
time. They would do it to poor dogs. A point to consider is that these men
are rowdies but not inherently evil characters, in spite of their social station.
Notice, again, the very common name Pedro Martínez, who happens not to
be the retired Dominican baseball pitcher. Being named Pedro Martínez is
like being called Peter Smith in English, so it is not unlikely that this coincidence would happen. He is a ruffian who participates in the blanket tossing
of poor Sancho.

　　These characters, like Don Quixote himself, tend to have physical defects or scars. The source here, if there has to be a specific source, is *Celestina.* Remember, this is the work I have mentioned several times in which
the protagonist is an old whore and go-between who has an ugly scar on her
face. The faces of these characters are scarred by time, by temperament, by
profession, by crimes, by illness, by class. In this, Cervantes is very much like

Velázquez; he finds beauty in ugliness, and this is very much a part of the modernity of Cervantes and Velázquez. He finds beauty in the deformed, even the monstrous; and some of Velázquez's and Cervantes' characters are monsters. These characters have features that make them apt to be displayed, to be seen, to be admired, like Velázquez's dwarfs.

As you can see, Velázquez has painted this dwarf with objects around him, so that you can gauge his relative size (fig. 8). He is tiny, indeed, and that physical feature is what makes him a specific individual, and it is that deformity that makes him aesthetically interesting. Some of them, like the one in *Las Meninas,* have an air of idiocy on their faces, as if they were also retarded. I think the most famous one is Sebastián de Morra (fig. 9). These

Figure 8. Diego Velázquez, *El bufón 'Calabacillas,' llamado erróneamente "Bobo de Coria."* © Madrid, Museo Nacional del Prado.

Figure 9. Diego Velázquez, *El bufón don Sebastián de Morra*
(c. 1645). © Madrid, Museo Nacional del Prado.

are characters in the court. They were used for entertainment and for amusement. This one has, as you can see, an air of idiocy in his face. And then if we
go back to *Las Meninas* there is the freak with that flat, round face and that
idiotic gesture (see fig. 5). I wonder if she suffered from Down syndrome or
something like that. Such characters can and were turned into spectacles—as
happens, by the way, to Don Quixote in several episodes—because of their
peculiar features. It is their defects that make them aesthetically valuable
and different. Velázquez was a master at showing individuals' features and
suggesting a relationship between them and the personality of his subjects.
He did this even in the portraits of kings. Some of these Hapsburgs had a
large jaw; because of inbreeding such features were emphasized genetically.
Velázquez would paint the kings like that, without flinching. It is the same

as Cervantes' penchant to characterize on the basis of peculiarities of body and mind.

Don Quixote is thin and cerebral, Sancho is fat and physical. Each, however, is mental or cerebral or physical in a particular way. But while focusing on these ugly characters, let us not forget Marcela's perfect beauty and that of other young women and men about to appear in the novel. These follow models of beauty derived from Renaissance art, which in turn derived from classical models. Think of Botticelli's Venus in *La Primavera*. Variety is the norm in the *Quixote*, with frequent contrasts between extreme ugliness and stunning beauty. You will find this in characters like Dorotea, who are about to appear.

At the inn the first character with a physical defect is Juan Palomeque himself, who is left-handed. Until recently, left-handedness was considered a defect, and in school left-handed children were forced to use their right hand. My Basque maternal grandfather was left-handed, and he was physically forced to use his right hand in school or otherwise he would be beaten. When he went home to do his homework he would do it left-handed, which was more comfortable, and as a result he could write with both hands. Nowadays we are far from thinking of left-handedness as a physical defect. But the most remarkable character in terms of physical traits is Maritornes. Her name, by the way, could suggest an inversion of virginity: Mari, Maria, Virgin Mary, -*tornes*, turns around. Maritornes would be the reverse of a virgin. She is, in fact, a whore. Let me read the description of Maritornes. First, on page 122 of your book: "Another girl was serving at the inn: an Asturian lass with broad jowls, a flat-backed head, a pug nose, blind in one eye and not very sound in the other. It's true that the loveliness of her body offset her other shortcomings: she didn't measure five feet from her head to her toes, and her shoulders, with something of a hump on them, made her look down at the ground more than she liked" (I, 16, 122). Remember, again, the dwarf in *Las Meninas:* the face is broad and flat, the nose deformed. Her being stooped or hunchbacked suggests her being inclined, literally, to the ground, to the base, to that which is low, not to the heights. Her defective eyes add a touch of grotesqueness but also signal limitations in perception that are at the core of what happens at the inn in the dark, when the characters cannot see each other very well. These are only her physical attributes. Later, when Don Quixote seizes Maritornes we get the rest of the picture:

> The Asturian girl [Maritornes], hunched up in silence, was creeping forward with her arms held out in front of her in search of her lover, when she bumped into Don Quixote's arms and he

seized her by her wrist and pulled her towards him and made her sit on his bed, and she did not dare utter a word. He felt her shift and, although it was made of sackcloth, it was for him the sheerest sendal. On her wrists she was wearing glass beads, but for him they had the sheen of precious pearls of orient. Her hair was more like a horse's mane, but he saw it as strands of gleaming Arabian gold, the splendor of which made the very sun grow dim. And her mouth, which reeked of stale piccalilli, seemed to him to exhale the gentlest of aromas; and, all in all, he depicted her in his imagination with every attribute of that other princess he'd read about in his books who, overcome by love, came to see the sore wounded knight, arrayed in all the finery there described. And the poor hidalgo was so besotted that neither touch nor smell nor any of the good maiden's other attributes could make him notice his mistake, even though they'd have made anyone but a muleteer vomit. (I, 16, 126)

We move here into a kind of phenomenology of ugliness as Maritornes's more contingent and secondary characteristics are itemized: how does it feel? how does one perceive ugliness or the repulsive? The reader is given these random features depending on what she wore and how she smelled on that particular night, and what her breath was like, owing to her last meal. The phrase "nor any of the good maiden's other attributes" is a polite circumlocution, a periphrastic way of sparing the reader from seeing her probably more revolting traits.

The aesthetics of the ugly and repulsive is very much contingent on temporality, on the passing of time, which wears down bodies and endows them with undesirable, though temporary, qualities. Deformities are contingent, individuating, particularizing, in contrast to perfect models, which are timeless. Contingency, by the way, since I am using the word a lot, means "that which may or may not happen, possible, happening by chance, accidental, fortuitous, conditional." This is the aesthetic counterpart of the statement Don Quixote makes when he is mauled by the windmills that he took for giants. Everything is subject to change. It is the realm of mischievous enchanters, who alter things, like walling up his library and turning this damsel, this beautiful princess that he thinks he is holding, into this repulsive whore.

Don Quixote's mistake is applying the Renaissance model of beauty, that of a blonde, beautiful young woman, to the grotesque Maritornes. His mistake reveals, however, that what he passes off as sublime love is really lust. The episode lays bare, appropriately in the middle of the night and in total darkness, Don Quixote's subconscious. We should not miss the point that as a prostitute, an embodiment of lust, Maritornes is the opposite of what one would normally consider amorously desirable. Here we are at the lowest point of desire, at its basest.

So the episodes at Juan Palomeque's inn, fraught with erotic violence and culminating in Don Quixote's and Sancho's violent bowel movements and vomiting, are like a phantasmagoria in which the most basic drives behind the protagonists' actions are staged. If we want to use Freudian terminology, they are reduced to their oral, anal, and even genital stages.

Don Quixote's desire for the innkeeper's daughter shows his physical desires, which are surely behind his transforming of Aldonza Lorenzo into Dulcinea. Aldonza Lorenzo is the young woman near Don Quixote's village whom he turns into Dulcinea, so we see how he turns Aldonza into the sublime Dulcinea. Aldonza is not ugly, as we will see. She is brawny but attractive. Don Quixote's lust for her is typical of an upper-class, older gentleman's lust for a lower-class woman whom he considers sexier and more sexual than women of his social class. Spanish literature is full of situations in which a lustful aristocrat tries to ravage a peasant woman; all of European literature is full of this. Don Juan, of the famous Don Juan tradition, is such a case, but there are others I will mention.

Don Quixote's and Sancho's bodily evacuations provoked by Fierabras's balsam dramatize the violent forces underlying their basic drives to live. Don Quixote claims to have the recipe or the prescription for this balsam, which he learned in the romances of chivalry and that if you drink will make you whole again, even if you have been sliced or cut in two. You drink the balsam and, boom!, you are made whole again, you are cured. He asks for the ingredients and makes it, and they drink it, and, of course, the results are horrendous because both Don Quixote and Sancho have violent bowel movements and vomiting.

This is particularly so with Sancho, who, by the way, will defecate again soon out of fear—if you have gotten to that funny episode with the fulling hammers. But note that the balsam is supposed to restore their bodies, to make their physiques whole again, erasing the ravages of violence and, more broadly, of time. The balsam would erase those ugly physical features or scars that identified them. Here, the balsam stands for something that would erase those marks on their bodies, the marks I have been speaking about. Excreting is a mock form of literal purification, a rejection of the material world they have ingested. Ironically, Don Quixote does get better; perhaps, medically speaking, he needed to be cleansed out, and so taking this balsam, which turns out to be a violent laxative, makes him feel better. But Sancho almost dies because he vomits and has diarrhea. I will return to this unsavory topic soon.

The flimsy construction of Juan Palomeque's inn leads us to a topic I have mentioned several times before: improvisation, evident in Velázquez's gesture with his brush and palette in *Las Meninas*. He is improvising. Juan Palomeque's inn is the most important building in Part I and is an internal emblem of the book's careless genesis and structure, or its deliberately careless genesis and structure. Here I am equating the inn and its construction with the composition of the *Quixote*. The inn is the sole shelter the protagonists find repeatedly in Part I, but they enjoy no protection or peace within its walls because it is so dilapidated that it barely keeps them out of the elements. It is not a meaningful, fulfilling end of the road but a way station. That is, it is not a home to return to, a substantial shelter that provides solace. Its parts are in a sorry state of disrepair and do not match harmoniously with each other. For instance, the place in which Don Quixote is going to sleep: "camaranchón" is the word for it in Spanish in the original. A *camaranchón* is a sort of attic where Don Quixote's bed is set up: "an attic that showed all the signs of having served for many years in former times as a hayloft" (I, 16, 122).

Sebastián de Covarrubias, whom you must remember from my earlier lectures—the lexicographer who wrote the first dictionary of the Spanish language and published it in 1611—says that *camaranchón* is derived from the Latin *camera*, 'chamber,' and that it is a disparaging term for the highest spot in a house, an attic or loft where old junk, heterogeneous by its very nature, is stored. This is the reason the stars can be seen through the gaps in its flimsy roof, which is why it is called in the Spanish an "estrellado establo," or "starlit barn'" in our translation (I, 16, 124).

From the inside you can see the ceiling with holes in it, and it is starry because you can see the sky through it. This suggests that the inn was originally a small house to which additions were made haphazardly, incorporating the stable and its hayloft into its living quarters to accommodate more paying guests.

A ceiling so full of holes that the stars are visible from within comically suggests that the inn has cosmic connections, as did Greek, Roman, and Aztec temples as well as their Renaissance counterparts through their alignment to celestial bodies. In classical architecture, in Aztec architecture, the temples were aligned with the stars, with the constellations, so that the building would be part of this cosmic world. Also, such a star-spangled ceiling would be nature's counterpart to the elaborate ceilings of certain palaces on which zodiac signs were often depicted. What is the closest example we have to that today, those of us who live in the Northeast, that we see all the time? Grand Central Station! The next time you go to Grand Central Station, look up—not too long or they might take your wallet—but look up and you will see that the ceiling has all of the constellations depicted on it. It is as if there were no ceiling, as if you could actually see the stars. It is a device used in Renaissance palaces. In Juan Palomeque's inn the holey ceiling is an ironic allusion to that.

Against the background of the inn's ramshackle, improvised architecture, such allusions are hilarious and highlight that it is no architectural jewel built by following a careful plan and classical models. It would seem as if during its construction, which was gradual and ruled by chance, everything in it had been transformed by contingency—there is *contingency* again—and the passage of time. "Many years," says the quotation I read you. The provisional nature of its furnishings is evident in Don Quixote's bed, which, "consisted of four bumpy boards on top of two torturous benches" (I, 16, 122). Predictably, during the free-for-all provoked by Maritornes's nocturnal appointment, the mule driver climbs on it and makes it collapse: "The bed, being somewhat fragile and insecurely founded, couldn't bear the addition of the muleteer and came crashing to the floor" (I, 16, 127).

The improvised patchwork architecture of Palomeque's inn reflects that of the structure of the *Quixote* Part I, with its interpolated stories, some of which you are going to read soon. And also Cervantes' notorious errors and even Don Quixote's practice of letting Rocinante's whim dictate the direction of his journey.

The *Quixote* is the only classic with a whole bibliography about its errors. All classics have them—you know, they say Homer fell asleep when something in the *Odyssey* is not perfect—but the errors in the 1605 *Quixote* are a notorious part of it. Much has been written about them. Improvisation can lead to errors, and there are quite a few in Part I. Let me list some of them. There are errors that the characters make that cannot be attributed to Cervantes but to their haste, that is, the haste of the characters, their carelessness, but all of that is within the fiction. These are the errors like those that—later on you will learn—Dorotea makes while playing Princess Micomicona. Don Quixote makes a few. In chapter 4 he says that seven times nine is seventy-three—this could be a typo. Later he says that the biblical

Samson removed the doors of the temple when it was the gates of the city of Gaza that Samson ripped off. And there are other kinds of errors that can be blamed on Cervantes and his editors. For instance, the mistaken chapter titles and numbers. The title of chapter 10 reads, "About what happened next between Don Quixote and the Basque, and the peril with which he was threatened by a mob of men from Yanguas" (78). But the episode with the Basque is over, and the fracas with the Yanguesans does not come until five chapters later, after the Grisóstomo and Marcela interlude. Chapter 44 appears in roman numerals as chapter 35, and so on. But the grandest mistake was the theft of Sancho's donkey, which you have not reached yet; but in chapter 25 the reader finds out that Sancho's donkey is not just missing, but that it was stolen! After twelve chapters we start learning about the lost or recovered donkey; he reappears gradually. His trappings are mentioned, until in chapter 46 he is there again, miraculously, in the inn's stable! This is all in the first Juan de la Cuesta 1605 edition—Juan de la Cuesta was the publisher of the 1605 edition.

Actually, the very first printing was late 1604, but it was given the 1605 year, if you want to be really pedantic. But it is the 1605 date that is given. This is all in the first Juan de la Cuesta edition, the *princeps* edition. But in the second 1605 printing—it sold so well that a new printing had to be made—also by Juan de la Cuesta, the theft of the donkey appears in chapter 23 and it is recovered in chapter 30, and Cervantes has added a series of paragraphs to justify all of this—these are hilarious paragraphs. The writing in these added passages reads much like Cervantes' prose to me—though not to other scholars who think this is somebody else writing—so editors have incorporated them into the final version of the novel.

A critic named Tom Lathrop thinks that the additions were by the editor and believes that all of these mistakes were put in the *Quixote* on purpose by Cervantes.[2] Once you have something like this, there are critics who can claim anything, that it was not a case of careless improvisation but a plan to simulate it. The issue is moot for me. In either case, willed or not, the mistakes reveal a hasty, shoddy composition and imperfection and lack of finish, as it were, and fit with the topic of improvisation introduced in the prologue, when the narrator or Cervantes claims he does not know how to write the prologue and presents himself as someone who is not in total control of his creation.

Back to Juan Palomeque's inn. I hope you have understood my equating the improvisation, the ramshackle character of the inn, and that of the 1605 *Quixote*. I must mention Sancho's blanket tossing, the last event at the inn, because Sancho never forgives Don Quixote for not defending him, and the failure of his master to act is something that casts doubts in his mind about Don Quixote's courage. Don Quixote justifies his inaction by claiming he is not supposed to enter into battle against commoners and also that Rocinante froze. The importance of this episode is that Cervantes is building up the relationship between his two protagonists, a relationship that will deepen in the next episodes, first when Sancho helps to cure Don Quixote when he is wounded by the shepherds defending their sheep, and later when Don Quixote, angry at Sancho for laughing at him, strikes him. You remember when Don Quixote hits him over the head. This deepening relationship is one of the great virtues of the novel. Cervantes displays a profound and caring knowledge of human nature and of the transformations of human relationships; it is something to learn from the book. This is new in fiction, that their relationship transcends the social differences between them and becomes deep and complicated because of the spats they occasionally have.

Subsequent episodes follow the same pattern. Don Quixote and Sancho mistake what they see with catastrophic consequences. It is the same pattern established in the episode of the windmills. The first is the battle with the herds of sheep, which I hope you found as hilarious as I always do when I reread it. Don Quixote is, again, fooled by a real world that seems to conspire to look like what he has in his head. In this case, the sheep reflect what you have read in Elliott about the importance of sheep farming and of the wool industry in Castile. It is still very important. I have been in a Castilian town, and suddenly a whole sea of sheep comes by; they are being herded to the north or to the south, as the case may be. Cervantes is reflecting here not only the reality of everyday life but also the broader, socioeconomic realities of Spain in the period.

Don Quixote translates everything that reminds him of the world of romances of chivalry into their language. His arguments with Sancho and others about the nature of the real are one of the sources of humor in the novel. In this episode Cervantes displays his own gift for linguistic invention and parody. The names of the knights involved are hilarious, as is his description of the imaginary battle, which has a mock epic quality. Don Quixote, hurt by stones—they are called almonds at one point to understate their ability to hurt—loses some teeth, just as before he lost part of an ear. These are the scars of time on his body that I have mentioned before. His body is diminished as the work progresses, contributing to his sorry appearance and leading to the name Sancho gives him in the next episode. Notice that Don Quixote kills several sheep and that he has, again, been involved in a fight. Hence, he has committed crimes that come under the jurisdiction of the Holy Brotherhood. So besides the disputes about the real and the parody of the romances of chivalry, Don Quixote and Sancho are criminals who are fugitives from justice.

I want you to notice that Don Quixote and Sancho vomit on each other. We already saw the purging involved in the characters' evacuations, but here, I believe, there is another suggestion. Vomiting here and in the inn suggests the existence of a concretely repulsive language of pure meanings, language whose effect is repulsion, mutual repulsion, but that is nevertheless a form of communication. One vomit elicits the other, as in dialogue. It is in this sense that it is a pure language, an ironic fusion of words and things.

If you think that words merely reflect reality, vomit is reality itself expressed as words through the mouth, this is what I am trying to say. Vomit contains objects, not signs, and produces bodily effects, as when, in the case of the next episode, Don Quixote smells Sancho's feces, another expression on the part of Sancho, and he asks him to move away. This consideration of language dovetails with all of the meditations about language and literature that are in the book. It is very appropriate, I think, that it should occur in an episode where there is such a marvelous display of literary language in the description of these battles and all of those knights. So we have that literary language, and then, by contrast, this concrete language of puke.

CHAPTER 6

Modern Authors

Cervantes and Ginés de Pasamonte

Required Readings

Cervantes, *Don Quixote*, Part I, chaps. 21–26, pp. 165–227.
Elliott, *Imperial Spain*, 77–129.
González Echevarría, Roberto. "*Don Quixote:* Crossed Eyes and Vision." In *Casebook*, 217- 39.

I am going to begin by briefly going over the episodes I did not get to cover in the last lecture because we ran out of time. I am not going to go over every single episode in the novel, or else we would be here for the whole year at least. But I thought I would say a few things about the adventure of the dead body.

We move from the brightness of the road to the darkness of the incident of the dead body. This is another instance in which appearances conspire to fool Don Quixote, although here it is without artifice because he does not turn the people with the corpse into characters from the chivalric romances. This is what is unique about this event. Reality as it is is strange enough. Don Quixote's reaction is still to attack, as he did the monks in the episode leading to the fight with the Basque. This incident of the dead body is another adventure with religious resonances. The episode of the merchants of Toledo is another one that comes to mind. This one has religious resonances because it is a funeral procession and because one of the men, the one injured by Don Quixote, claims to be an ecclesiastic. After all is said and done, it turns out he is not quite ordained yet. Sancho, again, fears the police because Don Quixote has injured a person of some distinction and may now be excommunicated for having injured someone who is going to become a priest. So Don Quixote is now not only a fugitive from justice but, in some ways, also a fugitive from the church.

This is the occasion where Sancho calls Don Quixote the "Caballero de la Triste Figura," or 'Knight of the Sorry Face' in the translation we are using, which brings us back to characters with physical defects that I spoke about before. Certainly Don Quixote has some marks and physical defects that make him stand out and that lead to Sancho's calling him that. When asked by Don Quixote why he called him such a name, Sancho answers, "I was just looking at you by the light of that poor bloke's torch and the truth is that at this moment you're the sorriest sight I've ever clapped eyes on. It must be because of being tired after your fight, or else losing all those teeth" (I, 19, 151). You remember that he has lost several teeth, having been struck by one of the stones the shepherds threw at him. So this is a passage about his physical defects, his injuries, and his uniqueness as a physical being. But at issue also is Don Quixote's awareness that his adventures will be written or, in fact, that they are *being* written. And Sancho's invention of the epithet has taken place as the text is being composed, the text we read. This is consonant with the issue of the novel being a work in progress, not a fixed text but one that is being made as we read it.

This is a very significant passage, one that I think has not been re-marked upon by criticism. When Sancho explains that he looks the way he looks for the reasons I have just given, Don Quixote replies, " 'No, those are not the reasons,' replied Don Quixote. 'It is rather because the sage whose task it is to write the history of my exploits must have thought it right for me to take some appellation, as all previous knights have done: one was known as the Knight of the Burning Sword, another as the Knight of the Unicorn, another the Knight of the Damsels, yet another the Knight of the Phoenix, that one the Knight of the Griffin, that other one the Knight of Death'" (I, 19, 151–52). If you read carefully you realize that Don Quixote assumes that his story is being written as they go, which is based on an impossibility. How can it be written as they live it? Are they following a script? or is the writing following what they do? This is left unclear, but it feeds into all of the speculations that you find in the novel about the nature of literature and of writing.

In addition, with this episode the presence of death in the novel be-comes apparent. During the brawl at the inn Don Quixote was taken for dead, which will happen again later, and Grisóstomo's dead body presides over the scene involving his tragic love for Marcela. So this episode of the dead body highlights that presence of death in the novel. Death brings an element of seriousness to these comical episodes; it lurks as a reminder of the characters' vulnerability and generally of the human need to create art in the face of certain extinction. Here I want to bring in three lines from a poem by Wallace Stevens, the great American poet, about whom you will hear a little more in today's lecture. The lines are: "Death is the mother of beauty, mystical, / Within whose burning bosom we devise / Our earthly mothers waiting, sleeplessly," meaning death drives humans to create beauty.[1] So this is why the presence of death in the *Quixote* in a general sense is so important.

Now the adventure of the fulling hammers. We do not know what a fulling hammer is, we do not know what *batanes* are in Spanish; they do not exist anymore. This was a kind of machinery to full wool driven by a river or a stream going by, and it makes an awful noise. We continue in the darkness, but there is also the strange noise that frightens the protagonist, although Don Quixote adamantly denies that he is scared. But this episode has four elements that I want to bring out. First is the story of the goatherdess Torralba. This episode, this *cuento de nunca acabar,* or 'never-ending story,' is the story about the sheep being brought across a river.

Sancho is telling the story, and he warns Don Quixote, "Please, do not interrupt me, and keep track of the number of sheep." The knight says, "Alright." So at one point Sancho asks, "How many sheep?" and Don Quixote says, "I can't remember," and that is the end of the story. Don Quixote is very angry and asks, "Why?" and Sancho replies, "Well, because I told you those were the conditions." This is a story that is very funny. It is also a love story, if you look into it, between these two goatherds, but it is also a story in which the issue of language and reality is underlined because here Sancho is demanding a strict kind of literality: you say "sheep" and there is one sheep, you say "sheep" again, there is another sheep. You have to count every single one because language cannot abstractly say forty-five sheep: it has to say one sheep, two sheep, three sheep, four sheep. This is a highly elementary way of conceiving language, but this is what Cervantes is bringing in: folktales sometimes contain interesting elements about the nature of storytelling.

The second element, which I have already mentioned, is the fact that in this episode Sancho defecates out of fear. He tries to hide it from Don Quixote, but Don Quixote smells it and tells him to please move away, that he cannot stand the stench. Classics of literature contain the whole range of human experience, including the most humble physical functions, and this is one instance. There are similar episodes in Chaucer, and in Dante's *Inferno* there are various scatological episodes but none as humble as this instance when Sancho cannot contain himself and has to discharge his bowels.

Another element is the fact that Don Quixote beats Sancho over the head in anger. This continues to fill out the relationship between the two characters. It is a relationship that includes tenderness but also anger, and that idea is thoroughly developed in the novel. This is something new that, in a way, Cervantes invented.

And finally, I would like to raise the question, How does Sancho know there is water in the vicinity? and how can he tell time by the stars? Well, here, we learn—you may remember, and I have always asked you to look for details—that Sancho says he was a shepherd once, and hence he learned how to find water for his animals and fresh grass for them. I think the notable thing here is that we begin to learn about Sancho's past retrospectively. It is not as if at the beginning the narrator told us Sancho was once a shepherd and then he began the adventures. Instead, we begin to learn retrospectively about Sancho's previous activities and how he came to be who he is now. This is a very effective device to fill out the character. I want you to notice it because there will be other instances where we will find out other things about Sancho's past. His life is filled in on the go, not following a conventional chronological progression.

And now we get to the second part of today's class, which has to do with this topic: Why does Cervantes focus so much on low-class types and even criminals? This is something I have talked about before, but I will be harping on it again today. I have spoken about Maritornes, who is a prostitute, but there are others, for instance, the servant who beats up Don Quixote in the episode about the merchants of Toledo, the rowdies who toss Sancho in the blanket, Andrés, who was being beaten by his master but who seems to be a pícaro himself, the first innkeeper, whom I have called a retired pícaro, and the prostitutes at the first inn. We will meet quite a few other such types. As we talk about the galley slaves episode today we will be attempting to answer this question: Why the focus on these kinds of characters? why the abundance of low-class types and outlaws?

By the way, galley slaves,—I say this because I am sure you have never heard of this before, it is not something we are familiar with—*galeotes* in Spanish, were prisoners or, legally speaking, slaves who were forced to row the galleys, whether private or, more often, owned by the Crown. That is, the ships move with sails but also with oars, and the oars were manned by the galley slaves, who sat in rows inside and were whipped to row harder and harder. It is a terrible kind of punishment. The fact is that most of them did not come back alive. That is what a galley slave was. The closest thing we have, I think, are those chain gangs of prisoners we see occasionally in some states going around in their striped uniforms.

Let me anticipate some ideas and redirect others I have already mentioned to give context to what I am going to be saying next. The Renaissance is interested in the nature of humankind relatively independent of God. Renaissance thinkers and artists focus on characters like wild men, for instance, who are close to nature rather than to the social world. The wild man is an individual lost in the woods or in some cave who lives in a state of nature away from civilization. In Spanish literature the best known example is Segismundo, the protagonist of *Life Is a Dream,* a play by Pedro Calderón de la Barca that I will be mentioning often during the semester. Renaissance thinkers and artists also concentrate on individuals who willfully become marginal to society, like madmen and criminals. The underlying idea is that society masks, erases, or attenuates fundamental traits of the human.

There is also an aesthetic reason behind this. Social individuals are types; individuals in society become types. Their features are determined by social conventions attached to their station or trade, whereas marginal figures are individual in their appearance and behavior. Don Quixote and Sancho will meet characters like Diego de Miranda, the "man in green" in Part II, who lead tedious lives because they conform to social norms. He is a rich hidalgo who lives a life of ease at his estate and who lodges the knight and his squire for several days in his comfortable house, until Don Quixote gets bored.

Don Quixote and the pícaros he meets, on the other hand, are not boring; they lead lives of adventure. They are appealing because of their eccentricities, just as they are physically compelling because of the deformities they bear, as we saw in the last class. Of course, epic heroes and protagonists of chivalric romances led interesting lives, full of adventures. But those adventures took place in a distant, vague past and in abstract countries with generic qualities drawn from literary conventions, whereas the pícaros and Don Quixote live in the present and in a society the reader recognizes as his own. The clash between the two is at the core of Don Quixote, but the point is that, except in his imagination, Don Quixote never inhabits a world other than that of Spain in the late sixteenth century, among people involved in ordinary activities who do not violate the laws of nature. No one flies, for instance, in the *Quixote* or performs feats that are beyond human strength, as happens in the epic and as happens in the romances of chivalry.

Figure 10. Barber's basin. Photo courtesy of Blackman Cruz.

We are about to come to an episode in which this clash between ideal-ized time and space meet real-time, present-day Castile. I refer to the in-cident involving Mambrino's helmet in chapter 21, and here is where the picture of a barber's basin is useful because no one in this room has ever seen a barber's basin, even myself, because they are no longer in use (fig. 10). A barber's basin is a device the barber would use—it has an indentation that allows it to fit under a person's chin, at the neck—to wash the beard and have the water fall in it. There are two important elements in the Mambrino hel-met affair, which is one of the most famous and most discussed in the *Qui-xote* because it brings to the fore speculation about the nature of the real that dominates the discussion among the characters but, particularly, between Don Quixote and Sancho, as happens here.

The first element I want to bring out regarding this occasion has to do with the oath Don Quixote made earlier, in chapter 10. By fulfilling it, he would close a loop in the plot. Upon seeing the shiny barber's basin, he re-members the oath he made when he discovered that part of his own helmet had been damaged in the fight with the Basque. So he says that the oppor-tunity now arises, when he sees the basin, to fulfill the oath: "about which I swore that vow" (I, 21, 166).

Don Quixote had sworn the following after the fight with the Basque: "I swear by the Creator of all things, and by the four evangelists and all their holy writings, that I will lead the life led by the great Marquis of Mantua when he swore to avenge his nephew Baldwin's death, and until then 'ne'er at table to eat bread nor with his wife to lie,' and other such things that, although I cannot remember them now, can be taken as spoken, until I have exacted full vengeance on the perpetrator of this outrage" (I, 10, 80). The outrage is the damage to the helmet, which he can now restore with a new one that suddenly approaches and that he plans to appropriate. The novel begins to acquire—this is the point—an inner density and substance by means of these links, these connections within the plot, one related to the other, the oath and the fulfillment of the oath.

The second element I want to bring up has to do with the confusion created by the wet, shining basin that looks like a helmet. Mambrino's helmet belongs to the tradition of Roland and his various incarnations as Roland, who becomes Orlando. This is the Carolingian cycle of chivalry that I mentioned in one of my early lectures. Mambrino's helmet appears in Rolandian literature in a poem by Matteo Boiardo called *Orlando innamorato,* 'Orlando in love.' Reinaldo de Montalbán kills the Moorish king Mambrino and wins his enchanted helmet. In Ludovico Ariosto's *Orlando furioso*—a poem I will mention several times in the course of the semester—the enchanted helmet had been won from the Moorish king Mambrino by Dardaniel de Almonte—not Sacripante, as Don Quixote misremembers—and Reinaldo de Montalbán wins it when he kills Dardaniel. So this is the background of Mambrino's helmet. In his imagination Don Quixote acts like the Carolingian hero in obtaining the helmet from the Moorish king. So Mambrino's helmet has an incontestable chivalric pedigree, a deep pedigree, which makes it all the more ridiculous that it be confused with a barber's basin. So you have to have this background to realize the distance between Mambrino's helmet and the barber's basin.

But there are attenuating circumstances to Don Quixote's error. Reality, contingency—when I say contingency I mean accidents—conspire to confuse him, as in the case of the dead body. The basin is not being used for what it was intended. The barber has it on his head to protect his new hat from the rain—remember the detail, he has a new hat, and he puts the basin over it to protect it from the rain. By the way, this is the only time it rains in the entire *Quixote,* if you want to notice a detail. It does not rain often in Castile. Castile is very dry, and this is consistent with the real conditions of the region. So it rains, and the basin is being used to protect the hat.

The poor barber is the victim of this mutation, of this circumstance. It happens with other things in the *Quixote*. As you know, the inn was originally a stable, or parts of the inn were originally a stable. In the real world things are adapted ad hoc for purposes other than those they were made for; their essence does not guarantee their usage, they are in flux. Remember what Don Quixote said after the episode of the windmills about mutations, how things are in a constant state of mutation. So reality is in a state of flux, as is Don Quixote himself. Hence, he takes the shining barber's basin for Mambrino's helmet.

This episode exemplifies the modern radical doubt about the power of the senses to grasp reality, which will become a topic of the baroque, the period almost immediately after the Renaissance and about which I will be talking a great deal later on. Remember what I said about the critical cliché, that the first part of the *Quixote* is Renaissance, the second part is baroque. But the topic of our senses not being able to really discern reality is one that is still with us. It is the sort of doubt about the real that we find even today in a modern poem like Wallace Stevens's "Man Carrying Thing." I bring up this poem because on one or two occasions the basin is referred to as a thing—"a thing that shines," Sancho says—as yet lacking ontological and phenomenological specificity; the ontological is being, it is not specific, it is appearance, it is phenomenology, it is not specific. And so it is called a thing. And so I always, when I come to this episode, think of this poem by Stevens, Wallace Stevens being one of my favorite, if not my most favorite, poets. He was an American poet, 1879–1955, who spent almost all of his life as an executive at an insurance company in Hartford, Connecticut. Nevertheless, he was really one of the major American poets.

"MAN CARRYING THING"

The poem must resist the intelligence
Almost successfully. Illustration:
A brune figure in winter evening resists
Identity. The thing he carries resists
The most necessitous sense. Accept them, then,
As secondary (parts not quite perceived
Of the obvious whole, uncertain particles
Of the certain solid, the primary free from doubt,
Things floating like the first hundred flakes of snow
Out of a storm we must endure all night,

Out of a storm of secondary things),
A horror of thoughts that suddenly are real.
We must endure our thoughts all night, until
The bright obvious stands motionless in cold.[2]

I do not think the "bright obvious" ever "stands motionless in cold" in
the *Quixote,* but I think this poem dramatizes what is happening in this episode with this thing that Don Quixote takes to be a helmet and that Sancho
knows is a barber's basin. This is a Cartesian problem, since it was Descartes
who first gave full attention to it: how do we really know the real? Doubt,
as the principle of modern philosophy, is present here, already. In this sense
Cervantes takes leave of Renaissance thought and poetics and moves toward
the baroque. The basin will reappear and provoke a full-fledged discussion
in the inn among various characters about whether it is a basin or a helmet,
with the basin present to be seen. It is a hilarious parody of a scholastic debate. The basin is one of those things that the novel focuses on and that I told
you to take notice of in connection with Alberti's theories about perspective
because the basin is seen in the distance, in the depths, and this is why it is
difficult to ascertain what it is.

The second part of the chapter contains what I call Don Quixote's own
chivalric romance. Here we see Don Quixote in the act of creating a chivalric
romance. Remember, Sancho asks him if they should not go and try to gain
some notoriety and fame by doing important things, and so Don Quixote
launches into this narrative, a chivalric romance, which he invents out of elements drawn from many of these romances. He has been able to condense
from various romances the essence of the chivalric romance, the basic story.
The story reveals what he has in his head. This probe into the mind of a character is also new in fiction. Here and elsewhere—as in the case of Cardenio,
whom you are going to meet right away—we get intimations of a character's
subconscious, not just of his actions, as in the case of the epic, the romances
of chivalry, and even the picaresque. Here we get something about Don Quixote's mind. This will happen several times in the novel.

The story of this chivalric romance is an exercise in narrative in which
Cervantes is underlining the conventions of the chivalric genre; the fact that
there is a kind of basic blueprint or structure upon which anyone can em-
broider. This is true, by the way, of popular forms of narrative, like James
Bond movies, of which they keep making more and more and more because
the basic blueprint is there, and all you have to do is to make a slight change
in one character here or a slight change in this kind of adventure there, and

you have a James Bond. The same was true of Conan Doyle and the Sherlock Holmes stories and, as I have mentioned several times, of soap operas.

So Cervantes, as in the case of the picaresque—and we are going to discuss it in the following discussion of the galley slaves episode—Cervantes is concerned that the conventions of literature, its topics, draw it away from real life; that even the new genres, new in relation to the classics, reassert their literariness by deploying these conventions, which turn into predictable codes. Awareness of this possibility is crucial to the whole *Quixote* and to Cervantes' entire work; how convention obscures the real and shields us from it; how literature quickly retreats into formulas, like those in Don Quixote's mind. Self-reflexivity helps to point out these conventions and to show their disconnection from reality; they are self-generated and self-contained. I am reminded here of a novel by Manuel Puig, an Argentine writer, titled *The Kiss of the Spider Woman*. It was later made into a movie. Those of you familiar with it will remember that Molina narrates to his cell mate all of these movies he has in his head that he has memorized; there are people who have memorized the plots of many movies and can condense them into a kind of a generic movie, the way Don Quixote is creating here a kind of generic chivalric romance.

This episode also plays into the game of mirrors that the *Quixote* is becoming; it is a story within the story, and the large story is a parody of a romance of chivalry. This is what is called in French *composition en abîme,* and in English it is the infinitely receding sequences. It is what we found in Velázquez's *Las Meninas,* the story within the story, like the painting within the painting, like the play within the play in *Hamlet.* I first visualized this as a child looking at the label on a can of condensed milk. The label depicted a condensed milk can that had the same label, within which there was another label with the same condensed milk can, and so on, and I had the vertigo of not knowing whether I was part of a larger condensed milk can. There is no without if you are within it. Everything is within literature in this case; there is no authority that orders the universe of fiction, which is continuous with that of reality. The only infinite being would be God, so to posit this kind of abyss-like universe is a form of radical skepticism on the part of Cervantes, and also of Shakespeare, by the way. Here the authority within that fiction, this house of mirrors—I am sure you have also gone to the house of mirrors—is a madman.

Another important point about the generic chivalric romance Don Quixote comes up with, in answer to Sancho's question, is that Don Quixote reveals insecurities about his lineage. He feels he has to acquire fame in

order to aspire to marry a princess. Behind this apparently naïve preoccupation lies one of the social issues at stake in the novel, the question of social
class and privilege and the possibility of acquiring it rather than inheriting
it. You remember that he speaks here about acquiring enough fame by dint
of his valor to merit being married to a princess. Even in the relationship
between the knight and his squire there are intimations of a leveling of social
classes. And you will see as we move to Part II that this leveling will increase
as Sancho's importance in the novel increases. So this is one of the central
topics of the novel. In addition, we get here another glimpse into Don Quixote's subconscious. He is worried about being of low nobility, about his thin
aristocratic background.

Now we get to the galley slaves, another famous episode in the *Quixote*. Famous because, among other things, it shows Cervantes dealing with
the question of literature or, more specifically, the picaresque. Notice, by the
way, the mistranslation (on page 179) when Rutherford renders *alcahuete*
as 'pimp' when it should be 'go-between.' Don Quixote actually praises the
alcahuete, which is what it says in the original. An alcahuete is someone
who arranges marriages and illicit encounters between lovers, not a pimp. A
pimp is an agent for prostitutes. Alcahuetes, go-betweens, have been praised
throughout the ages, even by Saint Augustine at some point; he praises the
job they do in arranging for couples to meet and become lovers.

Why such interest in the picaresque? You might be getting tired of
my talking about the picaresque, but the picaresque is the new fiction that
precedes the *Quixote*, precedes Cervantes' work, within which and against
which he writes. The picaresque comes up again, not only because Ginés
de Pasamonte, who is the main character here, is a criminal, but also, more
important, because Ginés de Pasamonte is an author. When asked by Don
Quixote if the book he is writing is good, Ginés replies, "'It's so good,' replied
Ginés, 'that I wouldn't give a fig for *Lazarillo de Tormes* and all the others
of that kind that have been or ever will be written'" (I, 22, 182). And when
asked for the title and if it is finished, Ginés answers, "'*The Life of Ginés de
Pasamonte*,' replied the man of that name. 'And have you finished it?' asked
Don Quixote. 'How can I have finished it,' he replied, 'if my life hasn't finished yet? What's written so far is from my birth to when I was sentenced to
the galleys this last time'" (I, 22, 182).

Picaresque novels tended to be called *Vida de . . .* , 'Life of . . . ,' as in
Vida de Lazarillo de Tormes, Vida de Guzmán de Alfarache. So *The Life of
Ginés de Pasamonte* is obviously a picaresque kind of novel he has written
about himself. Cervantes is taking on the conventions of autobiographical

writing. "How can you write an autobiography if your life is not over?" is what Ginés answers. Cervantes is poking fun at that convention of autobiographical writing, as in the *Confessions* of Saint Augustine where the conceit is the creation of a death and resurrection kind of scheme. That is, I am speaking about the man I formerly was until I had a conversion, by which the old man died and the new one arose. This is what is behind the little repartee between Ginés de Pasamonte and Don Quixote: a satire of autobiographical writing and of the picaresque novel specifically.

Ginés unwittingly underscores the fact that there is no way to put a stop to autobiography by alluding to the last time he went to the galleys; so every time he goes to the galleys he takes up the book again and writes it and writes it and writes it, and he says at one point here that he does not mind going to the galleys because there he will be able to finish his book. A kind of literal continuity between life and writing is what is being made fun of in this episode. Now, you remember the whole background of the picaresque because I have given it to you before, from *Celestina* to *Guzmán de Alfarache* in 1599, right? This is precisely the time when Cervantes was writing *Don Quixote*. In the *Guzmán de Alfarache* the protagonist is a galley slave at one point, so the reference to this novel is clear.

Ginés de Pasamonte is one of the most important secondary characters in the *Quixote*. This is not an oxymoron; there are important secondary characters and secondary characters that are not important. Important not only because this is a really fun and funny episode—Ginés is a lot of fun and will reappear—but also because he is one of the storytellers in the book and hence is part of the book's take on literature and the nature of narrative. Ginés is one of the many storytellers in the *Quixote*. By this I mean characters who not only tell a story or recite a poem but who are writing or have written a book. The most memorable of these are, of course, the narrator of the *Quixote*, who claims not to be the author, the apocryphal Cide Hamete Benengeli, and the translator; these are all characters who have written a book. There will be others; Cardenio, for instance, has written a book.

Through them Cervantes is considering the possibility of new genres, new forms of literature emerging—which they are, at the time he is writing—and showing the mechanisms by which a new genre is born; a new genre, meaning a new kind of literature that is not merely derived or copied from the classics, as was done or attempted to be done in the Renaissance. There are authors like Lope de Vega, who created, as it were, the Spanish national theater, the *comedia*. Ginés is as complex a figure as other narrators of the *Quixote*, like Cide Hamete Benengeli, and I remind you again—and I will probably do so again in this lecture—that at this point between the sixteenth and the seventeenth centuries the first professional authors are emerging, that is, authors who are trying to make a living from their writing. Lope did well because he wrote so many plays, while Cervantes did not do so well in the theater, as we know.

Such interest in the nature of literature and the figure of the author in the *Quixote* is prevalent because the novel, this novel, the *Quixote,* is not so much about the question of the book as it is about that of the books, in the plural, as we saw in the episode of the scrutiny of the library. It is about the proliferation of books made possible by the development of the printing press and the economic factors that encouraged editorial produc-tion in the sixteenth century. The *Quixote* is the first major work to consider how the dissemination of books unsettles received notions about the book and about authorship. These are—remember, again, turn of the sixteenth to the seventeenth century—new genres, new authors, like Mateo Alemán and Lope de Vega, who are professionals. This matter is tied to the whole issue of the books.

The proliferation of books is accompanied by a decline in the social class of authors and the author figure, by which I mean characters like Ginés de Pasamonte, who represent authors within the fiction. Take stock of this: Ginés de Pasamonte is a criminal, a prisoner, a galley slave; however, he has written a book. This is novel, I mean, that someone of his social class, which could not be lower, is writing a book. In addition, the production of many copies of a single book brings down the fetish value of each single copy of it: if you have too many of something the value declines, if you have few the value increases. I have a two-dollar bill in my wallet that somebody gave me, and I have kept it because they say it is good luck but also because there are so few of them. So this is the fetish value of things that are few; this we learned in economics classes in high school. But the opposite is true of the relevance of authors and the author figure, which increases as the value of each copy of his book decreases. The authors now become the guarantors of the work's worth as well as the persons accountable for it before the law. In the case of the comedia, the Spanish plays, where proliferation was rampant, to be *de Lope,* 'by Lope,' became a sign of excellence, like a trademark, ap-plicable as an indication of value to things other than plays. You could say, this thing is *de Lope,* and that meant it was very good. In the picaresque, author and protagonists are conflated, book and author become one, as in the case of Ginés, whose reductio ad absurdum of this textual strategy has been noted many times.

A rudimentary equation could perhaps be worked out. These new authors break with the strictures of Renaissance mimesis—the idea of imitating the classics—in the sense that they innovate, leaving behind classical forms and themes or subjecting them to substantial transformations. Hence, the descent in social status of the author appears to be accompanied by an increase in inventiveness and a rise in the importance of the author. The higher the social class, the less the invention because they practice mimesis, they imitate the classics. The lower the author's social class, the greater the invention, hence the more value attached to the author, which leads to the following: the more invention, the more value given to the author—for example, Ginés de Pasamonte, who prides himself on having written this book about himself.

This explains why, as Alemán did earlier with his *Guzmán de Alfarache,* Cervantes rushes to write his second part once he learns that Alonso Fernández de Avellaneda has written a second part of the *Quixote* (Avellaneda publishes his *Quixote* in 1614). Cervantes feels that the *Quixote* is his invention, his in every sense, including the monetary sense; that he is going to lose revenues if somebody else writes a *Quixote.* So it seems that the impact of these socioeconomic developments on books and authors is undeniable.

But there is another important factor at work that issues from the content of the books themselves and its relation to knowledge. Ginés de Pasamonte exemplifies the lowering of an author's social class. Cervantes himself was a petty nobleman, poor, and twice imprisoned. Ginés de Pasamonte is important because he exemplifies that drop in social class of the author. Anthony Grafton opens the introduction to his *New Worlds, Ancient Texts: The Power of Tradition and the Shock of Discovery* with these words: "Between 1550 and 1650 [precisely the time of Cervantes] Western thinkers ceased to believe that they could find all important truths in ancient books."[3]

The early Renaissance thought that all important truths could be found in books, but now this belief has waned. Grafton goes on to quote the Jesuit José de Acosta, who wrote the following in a book about the history of the new world called *Historia natural y moral de las Indias* (1590). This is Acosta quoted by Grafton: "Having read that what poets and philosophers write of the Torrid Zone, I persuaded myself that when I came to the Equator [he was traveling to the New World] I would not be able to endure the violent heat, but it turned out otherwise. For when I passed [the Equator] . . . I felt so cold that I was forced to go into the sun to warm myself. What could I do then but laugh at Aristotle's *Meteorology* and his philosophy?"[4]

Ironically, then, the proliferation of books begins at the time when the authority of the book was most severely tested and ultimately devalued. The ability to read many books did not bring one closer to the truth but to an inordinate, perhaps infinite enlargement of the library, and to Don Quixote's madness, or to Descartes' "Je pense, donc je suis," "I think, therefore I am." I know that I am only because I think, and in this way he discards the whole philosophical tradition contained in books before his. This, too, leads in the direction of an increase in the importance of the author. Just as the classical tradition is being refashioned or denied altogether, so received knowledge from the canonical books is being questioned. The function of books changes not only because the printing press makes them available in larger quantities, but also because they are no longer seen as reliable purveyors of truth.

Experience, not books, becomes a critical element in philosophy and literature. If Acosta in the 1590s can laugh at Aristotle, why not then pick up a picaresque novel and have a good laugh, or a chivalric romance and be entertained or aroused instead? Or the *Quixote* and have a good time? Reading books is not equated, as before, with the acquisition of knowledge but increasingly with pleasure, and the value of each book is dependent on an author whose ability to produce such pleasure is known. The scrutiny of the library and Altisidora's dream—which we will get to in Part II—clearly show some of the quandaries this new situation opens up. Altisidora's dream is this marvelous episode in Part II in which a character—you will meet her—named Altisidora has a dream in which she sees some devils playing something like a game of tennis in which the balls are books and the rackets are flaming rackets. When they hit the books, poof!, they explode and are pulverized. It is a magnificent dream about what I am trying to tell you. The book that is pulverized most easily is Avellaneda's apocryphal *Quixote*.

This is why Ginés de Pasamonte is so important. Ginés de Pasamonte is heavily shackled when he appears. He is covered with chains from head to toe; he cannot move his head down to reach his hands or reach his mouth with his hands. It is as if he were possessed of some demonic power. Here Cervantes is anticipating a kind of a romantic notion of the author as a demonic figure. But the most interesting thing is that Ginés de Pasamonte is also a self-portrait of Cervantes because at one point Ginés describes himself as being very unfortunate, and the line is obviously a self-allusive one on the part of Cervantes.

Ginés de Pasamonte is a figure of Cervantes in the book: he is of a lower class and is possessed of powerful inventiveness that has to be contained by all of these chains that hold him down. In Part II Ginés will reappear, and I anticipate having a lot of fun with him then, when he is a master puppeteer; he has a puppet theater, and I will not ruin the plot by telling you what happens then, but it is hilarious and it dovetails with what I have been talking about here. This slipperiness on the part of this author figure is connected to all of these games of authorship. The slipperiness of Cide Hamete Benengeli, the slipperiness of the translator who has the text translated; they are all contained within the figure of Ginés de Pasamonte, this pícaro.

One further aspect of Ginés I want to discuss is contained in an essay of mine that is in the *Casebook:* he is cross-eyed. Ginés is introduced as follows: "Behind all these [qualities] was a man of thirty, very good-looking except that he squinted a little" (I, 22, 181). Rutherford mistranslates "que al mirar metía el un ojo en el otro," as "squinted," but it means that Ginés was cross-eyed. We still say "meter un ojo en el otro" in Spanish for being cross-eyed. Vision is tied to representation. You represent what you see, and Ginés's being an author figure who is cross-eyed is highly suggestive, first of all because being cross-eyed gives Ginés a shifty look. When you look somebody in the eye to see if he is being truthful, if the eyes shift, then the person does not appear sincere. So being cross-eyed gives Ginés a shifty appearance to go with his slipperiness. He is also Janus-like: if you look at him from one side, you see one eye going this way, but if you look at him from the other side, the eye is going the other way. So he is two things at the same time, whether you look at him from one side or the other. There is no center, no stable figure of Ginés de Pasamonte because he is cross-eyed. He has a monocular cross-eyedness, that is, one eye is the one that goes into the other.

If you have two lines of sight that normally meet here on this object, that object is represented whole to your mind's eye as well; but if you are cross-eyed, they meet there, and therefore the object is distorted. This is what monocular cross-eyedness means. Also, it leads to a double vision, what is called *diplopia.* So Ginés suffers from this cross-eyedness, diplopia, meaning double vision; he sees two things at the same time. And he is this figure of the author, the figure of the author who, like the Cervantes of the first prologue, has to divide himself into two persons; he is two within his own vision because he sees double.

What I am trying to say is this: you will see that one of the topics in the *Quixote* criticism is perspectivism, that reality is seen from the various perspectives of the characters. In the end reality, the truth is the sum total of all of these perspectives. What I am saying here is that there is no such thing; that within each individual there is already perspectivism because there is more than one perspective of things within him. I want to emphasize this. Ginés sees two things; he is not just one perspective. There is perspectivism inherent in him, not just part of all of the others' perspectives. This complicates the issue a lot more, particularly when you take into account that Ginés is presented in the *Quixote* as an author figure, a storyteller. Storytellers in the *Quixote* tend not to be healthy, either physically or mentally, and Ginés is important because of that.

CHAPTER 7

Love and the Law

Interrupted Stories

Required Readings

Cervantes, *Don Quixote*, Part I, chaps. 21–26, pp. 165–227.

Elliott, *Imperial Spain*, 77–129.

Riley, E. C. "Literature and Life in *Don Quixote*." In *Casebook*, 125–40.

Wardropper, Bruce W. "*Don Quixote*: Story or History?" In *Casebook*, 141–61.

I want first to give you my final thoughts on the topic of Ginés's crossed eyes. Then we are going to move on to the character among the galley slaves whom I call the prisoner of sex and finally to the Sierra Morena and the complicated stories that take place there.

I said that Ginés's cross-eyedness is monocular and convergent—monocular meaning of one eye, one eye goes into the other. This prevents him from perceiving reality clearly; his perception is slanted by the conflicting angles of his visual axes. It is a sort of—this is the main point of what I am saying—innate or congenital, internal perspectivism, prior to any perspectivism based on the multiple points of view provided by several characters. Perspectivism in Cervantes, which, as I have mentioned before, is a topic of Cervantes' criticism, presupposes the unified visions of several characters who view something like Mambrino's helmet, that is, the barber's basin, and disagree on what it happens to be. Each sees reality in a way that represents his or her point of view and his or her way of being, but Ginés's being cross-eyed suggests that such individual visions are abstractions, hasty assumptions; the assumption that each look is singular and represents only one individual. But being cross-eyed means that within each individual there are conflicting views and therefore conflicting ways of seeing, and this is very much in line with the way Cervantes' characters often behave, at odds with themselves.

The final result is not a unified but a conflicted vision within each of the characters, a kind of double vision called diplopia. It is an awful-sounding word of Greek origin, *diplopia*. So the new model I propose, based on this observation that Ginés is cross-eyed, is that it is a new kind of conflictive being; conflicting being within him or herself, capable of seeing simultaneously in two ways. The conflict is an internal dialogue of sorts within each of the characters. Cervantes represents this condition, as he usually does, in a sharply funny way. When Ginés, who was the first to jump free, is released from his chains, the text reads as follows: "[Ginés] was the first to spring into action as he launched himself at the fallen sergeant, snatched up his sword and his firelock and, pointing this at one man and then at another, without firing it, made all the guards disappear as they fled from the gun and from the stones being hurled at them by the escaped convicts" (I, 22, 184).

Being cross-eyed allows Ginés to guard each one of the guards at the same time instead of one after another. With one eye he is looking at one, while with the other eye he is looking at his mate, with a sword in one hand and a gun in the other. This is, I think, the way Cervantes is representing this double vision of Ginés. If you do not read those lines carefully you miss the subtle point that Ginés can do that because he is cross-eyed. Details.

I now move on to another prisoner, one who has been generally overlooked and who occupies all of one paragraph. It is the prisoner or the galley slave whom I call the prisoner of sex, and it shows Cervantes' remarkable ability to create a character in a few brushstrokes.[1] He has been asked, like all the others, why he is going to the galleys, and he replies,

I'm here because I fooled around too much with two girl-cousins of mine, and with two girl-cousins of somebody else's; and, in short, I fooled around so much with the lot of them that as a result the family tree's become so complicated that I don't know who the devil would be able to work it out. It was all proved against me, there weren't any strings for me to pull, I hadn't got

any money, I was within an inch of having my neck stretched, I
was sentenced to the galleys for six years and I accepted my fate:
it's the punishment for my crime, I'm still young, long live life,
while there's life there's hope. If, sir knight, you've got anything
on you that you could spare for us poor wretched, God will repay
you for it in heaven, and here on earth we'll take care to pray to
God that your life and your health may be as long and as good as
you obviously deserve. (I, 22, 180–81)

He has been sentenced to the galleys because he was having simultaneous
affairs with four women, two of whom were his cousins and two others who
were not but who were cousins to each other. As a result, he had a series
of children whose family ties were difficult to untangle. They were cousins,
brothers and sisters among themselves, as you can imagine. Now, the historical reasons for his being on his way to the galleys—Cervantes is careful in
backing up all of these stories with precise historical facts—is that men were
needed for the galleys at the time because of Spain's overseas adventures, and
so sentences were changed to send more prisoners to the galleys, and the age
limit was lowered—to sixteen, I think. So this is why the prisoner was sentenced to the galleys. Now, he is a brazen young man, and, to judge by his good
Latin and his robe, he is a law student, which is noteworthy. There were many
law students at the time, and they were masters of rhetoric and syllogistic
thinking and arguing, these being the skills lawyers presumably developed.
    The other precise legal detail here is that he was engaged in what was
called complex fornication. There was simple fornication and complex fornication. Simple fornication was consensual sex between two individuals of
different sexes who were unmarried. Complex fornication, as you can imagine, is when one of the partners is married, both of the partners are married
to other people, or they are of the same sex. The sentences for complex fornication were more severe. This prisoner has engaged in complex fornication
because he has committed incest, having had sex with his cousins, two of
them, for good measure.
    His legal training is evident in that he is trying to turn what is a crimi-
nal case, incest, to put it in modern terms, into a civil case. For him, it is a
question of inheritance law; how are we going to figure out the inheritance
when these children's family ties are so complicated? As you can see, he has
subtly, in his discourse, tried to diminish his culpability; but he is guilty of
incest and therefore has been given the maximum sentence, six years in the
galleys. So he shuffles the issue, which is a case of incest, to a question of

inheritance law, a civil case. Incest is to engage in sex with someone you cannot marry according to canon law, canon law being religious law. According to canon law there are all kinds of prohibitions, but cousins are not supposed to marry, although dispensations can be obtained from the church. Of course, you cannot marry your mother, you cannot marry your sister, but the prohibition goes all the way down to your cousin. You cannot marry a nun either; all of that falls under the prohibition of incest.

The sentenced lawyer is certainly guilty of incest, and this is why he is being sent to the galleys. Notice that he says, "It's the proper punishment for my crime," as if he knows the law. Being a budding lawyer, he is saying, "I accept this," and he adds, "Well, life will go on, I'm young, I'll come back from the galleys," which was unlikely, and then he disappears—but not before jumping on Don Quixote, taking the basin from his head, and whacking him a few times with it. That is the last we hear of this prisoner of sex, who is a kind of libertine in the making. He and the others vanish into the woods, the same woods where Marcela disappeared, by the way, and the same woods into which Don Quixote and Sancho are also heading to get away from the law. Notice, again, what I said at the beginning about how Cervantes has created this rather complex character in just one paragraph and by just this speech; by what he says and how he says it.

We now go into the Sierra Morena and enter what is really the core of Part I of the *Quixote*, which is made up of all of these love stories we will be hearing about in the next few classes and that you are reading now. Don Quixote and Sancho are running away from the Holy Brotherhood, about which I have spoken several times, because they are fugitives from justice. This is the overarching plot; they are running away from justice. In the real context of the period, they are, in fact, as you will see later when they are captured, being pursued by the Holy Brotherhood, who have an arrest order for them.

Don Quixote and Sancho are criminals who, in some way, are expiating their sins in the woods. The woods are a kind of labyrinth or a vision of hell, remindful in various aspects of Dante's *Inferno*. They are located as far as possible from civilization. It is a world of disorder and madness; it is also the *despoblado*, the unpopulated, which in Spanish law meant areas not covered or protected by the law. These are areas where neither the law nor the power of the Crown reached. Cervantes uses those zones to send his characters into danger, into confusion, and into violence. The Sierra Morena will be the setting of a series of tightly related events, all dealing with the question of love and, more mundanely, the issue of marriage.

The interpolated stories that come after the Marcela and Grisóstomo episode, which prefigured them, and Rocinante's disastrous flirtation make up, as I said, the core of Part I of the *Quixote*. These stories peak and are resolved, for the most part, together with the main plot, the plot involving Don Quixote and Sancho, which, as I said, resolves itself when he is captured and sent back home. This is a set of narrative trends woven around two of the principal drives in the book: Don Quixote's love quest for Dulcinea and the series of crimes and misdemeanors perpetrated by the hidalgo and his squire that lead to his pursuit and apprehension. The interpolated stories have in common with the central plot, with the Marcela and Grisóstomo interlude, and with each other the perpetration of offenses due to passion that result in injuries to honor, body, and property, with the resulting need for restitution, recompense, requital, pardon, or revenge. In all of them marriage looms as the inevitable and most appropriate form of reparation as well as the most effective kind of narrative closure. Marriage is also, in this context, a form of punishment.

These love stories involve potentially unequal marriages, and most of them contain violence of some kind. Unequal in the sense that the individuals involved come from different social classes, that difference being what motivates many of the conflicts, but not all. Although penal law looms over the episodes—the penal law applied to criminals like Don Quixote and Sancho—the most developed legal aspect in them derives from testamentary law, something at issue in the Marcela–Grisóstomo conflict. Remember how much importance was given to the fact that they had both inherited wealth and how they had inherited it, she being a woman, he being a man. Inheritance and marriage codes, both regulating succession, drive and constrain the characters.

Restitution and compensation cooperate to make whole what the characters damage in the process of channeling their desires—if you know something about law, you know that to make whole is to bring restitution for some damage or loss incurred. So the same symbolic topology that we have already seen between the road and the inn reappears here; it is between the woods and the inn, between the inn and the wilderness, which is a good way to translate despoblado, the wilderness. And the going back and forth from one to the other is punctuated, often, by interruptions in the narratives, interruptions that I will consider carefully.

Marriage has to do with the law as well as with the closure of stories. So it is an important structural issue, too, in terms of the narrative. Marriage is the ending of many tales and plays; "and they married and lived happily ever after," so to speak, is the end of many tales. That is how things are resolved, how order is restored and succession is insured. The questions of love and marriage which were important issues both from a social and literary point of view surface here, as in the episode of Grisóstomo and Marcela, I underline, through stories of young people: Cardenio, Luscinda, Don Fernando, and Dorotea.

These are decisive episodes in which Cervantes is dealing with love and marriage at a significant point in Western history, both in social and literary terms. Is love an integral or even necessary part of marriage? or is marriage principally a social and economic contract? Do young people have the right to choose whom they marry? All of these questions have obvious answers today, but not then, and not for a long time. Even now, well into the twenty-first century, in some societies marriages are arranged. I remember Gayatri Spivak, the critic and theoretician, telling me—she is from India— that her mother had heard her father's voice only once, in another room, before the day on which she married him. The issue of marriage was being debated in the sixteenth century, and it will continue to be debated through the centuries. It is an important topic in Cervantes because it has to do with the social, the legal, and also with the question of love. It has to do with narrative too.

It is at this point that Sancho, to his astonishment, learns Dulcinea's real identity: Ah, she is the daughter of Lorenzo Corchuelo! He knows who this woman is! Is that Dulcinea? The story of Don Quixote's love for her is the background for the stories of Cardenio, Luscinda, Don Fernando, and Dorotea because Don Quixote's love of Aldonza Lorenzo could have led to an unequal marriage, that of an aristocrat, even if a minor aristocrat, with a country lass. I have already said that unequal marriages are one of the constants in all of the stories in the Sierra Morena and reflect a society in flux where there is incipient class mobility. Sixteenth-century Spain was called by Américo Castro, a famous historian and critic, a "conflictive age," and part of the conflict was this social effervescence, this social instability, about which I will speak more in the course of the semester. Aldonza appeals to Don Quixote or Alonso Quixano because of her manly qualities, which he transforms into sublime, courtly love beauty. She is manly in the sense that she is brawny, strong, used to hard labor in the fields.

I imagine this is the fetishistic appeal she has for Alonso Quixano: as opposed to the women in his class, Aldonza would be sexual in a more physical and unabashed way. What does Alonso Quixano's love of Aldonza tell us about love? Aldonza/Dulcinea. This is one of those life lessons I told you about in the first lecture; you might learn something from reading the *Qui-xote*. The *Quixote* is also about life, your lives. What we learn from Alonso Quixano's passion for Aldonza, whom he turns into Dulcinea, is that when in love we invent the object of our desire and that that object depends on the projection of our own inner demons. This is perhaps the most important and urgent thing for you to learn from the *Quixote*, at least today.

Let us set up the cast of main characters in the stories in the Sierra Morena so that we can untangle this narrative knot as much as we can; because it can get complicated, and I am also going to unravel the socioeconomic background behind all of this. Let us begin with Cardenio. Cardenio, the name, suggests *cárdeno*, which means 'purple,' bright purple, bright purple with passion. In terms of literary history Cardenio is a minor Orlando, Ariosto's protagonist in the poem mentioned before, who goes berserk when he suspects that Angelica has betrayed him with Medoro, a youthful Moor. This is that famous poem *Orlando Furioso*, which I have mentioned and which you should read at some point. Cardenio is mad as a result of a lover's treason. He roams about nearly naked, an image of his savagery, of his regression to the world of nature; he is a wild man in the Renaissance tradition—in the Renaissance the figure of the wild man appears often. Madness and love are embodied in Cardenio as they are in the mad knight Don Quixote because Cardenio is a double of Don Quixote, and, in fact, Don Quixote has a feeling of uncanny recognition when he meets Cardenio for the first time: "[Don Quixote] walked with graceful elegance to embrace him, and held him for some moments in his arms, as if he knew him from distant times" (I, 23, 195).

Perhaps he had been acquainted with Cardenio by being acquainted with himself, and this is what the line suggests. So Don Quixote discovers in Cardenio a kind of double. Cardenio is a poet. We discover this when Don Quixote and Sancho find a rotten bag in the woods that contains a book of poems and other texts by Cardenio. We have, again, a literary text read in the novel, as we did with Grisóstomo's song. Like Grisóstomo, Cardenio is a Petrarchan or a Garcilaso-like poet, sick with love. Petrarch was the great Italian poet about whom you have all heard, the one who is the creator of modern poetry. He lived in the fourteenth century. And Garcilaso, whom I have mentioned before, a Spanish disciple of Petrarch, was the great poet of the sixteenth century who brought about a whole revolution in Spanish poetic language. He lived in the sixteenth century, from 1501 to 1536, a short life. Don Quixote is happy to have found the poem and is curious about whom the author might be, whereas Sancho is very happy to have found a

hundred gold coins. As you may have noticed, Sancho is not all that interested in discovering who the owner of the bag is because he does not want
to have to return the money.

Cardenio and Luscinda belong to the low nobility. They are hidalgos,
like Don Quixote, with sufficient wealth to make their marriage desirable.
Both would gain: she would gain social status because Cardenio's status is
higher, and he would gain wealth because she is rich, like Marcela. Her estate would become Cardenio's dowry, guaranteeing succession, a reassuring
prospect to her parents because she is a woman, and there will be—again,
as in the case of Marcela—some concern about the legacy being lost. The
added capital would even improve the lineage. Dorotea, on the other hand,
is a commoner. She is a rich farmer's daughter, and she is far below Don
Fernando's social status; if Don Fernando were to marry her he would anger
his father because she is his vassal. Her name, as you may have already noticed, rhymes with Dulcinea. We will see other instances where Cervantes
uses rhyme echoes of this nature to establish connections. In the rhyming
with Dulcinea there is something of a mirroring or echoing effect, a version
of what Don Quixote's and Dulcinea's romance could have been; as I told
you, the same relationship except that Don Quixote is old. The duke, Don
Fernando's father, is so wealthy that while the increase of the estate would be
welcome, it would not be much of an incentive.

Don Fernando is the most complicated of these characters. He is not
exactly a hero. Having seduced Dorotea and married Luscinda under false
pretenses, he is the character most vexed by judicial and economic pressures, the source of most of the troubles in these stories. He is guilty of *estu-
pro,* 'rape,' and the priest, at some point, plans to denounce him, whereupon
he will become a fugitive from justice like Don Quixote. Don Fernando's
actions have sent Cardenio and Dorotea into the wilderness and left Luscinda in a dangerous situation from which she too wants to escape, but she
is abducted by Don Fernandò in that story that is told somewhat laterally. If
Cervantes had gone into that story we would have had an endless sequence
of stories, so what happens to her when she is abducted from the convent
is left hanging. Don Fernando is a Don Juan type; Don Juan, the serial se-
ducer, who first appeared in Western literature in a play by Tirso de Molina,
a Spanish playwright of the seventeenth century. Don Fernando has injured
Cardenio's and Dorotea's families, not just them individually, by compromising their honor and estate, meaning their social status and economic
position. There is an implicit cause, an implicit, subtle, but strong cause for
Don Fernando's criminal actions. Don Fernando is an anxious *segundón.*

The word comes from the word *segundo* in Spanish, which means 'second.'
Segundón means 'second-born son,' and it has pejorative connotations.

To explain Don Fernando's socioeconomic status I must expound a
little on a Spanish institution, the *mayorazgo*. In the Middle Ages, Castilian
law had elaborated the institution of the mayorazgo, an entailed state, a mass
of wealth and property whose integrity and continuity were guaranteed by
exceptional testamentary laws. An entailed state, in law, is to limit the inheritance of property to a specific line of heirs in such a way that it cannot be
legally transferred—I am giving you the definition from Webster's because
not everybody knows what an entailed estate is. As the name implies, mayorazgo, *hijo mayor*: *hijo* / 'son,' *mayor* / 'eldest'; mayorazgo. The mayorazgo
consisted in the privileging of firstborn males in matters of inheritance. The
firstborn son inherited the title and the bulk of the endowment. The mayorazgo was an entailment devised to ensure the accumulation and retention
of wealth within one family by preventing its dispersal through marriages—
because if you had three sons and each inherited the same amount and each
married a different woman, the estate would be dispersed and diminished.

By the middle of the twelfth century, the king allowed the establishment of mayorazgos that comprised entire villages. A mayorazgo could also
be a royal grant from the king as a reward for some special deed. In the *Siete
Partidas,* a thirteenth-century legal code that is the foundation of Spanish
law, the mayorazgo is already established. The legal foundation of the mayorazgo was ultimately grounded in the specific mention of God's command to
Abraham to sacrifice Isaac, his first and most beloved son.

So the ultimate authority was the Bible. The *Siete Partidas* also explic-
itly allowed the *testador,* that is, the one whose legacy is being passed down,
to forbid his heir from alienating the inheritance by sale or other means,
obliging him to pass it on to his own firstborn son. In the sixteenth century
commoners were allowed to begin mayorazgos. The proliferation of mayorazgos generated a class of segundones, or second-born sons, who were left
out of the patrimony. If only the firstborn could inherit, and families had
many sons and daughters, there were a lot of segundones. They had the social status that their usually illustrious names conferred on them but not
financial substance or position in society and an uncertain future. Elliott
writes in *Imperial Spain,*

> Just under these two groups of magnates [grandees and *títulos*],
> who formed the élite of the Spanish aristocracy, came a group

which differed from them in having no corporate entity of its
own, but which none the less enjoyed an acknowledged position
in the social hierarchy. This group consisted of the *segundones*—
the younger sons of the great houses. These possessed no title
of their own, and were generally victims of the *mayorazgo* system which reserved the bulk of the family wealth for their elder
brothers. Since their resources tended to be limited, they were
likely to devote themselves in particular to careers in the Army
or the Church, or to serve the Crown as diplomats and adminis-
trators. (114)

The term *segundón,* by the way, by virtue of its suffix *-ón,* is an augmentative.
It is derogatory, as in *grandulón,* a lummox; *regalón,* someone who is spoiled;
coquetón, a flirt; *empollón,* a nerd; *huevón,* lazybones; and so forth. Some of
these are not nice words, but they clearly point to the embarrassing position
of the segundón. I am trying to give you the background so you understand
Don Fernando's situation. It points to the embarrassing position of someone
who, because of his heritage, can act with the self-sufficiency of his class but
has little substance to back it up. The way out of the situation was contained
in a refrain of the times, "Iglesia, mar o casa real." We will encounter it later
in the captive's tale, where it is applied to the sons of a man. It meant that
the segundón could go into the *iglesia,* 'church,' obtaining a position of some
importance because of his family's connection; *mar,* 'sea,' he could go to sea
to seek adventures and wealth, go to the colonies; or to a *casa real,* 'royal
house,' that is, attach himself to the court or to the house of a grandee.

Cut off from their parents' legacies, segundones became social and economic climbers, anxiously trying to make up for their deficiency in status.
In the Spain of the sixteenth and seventeenth centuries they became a class
unto themselves, a laborious one, one should say, desperately seeking social
and economic advancement. Don Fernando's situations and actions betray
all of the features of this class. Don Fernando is a segundón, the second son
of Duke Ricardo. In fact, the text reads in Spanish, "Un hijo segundo del
duque," 'one of the duke's second sons.' Because it included all of the sons
who were not the firstborn, not only the second son but also the third, the
fourth, the fifth. They were all segundones, so the segundón is essentially
he who is not first, the only position with entitlement. When Cardenio appears at Don Fernando's home, having been summoned by the duke explic-
itly to be the companion of his older brother, who is in line to be the father's

successor and is already a marquis, Don Fernando ingratiates himself with the visitor and wins him over to his side.

Cardenio is like a rival, or someone who reminds Don Fernando of the role he would be called on to play if he chose casa real, to join the house of a grandee. He could be a competitor in that by becoming the ally of his older brother he could come closer to gaining wealth and power than Don Fernando himself, prevented as he is by law from acquiring them from his father. Don Fernando is the odd man out, literally number three in this case, which is worse than second. So he lures Cardenio away and soon finds himself as his rival for Luscinda's favors. His seduction of Dorotea could have an economic motive, too. In fact, when he does agree to marry her later, Don Fernando is potentially founding an estate that could conceivably become a mayorazgo of his own if it is rich enough and wealthy enough. Restitution takes on a whole new meaning when viewed from this perspective.

Readers of Cervantes' time would have immediately recognized all of the testamentary conflicts involved in Don Fernando's actions and how the law impinges on his love life. It is his anxiety that drives Don Fernando to this frantic love life. The economic, social, and ultimately judicial context that was the background of the Marcela–Grisóstomo episode is greatly expanded here to encompass deep social and economic issues in Castile during the sixteenth century. The judicial situation is historically accurate.

The source of the conflict in which Don Fernando, Cardenio, Luscinda, and Dorotea are entangled is very precise. The impending marriage of Luscinda and Cardenio is, again, dictated by circumstances as well as by mutual attraction. Cardenio says that Luscinda is "a maiden as noble and wealthy as I" (I, 24, 198). The description he gives of their youth and early love is like the implicit blueprint for the marriage of Marcela and Grisóstomo, except that it was nearer to taking place.

Actually, their marriage is about to take place when Don Fernando intervenes. But the ambition of social advancement first postpones the marriage because Cardenio's father feels that the young man should go and answer the duke's summons, and then Luscinda's parents are keen on her marrying Don Fernando because it would be a leap up in social class. So, in fact, Cardenio accuses Luscinda of acting out of economic and social interest, and this is why she left him, and her leaving is the source of the feeling of betrayal that has sent him into the woods.

Dorotea is the victim of Don Fernando's treachery, but she is not a passive character—I told you Cervantes' female characters tend not to be passive. Her actions are dictated by the same economic and legal determinations that drive the others. She is the daughter of commoners who are, however, all Christians, and the characters boast of this at a time in Spain when being suspected of having Jewish or Moorish blood could be a disabling condition. So they are proud, old Christians, wealthy, and therefore capable of social advancement. Her father is Clenardo the Rich; a great name. Clenardo and Dorotea's mother have great ambitions for their daughter. In fact, later, when Dorotea, disguised as Princess Micomicona, makes up a story (I will talk about it soon), she reveals that she is fearful of Don Fernando taking her wealth. She runs the farm; she boasts that she is the one who did all of the administrative work for it.

Dorotea may be a woman and a vassal, but she is well aware of her rights and legitimate aspirations, not to mention what an asset her physical beauty can be. When Don Fernando sneaks into her chamber, determined to possess her by any means, she decides to surrender, motivated by love, pragmatism, and greed. In telling her story to the priest, the barber, and Cardenio, Dorotea repeats what she told herself at that crucial point. She is telling the story of what she thought at the moment Don Fernando was pressing the issue:

> All right then, I shan't be the first girl to rise by means of mar-
> riage from humble to high estate, nor will Don Fernando be the
> first man to be led by beauty or, more likely, by blind desire, into
> taking a wife beneath his rank. Well, since I'm not going to be
> changing the world or creating some new custom, it'll be best to
> accept this honour that fortune's offering me, even if the love this
> man professes does last no longer than it takes him to have his
> way—for, after all, in God's eyes I'll be his wife. And if I scorn and
> reject him, I can see he's in such a state that he'll ignore his obli-
> gations and use violence, and I'll be dishonoured and left without
> the excuses that anyone who doesn't know how innocently I have
> come to this pass would otherwise have made for me. Because
> what arguments will be powerful enough to persuade my par-
> ents and others that this gentleman entered my room without my
> consent? (I, 28, 255)

She draws a balance and decides that the best thing is simply to give in. She has made him swear they are going to marry, and she has made him swear in front of her maid, the one who let him in, that he would marry. In the Spain of the time—I will talk about this much more—secret marriages were allowed, meaning, if you told your beloved in the darkness of night and in a fit of passion that you wanted to marry her and she said yes, then you were married because God is listening everywhere; therefore, presumably you are married. It is no surprise that the temptation not to abide by such vows was great. There were debates about it in the Council of Trent, as we will have reason to discuss in classes concerning other marriage situations in Part II.

Dorotea is faithfully following both religious doctrine and Castilian law, which condoned premarital sexual relationships after a betrothal, such as the one she has forced Don Fernando to make. He has sworn to marry her not only before herself and her servant but also before God. When she later pleads her case at the inn, Dorotea invokes this oath, appeals to Don Fernando's conscience, and assures him that by law he is not compromising his or his family's status because nobility is transmitted by the father, not the mother's blood, in Castile—as we had occasion to see in the case of Grisóstomo and Marcela. She convinces Don Fernando in a speech that has as much verve as Marcela's and is also couched in forensic rhetoric and terminology. So this is the legal, socioeconomic background of these stories, about which I will talk more.

But I am now going to speak briefly, and in conclusion, about an important aspect I mentioned before, and that is interruptions. You may have noticed that many of the stories are interrupted at some point. The whole novel is interrupted once, in chapter 8, when the narrator claims to have run out of text. This is perhaps the most famous interruption in Western literature, but there have been many others, including the story of Marcela and Grisóstomo being told by Vivaldo, Ambrosio, and others, which is interrupted several times. The funniest interruption occurs when Sancho is telling his story about Torralba and her boyfriend and the goats having to cross the river. Remember that interruption?

Here we have other interruptions, however. The most important and most spectacular is that of Cardenio. Cardenio says he will tell the story, but he will not be interrupted; he does not want to be interrupted with questions or anything. That is the precondition for his telling the story. But at one point he mentions Amadís de Gaula, and that is simply too much for Don Quixote to resist, so he breaks in and interrupts Cardenio, and Cardenio goes berserk. He brings up this story about Queen Madasima having had an affair with a lowly surgeon—surgeons at the time did not have a very high status—and attacks Don Quixote and Sancho and runs wild.

What is behind all of these interruptions is that they allow for a certain truth to come out because what Cervantes is showing is that stories have a self-generating thrust, they follow a certain implicit script, and they veil the truth instead of telling it, and, unless the teller is interrupted, the truth will not come out. So what is the truth here? The truth here, in the case of Cardenio, is that he has this paranoid fantasy that Don Fernando has already possessed Luscinda and that therefore Luscinda is not fit for marriage to him. It is unclear whether this happened, but the story Cardenio tells, translated into literature, is that this Queen Madasima had an affair with a surgeon. The idea of the surgeon, of cutting, is a story of deflowering that is deep in his mind; that Luscinda has been deflowered by Don Fernando. So he has transformed that story in his imagination into his paranoid fantasy. What the interruption truly reveals is his subconscious. This is similar to what we saw in the case of Don Quixote making up that chivalric romance; telling the story, or, in Cardenio's case, interrupting the story, reveals another story.

The *Quixote* shows us how to read stories. It is a primer on how to interpret them. This is the second life lesson you are learning here today, particularly if you are going to be a lawyer. Why? Lawyers do not allow witnesses to go on speaking for a long time. They are taught to interrupt them because a witness can go on and on and let the story get away and create facts that do not exist. What is most important to remember about these interrupted tales is to look not for the story being told but for the story being told obliquely. That's what we did when considering Don Quixote's invention of the generic chivalric romance, which was a roundabout way of speaking about his anxieties concerning his lack of social status. This is why in the psychoanalytic session the analyst will interrupt you and ask questions: "Oh, what did you say about mommy? Hmm. . . . What did you say about daddy? Hmm . . . ," and does not let you go on. It is in the give and take that the truth may emerge. So this is what the *Quixote* is telling us. We will see the same narrative device appear again when Dorotea, disguised as Princess Micomicona, makes up a story that is really the story of her own turbulent love affair with Don Fernando. She cannot make up a fictional story without her story emerging in the background, and there are little details that betray that it is the real story. So the *Quixote* is, among many other things, a book about how to read and how to interpret stories, and we are surrounded by stories of all kinds, not just in literature but also in life.

CHAPTER 8

Memory and Narrative

Stories within Stories

Required Readings

Cervantes, *Don Quixote,* Part I, chaps. 27–35, 228–337.
Elliott, *Imperial Spain,* 130–63.

We are coming to a part of the *Quixote,* the core of Part I, in which Cervantes makes a display of narrative mastery by combining the sequential structure of the chivalric romance, whose form he is parodying, with the multiple story design of collections of *novelle,* the long short story favored by Italians from Giovanni Boccaccio (1313–75) to Matteo Bandello (1485–1561). How can these two genres be merged and mixed? Cervantes achieves it by taking his protagonist away from the center of the story while still engaging him in the unfolding and resolution of the intercalated tales involving Cardenio, Don Fernando, Dorotea, and Luscinda. We will get to that today and in the next class. But, first, I want to begin by talking about the role that memory plays in the narrative and the development of characters.

In the last class we saw how interrupted stories being told by characters led to the revelation of other stories not being told or being told obliquely. In all of those cases memory is the key element. Don Quixote makes up the generic chivalric romance by drawing from his recollections of the chivalric romances he has read in the past. In the episodes in the Sierra Morena there are three moments when memory plays a crucial role. The first is when Cardenio speaks about how painful the memory of his betrayal by Luscinda and Don Fernando is and how he would like to evoke it, if only to give him the strength of mind to commit suicide: "O memory, the mortal foe of my repose! Why bring before me now the incomparable beauty of that adored enemy of mine? Won't it be better, cruel memory, to recall and picture to me what she did next so that, moved by such a manifest affront, I can at least, since vengeance is impossible, put an end to my life?" (I, 27, 239). The agonizing recollection of the betrayal constitutes Cardenio's defining story and the source of his madness. It is not just what others did to him, but what he failed to do at the decisive moment, his cowardice, as he twice refers to it.

The second instance in which memory plays a significant role is when Cardenio says he vaguely remembers the fracas with Don Quixote when the knight interrupted his narrative; the episode is like a hole in his memory. This is an example of Cervantes' psychological sophistication in that Cardenio can remember the fight with Don Quixote only as if it had been a dream and cannot recall what provoked it: "Cardenio recalled, as if from a dream, his fight with Don Quixote, and told the others about it, but he couldn't say what the cause of their disagreement had been" (I, 29, 262). Cardenio's story has a gaping hole, a crack at the climax that is contained within another crack, Don Quixote's interruption. It is like a scar left by a deep wound. This lapse is a clear symptom of trauma, we would say today. Cardenio's story is full of holes, gaps, and discontinuities.

The third instance in which memory is highlighted is when Dorotea, as Princess Micomicona, forgets her name even as she plays that role when telling the bogus story of her life: "'First of all, I'd like you to know, gentlemen, that my name is . . .' And here she hesitated, because she'd forgotten the name which the priest had christened her; but realizing what the trouble was he came to the rescue and said: 'It is no wonder, my lady, that Your Highness should be overcome by confusion and embarrassment . . .'" (I, 30, 272). As Dorotea says, she will make up the story by basing it on her recollection of reading romances of chivalry. This, by the way, is an inconsistency either in Cervantes' case or in Dorotea's recollections. When she told of her life, she said that one of her entertainments was reading mostly devout literature. She did not mention anything then about reading romances of chivalry, but she does now. So she will make up the story by basing it on her recollection of reading romances of chivalry, but the name she forgets was not of her own invention but the priest's, so she quickly forgets it and has to be prompted. Since, as I commented, her story is a translation of her current predicament into the discourse of the romances of chivalry, her forgetting of her name is indicative of her traumatized self. She has, after all, assumed other roles after being abandoned by Don Fernando, which is the traumatic event in her life. Her sense of identity is frail and in the process of being remade.

Connected to all of this—and perhaps the overarching memory lapse of them all—is the loss of Sancho's ass. The ass, by the way, is not named in the Spanish original. The theft of Sancho's ass was left out of the first edition, and Cervantes hastily restored it in the second printing, a few months later. Memory is not just a repository of recollections and stories from the past. It is that which structures the self in the present and the archive whence narratives issue, flawed and misshapen, no longer a true reflection of what happened but revelatory of a truth about a character's state as he or she talks in the present. So it is a truth about now, about the present, that may be full of holes, of misrepresentations about the past. It is nevertheless the repository of stories about the past. So it is in that interplay between flawed recollections and the present that the stories are told.

The representation of all this interplay of memory and narrative is the overall network of interrelated and intertwined stories that take place or are told in the Sierra Morena and resolved at Juan Palomeque's inn, after Don Quixote's battle with the wineskins, about which I will speak in the next class. Now, Cervantes was very much aware of the complexities of that construct, that network of stories. We read this at the beginning of chapter 28 after we have heard Cardenio's tale in two installments. It is a remarkable, self-referential mock admonition on the part of the narrator: "No sólo la dulzura de su [Don Quixote's] verdadera historia, sino de los cuentos y episodios de ella, que en parte no son menos agradables y artificiosos y verdaderos que la misma historia, la cual prosiguiendo su rastrillado, torcido y aspado hilo, cuenta que así como el cura empezó a prevenirse." Charles Jarvis's translation pares this down to the following: "Enjoy the sweets of his [Don Quixote's] true story but also the stories and episodes of it which are in some sort no less pleasing, artificial and true than the history itself, which resuming the broken thread of the narration relates that . . ." Tobias Smollett's version, with some emendations of my own, reads as follows: "In this our age, so much in need of enjoying agreeable entertainments, not only of his [Don Quixote's] true and delightful adventures, but also of the intervening episodes, which are no less real, artful and delicious than the main story itself, the twisted reeled and rattled thread of which is continued thus, just as the curate was ready to offer some consolation to Cardenio." You can see how much Jarvis left out. In the translation we are using, Rutherford renders the passage thus: "We can now enjoy, in this age of ours, so much in need of amusing entertainments, not only the delights of his [Don Quixote's] true history but also the stories and episodes inserted into it, for in some ways they are no less agreeable or imaginative or true than the history itself; which, resuming its thread (duly dressed, spun and wound), relates that as the priest was preparing himself to comfort Cardenio . . ." (I, 28, 247).

I want to call attention not just to what the text says but also to the interruption itself, which is a speech act that performs the function of interrupting the narrative. A speech act is an act that a speaker performs when making an utterance. Just as the priest is about to reply to Cardenio he is "prevented," in Smollett's version, "hindered," in Jarvis's version, and "checked," in Rutherford's version by Dorotea's voice, which will provide part of the missing information in Cardenio's account. There can be no comforting of Cardenio yet. Interruptions rarely promote comforting. The words Cervantes used to refer to the buildup or spooling up of narrative threads brings this out. They are drawn from spinning linen thread, "rastrillado, torcido y aspado," and are reasonably well translated by Smollett as "twisted, reeled and raveled" and by Rutherford as "dressed, spun and wound." But in the original they have, at least for me, perhaps because Spanish is my native language, a more violent or literal inflection. In other words, "twisted," "reeled," and "raveled" and "dressed," "spun," and "wound" are common English terms whose remote, metaphoric origin has now faded. In Spanish, the words used by Cervantes, applied allegorically to narrative, are shockingly fresh and evoke more directly the physical actions they describe. *Rastrillar* is to rake out the excess fibers from the thread; *torcer* is to twist together many strands in order to make a string or thread; and *aspar* is to twist two sticks to weave together, to weave strings together, as is done on a smaller scale with the needles in knitting.

The cross-marriages, Luscinda with Cardenio—although she had been married to Don Fernando—and Dorotea to Don Fernando—although she had been in Cardenio's care—replicate the positioning and action of the two sticks used for *aspar*, if you understand what I mean. In short, the relation among the stories, including the main plot, is predicated on blunt cuts and crisscrossing, not on smooth transitions. These are made possible by traumatic interruptions which jostle the memory of the tellers and drive them to reveal other stories behind the one they tell and also make them disclose their inner thoughts, thereby rounding out their characters. But, in addition, the whole network of stories, which is like a quilt—to extend the metaphors having to do with cloth—is itself a superb display of narrative skill and variety, which is one of the aims of Renaissance art. But the question will always remain, in spite of what the narrator says, about the relationship of all of these stories to the main story of Don Quixote and Sancho. I am sketching an answer here today, but I must inform you, as you will learn in the prologue of Part II, that Cervantes was criticized for including these stories, and in the sequel he was careful to integrate stories more seamlessly into the main narrative. He did not include a story like "The Tale of Inappropriate Curiosity," about which I will be speaking in the next class, whose relationship to the main story is questionable.

In the last class I focused on Don Fernando—remember when I talked about the *mayorazgo* and the *segundón* and that whole background. Let us concentrate today on Dorotea and Cardenio. Edward Dudley writes the following about Cardenio in his essay "The Wild Man Goes Baroque": "This Wild Man is Cardenio, the soul brother of Don Quijote and, like him, a victim of madness. Their meeting in the Dark Sierra occurs in an atmosphere of unspoken attractions, and Don Quijote, already mad, is driven farther into the shadowed wilderness of his insanity. His subsequent imitation of Cardenio's madness is the high point of his lunacy."[1] Dudley is referring to the episode I quoted earlier about the meeting of Cardenio and Don Quixote, when the knight seems to remember having seen him before. The difference between the two is that Cardenio is a poet, in the Petrarchan or Garcilaso vein, like Grisóstomo. So there are parallels with Don Quixote but also differences. Dudley goes on to give context to the figure of the wild man. He says, "The approach to a Wild Man hidden in a threatening wilderness is an archetypal pattern familiar in world folklore and one utilized by artists again and again."[2]

He even alludes to a modern work like Joseph Conrad's *Heart of Darkness,* which is from 1900. So the story of finding a wild man in the wilderness is something that is a folkloric story. Dudley cites he-goats and wolves as being akin to Cardenio in his moments of madness. I mean these figures assume the role of he-goats and of wolves, two images that suggest, respectively, the problems of sex and violence that haunted the seventeenth century; I would say that haunted all centuries, but Dudley knows because he has studied stories in the seventeenth century. Dudley claims that "Cardenio's problem is that he cannot talk effectively, that he cannot communicate by means of the spoken word." And he adds, "Clinically Cardenio's condition has been diagnosed as a case of zoanthropy (animal-man)."[3]

Zoanthropy, animal-man, man becoming like an animal. As for the relationship between Don Fernando and Cardenio, Dudley sees a homosexual pattern. He suggests that the relationship between Cardenio and Don

Fernando shows some mutual attraction that, in a way, anticipates the relationship between the two protagonists of "The Tale of Inappropriate Curiosity," which I will be discussing in the next class. That is, that the relationship between these two men is mediated by Luscinda but that actually it is a homosexual relationship between the two of them. More in line with what I have been saying about interruptions, Dudley says that in asking Cardenio to tell his story, "Don Quijote in this way anticipates the twentieth-century analyst who begins the cure by having the patient tell his story, and it is in the story that the cause of the madness is found, just as it is by means of Don Quijote's intervention that the cure is initiated. . . . But as he proceeds it becomes apparent that the real reason is that he is autistic and wants above all not to be challenged in his dubious interpretation of the events."[4] I will say that it is not that he is autistic but that he has been traumatized and that trauma has caused something akin to autism, but it is not autism. And then Dudley says that Dorotea plays an important role because she appears before Cardenio, and he admires her beauty but does not lust after her, and that in that process Cardenio's cure has begun.[5]

This is a typically Renaissance idea of a cure brought about by the contemplation of beauty. This is the role Dorotea plays in the cure of Cardenio. Cardenio's character flaws and his intermittent bouts of madness are perhaps the reason Shakespeare found Cardenio so compelling and wrote a play about him, a play that was lost. The *Quixote* appeared in English in 1612, so Shakespeare had time to read *Don Quixote* and to write a play based on this character. Unfortunately it was lost, but one is left to wonder what Shakespeare found compelling in the character of Cardenio. I would say there is a Hamlet-like tendency to hesitation in Cardenio that Shakespeare may have found attractive.

Dorotea's story. As we saw in the last class, Dorotea is seduced by Don Fernando, who marries Luscinda. Is there some kind of culpability in Dorotea? Did she not also consider at the crucial moment what a good match Don Fernando would be? Was she not trapped by the fact that if she resisted no one would believe she had not allowed Don Fernando in her room? Like Cardenio, she hesitates at the moment of truth, but unlike Cardenio she makes a decision and takes action. Hers is not a submissive surrender. It is a calculated surrender. When Don Fernando disappears she goes in search of him but then discovers that the marriage to Luscinda may not be final and that she may have a chance to force him to make good on his promise. Remember that Don Fernando, as she discovers, has been out hunting after he left her, completely oblivious to her. Cardenio, on the other hand, is pusillanimous, cowardly, and Luscinda cannot bring herself to commit suicide at the crucial moment, as she intended to do. Dorotea, on the other hand, is not passive. Like Don Quixote, she invents herself and, like him, ultimately raises herself in social class because she does marry Don Fernando. We will soon see the role she plays in bringing a resolution to the conflicts and preparing the way for Don Quixote's return to his village.

Dorotea's story is as compelling as Cardenio's, but she is more composed and determined to obtain some sort of restitution. Her situation is complicated by the fact that her father is Don Fernando's vassal, and she could hardly be the one to seek revenge or compensation according to custom. But by law she had recourse to both revenge and compensation, but usually this happened with the help of a man. Legislation in the wake of the Catholic Kings' program to rein in the aristocracy made it a crime for noblemen to take advantage of peasant women. Cardenio, being a man and an aristocrat, like Don Fernando and the duke, offers to stand up for her, clearly because it is also in his interest. He promises to defend her in strict accordance to law and custom. Cardenio says he will challenge Don Fernando to a duel, implicitly alluding to the concept of *riepto*, which is an old Spanish word for *retar*, 'to challenge,' and was part of Spanish legislation in the Middle Ages but had been banned by legislation in the sixteenth century. That is, by the sixteenth century noblemen were not allowed to duel with each other over an issue. But there was a great deal of debate because the aristocracy wanted to retain that right, which went back to Visigothic times, when noblemen took care of conflicts by fighting each other. Now that he is reassured of Luscinda's virginal condition—and this is crucial—and the questionable legality of her marriage to Don Fernando, Cardenio is encouraged to take action, and he invokes what he believes to be his right to defend her. Dorotea's story is briefly interrupted by Cardenio, who cannot refrain from saying something when he hears about his own misfortunes from her point of view. This is the rest of his own story, which he himself did not know, and when he reveals his identity to Dorotea, parts of her story that she did not know fall into place.

Interruptions are like the lines between the pieces of a large puzzle. For Cardenio, the crucial piece is the scene of the wedding of Luscinda and Don Fernando, which had appeared proleptically in the chivalric story he blurted out when Don Quixote interrupted him, the business about Queen Madasima and the surgeon having had an affair—that psychotic vision he had in his mind about the deflowering of Luscinda. But now he and Dorotea begin to discern a potential happy ending to their misfortunes at the intersection of their stories, when they hear each other's tales. The deleted motive, the gap in the story, concerns the legality of Don Fernando's and Luscinda's marriage and her retaining her virginity. It is that chasm, fraught with violence and erased from Cardenio's memory, that needs to be filled in the melodramatic conclusive scene at Juan Palomeque's inn. Cardenio expresses his desire for restitution in legal terms, describing the damage inflicted on him and Luscinda: "We can well hope that heaven will restore to us what is ours, because it's all still valid, it hasn't been alienated or damaged" (I, 29, 261). These are crucial words. The original reads, "Bien podemos esperar que el cielo nos restituya lo que es nuestro, pues está todavía en su ser y no se ha enajenado ni deshecho."

The last part is a notarial formula used in contracts involving the assessment of properties and their resale value when returned to the original owner. I think, too, that "todavía está en su ser," 'it remains whole in its integrity,' is a euphemism to say that Luscinda is still a virgin, as does "deshecho," 'undone.' This invocation of heaven means that, once they are rescued from the wilderness, the law, both human and divine, will again take effect, and their story will have a happy ending.

Dorotea is ogled by three men in one of the most explicit and sophisticated erotic scenes in the *Quixote*. Like Cardenio, Dorotea is first a voice, heard by the barber, the priest, and Cardenio, who laments her fate. She is sound before she is a visible body, and she will become a quite visible body indeed. Sancho has left to fetch Don Quixote and Cardenio, and the priest and the barber discover the beautiful Dorotea in a shady spot, washing her feet in a brook. She is disguised as a farmhand but soon, by spreading her gorgeous blonde hair, she reveals herself to be a very beautiful young woman. Her graceful, harmonious body is seen in stages by the men, who spy on her without being seen—the pleasure of voyeurism is not just seeing but also not being seen.

Dorotea is the object of converging gazes that possess her by parts; first, fetishistically, her feet. Their desiring gazes cut the body into parts, a violent act of possession. Dorotea, who as an ensemble embodies perfect beauty, is consumed by the men looking at her in pieces. She is a version of Diana in Greek mythology and of Susanna in the book of Daniel, naked women who were ogled by voyeuristic men. Dorotea is not naked but, even more alluringly, dressed as a man.

In Roman mythology Diana was the goddess of the hunt, associated with wild animals and woodland, and also of the moon. Among her main attributes, Diana was an emblem of chastity. Oak groves were especially sacred to her. In art she appears accompanied by a deer because she was the patroness of hunting, although the deer may also be a covert reference to the myth of Actaeon, who saw her bathing naked. Diana transformed Actaeon into a stag and set his own hunting dogs on him to tear him apart. Susanna or Shoshana, Lily, is one of the additions to the book of Daniel accepted by the Catholic and Eastern Orthodox churches. As the story goes, the lovely Susanna, a beautiful Hebrew wife, is falsely accused by lecherous voyeurs. As she bathes in her garden, having sent her attendants away, two lusty elders secretly contemplate her. When she makes her way back to her house, they accost her, threatening to claim that she was meeting a young man in the garden unless she agrees to have sex with them. She refuses to be blackmailed and is arrested and about to be put to death for promiscuity when a young man named Daniel interrupts the proceedings and finally gets the two old men to contradict themselves when he cross-examines them. The two men are executed, and virtue triumphs. But the crucial images here are those of Susanna being observed, gazed upon by the two old men, and of Actaeon looking at Diana bathing naked.

These allusions are implicit in this beautiful scene. The voyeurs here are Cardenio, the priest, and the barber; Sancho is not with them. The three men are looking at her:

> They approached him [they think she is a man] so quietly that he didn't notice them, being so engrossed in bathing his feet, which looked like nothing so much as two pieces of white crystal lying among the other stones there. They were astonished at the whiteness and the beauty of those feet, which didn't look as if they were accustomed to treading the clods or trudging behind the plough and the oxen, as the lad's clothes indicated they were.
>
> And so, seeing that they hadn't been noticed, the priest, who'd gone on ahead, motioned to the other two to crouch down and hide behind some rocks, which they did, watching every movement made by the lad. (I, 28, 248)

The text goes on to describe how Dorotea washes her feet, how her hands are beautifully white and her hair cascades down to the point that it makes Apollo envious. Eventually, they disclose to her who they are, and the episode ensues. This is a scene that could be a Renaissance painting. And, in fact, Cervantes was well acquainted with Italian Renaissance painting, for, as you know, having read it in the *Casebook,* Cervantes spent a good deal of time in Italy. Frederick de Armas, at the University of Chicago, has written two books about the impression Italian art made on Cervantes' work.[6] This is obviously one of those instances.

Why is Dorotea a version of the classical and biblical myth? It is a Renaissance move, as it were, on the part of Cervantes. The background enhances the figure; it enhances the figure to make of her a version of a classical myth. It adds to her beauty and to the prestige of the creation, and it also shows that art can make the present, or a present scene, be like a classical myth. This is crucial to understanding why the scene is so much like a Renaissance painting. Dorotea's beauty shines through her coarse, cross-gendered dress. In fact, it is enhanced by it, the contrast, the misled anticipation—you begin to see what you think is a male and suddenly, as the person disrobes, it begins to show female features and the gradual revelation of body parts. These are all highly erotic features, particularly the gradual revelation of the body. Transvestitism is rampant in the Sierra Morena, as you may have noticed.

First, the priest dresses like a princess; then, when the priest becomes a little squeamish, the barber puts on the dress. Here we have characters in drag ogling characters in drag. The barber, dressed as a woman, looks upon the beautiful Dorotea, who is dressed like a man. What does it all mean? It suggests that in the disordered world of the woods sexuality is so primal that it antecedes gender distinctions. It is a form of generalized desire. Transvestitism is thus rampant in the Sierra Morena. When the priest addresses Dorotea later, he simply tells her she can claim to be whatever she wants to be, man or woman, meaning that she can use feminine or masculine endings and pronouns, as Spanish allows for gender distinction in the speaker: "My dear lady, or my dear sir, whichever you prefer to be" (I, 28, 249).

The *despoblado,* this area in the wilderness, is a place so far outside the law that genders have yet to be defined, and it is even pregrammatical in the sense that it exists before endings can determine or express gender. This is suggested by the locus amoenus—remember, I discussed the locus amoenus, or the pleasant place, before, like the one we found when Rocinante was aroused by the mares after the Marcela and Grisóstomo episode. The locus amoenus, the perfect site for amorous exchange, enhances Dorotea's appeal. There are light and shade patterns, there is water that reflects and distorts. The waters of the brook are full of reflections and refractions that repeat and distort her image and increase her erotic appeal. First, her feet in the water look like pieces of glass, as transparent as the water itself. Later, her hands acquire the whiteness of snow. Her golden hair would provoke the envy of Apollo. These are symmetries and reflections concurrent with the larger ones concerning the various characters and plot strands. I am trying to establish here a relationship between this locus amoenus and what takes place in it and the overall pattern of these stories. All of these episodes are made up of correlations between the plot, the characters, the settings, and the scenes. Dorotea is the correlative opposite of Luscinda, who is aristocratic but has little money; Dorotea is rich but not aristocratic. Dorotea is also Cardenio's counterpart, lost as she is in the solitariness of the woods, fleeing, disguised, from her fate.

Symmetry and order contrast with the disorder caused by the "pestilencia amorosa," 'the amorous pestilence' Don Quixote spoke about in the speech of the Golden Age. That imagined Golden Age and this locus amoenus are shown to be artifices that conceal desire in a semblance of order but which ultimately cannot contain it and, as a result, violence ensues. I want you to be clear in your mind what is at stake here in this locus amoenus and this violent (not overtly violent) possession of Dorotea by the gaze of these men and the relationship all of this has with the overall pattern of the stories I am analyzing here. Dorotea hurts her feet when she tries to flee barefoot over the rocky ground. She is physically wounded, as she was when she lost her virginity to Don Fernando, and she was almost wounded again when the servant tried to rape her and she threw him over a cliff—we do not know if he is dead—and yet again when her employer tried to possess her. These are dangerous woods.

The story of Cardenio, Luscinda, Don Fernando, and Dorotea is told from at least two perspectives, Cardenio's and Dorotea's. It is also told at various moments and with the attendant interruptions I have been mentioning. All is assembled under the umbrella of the main story of getting Don Quixote out of the Sierra Morena and back home. The stories are united by the theme of love but considered at many different levels.

I move on now to the hilarious invention of Princess Micomicona by the priest. This whole episode is conceived to try to get Don Quixote back home by inventing a fictional chivalric romance that will return him to his village because to reach the kingdom of Micomicón he will have to, according to the story they tell him, pass by his unnamed place in La Mancha. Dorotea's story in her guise as Princess Micomicona is a translation of her real situation. Javier Herrero summarizes the situation thus: "Princess Micomicona, of the kingdom of Micomicón, is the daughter of a magician king—Tinacrio the Wise Man—and the queen Jaramilla. By means of his science the king finds out that someday the princess will be an orphan, and a terrible giant, Pandafilando de la Fosca Vista (so called because he squints to frighten people) will usurp the kingdom. The king further prophesied that only one knight could defeat the giant, the famous Spaniard don Quijote de la Mancha."[7] There is substance to characters invented by characters; that is, Pandafilando de la Fosca Vista, Princess Micomicona, and Tinacrio the Wise are all characters trumped up by the priest and performed by Dorotea! These characters invented by characters acquire solidity within the fiction even though they are metafictional characters.

Pandafilando's name suggests lust. He is a 'pan-philanderer.' What is a philanderer? A philanderer is a man who has many love affairs. So 'pan,' generalized, 'philanderer.' Actually, if you go back to the Greek, it means 'lover of man,' but pan philanderer, he is a 'pan lover,' a persistent, recidivist, insistent, prolific lover; this is Pandafilando, the made-up giant.

The name Micomicona is funny at first glance. It has multiple resonances because it has to do with monkeys. The princess is from Micomicón, the kingdom of monkeys. *Mono* is the most common word for monkey in Spanish, but *mico* means 'monkey' in a more general way. What do monkeys do? Monkey see, monkey do. Monkeys imitate humans in a comical way, only in form, not substance; they are like parodies of us. When you stand in front of the monkey cage at the zoo you see they seem to be making fun of us by imitating us. Indirectly and humorously, the issue of mimesis is brought up here by Cervantes. Mimesis was the Renaissance doctrine of imitation, the imitation of the classics; the imitation of the classic models in order to come closer to the imitation of reality. Mimesis has to do with representation. You can hear its etymological relatives: to mimic, to mime, and mimetic, one can even hear a faint echo of *mimesis* in Micomicona.

But Micomicona, here, means that she is from the kingdom of monkeys, from a kingdom of representation, a kingdom of parodies. Micomicona is also Dulcinea's rival because Sancho badly wants his master to marry the princess so he can get his kingdom. Micomicona is a copy of Dulcinea or an echo of Dulcinea—remember that *Dulcinea* and *Dorotea* rhyme. The Dulcinea who now appears is the one Sancho makes up in his lie about his visit to her—remember, the kind of brawny, smelly Dulcinea who gives him a piece of cheese. He gets next to her and he says that she is tall and that she smells, and Don Quixote says, "How could she smell? You were probably smelling yourself," and Sancho replies, "Yes, it could be because I smell like that sometimes." It is all very funny. But why is Sancho telling the lie?

Because Sancho wants Don Quixote to marry the princess, so he is trying to bring Dulcinea down, to make her look bad; but Don Quixote is not deterred, he says, " 'No, no, no, you must have this all wrong' " (I, 31, 281–82).

So remember that *Dorotea* and *Dulcinea* rhyme, which underscores the relationship they have at this heady, metafictional level. This is a fiction within the fiction that the characters are creating, that the priest is creating, that Dorotea is creating by performing the story, and that Sancho is creating with his lie. We know now what is behind Sancho's lie. All of these stories always have another story behind them; they are always telling another story. The story being told here is that Sancho wants Don Quixote to marry the Princess Micomicona, not Dulcinea, so he is trying to make her look bad. Another rhyming echo here reveals to what extent the story Dorotea is telling is a version of her own predicament: Pandafilando, Fernando. . . . Can you hear it? There is a connection here, an aural connection between the two characters. So this character who is lustful—and who Herrero will claim is an allegory of lust itself—is equated with Don Fernando.

At one point or another, nearly everybody here is in disguise. Some men have been in drag playing various roles, and even Sancho is playing the role of the squire of a bogus knight-errant. The deep question about this episode with these metafictional levels is about the theatricality of life. This is where the *Quixote* leads us, again, to ask questions that are pertinent and relevant to our own lives. Is living the playing of roles? Are we characters in somebody else's fiction, as these characters are here? And if so, for instance, are we bound by ethics if we are just mere characters in somebody's fiction? There are stories within stories creating the infinitely receding sequence I spoke about before. We can lose track of the real and of the self in such a construct. Who are you?

I have heard that under hypnosis we cannot be made to do anything that goes against our sense of values, against our morals. However, in dreams we do transgress principles and engage in wish-fulfillment fantasies. Freud's *The Interpretation of Dreams*, published in 1900, has suggested for the twentieth century and beyond an analogue for literature and for these levels of fiction. Where does literature stand among all of these states of mind? In his own dream, as we shall see in Part II in the Cave of Montesinos episode, Don Quixote will go on with his madness, he will continue to be mad in his dream. In the stories they make up here, however, Micomicona and Sancho do reveal their deeper desires and apprehensions; a subconscious force that is stronger than their will to lie. They want to lie but they tell the truth indirectly. These are the issues that this complex set of stories suggests.

Let me talk, for comic relief, since we are talking about values and principles, about an obscene passage in the *Quixote*. Herrero claims that the *rabo*, 'the tail,' the barber borrows from the innkeeper's wife means her genitals and that the obscene reference to it leads to an identification of Pandafilando with the phallus. Hence, Don Quixote cuts off a phallus, the symbol of lust, when he slashes the wineskins in the belief that they are the giant. I think the whole thing is mostly just a dirty joke by Cervantes, who is having fun with the keen reader who he imagines could understand the obscenity behind all this. The innkeeper's wife says—and I am going to read it first in Spanish,

"Para mí santiguada [you remember that they borrow the oxtails she had placed where she kept her comb, so first the priest and then the barber can make a beard and look different] que no se ha aún de aprovechar más de mi rabo para su barba, y que me ha de devolver mi cola, que anda lo de mi marido por esos suelos que es una vergüenza; digo, el peine, que solía yo colgar de mi buena cola." "By all that's holy, you aren't using my tail as a beard any more, you've got to give it back to me, it's shameful how my husband's thingummy's bandied about all over the place nowadays—I mean his comb that I used to stick into my fine tail!" (I, 32, 289).

Herrero writes, I think overinterpreting, "This is, then, the extended joke: the barber has taken away the innkeeper's wife's tail, into which the innkeeper used to put 'his thing' [this is a literal translation] (also referred to as 'his comb'). When the barber gave it back to her, she complained that it is completely spoilt, that it has lost its hair, and that it will not serve any longer for what her husband used it." Herrero continues, "As we are going to show immediately [I will spare you his proofs], 'tail' ('rabo,' 'cola') means 'the loins' (both male and female genitals) and also the 'arse' ('culo'); and 'beard' has a similar meaning. Cervantes has created with his multiplicity of obscure meanings [I do not think they are all that obscure] a constellation of sexual images which are finally conveyed on the giant himself."[8]

I cannot go there with my friend Javier. I think the joke is very clear and funny, but I do not think it is so obscure. I do not see how it can be extended to the giant, but one wonders, why did Cervantes include this obscene joke in the text? As I said, I think he is just having fun for the sake of the reader who can pick up on it.

The stories, side stories, and interruptions in relation to memory bring to mind—going back to the beginning of my lecture today—the issue of Cervantes' oversights, particularly the one about Sancho's stolen donkey. What does it all mean? Perhaps that creation is the flawed product of memory. One critic has suggested, as I believe I said before, that Cervantes included errors in the *Quixote* purposely. I doubt it because within months he tried desperately to fix them. But the errors are consistent with certain other characteristics of the *Quixote,* such as improvisation and the faulty or creative nature of memory. In making mistakes we create by deviating from models. The mistakes of memory, as we have seen in the stories told by the characters, are creative.

What is the value of the subtexts—if I can use that word—we found beneath the stories being told, like the one about Dorotea's predicament and the one that Cardenio is really telling? To learn that sometimes, perhaps all of the time, a story is the deflected version of another. So what? So the plea-sure lies in the gradual discovery of the story within the story, as in the entire *Quixote.* All this has to do with the nature of narrative and with the nature of literature, a multilayered discourse whose gist is precisely the hidden mean-ings that surface in odd ways as we read.

Why did Cervantes embed these stories about Cardenio, Luscinda, Dorotea, and Don Fernando within the overall story of the *Quixote?* Did he think that they, or the main story, could not stand on their own? The stories are reflections of the main story, as we have seen, both in their themes and in their inner structures, the characters create other characters, the stories are broken up and started again, many characters display some sort of madness, they are like mirror images of Don Quixote. Mostly, I believe, Cervantes was searching for a way to create a new genre, a new kind of writing, he did not know yet which, that would allow for this mixture of the sequential plot of the chivalric romance and the multistory kind of book produced by the Ital-ians. A new genre that would also allow for this mixture of main story and lateral stories; and he did create it, he created what came to be known as the novel by doing this. Beyond literature, the most significant idea behind this intermingling and the errors is to posit that memory is the self, that the self is memory with all of its flaws and its holes and its gaps. Remember that the novel, the *Quixote,* begins with a willful act of forgetting: that village in La Mancha, whose name the narrator does not want to remember.

CHAPTER 9

Love Stories Resolved

Fictions and Metafictions

Required Readings

Cervantes, *Don Quixote,* Part I, chaps. 27–35, 228–337.
Elliott, *Imperial Spain,* 130–63.

I am going to talk today mostly about "The Tale of Inappropriate Curiosity." Cervantes was criticized in his time for including this short novel in Part I of the *Quixote.* He answered his critics through characters who speak about that criticism, chiefly a character called Sansón Carrasco—whom you will meet when you begin reading Part II. Cervantes also talks about it in the prologue to Part II, and he refrained from inserting any novels like this one in Part II. So he took the criticism to heart. As I said in my last lecture, Cervantes was trying to combine the sequential kind of plot of the chivalric romance, one adventure after another, with the collection of stories in the style of Boccaccio.

It is known that Cervantes contemplated publishing a collection of stories to be called *Semanas del jardín, Weeks in the Garden,* and he did publish, in 1613, the collection of stories you have and from which you will read called the *Novelas Ejemplares.* This collection, as you will discover, does not have, like Boccaccio's *Decameron,* an overarching fiction involving character-narrators leaving the city, fleeing the plague, and gathering to tell stories. The overarching fiction in the *Decameron* is that a group of young people leave the city because there is a plague, gather in a pleasant place, and each tells one story per day. The *Exemplary Novels* of Cervantes do not have such an overarching fiction; it is just a collection of stories by Miguel de Cervantes with a prologue also by him. *Weeks in the Garden,* or *Semanas del jardín,* does sound as though it would have had that kind of canvas-like plot, meaning that characters would get together in a garden and tell stories. The point is that in the *Quixote,* Part I, Cervantes is attempting to mesh these two forms of narrative, as I said. The result may seem awkward, but it is really quite innovative, and it leads to the creation of the modern novel, with this very loose structure in which this kind of insertion is possible.

We saw how those commingling stories about Don Fernando, Dorotea, Cardenio, and Luscinda are correlated. My colleague from the Department of Comparative Literature, David Quint, calls this "interlacing"—how the stories are interconnected—in a recent book on Cervantes.[1] And I proposed that they are structured, with their cuts, faults, and gaps, like a representation of human memory; human memory upon which fiction depends and on which the very makeup of the creative self of the author is based. As we will see today and in the next class, the final resolution of the conflicts in those stories is a narrative tour de force, a veritable boasting of his artistry by Cervantes. But "The Tale of Inappropriate Curiosity" does stick out as being very different and apparently only tenuously related to the main plot and to the other stories. Why is the story inserted here in the *Quixote*? You could say it is padding. Or does it have something to do with the love stories that we have been discussing and that are about to be resolved at the inn where "The Tale of Inappropriate Curiosity" is read out loud?

First, let us go over how Cervantes justifies the inclusion of the novella at the most elementary level of the plot. The innkeeper, Juan Palomeque, reveals that he keeps a suitcase somebody left behind that contains some papers and that he owns a number of chivalric romances. This is the second suitcase we find; the first was Cardenio's, which the characters found rotting away in the middle of the Sierra Morena, and it too contained writing—Cardenio's manuscripts and poems—in addition to some shirts and, most important to Sancho, money. A discussion among the innkeeper, his wife and daughter, and the priest ensues about the value of the chivalric romances. This is a return to the scrutiny of the books episode earlier, and the scrutiny of the books, in fact, is mentioned by the characters. The priest wants to burn these chivalric romances, as he did Don Quixote's, but the innkeeper will have none of it. Juan Palomeque, as he himself says, is not mad, he is not insane, he knows that what those books relate happened a long time ago and not in the present, as Don Quixote does; he knows that the romances of chivalry are not applicable to the present. In addition, Palomeque maintains that they provide entertainment when, at harvest time, the workers gather around at the end of the workday and someone reads out loud from one of them.

The tradition of reading out loud goes back to the Middle Ages, to convents and monasteries, as rituals in those institutions. Palomeque says that they provide solace, rest, and relaxation at the end of work. The innkeeper's wife and daughter, for their part, are fond of the love scenes particularly. The daughter talks about the love scenes that moved her so much. Palomeque defends the veracity of the chivalric romances, saying that these books are published with the approval of the Crown's councils; they have the stamp of the Crown council. How could the Crown allow books of lies to be published? Of course, he has a primitive notion about printed books. Palomeque is corrected by others—the priest mostly—but to no avail: he sticks to his guns, so no books are burned.

There will soon be another scene in which the romances of chivalry are discussed, but at a theoretical level by well-educated and well-read characters like the priest, the canon of Toledo, and Don Quixote. But here at the inn, Cervantes seems to be emphasizing, the romances of chivalry do have a function in society in that they provide relaxation to the common people. It is foolish to take Cervantes at his word when he says he has written the *Quixote* to demolish and banish the romances of chivalry. There are people who still take him at face value on that, but, in fact, the *Quixote,* like all parodies, is both a critique and a homage to the romances of chivalry, and it is perhaps the last of the romances of chivalry. So we must not take Cervantes seriously when he says he wrote the book simply to do away with the romances of chivalry. Remember what I said before, that by his time the fashion of publishing them had ended; but they continued to be read, at least if we take the *Quixote* as evidence of their being read by the common people.

The innkeeper then speaks about the papers in the suitcase and mentions the story, "The Tale of Inappropriate Curiosity," which, he says, had been approvingly read out loud at the inn. It is in manuscript form. Much literature, including Cervantes' own stories, still circulated in manuscript even after the development of the printing press, as printing was complicated and expensive. So you must not assume that once printing became available literature did not circulate in manuscript form any more. It did, and some of Cervantes' stories later included in the *Exemplary Novels* had been circulating in this form. This is, then, another self-referential moment in the *Quixote.* It is clear to me that it is Cervantes himself who left that suitcase there with the manuscript, and Cervantes is, again, winking at the reader: "I'm the one who left this suitcase here." It is clear too that he has found a way to publish the story by inserting it here in the *Quixote.* That does not mean he is just padding the novel. The long short story, the *novella* or *nouvelle,* in the manner of Boccaccio, was a form with which Cervantes felt very comfortable, as you will discover when you read the *Exemplary Novels* and as you have already discovered in these intercalated stories in Part I. Cervantes favored this sort of long short story.

Now, let us not miss the irony, which is easy to miss. You have to read carefully for details. The irony is that it is the priest who reads out loud "The Tale of Inappropriate Curiosity." This perverse, twisted love story is told in the voice of a representative of the Church. This priest is a complicated character, as you are discovering; he invents chivalric romances, and he is out on the roads chasing Don Quixote, and it is, to me, very ironic that you have the priest reading this erotic story. Cervantes loves these ironic games. It is the priest who at the end critiques the story and asks permission to have it copied later. Cervantes is engaging here in some self-criticism but also in some self-praise, having one of his characters praise the story, even with some reservations. This priest is also a literary critic, as we discovered in the episode of the scrutiny of the books.

"The Tale of Inappropriate Curiosity" is the most blatantly literary story in the *Quixote,* that is, the most artful and obviously derived from literary sources. The action is set in Florence in a vaguely defined past. It is a time and place of fictions, not the present in which the *Quixote* takes place. It is drawn from known Italian sources and written in the style of Boccaccio—whom you now know—and Matteo Bandello, one of the great short story writers of the sixteenth century. He was much read throughout Europe, and, in fact, one of his stories inspired Shakespeare's *Romeo and Juliet.* Shakespeare was fond of reading Italian literature.

"The Tale of Inappropriate Curiosity" is actually drawn from Ariosto's *Orlando furioso.* I have mentioned Ariosto several times, but I will mention him again. His famous poem is *Orlando furioso.* Ariosto lived from 1474 to 1533, and the *Orlando furioso* was published in 1516, then again in 1521 and 1532. It is a mock epic poem that Cervantes much admired, as you should know by now. So we have here these three Italian authors to whom Cervantes was indebted: Boccaccio, Bandello, and Ariosto. Other, more distant sources have been found, but Ariosto is the obvious one. One very distant source is the story of a king who wanted to put his wife to the test and had somebody seduce her; so this is the same story but remote. The most obvious source is a passage from the *Orlando furioso.* I underscore, again, Cervantes' indebtedness to Italian Renaissance literature, as he was also to Italian Renaissance art. If you have been reading the *Casebook* and your introductions, you know Cervantes spent a good deal of time in Italy, the cradle of the Renaissance.

"The Tale of Inappropriate Curiosity" has been variously interpreted, but the most apt analysis, the most current analysis, the most accepted one is by René Girard. Girard was a French professor who taught in the United States nearly all his life. His most famous book was called, in the original, *Mensonge romantique et vérité romanesque,* known in English as *Deceit, Desire and the Novel.* The original, the first publication, was 1961. Girard's whole theory revolves around the concept of triangular or mimetic desire. This desire is both external, when it applies to a novel and its sources, the previous books it imitates; and internal, when it applies to the protagonist's love relations. In fact, Girard will claim that the kernel of all novels is this kind of mimetic, triangular desire, and his book contains analyses of famous novels in the European tradition like *Madame Bovary, Le Rouge et le Noir,* and the *Quixote.*

"The Tale of Inappropriate Curiosity" is crucial to the development of Girard's theory, and indeed it may have inspired his theory. He writes,

> The existence of "The Curious Impertinent" ["The Tale of Inappropriate Curiosity"] next to *Don Quixote* has always intrigued critics. The question arises of whether the short story is compatible with the novel; the unity of the masterpiece seems somewhat compromised. It is this unity which is revealed by our journey through novelistic literature [his journey in the book through novelistic literature, in which he shows that this triangular desire exists in all of those novels]. Having begun with Cervantes, [he begins his book with him] we return to Cervantes and ascertain that this novelist's genius has grasped the extreme forms of imitated desire. No small distance separates the Cervantes of Don Quixote and the Cervantes of Anselmo since it encompasses all the novels we have considered in this chapter. Yet the distance is not insuperable since all of the novelists are linked to each other; Flaubert, Stendhal, Proust, and Dostoyevsky form an unbroken chain from one Cervantes to the other.
>
> The simultaneous presence of external and internal mediation in the same work seems to us to confirm the unity of novelistic literature. And in turn, the unity of this literature confirms that of *Don Quixote.* One is proved by the other, just as one proves

that the earth is round by going around it. The creative force of Cervantes is so great that it is exerted effortlessly throughout the whole novelistic "space." All the ideas of the Western novel are present in germ in *Don Quixote*. And the idea of these ideas, the idea whose central role is constantly being confirmed, the basic idea from which one can rediscover everything is triangular desire.[2]

I am sure this sounds strange and obscure to you if you have not heard it before, but I tell you, once you understand it you may glean something useful about your own love life. I have said that reading the *Quixote* would provide lessons for living.

For Girard, desire is never spontaneous, never a self-generated, one-to-one relationship, but mediated; one desires a man or woman because he or she is desired by another. It is that presumed desire by the mediator that makes her or him attractive. I say presumed because then the mediator's desire must have yet another mediator to exist as such, and then there will be a sort of endless series of mediations, but we are focusing on one triangle at a time. Jealousy, a kind of envy in other words, is a requirement for desire, for love to exist.

You can now think of all the novels you have read in which jealousy plays an important role. Proust is full of jealous characters. Hence imitation of the mediator, the one of whom one is jealous, is of the essence because of the belief that she or he is loved by the object of our desire. This is the mimetic part of desire, which may lead to desire for the mediator in the guise of desire for the original object of desire. That is, you love the mediator so much that you wind up loving the mediator, not the person you thought you began loving. We will see some of this switching in "The Tale of Inappropriate Curiosity." In the context of that story it works like this. Anselmo cannot really love Camila until he gets Lotario to love her. This is the gist of this man's twisted desire and why he must put her to the test. So Anselmo loves Camila, but only once Lotario is inserted as the mediator. Then, eventually, when Lotario loves Camila, he does so—a second triangle—because she has loved Anselmo before. So we have these two triangles.

This story may well reveal a hidden substory of the kind we have been finding when characters tell stories, and the story may very well be, and it has been proposed, a homosexual love between the two friends, using Camila as the mediator, a third triangle. Anselmo really loves Lotario via Camila as the mediator. Nicolás Wey-Gómez has written a persuasive article that not only discusses the relationship between the two men but also shows that Anselmo's illnesses, both physical and psychosomatic, are feminine in the medicine of the time, to underscore the nature of the relationship between these two.[3]

This structure sheds light on the intertwined stories we have been discussing. We have the Don Fernando, Cardenio, Luscinda triangle, in which Don Fernando loves Luscinda, really because she is Cardenio's girl or is going to be his girl. Eventually—I suggested this in another class—there are intimations of a homoerotic relationship between Don Fernando and Cardenio. Don Fernando, when it comes to Dorotea, loses interest in her once he has possessed her because there is no mediation; but he marries her once she appears at the inn and is defended by Cardenio. Once Cardenio appears as a potential mediator, Don Fernando goes ahead and marries Dorotea (fig. 11). Now, Don Quixote's mediations are the romances of chivalry and the heroes therein, particularly Amadís de Gaula, whom he imitates, just as he imitates Orlando in the *Orlando furioso*. The object of his love, Dulcinea, is a projection of the loves of those famous lovers, Oriana in the case of Amadís, Angelica in the case of Orlando, which is why he desires her and, in a way, invents her from their constructions of her. And we will see Dulcinea's transformations, which are remarkable, as the novel progresses, especially in Part II.

"The Tale of Inappropriate Curiosity" holds up the mirror of literature to the young people involved in the love stories that are about to culminate in marriage. It provides a contrast to the comedic-like ending of the stories of Don Fernando, Dorotea, Cardenio, and Luscinda. "The Tale of Inappropriate Curiosity" is not so much an admonition, though it is that too, as a lesson about the complexities of love and how no enduring stability can be achieved through it, particularly not by marriage. It is also a wink at the reader, I think, a wakeup call. I mean, can anyone—you will soon see someone who does—but can anyone really believe in the sincerity of the constancy of Don Fernando's conversion? Is it likely that Don Fernando will be a faithful husband? What about Luscinda? She was tempted once by money and status and could be again. Literature teaches through pleasure a harsh lesson about the human condition. Ultimately, "The Tale of Inappropriate Curiosity" is about the death drive concealed within desire; coeval and coevil with love. It was Freud, not me, who called it the death drive. There is no stability where there is desire. The perfection of the socioerotic situation involving Anselmo, Camila, and Lotario is a mirage and an invitation to tragedy.

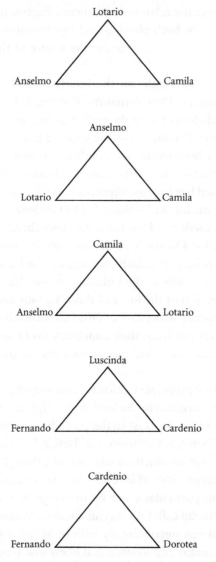

Figure 11. Girardian triangles in the *Quixote*.

This is an even harsher lesson than the one about triangular desire concerning the human condition. What the priest says at the end is that he finds the story to be well written, but he cannot believe—or the author has not shown—that it is a real situation because a husband would never do something like that. That maybe young people in love before marriage would, but not a husband. What he is saying is something that is a given in all Golden

Age Spanish literature, and the given is that everything that happens before marriage is the stuff of comedy and everything that happens after marriage is the stuff of tragedy. This is not a lesson to be taken too literally, but it is something to be pondered, and I think this is what the priest notices. Marriage is usually the ending of a comedy. Comedies tend to end in marriage because marriage is a return to stability; and in theater, comedy is a return to an order that has been upset, whereas tragedy does not return to order. Whether this is applicable to life or not is for each one of us to discover.

I move now to the ending of all of the intertwined love stories at Juan Palomeque's inn. Don Fernando accepts Dorotea after everyone pleads with him, and a good deal surfaces about the concept of *hidalguía,* from *hidalgo.* Dorotea pleads her case with as much verve as Marcela did in an earlier episode and having a thorough knowledge of Castilian law. Dorotea is lacking hidalguía, or nobility, but hidalguía is passed on through the male line, not the female line, as I have mentioned before. This is what Dorotea underscores in her defense. Cardenio has his Luscinda, who has the hidalguía but not the wealth that Dorotea has. There is, as I mentioned in an earlier class, a sort of crisscrossing here, a mirror image of the two women. That is, Dorotea has no nobility, but she has money, and Luscinda has little money, but she has nobility. In the midst of all of this, Luscinda had been kidnapped from a convent and brought to the inn in what turns out to be a side story not told in detail. These stories could be extended ad infinitum if you pursued every one of them. But Luscinda, who had been kidnapped, is brought back for this ending.

I mentioned Javier Herrero in the last class, and I mention him here, again, with respect. But sometimes I disagree with good old Javier, who is—or was, he is retired now—a very competent critic and also, I should say, a very Catholic one, as you will see from what I'm going to read here. There is no sin in that. Herrero interprets the battle of the wineskins that leads to the resolution of the conflicts in Christian terms. He also has a kind of symbolic, sexually symbolic, interpretation of the whole thing, but it is good to hear it in order to correct it a little bit and to learn from it. He says,

> The meaning of the battle against the wineskins is now clear. Don Quijote, in a state of hallucination (since he is really possessed by an intense dream and acting with closed eyes), takes the two superimposed wineskins, which he saw in his room when he went to bed, to be the giant Pandafilando and, to behead him, he cuts the head around and pierces the body; the wine floods the

room and fills the inn with its smell. Don Quijote has destroyed an erect penis, and has filled the inn with the smell of wine. . . . Don Quijote has certainly cut down the power of lust. This blood transformed into wine must certainly be taken as a sacramental symbol: a symbol of the mysterious power of the knight against the "amorosa pestilencia." Metaphorically, the courage and courtesy of don Quijote have vanquished the arrogance, cruelty and lust of don Fernando. It is true that don Quijote is wrong, that his adventures have created havoc, and morally his motivation is mixed, but it is also undeniable that he is courageous, truthful and chaste. His foolishness brings him blows and ridicule, but his greatness makes him a worthy instrument of Providence.[4]

He writes the following in another piece:

We see clearly that the spiritual movement has been completed by Don Fernando's descent from lust and pride to a Christian humility and fraternity by which he raises his victims to the level of his affection and, now reunited in love, a common embrace is possible. The giant is dead, and the true man, the Christian gentleman, has replaced him. But which powers have brought about the conversion? Has it been the beauty, the tears, the truths of Dorotea? The priest's persuasion? They certainly all have a part in it; but the text leaves no doubt that all these elements, together with don Quijote, have been but the instruments of Providence. . . . While men and women had been acting through the impulse of their passions, which brought them to the labyrinth of the Sierra Morena, not a reference has been made by Cervantes to Heaven's will; but as soon as Cardenio meets Dorotea and is told that don Fernando did not take Luscinda with him, he expresses hope that Heaven has decreed their salvation. From that moment on, their destinies began to escape from the darkness and confusion of the labyrinth. At the inn, the *locus* of social reunion and consequently of the transition from wildness to civilization, Luscinda, having been released by don Fernando in the scene just as described, exclaims "observe how Heaven by unusual and to us hidden ways has brought me into the presence of my true husband, and well you know by a thousand dear-bought experiences that death alone can efface him out of my memory." Immediately, and in the long scene of reconciliation, all the participants claim that their meeting in the inn is not accidental, but, on the contrary, the work of Providence.[5]

The question to be considered is whether the conflicts would have been solved without the intervention of Don Quixote. I think he was the agent. Herrero's article ultimately deals with the whole issue of marriage, which is so important in the *Quixote* and so much discussed in the sixteenth century. The likes of Erasmus and Juan Luis Vives wrote about it. The Council of Trent, which is taking place in this period—as you know, from reading Elliott—pondered the issue of marriage. Because marriage is at the core of social stability and social transitions in society; it is the way that society renews itself, so it is crucial. This is what Herrero wrote, and it is important because he is bringing in, first, the Neoplatonic notions of love derived from the courtly love tradition, then pitting it against a certain movement in sixteenth-century Spanish society and in philosophy in general toward a more bourgeois sense of marriage. You remember the courtly love tradition, which is one of the great spiritual revolutions in the West, in which the idea was that the woman had to be adored at a distance, that love could not be consummated. Love was reserved for a woman who was unattainable, preferably married, and the lover paid homage to her. We hear echoes of the courtly love tradition in modern poetry, in Pablo Neruda and Octavio Paz, for instance, and in other great modern poets. Don Quixote is a courtly lover in that sense, an aged, out-of-fashion courtly lover, and that is what inspires his love for Dulcinea. Neoplatonism was at the core of the courtly love tradition. So Herrero says the following:

> Against a sentimental and Neoplatonic tradition which made of woman a goddess, Cervantes takes the side of the conjugal love presented by Erasmus and Vives [Erasmus of Rotterdam—I will speak more about him in the following classes; he was a very important sixteenth-century humanist, and so was Vives] as the Christian ideal which allows man not only to enjoy the legitimate pleasure of the sexual union, but to help each other to fight against the inevitable weakness and imperfection of the human condition. By emphasizing the social, civilizing aspects of marriage, Cervantes . . . was closer to the new doctrines of reform than to the Renaissance ideals of love [he is thinking of Petrarch and Garcilaso and the poets I have mentioned before]; indeed,

with his attacks on the pastoral and by the story of "El curioso impertinente" ["The Tale of Inappropriate Curiosity"], Cervantes is precisely marking his distance from the great aristocratic tradition of the Renaissance and joining the new, to a great extent bourgeois, Christianity which descended to the south of Europe from the Low Countries. In opposition to Amadís, Palmerín, Belianís [these are the chivalric heroes of the romances], the new bourgeois lover is not a knight but a Christian gentleman. Such love, as we have seen, has two elements. It is Christian, and the activity of Providence and the priest shows the role that God and His Church play in its growth. But it's also gentlemanly; both Cardenio and don Fernando become through love not only Christians, but Christian gentlemen. Courtly love brings the knight to madness; but Christian love saves him. Such a rescue is metaphorically expressed in our story by the great classical myth of the labyrinth, lost in the wilderness of Sierra Morena, their lives twisted into the intricate maze of the labyrinth, on the brink of being devoured by the Minotaur of lust and madness, Cardenio, Luscinda, Dorotea, and Fernando are finally rescued by don Quijote's courageous battle and by the civilizing force of an Erasmian Church. Divine Providence, in fact, has provided as Ariadne, the saving thread.[6]

All of this sounds fine, and it is instructive, particularly the references to Erasmus and Vives, until we take into account the hilarious convolutions and the mixture of madness, dreams, and lies that bring about the resolution of the conflicts. The conflicts have been solved by Don Quixote's intervention, but how can such a ridiculous figure be the instrument of Providence? They have been solved by Don Quixote's agency because they are truly worldly conflicts involving tensions of a world in social flux, where the older values, let us say, the values of the Renaissance, the values of courtly love, no longer hold sway. Don Quixote embodies the mixture of values in transition, so he can mediate the various conflicts and solve them. He would not have been able to do so had he been a real knight or had he been an ordinary man of his time. But to say this is not to do justice to the multilayer plots unraveling in these episodes.

I am mostly struck by Cervantes' inventiveness, by the wild yet disciplined imagination at play which, I think, cannot be reduced to this providential scheme that Herrero offers. Don Fernando is, at one level, Pandafilando de la Fosca Vista, a giant. Remember, the rhyme, Fernando, Pan-dafilando. The figure of Pandafilando, though invented ad hoc by the priest, is presented as an effective factor in the outcome of the conflicts, as are Tina-crio the Wise and Princess Micomicona, although not as real and grotesque, not as real in relation to the fiction of the novel; this whole ensemble exists and performs on a level not unlike that of the characters who invented them. The story of Pandafilando is like a dream version, a recognizable distortion of Dorotea's real conflict. Again, the hidden meaning of Micomicona: in her name there is an allusion to mimicry, to representation, to mimesis, to the very process by which she was invented. Does Micomicona not in a way represent representation itself? I mean, she is the representation itself taking place before our eyes. Are all of these inventions of characters by other char-acters similar to Cervantes' invention of his own characters in the *Quixote* and is this what this whole thing is telling us?

What is truly dazzling about the resolution of all of these conflicts is that they unravel at every level simultaneously. That is to say, first, Don Qui-xote's dream, which involves Don Quixote, Pandafilando, and Micomicona; he cuts the head off of the giant, he thinks, in the dream. Second, the meta-fictional creation by the priest, the story the priest invents and Micomicona then performs, meaning Dorotea. Don Quixote, Pandafilando, Micomicona, Tinacrio, all these characters in that novel the priest and Dorotea invent. Then, third, there is the fiction of the novel, which includes Don Quixote, Don Fernando, Dorotea, and the others. All of those levels collapse together, and the conflicts are resolved by Don Quixote's slaying of the giant, that is, cutting and bursting poor Juan Palomeque's wineskins, to his horror.

It is a stroke of genius that the process of restitution will be motivated by Don Quixote's nightmare, which comes to interrupt the reading of "The Tale of Inappropriate Curiosity" at the point near the end, when it is about to unravel. This is another case of an interruption. In the dream, Don Quixote completes the story of Princess Micomicona, that is, Dorotea's predicament translated into the language of chivalry, like Cardenio's psychotic delusion about Queen Madasima having had an affair with a surgeon, which was his version of Luscinda being deflowered by Don Fernando. This version of Dorotea's imbroglio, true to the name she assumes, is a grotesque parody of her story. I go back to what I said earlier: *mico* means "monkey," Micomi-cona is 'the twice monkey,' with an augmentative like that in *segundón*. Mi-comicona is a big, blown-up, distorted copy of Dorotea.

The ending of Dorotea's story in that register is what breaks off the reading, as I mentioned, of "The Tale of Inappropriate Curiosity." That story will be resumed, and it comes to its tragic ending, while those of Cardenio, Luscinda, Dorotea, and Don Fernando have purely comic ones, with marriages that are typical of comedy. This is yet another intersection of the two stories, with the accent on *section,* on crossing, on cutting. The ending of "The Tale of Inappropriate Curiosity" reveals its artificial literary quality once the reading is concluded and, as I have mentioned, the priest remarks that it does not sound right for a husband to have done what he has done, so it is not good mimesis; and then there follow the courtlike scenes of reconciliation among the various couples and restitution made, including restitution to all the characters who have been injured or damaged in some way. The inn becomes like a court of law where these restitutions are made. I want to quote Herrero in a more positive light now. He is right, in the sense that values are changing and there is an emerging bourgeois sensibility: "It is true that Neoplatonism, associated with the tradition of courtly love, was still the accepted poetic and artistic vehicle for aristocratic sentiment; but through the influence of Christian humanism, and as an expression of the strength of the new bourgeois, the preoccupations with secular life and, above all, marriage, replaced the stylized conventions of chivalry and the austere ideals of monasticism."[7] This may be true, particularly if we take into account all of the economic and legal background I have given you about the relationships between these characters; the fact that Don Fernando is a *segundón* and is not going to inherit the estate, which makes him anxious, the fact that Dorotea runs a farm and has money and all of that; it does give the impression that there is a kind of a bourgeois sense of marriage and stability that is replacing the old idea of the Neoplatonic ideals contained in the aristocratic versions of love in the poetic traditions.

The idea also seems to be that to cure the characters in the real world of the novel's fiction, where they live, they also have to be cured in their dreams and inventions, which is one of the overall plot strands now being resolved in the *Quixote.* The knight is the only one missing here. I mean, everyone is going to be cured of his or her dreams and hallucinations, but Don Quixote still has not. They have to be cured of those hallucinations, and their situation has to be stabilized in social terms. The priest, the barber, and the rest of the characters engage Don Quixote at his level of madness in part because they are also mad in their own way. What are the priest and the barber doing traipsing all over Spain after the hidalgo? I said before that this is a very strange priest, a reader of romances of chivalry.

What has become of the priest's duties at church or the barber's customers? They too have left normal lives, as Sancho has—he left his wife and children—to engage in an insane quest for an insane man. The point is that life, mental life, is made up of levels that mirror and distort each other and that literature appears to emerge from this interplay. The creative mind of the author is capable of reflecting or expressing the multilayered essence of that mental life. After the captive's tale, a fascinating, highly entertaining tale based on Cervantes' life—I will be talking about it in the next class— the priest and the barber and the others will send Don Quixote home. They will put him in a cage and send him home, a return that will engage them in further adventures still. The end of Part I is near, and we will get to it next week.

CHAPTER 10

Fugitives from Justice Caught

Restitutions as Closure at the Inn

Required Readings

Cervantes, *Don Quixote*, Part I, chaps. 36–52, pp. 338–479.
Elliott, *Imperial Spain*, 164–211.

We are moving toward the end of Part I, the 1605 *Quixote*. I am sure you will
have noticed that there are a number of returns and repetitions which give
facticity to the fiction by its being cross-referenced, as it were, within itself.
I mean that there are characters that reappear and incidents that—if not
repeated exactly as before—recall previous incidents. There are three such
characters and incidents, one of which I will discuss in detail and two that I
will just mention briefly here at the beginning of today's lecture. One is the
galley slaves, two is Andrés, and three is the postprandial speech.

The galley slaves are mentioned again when the priest and the barber
bring up the incident to explain their presence at the inn. They say they were
assaulted by the freed prisoners as they were on their way—not the prisoners
but the barber and priest—to collect some money sent from America. They
do this to embarrass the knight and to persuade him that what he has done is
not right; that, in fact, it is a crime. The priest gives a correct legal interpretation of Don Quixote's actions in freeing the galley slaves. He has committed
a crime against the Crown because the prisoners were under its jurisdiction,
given that they were being sent to the galleys, that they were on the road, and

that they were being guarded by agents of the Crown, as opposed to other branches of justice. Because of the regional independencies in Spain there were various kinds of police, but these galley slaves were under the purview of the Crown, which makes Don Quixote's crime very grave.

This prepares the second mention of the incident of the freeing of the galley slaves, which is when Don Quixote is, in fact, nabbed by the Holy Brotherhood, precisely for that crime. I will speak about this later, but notice that the characters, who are presumably out to bring Don Quixote to his senses and return him home, enter and exit his madness, participating in and expanding his delusions with their lies; notice also that this lie the priest comes up with is an elaborate one.

One of the larger themes of the *Quixote* is that, although society cannot cope with his madness because it shows the arbitrariness of laws from outside of the judicial system, members of society are themselves toeing a thin line between their compliance with societal laws and norms and acting insane themselves. Ultimately, and this may well be beyond anything Cervantes intended, the figure of Don Quixote being a mad individual questions the very core of the rules and regulations that sustain daily life. Don Quixote's most original feature as a character of fiction is his insanity. It gives him a certain transcendence. He is truly the first insane protagonist in Western literature; there have been others since but none with this kind of transcendental form of madness. So that is the first of the returns.

Now to the second one: Andrés. Andrés returns. Andrés was a young man who was being flogged by Juan Haldudo, and Don Quixote intervened on his behalf. He returns and reveals that what Don Quixote did for him made his situation worse. This is parallel to the mention of the galley slaves because it points out that Don Quixote's actions have had the opposite effect of what he intended. In both cases he defends himself by saying he was upholding the laws of chivalry, which are superior to the laws and customs of the time in which he and the others live. But the crucial detail here is that Andrés is on his way to Seville, which, as we now know, was the center of picaresque life. This fact is reinforced by the exemplary story "Rinconete and Cortadillo," which takes place precisely in Seville, as you will see. So the fact is that Andrés's return shows or suggests retrospectively that he was a pícaro all along and that he was probably guilty when Haldudo whipped him. So these returns cast light retrospectively on previous episodes. As I said, the returns establish this kind of world of inner references in the fiction. Sancho has to give Andrés something to get rid of him. The reappearance of characters is a narrative device Cervantes will use more frequently in Part II, which is a more tightly structured novel than Part I. And the return of characters is a technique that some of Cervantes' followers in the eighteenth century, like Henry Fielding, will use, if you remember *Tom Jones*, for instance.

The third repetition is the postprandial speech. I am referring to the discourse about arms and letters. The speech about arms and letters is the near repetition of a previous happening: the speech about the Golden Age that Don Quixote delivered to the goatherds right before the Marcela and Grisóstomo episode. The speech on arms and letters harkens back to medieval debates, like those pitting wine against water, clerics against knights, and so forth. These were topics for rhetorical exercises, like the topics debated by debating teams nowadays. Arms against letters was a set topic. This is the reason Don Quixote delivers the speech. It is part of the storehouse of topics he has in his mind. But it is also true that Cervantes practiced both arms and letters and that he valued both, as did Don Quixote himself.

The topic of the speech also refers to utopian models of behavior, roles codified by the Renaissance: the courtier, the knight, the poet or man of letters, and, in Spain, the saint. Baldassare Castiglione (1478–1529) published *The Book of the Courtier* in 1528. It is a book in which these models of behavior are codified. The result of the debate in the *Quixote* is that the ideal individual is Don Quixote's own ideal of a reflective man of action, personified by the captain in the next tale, who becomes a captive. This debate would be like the current one between the politically committed individual and the intellectual in the ivory tower.

Again, the focus is on the intersection between literature and current history, between fiction and reality. Américo Castro wrote something relevant to this issue in a book called *El pensamiento de Cervantes* (*Cervantes' Thoughts* or *Cervantes' Way of Thinking* or *Cervantes' Ideas*), published in 1925. It is one of the best books ever written about Cervantes. In it, Castro dispelled the notion that Cervantes was, as the phrase went, an *ingenio lego*. You remember the word *ingenio* from one of the earlier classes, 'wit'— *Examen de ingenios*, remember the book by Huarte de San Juan, the doctor, and remember also that *ingenio* is in the title: *El ingenioso hidalgo Don Quixote*. *Ingenio lego* meant that Cervantes was an unlearned wit, a natural, that is, that Cervantes had an innate ability as a great narrator but lacked culture. This was a romantic idea, the idea of the creator who invents his stories out of nothing. It was also a highly nationalistic reading of Cervantes because those critics would say that this was the spirit of Spain expressing itself through Cervantes. Castro demonstrated that this was all hogwash, that Cervantes was steeped in Italian Renaissance literature and thought and that therefore he was no ingenio lego at all. In his book Castro writes, in my translation, "The debate between arms and letters is a harbinger of the importance that learning and reason acquire over traditional life. The intellectual, armed with theoretical reason, is getting ready to intervene in the fate of Europe."[1]

Absorb that: "The intellectual, armed with theoretical reason, is getting ready to intervene in the fate of Europe." In other words, government will not be left simply in the hands of kings and aristocrats, whose expertise in ruling countries was based on traditional knowledge and on practice passed down over time; instead, the practice of government was now becoming the object of serious, sustained reflection. It is the birth of political science as a discipline that we are witnessing in the sixteenth century and that is reflected in Don Quixote's speech. In this regard, the figure to keep in mind is Niccolò Machiavelli (1469–1527) and his famous treatise called *Il principe, The Prince*, which was written in 1513 and published in 1532. It is the founding work of political science.

I know you may have a vague idea of Machiavelli, mostly centered on the cliché that the ends justify the means. But his book is much more than that; it is complicated, influential, and important. One of Machiavelli's models of a cunning ruler, by the way, was Ferdinand of Aragón—whom you have met extensively in reading your Elliott—who knew how to apply the rules of government. Castro adds the following with regard to Don Quixote's speech, again in my translation: "We are, again, faced with the essentially Cervantean dualism, epic heroic fantasy versus reason and reflexive criticism. At a point in his speech, Don Quixote exclaims, 'But let us leave this aside, because it is a labyrinth with no easy exit.' The fulcrum of Cervantes' soul where the two planes intersect each other [heroic fantasy and reasonable effort] belongs to both; thus this theme that dwells within [within Cervantes], which is of a primarily formalistic nature is also a model for the sociological concerns of the Renaissance."[2] However, Don Quixote does favor arms over letters, and the fact is he has just won the battle with the giant, a victory which the speech in a sense celebrates; so he opts for arms over letters, perhaps like Cervantes himself, who always had a fondness for his life as a soldier, as you no doubt noticed in reading the tale of the captive.

To get back to our speech and dinner's topic of conversation: This is the second postprandial speech by Don Quixote. The Russian critic and theoretician Mikhail Bakhtin, in his book *Rabelais and His World*, endows dinners with a great deal of importance because his metaphor for the novel genre is the dialogue, and dinners are essentially dialogic. François Rabelais is yet another Renaissance figure you must keep in mind. He was French, for a change, not Italian, and lived from 1492 to 1553. He wrote outrageous stories about Gargantua and Pantagruel, as you may have heard. Bakhtin writes the following:

> Eating and drinking are one of the most significant manifesta-
> tions of the grotesque body [he is talking about the grotesque
> bodies of characters in Rabelais]. The distinctive character of this
> body is its open, unfinished nature, its interaction with the world.
> These traits are most fully and concretely revealed in the act of
> eating; the body transgresses here its own limits: it swallows, de-
> vours, rends the world apart, is enriched and grows at the world's
> expense. The encounter of man with the world, which takes place
> inside the open, biting, rending, chewing mouth, is one of the
> most ancient, and most important objects of human thought and
> imagery. Here man tastes the world, introduces it into his body,
> makes it part of himself. Man's awakening consciousness could
> not but concentrate on this moment, could not help borrowing
> from it a number of substantial images determining its interrela-
> tion with the world. Man's encounter with the world in the act of
> eating is joyful, triumphant; he triumphs over the world, devours
> it without being devoured himself. The limits between man and
> the world are erased, to man's advantage.[3]

Following Bakhtin, you can see that in all of these scenes of eating, of which there will be many more in Part II, the barrier between the individual and reality is broken when he or she incorporates reality into himself or herself, making it part of the self by eating it; this is what is celebrated in these post-prandial speeches. To Bakhtin, dinners are the privileged occasion for dia-logue; dinners celebrate the end of work and the defeat of the world, which is, in fact, consumed: animals, vegetables, wine, which is like the blood of the earth. Wine loosens the tongue, and the truth comes out unguarded—recall the Latin phrase *in vino, veritas*. Plato's *Symposium*, which I am sure you have read and is really called the *Banquet*, and the scene of the Last Supper in the Bible, for example, all mark ritual occasions at which the truth is to be spoken over food or after food. There are two other functions of the mouth that are not mentioned here but that do occasionally come into play: the erotic and the aggressive. The erotic I do not have to and will not go into here; it is too obvious. The aggressive is to bite or to spit and, as we have seen in an earlier episode, to vomit on somebody. I am assuming a Bakhtinian persona as I make these comments because he was so interested in these bodily functions. So the truth has prevailed in the resolution of all the conflicts at the inn, and Don Quixote celebrates with his speech because he, the madman, has been the vehicle of that resolution.

The speech also serves as a transition to the captive's tale, which will narrate episodes of war to corroborate Don Quixote's ideas. In fact, the captive's tale will narrate the Battle of Lepanto, which occurred on October 7, 1571. Through Bakhtin we concluded that this was a moment of truth ironically represented through the scene of the dinner. There seems to be a whole movement in the *Quixote,* as we approach the end of Part I, toward a truth that culminates in the story of the captive, which is based on Cervantes' own life and on episodes of recent Spanish history but, more important, on episodes during which Cervantes was present.

Could Cervantes' circling back to himself be a part of this move toward the truth? Is it a shift away from literary stories to stories based on his own life? and what would that mean? Ciriaco Morón Arroyo has said that Cervantes was moved to create art with the truth, to create art out of lived experience.[4] One might add that Cervantes' self as author has been presented as a thin, ambiguous, and shifting fiction and that what stands behind it are these snippets of autobiographical revelation underlined by self-allusions, like those to his own pastoral romance *La Galatea* in the scrutiny of the books episode and to "Rinconete and Cortadillo" as Don Quixote leaves the inn. The story of "Rinconete and Cortadillo," which the innkeeper says is among the papers somebody left there—I wonder who that somebody would be—will be included in the *Exemplary Novels,* the book you are reading. So this is one of Cervantes' teasing allusions to himself, the real author of the *Quixote.*

The captive's tale is the culmination of the group of intertwined stories, not quite the last one, but it is the culmination of the group of intertwined stories. It is one in which religious conversion intimates a synthesis of contraries that not only surpasses social barriers but also transcends the Neoplatonic convergence typical of Renaissance plots. In other words, this story entails not just an unequal marriage in social or economic terms but a marriage that crosses racial and religious boundaries. The union at the end will not be just a Neoplatonic fusion of Renaissance ideas. Zoraida is a Moor and a Muslim, and Ruy Pérez de Viedma a Spaniard and a Christian. Their union is more transcendental because it involves the coalescence of the two religions.

The tale could be seen as the counterpart of sixteenth-century Spanish mystical poetry, in which courtly love, about which I have spoken at length here, and Petrarchan conventions are adapted to express religious fervor and union, not merely with the beloved but also with God. I am alluding here mostly to the poetry of Saint John of the Cross (1542–91), a mystic and one of the greatest poets of the Golden Age or of any age. What I am saying is that the captive's tale and its story of religious convergence is akin to mystic poetry in the Spain of the sixteenth century, and it is a culmination of all the previous stories because it is much more transcendental; the obstacles to be overcome are much more transcendental. There is, at the end of Part I, a concluding and unfinished story about one Vicente de la Rosa, who is a kind of minor Don Juan, and Leandra, who is a bit of a fool. It is unfinished because its resolution converges with the end of the novel, and, of course, a current event cannot have an end precisely because it is current and ongoing. That is why that story is left unfinished. We will probably talk about it in the next class because it is really quite near the end of Part I. I mention it just so as not to leave any of these stories unmentioned.

The captive's tale follows a traditional formula. It has a biblical resonance; the prodigal son, the father who sets his son off to experience life. We encounter that saying "Iglesia, mar o casa real" that I mentioned earlier, which counseled a young man, particularly if he is not an aristocrat or if he is a segundón, to join the church, to seek adventure at sea, or to join the retinue of a great aristocrat or, if possible, of the king. The story of the captive illuminates, retrospectively, that of Don Fernando. It has provoked controversy among critics because of its religious background. Francisco Márquez Villanueva, who was a professor at Harvard for many years and is now living in retirement in Seville, was a friend of mine but not of Morón Arroyo, with whom, as you will see, he had a debate over this story. Márquez Villanueva claims that Zoraida, a typically Cervantean character like Marcela and Dorotea, exercises her desire for freedom within a religious context but is not motivated by religion per se.

Religion, that is, becoming a Christian, merely allows her to be free, even at the expense of bringing grief to her father, Hajji Murad. Morón Arroyo claims, on the contrary, that the whole tale takes place within precise theological guidelines, which he presents by quoting mostly from Saint Thomas Aquinas. His point is that the issue of baptism is dealt with in a strict theological way. Zoraida has not been baptized, as the captive says, because she has not been in mortal danger, and the baptism of adults in the Catholic Church should take place after they learn about the faith, except if faced by a life-threatening danger. So Morón Arroyo observes that this precept has been closely followed in the novel. The same is true, he maintains, regarding Zoraida's use of her father's wealth and her leaving him behind in grief; conversion to the Christian faith justified doing violence to nature, that is to say, to relatives. I quote Morón Arroyo: "Conversion to Christianity justified any break with natural relations of kinship if this came into conflict with the duty to convert that anyone who had learned of Christian doctrine had."[5]

All of this sounds plausible, but it is hard to imagine Cervantes as a theologian, much less as a scholastic theologian. What he is reflecting here, I think, is simply the mores of the time, which were thoroughly Catholic. Morón Arroyo is much more persuasive, it seems to me, when he compares Hajji Murad to Othello, after Hajji Murad first threatens Zoraida and later pleads with her in that very dramatic scene when they leave him behind. Morón Arroyo says, "The scene in which all of this develops is one of the great achievements of world literature; in the impulse both to curse, insult and also to cry and plead, Cervantes has portrayed a real man."[6] It is the most dramatic scene in all of Part I. Morón Arroyo is also good when he says, "I agree with Spitzer's definition of Cervantean perspectivism: 'In terms of morals Cervantes is in no way a perspectivist.' Later he adds, in a footnote: 'Perhaps we ought to point out here that perspectivism is inherent in Christian thought.' Perspectivism in the sense of a form of modesty that recognizes the limits of all judgment and human knowledge is indeed Christian humility and intelligence in its strictest sense. The capacity to perceive the limit of our own creations, i.e., *ironea*."[7]

But Morón Arroyo is at his best when he points out the following, referring to a critic called González López: "I find magnificent his observation that the marriage between the captive and Zoraida, the new Christian, is accepted by the audience at the inn by the *oidor* [the judge] makes no allusion to the impurity of blood that could result from it."[8] This is true. Once Zoraida converts to Christianity there is no impediment for them to marry and no stigma attached to their potential issue; there were stigmas attached to having Moorish or Jewish blood in the Spain of the time, but here in the *Quixote* there is no inkling of that at all. And Morón Arroyo is also perceptive when he points out that "the lingua franca of *Berbería* is the most beautiful expression of the efforts to communicate in that confused world. . . . The story of the captive demonstrates without any doubt that primeval state of communication in which human beings create a language if there is none. Algiers is an experiment with secular communication; the renegade's love and language are its fundamental forms of expression,"[9] meaning the renegade and all of these characters who speak this mongrel language made up of all of the languages of the Mediterranean, a language that he says is a form of the expression of the human overcoming linguistic barriers because of their love and their desire to communicate with each other.

In terms of the captive's tale, I would emphasize that Zoraida is a woman of action, that she is indeed much like Dorotea. She is the one who orchestrates the whole escape, the one who gets the money for it and who helps to organize it. Like Dorotea, she chooses her destiny; in her are combined figures of the renegade, the saint, and the seductress. Hajji Murad is the most dramatic and well-rounded secondary character of Part I. His despair at losing his daughter and his plea that he will accept her back on her own terms are full of pathos and tragic depth; in this I agree with Morón Arroyo and underline the fact that Hajji Murad is a very critical character in Part I and perhaps, as I said, even the most important and most dramatic secondary character in the whole novel, Parts I and II.

Now we move to a very strange episode: Don Quixote hanging from the window. It is a strange episode for which I have an explanation of sorts; I have never been able to fully explain this episode to myself, which involves Maritornes and the innkeeper's daughter having fun at Don Quixote's expense. Don Quixote had been aroused by the innkeeper's daughter, and he had actually grabbed Maritornes and pulled her into bed, bad smell and all. They are, in a sense, getting back at him here with this rather cruel joke of having him hanging from the window. This seems to be a distorted version, that is, a perversion on the part of Maritornes and the innkeeper's daughter, of scenes in the captive's tale, as if every important episode had to be projected in a different register.

At the *baño*—that is what they call the area where the captives are kept—the captive sees a hand appear through a window. He sees the hand of Zoraida, it turns out, and there is an exchange of messages with that gesturing hand through that high window. The window and the hand reappear in this episode. The relationship has no correlation with the action or with the plot; it is simply a remembered image. To me it is like a symphonic motif, a motif repeated and expanded on in a different key. I do not know if I can convince you of this, but it is the only way I can explain this episode: there are echoes and remembrances of this window and this hand as they appear here. Otherwise it is simply another act of cruelty toward Don Quixote, of which there are quite a few throughout the book. You could come up with all kinds of symbolic and allegorical readings of it: he is hanging from the window and his feet are just barely touching the ground, he cannot quite touch it, so you could say that Don Quixote's state in the world is like that, that he is in midair, just barely touching the ground with his feet. It is possible. But I would propose the other reading of it, as bizarre as it may be.

I said at the end of my last lecture, and I repeat it today, that we are coming to the end of Part I. Do not forget that Cervantes had no idea at this point that he would write Part II, so this ending is the conclusion of the novel he began to write. Because the two parts are bound together, you may not have the sense that you are coming to an end because you have another big chunk of book to read; but this is the end of Part I that we are coming to, and it was the end of the novel Cervantes set out to write or wound up writing. The sense of endings in fiction is crucial, as Frank Kermode established in his book *The Sense of an Ending,* which I recommend to everyone. The ending invites us to read retrospectively into the story that precedes it and suggests an author's conception of history and of the loop of life, as it were, as his characters meet benign or violent deaths, as conflicts are resolved, and as a feeling of completion is felt by the reader.

Aristotle's *Poetics* established how plots should be ordered, linking beginnings with ends and both with middles. Cervantes had that in mind, but also the endings of chivalric romances and picaresque novels, in which the plot essentially followed the development of the hero's life from birth to death or to the point at which the pícaro began to write, which involved death and resurrection, a conversion. But the *Quixote* is neither. It is not a chivalric romance, and it is not a picaresque; it was totally new. At best it could be said to be a parody of a chivalric romance, hence a deliberately distorted version of it. As such, it is a kind of a meta-chivalric romance, a chivalric romance about chivalric romances. So ending it will be no easy matter for Cervantes, as we shall see. At least two strands of the plot are closed in the episodes at Juan Palomeque's inn. This is done by appealing to the judicial or legal cast of the novel, which, as we have seen, involves the perpetration of crimes and misdemeanors by the protagonist and by the implied or actual presence of representatives of the Crown. So the first conclusion or conclusions we have here have to do with resolutions, restorations, and the capture and arrest of Don Quixote.

I pause here to explain this turn to the legal, which I have explained in further detail in my *Love and the Law in Cervantes,* which is in your bibliography. I'll give you a brief synopsis of it here so you can understand why I read the endings of these episodes in this fashion. I have maintained in that book that the picaresque, and hence Cervantes' novel, reflects the importance of the elaboration of a dense, complicated legal system in sixteenth-century Spain. You may have observed some of these while reading Elliott. This expansion was due in part to the development of the printing press, which made the issuance and dissemination of laws much easier, and also to the development of a modern state organized as a bureaucracy to administer the precariously united peninsula and its vast overseas empire. If you have read Elliott, you understand that Spain was a modern state in the making.

This situation brought about the creation and maintenance of state archives, in which myriads of cases, both criminal and civil, were kept and classified. The distinction between criminal and civil was not quite established as such, although in practice it was. A criminal act is perpetrated against the state, in this case the Crown; a civil crime is committed against somebody, another person. So the archive was a form of state control containing many stories from which the picaresque novel derived or drew its cases, like the ones involved in *Lazarillo* and *Guzmán*. Lazarillo's story is like a deposition given to a judge to justify his present predicament. He is the husband of an archpriest's mistress. Legal discourse made possible the minute description of the real, as opposed to Renaissance genres like the pastoral, which gave an ideal description of the world. Legal discourse is, in my theory, the foundation of the novel, a narrative that deals in the beginning mostly with criminals, like Ginés de Pasamonte and Lazarillo, and continues to deal with criminals; it describes, as only legal documents can, the business of daily life.

The intertwined stories of Part I involving legal issues, mostly focusing on testamentary law, read like cases taken from those archives. Not so "The Tale of Inappropriate Curiosity," which is obviously drawn from Renaissance literature. In Don Quixote, who is a fugitive from justice, an outlaw, Cervantes has created the first important novelistic protagonist drawn from the archive, as it were. His is the case of the insane hidalgo who set out to act out chivalric fantasies and, in the process, committed a series of crimes. He is the first hero-fugitive from justice in the Western tradition. In the process, Cervantes uses settings like the *despoblado*, which I have explained here, drawn from Spanish law, and in the Holy Brotherhood has drawn into the fiction the police of the times. The depiction of a real world for Cervantes involved a world held together precariously by the law and whose representation could not be accomplished without recourse to legal language and concepts. All of the situations in the *Quixote* are framed within legal discourse. This is why endings begin with resolutions, restorations, and the capture of Don Quixote. Let us get back to these partial endings I am now going to describe and analyze.

The episodes toward the end of Part I are the climax of the first *Quixote*. Don Quixote's defeat of Pandafilando is the culmination of his adventures, his most resounding deed. These adventures, for all of their humor and in spite of Don Quixote's ridiculous behavior, are successful in bringing about peace; Dorotea admits as much. Don Quixote does not meet an angelic Beatrice, as the pilgrim does in the *Divine Comedy* toward the end of *Purgatorio* as he prepares to enter *Paradiso*; he is not an epic hero, like Aeneas, who winds up founding Rome; but he does bring about peace and justice in the world it has been his lot to be thrown into. This is, as I have said earlier, part of the overall irony of the book: that such a preposterous figure is the agent of Providence. Through Don Quixote's intervention, Don Fernando agrees to marry Dorotea and make good on the promise he made to her the night he stole into her room and deflowered her, swearing to become her husband; Luscinda is returned to Cardenio, who had been wronged both by her and by Don Fernando. Crossed marriage vows bring these conflicts to a happy, comedy-like ending, but such an elevated kind of justice is not the only kind of finale that takes place at the end.

Resolution also takes place at a legal level in the most concrete and minute fashion, as restitution is made to those who have suffered injuries or damages and are owed money as a result. Don Fernando and the priest compensate the second barber and the innkeeper, who had been complaining about the destruction of his business, not to mention the cost of feeding the knight, his squire, and their mounts. The second barber had had his basin stolen and dented, and his donkey's harness had been stolen. Financial restitutions such as these are a form of closure drawn from the law. It is what making whole means in current legal terminology. An individual is brought back to the state he or she was in before the damage occurred. Restitution is the ending to a story that began with harm and the decrease of one's property or wealth.

Don Quixote, for his part, is finally apprehended by the Holy Brotherhood. This is consonant with the all-encompassing closure of the novel's plot. Don Quixote and Sancho had been pursued by the Holy Brotherhood with an order of arrest for the knight because of his having freed the galley slaves, as Sancho had feared all along. They had committed other crimes such as killing sheep and breaking a man's leg and stealing property from him and his companions. In one of the most hilarious scenes in the book the Holy Brotherhood officer reads the arrest order, comparing the description in the order with Don Quixote's features:

> But one of them [the officers], the one who'd been trampled and
> kicked by Don Fernando, recalled that among the warrants he
> had on him for the arrest of various criminals there was one for
> Don Quixote, whom the Holy Brotherhood had ordered to be

detained for setting the convicts free, as Sancho had so rightly feared. With this in mind, the peace-officer decided to check whether the description of Don Quixote fitted the man before him, and he pulled a parchment folder out of his shirt and found the warrant he was looking for, and he began to peruse it with the utmost deliberation, not being very good at reading, and he looked up at Don Quixote at every word to compare his face with the description in the warrant, and found that this was most certainly his man. Once he'd reached this conclusion he put his folder away, took the warrant in his left hand, with his right hand seized Don Quixote so tight by the collar that he couldn't breathe and cried: "Help, help the Holy Brotherhood! And to see that I really mean it, just read this warrant, where it is says that this highwayman must be arrested." (I, 45, 423–24)

"Highwayman": that is how Don Quixote is described and that is, in fact, literally what he is. Why is this funny? Because the law should be the ultimate and most reliable institution in the representation of social reality, particularly of individuals entrusted with upholding it! Yet its agent is a dolt who can barely read. Beyond that, because the interpretation of the real is always problematic and difficult, as is reading itself, and here those difficulties are minutely reenacted by the police officer. This is expressed brilliantly by his looking at each of Don Quixote's features after reading it in the warrant and comparing it with the knight. Like Velázquez checking to see that what he is painting corresponds to his models in *Las Meninas.* It is the exact same act; it is the same kind of moment. Here we have an agent of authority experiencing difficulty in establishing who a person is and in reading, the very vehicle through which the new legislation establishes its power over individuals. One can only imagine how Don Quixote's description was obtained from the guards from whom he freed the galley slaves, taking down notes as they spoke. It is a whole take on the difficulties of representation dramatized in this remarkably comical scene.

All of these restitutions that are drawn from the legal context of the novel are part of the closure of the book. But the most important incident within that legal context is the apprehension of Don Quixote himself by the Holy Brotherhood. This closes the circle of the plot, as it were. But next we will see the charade organized to cage Don Quixote and bring him back home.

CHAPTER 11

The Senses of Endings

Finishing the *Quixote,* Part I

Required Readings

Cervantes, *Don Quixote,* Part I, chaps. 36–52, pp. 338–479.
Cervantes, "Rinconete and Cortadillo." In *Exemplary Stories,*
71–105.
Elliott, *Imperial Spain,* 164–211.

I have been speaking in the past few lectures about the ending of Part I of the *Quixote,* and today we finally get to the end of the novel. I remind you, again, that although you have both parts bound as one book this is the end of the novel Cervantes set out to write and that he had no specific plan to write a second part, which would not be published anyway until a decade later, in 1615. It is easy to make the mistake of thinking that what we are coming to now is a provisional ending, so avoid that thought. It is also easy to fall into that mistake because you know that Part II is coming as part of your course and that you are going to read it. But the readers of the 1605 *Quixote* didn't know that. They did not have a second part they knew they were going to read; so I want to dispel the notion that this is a provisional ending. This is the ending of the novel as Cervantes conceived it.

There are critics who seem to see in the ending hints that Cervantes planned a second part, but they are at best hints. Because second parts were often written in the sixteenth century, second parts of chivalric romances, which tended to have many parts. *Celestina* had many second parts, the

Lazarillo had second parts, the *Guzmán de Alfarache* also had a second part, so it is conceivable to see in some of those works hints of the possibility that Cervantes thought of writing a second part. But it is not in the plan of the 1605 *Quixote,* which stands on its own, or was designed to stand on its own, as a book. It is almost impossible to buy it today separately.

Ending the *Quixote* was a difficult thing to do because it is no ordinary story with a clear beginning; that is, the birth of the hero, for instance, and a linear plot in which the protagonist pursues a goal that he either attains or fails to attain; hence, he is defeated or he dies. It is not a love story like the subordinate stories we have just seen being resolved at the end in which the lovers get married and presumably live happily ever after. The *Quixote,* as we have seen from the start, from the prologue, to be specific, is a meta-novel, a novel about the writing of a novel, among other things. It is a kind of meta–chivalric romance in that it is a parody of a chivalric romance. A meta-novel is a novel that includes a novel about the writing of the novel. This is quite common in avant-garde fiction in the twentieth century, but the *Quixote* is the first time it happens in literature; to have this dimension of criticism of the novel included in the novel itself. So the business of bringing it to a close is a complicated one that involves closing several narrative strands plus the commentary or meta-novel part about the composition of the novel. You cannot just come to the end and say, the hero failed, died, or got married. No, you still have to deal with all of this commentary on the writing of the novel, which is part of the novel.

How do you end that? How do you close that? I will anticipate that you have already read that ending because the only possible ending to that narrative level is the prologue, with all of its hesitations about how to write it, which means, with all of the problems about how to close the book. The last episode of that metafictional level is the prologue because closing the book, which we literally do when we finish, has many implications, the most important of which is that it implies or includes a statement, by just doing it, about the structure, about the shape of the book. Endings, as I have mentioned, are very important, and I believe I mentioned the best book on the subject, Frank Kermode's *The Sense of an Ending.* It is a brief but exceedingly smart book, and I recommend it. So closing the *Quixote*—after you have got to the end—has many implications about the structure of the book; the very fact that it has an ending, that you can close it.

These are the reasons we have several endings or closures and why the prologue has to be the final or overarching one, which necessarily suggests circularity and self-enclosure—if you come back to the beginning and make it the end—and this circularity and this self-enclosure, we saw, is one of the characteristics of the novel, of the *Quixote,* which is a fiction based on fictions where there is, or there seems to be, no way out of the fiction, because even the author whose name is on the cover is contained within that fiction. Miguel de Cervantes is mentioned in the scrutiny of the books; and then there is a Juan de Saavedra mentioned in the captive's tale; Saavedra is one of Cervantes' last names, so it is also an allusion to himself; "Rinconete and Cortadillo," the story you read for today, is a Cervantes story that is contained in the *Quixote* too, so even the author whose name is stamped on the cover is inside the fiction.

I will discuss several episodes that constitute partial endings, but I remind you that the ending is the prologue. The first of those episodes has to do with the en-closure, with the enclosure of Don Quixote. I am playing with the word *enclosure*—by which I mean his caging. Caging Don Quixote is a literal form of closure, you close him in. It takes him out of circulation for good, as the character he invented himself to be. So I see even in the act of enclosure of the character a form, a kind of ending, a formal enclosure. Now, Don Quixote is an outlaw, as we saw in the arrest order read by the Holy Brotherhood trooper—remember, the one who cannot read very well—who apprehends him after the fracas at the inn. Because he is a criminal, others, particularly the priest, have to argue Don Quixote's case to prevent the Holy Brotherhood from taking him prisoner. Remember, his crime is against the Crown because the galley slaves were under the purview of the Crown, so he would have been taken by the Holy Brotherhood, arrested, and perhaps even executed. Remember that Sancho says, at some point, that he can hear the arrows of the Holy Brotherhood buzzing around his ears because Sancho, being a commoner, is more liable than Don Quixote to be arrested by the Holy Brotherhood, whereas Don Quixote, being an hidalgo, perhaps thought he was above the law. But in any case, the others, the priest in particular, have to argue for Don Quixote's release into their custody because, being insane, Don Quixote would never be convicted. The insanity defense existed in Spanish law since the thirteenth century.

Again, Don Quixote's insanity puts him above or beyond the law. It is his most significant characteristic as a literary character, and, being insane, he accepts no law. But why is he caged and not simply arrested and taken home in shackles, sitting on Rocinante? Why is it that at the end Don Quixote's freedom has to be denied in such a spectacular fashion? And I mean spectacular because this caging of Don Quixote and being carried home in this case is a spectacle. Two plot strands are winding up here. First, Don

156   The Senses of Endings

Quixote's quest, and second, the priest and the barber's own quest to return him home, possibly to be cured. This is what justifies the charade of the masks. Pragmatically, the farce is staged because if Don Quixote recognizes the barber and the priest he will catch on to their plan to return him home, and he might resist. But there is more to it. It is really only at the level of fiction that Don Quixote, the character that he himself has created, can be captured. Alonso Quixano, the hidalgo, the modest hidalgo from that unnamed place in La Mancha, can be arrested or apprehended, but not Don Quixote, who is an invented literary character, unless it is within the world of his fiction; hence the make-believe. This is the scene of the caging:

> They constructed a cage with wooden bars, large enough to hold
> him comfortably, and then Don Fernando and his companions,
> Don Luis's servants, the peace-officers and the innkeeper, all tak-
> ing their order from the priest, masked their faces and disguised
> themselves, some in one way and some in another, to make
> Don Quixote think that they weren't the same people he'd seen
> at the inn. Then they all tiptoed in to where he lay recovering
> his strength after the recent skirmishes. They crept up to him,
> fast asleep and oblivious to what was going on, seized him and
> bound him hand and foot, so that when he awoke with a start he
> couldn't move or do anything other than gaze in bewilderment
> at all those deformed faces before him. And he believed what his
> tireless and delirious imagination was telling him, that all those
> figures were the ghosts of that enchanted castle and that he him-
> self was obviously enchanted again, since he couldn't move or
> defend himself: exactly as the priest, the designer of the scheme,
> had thought would happen. Only Sancho, of all those present,
> was both in his right mind and in his right clothes, and, although
> he wasn't far from suffering from his master's disease, this didn't
> prevent him from recognizing the men through their disguises;
> but he didn't dare to part his lips until he saw what came of the
> attack and arrest of his master. (I, 46, 431)

The irony in this episode is that Don Quixote has communicated to the others the freedom to act out whatever fantasies they have. Is this not contradictory? He is caged. He has forgiven them, allowing them the freedom to cage him. He has contaminated them with the imaginative freedom that he practices. This theme began with the story of Dorotea becoming Princess

Micomicona and her acting out a chivalric romance invented on the spot by the priest and performed by her. This whole charade of the caging, which is like a brief theatrical piece or interlude taking place in the darkness of the inn, is also like a scene in a nightmare. Don Quixote awakens to find himself bound and surrounded by what seemed like goblins that put him in the cage.

But is this a dream? or is this reality? Cervantes is dealing here with a theme that was common in the sixteenth and seventeenth centuries and that was made famous in a play called *Life Is a Dream*, by a playwright called Pedro Calderón de la Barca. This is a play from the 1630s, but you can see that the theme is here. Don Quixote has gone from being asleep to finding himself surrounded by these strange figures in the darkness of the inn, so what could it be if not some sort of nightmare? So he believes he is enchanted. In the cage, Don Quixote is like the prisoner he is because prisoners were paraded through the streets as a lesson to others. Prisoners were routinely—I think even up through the nineteenth century—paraded through the streets of town in carts or walking or being flogged as a warning to others. Part of their punishment was their punishment being made public, so it was not unusual for them to be riding donkeys, but they were also in carts. Don Quixote is also like a circus freak show, and you will see one or two such shows in the second part of the *Quixote* traveling around in carts. In fact, plays were staged in carts in town squares throughout Spain. That is, the company came in the carts, and the carts opened up and became the stage; so the cart is a significant means of transportation for taking Don Quixote around as a prisoner and also as some sort of a freak show, the continuation of the theatrical episode of the charade to put him in the cage.

An important part of the charade is the prophecy contrived and delivered in dramatic, highly affected tones by the barber, the prophecy which foretells the future of Don Quixote as knight, projecting a potential ending to the story on that fictional level which satisfies Don Quixote. Like the priest, the barber is an author, but also an actor. This is the prophecy by the barber:

> O Knight of the Sorry Face! Be not abashed by the captivity to which you have been reduced, which is needful for the more speedy accomplishments of the adventure in which your valour has engaged you. And it will be accomplished when the livid lion of La Mancha shall lie with the white dove of El Toboso, once their lofty necks have been humbled by the gentle yoke of matrimony;

from which unique coupling shall come into the light of the world brave cubs that will emulate the rampant claws of their valiant sire. And this will come to pass before the bright pursuer of the fugitive nymph shall have twice performed his round of visits to the luminous signs in his natural and rapid course. And you, the most noble and obedient squire that ever had a sword in his belt, a beard on his face and a smell in his nose, be not dismayed or grieved to see the flower of knight-errantry thus borne away before your eyes; for ere long, if it so please the Fabricator of this world, you will find yourself so ennobled and exalted that you will not recognize yourself, and you will not be defrauded of the rewards promised you by your noble lord. And I assure you, on behalf of the sage Mentironiana, that your wages will be paid, as you will duly see; so follow in the footsteps of the valiant and enchanted knight, for it is necessary that you travel together to the end of your journey. And because I am not permitted to say any more, God be with you. I am returning now to I know where. (I, 47, 431–32)

So this is the prophecy invented on the spot and delivered by the barber, who is, as we can see, quite a ham himself and also quite able to imitate the speech of chivalric romances.

This is the peak of playacting in the *Quixote*. By the way, you can see in the prophecy that this is a projected ending of the novel; that is, Don Quixote and Dulcinea will marry and have children. This is the projected ending within, or beyond even, the fictions Don Quixote has invented. So this is yet another level, those levels that the novel shows throughout, created by characters. This peak of playacting in the *Quixote* is a culminating performance that, among other things, displays Cervantes' talents as a playwright, particularly a playwright of the interludes, the *entremeses,* the funny skits he wrote. Juan Palomeque's inn, which has been used as a court of law and as a debate meeting room where they argue about what the basin is, now is transformed into a theater, as Don Quixote is finally dismissed from it. This, too, is one of the endings of the 1605 *Quixote,* and the novel has several, as I mentioned and as we saw in the last class when I discussed the restitutions made. This ending is the most consistent with the fiction; the prophecy takes place within the fictional world generated by Don Quixote and now inhabited by all of the characters around him, except for Sancho, who knows what is going on but prudently chooses not to intervene.

Now, we go on the road and meet one of the most memorable characters in Part I, the canon of Toledo, who is traveling with a retinue and meets
this strange caravan carrying Don Quixote and stops to find out what this is
all about. After he does so, the canon, Don Quixote, and the priest engage in
a discussion about commonplaces of literary theory, about the romances of
chivalry, and mostly about Aristotle's *Poetics*.

The relevant background texts here are the *Filosofía antigua poética*
(1596), by Alonso Lopéz Pinciano, known as el Pinciano, and Lope de Vega's
Arte nuevo de hacer comedias en este tiempo (1609), published after the *Quixote* but dealing with topics that are relevant to this episode. *Filosofía antigua poética* is a book in which el Pinciano expounds literary theory mostly
derived from Aristotle's *Poetics*. It is one of the great ironies of literary history that Cervantes was wildly innovative in narrative fiction but exceedingly conservative in the theater, except when writing his brief comic interludes. I do not have to emphasize by now that he was wildly innovative in
narrative fiction. Dealing with the theater, this episode is a vicious critique
of Lope de Vega, Cervantes' rival, because Lope de Vega wrote plays that did
not follow Aristotle's *Poetics*. Lope flouted all of these rules. His plays were
historical plays that were dubiously accurate about the history. He just made
it up, like Shakespeare.

Lope was a great innovator who wrote hundreds of plays and really
could not have cared less about the rules. He invented the Spanish national
theater by not following the rules. But there were those, like Cervantes, who
criticized him for that, and he replied in 1609 in a hilarious poem called *New
Art About How to Make Plays at This Time*—the title is very polemical, as
you can see. *Arte* is supposed to be eternal, and it says "new art," new art is an
oxymoron because art cannot be new or old; it is always the same, supposedly, if you follow the *Poetics;* to write comedies "at this time," now, not in the
past: now. And so Lope was wildly innovative. As I have mentioned, he just
took over the Spanish theater, and Cervantes, with his plodding plays that
followed the *Poetics,* did not have much success. He did have a few staged,
and then he had interludes also staged, and a book of them appeared. I will
speak about that when I speak about the transition between the first and
second parts. But it is an irony that Cervantes, who was so bold in prose fiction, was so conservative in the theater. He is using the canon and the priest
to criticize Lope de Vega for all of the irregularities in his plays.

Peter Russell, a reputable English *cervantista*, wrote, "The discussion [among the three characters about theory] has little direct bearing
on the kind of discoveries about fiction that Cervantes has been making

empirically in his book. Hardly a word is said in it, for example, about comic writing."[1] This is true. I think Russell is right that Cervantes considered all of the theoretical issues the canon puts forth, but that in practice he did not adhere to any of them, except that of verisimilitude in that the novel does not deviate from the imitation of nature, that its characters never engage in supernatural actions, and that there are no events that are beyond the credible. The most interesting part of the discussion is when the canon and Don Quixote explore the possibilities of the romances of chivalry, which, in the end, the canon winds up praising because they afford the possibility of introducing variety, one Renaissance principle Cervantes did follow. Besides, the canon himself confesses that he has written the first hundred pages of a chivalric romance. This is hilarious, coming from a critic of chivalric romances; it is a typical Cervantean twist. We have seen that it was the priest who read "The Tale of Inappropriate Curiosity" out loud, and here the canon says,

> "I myself," replied the canon, "have been tempted to write a book of chivalry, observing all those points I've just been making, and to tell the truth I've written more than a hundred pages of it. And to find out how accurate my own opinion of it was, I gave it to men who like reading such books and who are learned and intelligent, and also to others who are ignorant and only concerned with the pleasure they derive from reading nonsense, and I'm pleased to say that all of them have expressed their approval; in spite of that, however, I haven't written any more, both because it seems rather inappropriate to my profession and because I'm aware that there are many more fools than wise men in the world and, although the praise of the wise few is more important than the mockery of the foolish many, I'm not willing to subject myself to the indiscriminate judgment of the fickle mob, the principal readers of such books." (I, 48, 442)

Don Quixote, in reply, makes up a quite remarkable chivalric interlude based on the story of the Knight of the Lake, and with it, in a sense, he wins the debate. Both the canon and Don Quixote are authors, as are the barber and the priest.

Now, there is a very elegant joke embedded in this discussion. The canon, I maintain, is the "idle reader," the "desocupado lector" that Cervantes addresses in the prologue. The joke is that canons were supposed to have cushy jobs that allowed them time to read and devote themselves to other leisurely activities. *Vida de canónigo* was, and still is, a way of saying 'a carefree life.' Canons were supposed to read canon law and pass judgment on issues germane to it. Canon law is church law. When we talked about incest and the prisoner of sex, I noted that canon law would determine what incest was and was not, whom you could marry and whom you could not marry, and what was a sin and not a sin. Canon law was critically important then; it is not to us anymore. The distinction between crime and sin was beginning to gain currency in the seventeenth century, but it was not quite accomplished until the nineteenth.

Canons had all the time in the world to sit around and read; they were supposed to be well-fed, fat, with time on their hands to read romances of chivalry and pass judgment on what was harmful to read. All figures of authority in Cervantes—like the canon—are always slightly ridiculous. They have some flaw or other, but here the flaw is being yet another author, another internal author. We have seen many in the *Quixote:* Don Quixote himself, the priest, the barber, Ginés de Pasamonte, Cide Hamete Benengeli, the translator, and also Grisóstomo and Cardenio. The *Quixote* is literature within literature. Literature with its own internal rules discussed not from the outside; this is what is important here, the characters are discussing the nature of the work within which they appear. That is to say, there is a seamless continuity between theory and practice at the level of discourse but not at the level of ideology. In other words, the novel does not comply with the theory propounded by the canon of Toledo but develops from within its own practice.

Notice that the canon has not finished the novel he began and that he also confesses to never having finished reading the novels he began reading; he never gets to the end. I think Cervantes is pointing out here the difficulty of finishing a novel, finishing this novel in particular, and that is more important than all of the commonplaces about Aristotelian theory that the characters discuss. This passage about the canon of Toledo has generated a great deal of criticism because all you have to do is give a scholar a set of rules that were presumably being propounded and a text, and they will proclaim that literature is written by following prescriptions. It is a common delusion of scholars and critics. But none of this theory can contain Cervantes' narrative, the experiments we have been observing in the *Quixote*: all of the various levels of fiction, all of the intertwined stories, all of the very wild and at the same time disciplined experiments about the nature of fiction we find in the novel. All of that surpasses any theory expounded in the

Spanish Golden Age in the sixteenth century or, for that matter, in Europe
in the sixteenth century.

So we should not be blinded by the *Filosofía antigua poética,* by Aristotle's *Poetics,* by Plato, and all of those theories because the poetics of the
Quixote are contained in its own performance, which includes the discussion of its own poetics. Cervantes does not take theory from outside and
apply it to the *Quixote.* He was above what really was a bandying about of
commonplaces only tangentially relevant to writing. What takes place in the
sixteenth century in literary theory is the well-worn debate between Plato
and Aristotle. Plato was the first spoilsport in the history of criticism because he thought that art was a negative influence in the Republic, and he
wanted to banish the poets because art appealed to the emotions and because art was based on imitation; it could not be itself, it was always an imitation of something. Although Neoplatonism is important in other realms
of sixteenth-century literature, that view of art and of poetry was countered
by Aristotle's critique of Plato, in which his point of departure, his baseline,
is that humans tend to imitate; imitation is part of the human condition,
and therefore art is inherent in the human animal because he imitates. That
is, we are all micomicones, if we remember that Princess Micomicona was
about imitation, was about mimesis, that we are all monkeys, we imitate just
like monkeys, and this is what Aristotle really propounds: that imitation is
a good thing and that in art it leads to a pleasurable intellectual process that
he favors; that is at the base of Aristotelian theory.

In the *Poetics,* Aristotle gives a series of rules that he bases on his own
experience of reading the epic and the theater. These rules were applied,
slavishly sometimes, in the Renaissance because of the Renaissance penchant for reviving the classics. That is basically what is at stake here. It is
akin to what I mentioned in the last class about the rules of government that
are being drawn up from Machiavelli on, and the rules of behavior that were
contained in Castiglione's *The Courtier.* These are all related movements. But
in the case of the *Quixote* none of this theory is ultimately relevant. It is contained within the book; it is discussed, but it does not drive the book, it does
not control Cervantes' poetics in the *Quixote,* which surpasses all of that by
quite a bit. So I will not expound much beyond this on the presence of Aristotle's *Poetics.* There is a lot of criticism, and one of those who have written
about it is E. C. Riley, whom you have met in my *Casebook* in the essay about
life and art in *Don Quixote.* He wrote a book titled *Cervantes's Theory of the
Novel,* a classic of Cervantes criticism, but I think that ultimately what I have
said here today takes care of it.

Cervantes expounded on literature in other books. He wrote a long poem called *Viaje del Parnaso, A Voyage to Parnassus,* which is a book of literary criticism about the poetry of his time, and in the prologues to his various books he expounds on criticism. But the problem is that Cervantes, like all writers of fiction, always has such theory appear in a dialogue among various characters. You cannot really pinpoint what Cervantes' preference is in all of this, but I think what must be remembered is that the canon is a slightly ridiculous figure, that we cannot take him as a figure of authority who has given us the poetics of the *Quixote* by any means, and that he himself has tried to write a romance of chivalry.

Another element present in this episode is the criticisms leveled against the romances of chivalry. These books were criticized severely in the sixteenth century by figures as important as Erasmus of Rotterdam, another of the Renaissance figures I have mentioned before. Luis Vives and others criticized the romances of chivalry for being potentially a bad influence on society, in terms that Cervantes echoes mockingly in the *Quixote* when he says he has written the book to do away with the romances of chivalry. So there is in this episode, too, an echo of those debates about the romances of chivalry because, as I mentioned, they were quite popular at one point, aided by the fact that they could now be printed and distributed in relatively large numbers for the period.

You will see religious figures such as the canon appear in the *Quixote,* and the priest has been around the whole first part. Others will appear in Part II, one in particular who is depicted in highly negative terms, as you will see. The canon is not, the canon is very learned, very well read, and funny in his own contradictions. Notice that the whole debate takes place over lunch, a picnic they have organized in this nice valley with food they have brought from the inn. In this locus amoenus we encounter a pastoral interlude, which is another one of those stories that almost repeats previous ones toward the end of the *Quixote.* These inner references are, again, a way of lending substance, facticity, to the book. This pastoral episode is like a new version of the Grisóstomo and Marcela story, but it also recalls parts of some of the intertwined love stories. Leandra is a young beauty in her father's care who is desired by many men; Eugenio, the goatherd, and Anselmo, another goatherd, are Leandra's principal suitors. They appear to be perfect candidates to marry her, as in the earlier story of Grisóstomo and Marcela. They are both well off. Then Vicente de la Rosa appears and woos her with his wiles and lies. Leandra is no Marcela, and she allows herself to be seduced by Vicente, who is a modern man in that he has, almost literally, made himself. He has three suits that he switches around in such a way as to make it appear he has many. He is a *miles gloriosus,* Latin for a self-glorifying soldier derived from classical comedy. This is a soldier who boasts of his great feats of arms, even showing scars he has from battles, as Vicente de la Rosa does here. Vicente also plays the guitar, another way he woos Leandra. They run off to the wilderness, the same kind of landscape we saw in the Sierra Morena, and there she is robbed but, surprisingly, not sexually ravaged, a curious detail I have never been able to understand.

What does that reveal about Vicente de la Rosa? It may be as bad as that he was impotent and that all of these Don Juan–like adventures he seems to be engaged in are really a cover for that. But I find it amazing that she is left untouched, which greatly satisfies her father. But the story is left unfinished; it has not yet concluded. No one knows what is going to happen, and I have wondered why. I think the reason is that we are now coming to the end of the novel and what is being narrated is a kind of present, and a present cannot have a conclusion because current events are current and to give them a conclusion is an artificial way of finishing them. I think that is the only way to explain this unfinished story that is just left unfinished.

We come to the end. The priest, the barber, Sancho, and Don Quixote finally arrive back in Don Quixote's village on a Sunday. Is this meaningful? It is the day of rest, of leisure, of feasts, consonant perhaps with Don Quixote's arrival in a cage, as if he were part of a fair. But to me the most moving and interesting detail is that Don Quixote does not know where he is: "While Sancho Panza and his wife Juana Panza chatted away like this, Don Quixote's housekeeper and niece welcomed their master, undressed him and laid him on his ancient bed. He was peering at them through unfocused eyes, and couldn't fathom where on earth he was" (I, 52, 474). After all of the adventures, home is no longer familiar to Don Quixote. It is not, if it ever was, the abode of the canny, but of the uncanny. Instead of curing him, it seems to me, bringing him home has made him madder than ever. Perhaps the circularity of the event, coming back, has made him dizzy to the point that he cannot recognize even his own bed. I find this very moving. He is in his own bed, and he cannot recognize it. He will, again, get out of it when we meet him at the beginning of Part II, but not soon. In the fiction of Part II he will get out of it shortly thereafter, but in real history it will be a decade later.

I was going to end today by talking about "Rinconete and Cortadillo," which you were supposed to read for today, and I am going to do so briefly. But we will come back to the *Exemplary Novels* again to discuss "Rinconete and Cortadillo" a little more, and also because we will be reading several of them. The date of the *Exemplary Novels* is 1613. *Exemplary Stories* is the title of the book you are using. It is impossible to find a good title for the collection because novellas at the time meant short novels or long short stories, but today if you say exemplary novels you are thinking of longer novels. The short story did not really emerge until the late eighteenth century or early nineteenth, with the appearance of newspapers, so this is why there is no good way of translating the title of the book. When a Spanish speaker reads it today he is misled by the title, *Novelas ejemplares.*

The point is that as Cervantes became well known because the *Quixote* did so well, publishers, for a change, became interested in bringing out his works. They had fleeced him with the *Quixote,* and they were ready to do so again with other books. So he was able to publish his collection of stories, which, as I told you in an earlier class, does not have the overarching fiction the *Decameron* and other such books have. In Boccaccio all of the characters leave the city because of the plague, gather together somewhere, and then each one tells a story on a different day. The *Exemplary Novels* does not have that; it is a one-man show, twelve stories with a prologue by Miguel de Cervantes. Cervantes, as I have mentioned, favored the long short story, like those we have encountered intertwined in the *Quixote* and individually in "The Tale of Inappropriate Curiosity," and he had a few in reserve, obviously, as we recall the papers that someone left at Juan Palomeque's inn, including at least a couple of stories by Cervantes.

These were stories that were circulating in manuscript. Remember I told you that stories still circulated in manuscript in spite of the development of printing. In the *Exemplary Novels,* Cervantes collects stories with diverse themes and styles; it is like a series of narrative experiments. Some, like "Rinconete," are akin to the picaresque, others to the Byzantine romance, others are love stories, etcetera. We are going to be reading several here. They are superb. I think that even if Cervantes had not published the *Quixote* he still would have become a major author with just this collection of short novels. You will see that "The Glass Graduate" and all of the others we are going to read are really excellent stories.

"Rinconete and Cortadillo" is obviously of a picaresque thematic and ambiance, and it takes place in the center of picaresque life, Seville, but it does not follow the autobiographical form of the picaresque that Cervantes made fun of through Ginés de Pasamonte. Remember him? When he says, "How can the book be over if my life is not over?" Cervantes is making fun of that. You will see that he does use autobiography in "The Dialogue of the Dogs" at the end, but you will see that he does so in experimental fashion. To me, the point is that Rincón and Cortado, known by the diminutives

Rinconete and Cortadillo, become pícaros because the pícaro is already a stock literary character; so they become pícaros the same way that Don Quixote becomes a knight. There are hints of this in the first inn in the *Quixote*, when we learn that the innkeeper had been a pícaro and he tells stories. We get the sense that some of these pícaros the innkeeper assembled within those emporia of picaresque life that he mentions had chosen that life. It was not that they were just simply poor boys who were out looking for a way of making a living, but that they had chosen that life, so they had dropped out of society to become pícaros. And this is, I think, the case with Rincón and Cortado, who in the end decide not to be pícaros any more, and that is the end of their adventures. It is not that they go to the galleys or are nabbed by the police or have to write a story because they are married to the mistress of an archpriest—I am alluding to *Lazarillo de Tormes*.

I think the other noteworthy element in the story is Monipodio's brotherhood. Monipodio is the chief criminal here, and he runs a whole brotherhood in a well-organized fashion. He is, again, one of these figures of authority who is slightly ridiculous. He is surrounded by a bevy of petty criminals, prostitutes, and pimps, all of whom have their own distinct physical features. The picaresque life depicted here is not a somber, sordid life. On the contrary, it seems like a lot of fun. Everybody is having a good time, even the prostitute who complains about her pimp beating her up; she actually reveals that it was really a bit of S&M, sadomasochistic sex, a little consensual erotic game they were playing.

There is nothing evil in any of these pícaros. This is very typical of Cervantes. As I have said repeatedly, even the worst characters have some good qualities and are never totally evil; certainly none of these people are totally evil. Repolido is the pimp's name. His name means that he is bald, probably from some venereal disease. Cervantes deals with the most sordid elements but in a way that does not read as a sordid story. Also interesting here is that Monipodio's brotherhood seems like the blueprint for society. It is a kernel of society where rules are being created and where there is a kind of self-enclosed atmosphere made possible by those rules, as if this were the beginning of laws and the beginning of a certain mode of speech. This is, I think, what is behind the brotherhood: Utopia is one of the Renaissance topics, and this is a counterutopia—I am referring now to Thomas More, another Renaissance figure I want you to remember. Utopia refers to a well-ordered society, one in which everything has been thought of in advance and where there are rules. This is what Monipodio's brotherhood is like, a counterutopia that is organized with the well-wrought polish of a work of fiction.

CHAPTER 12

On to Part II

The Real and the Bogus *Quixote*

Required Readings

Elliott, *Imperial Spain,* 212–48.

Today I am going to talk about the transition from Part I to Part II of the *Quixote;* our transition, not Cervantes' transition. He did not know for sure he was going to write a second part. When he wrote the second part, he obviously knew he had written Part I. It is a transition for us and also a transition in his life, but not one that was envisioned when Part I was being conceived. I underline that fact; I have said it several times because the fact that both parts are usually bound together creates the illusion that the *Quixote* is one book. You will see that they are quite different books because we will be looking at their title pages.

I will begin by reviewing what I call the grand themes of criticism regarding Part I before moving on to Part II. The first of these are ambiguity and perspectivism. Leo Spitzer, whom you will be meeting in a week or so when you read his piece in the *Casebook* called "Linguistic Perspectivism in the *Don Quixote,*" says the following—I am only going to talk about his conclusions; we will talk more about how he comes to those conclusions after you have read his piece, but I need to go over his conclusions. He writes,

> This means that, in our novel [the *Quixote*], things are represented not for what they are in themselves, but only as things

spoken about or thought about; and this involves breaking the narrative presentation into two points of view. There can be no certainty about the "unbroken" reality of the events; the only un- questionable truth on which the reader may depend is the will of the artist who chose to break up a multivalent reality into dif- ferent perspectives. In other words, perspectivism suggests an Archimedean principle outside of the plot—and the Archimedes must be Cervantes himself [meaning the Archimedean principle, the focus, the center, the fulcrum is Cervantes himself, who has created this perspective]. (181)

Spitzer adds, "And we may see in Cervantes' two-fold treatment of the prob- lem of nicknames [which he studies in great detail in his article] another example of his baroque attitude (what is true, what is dream?)—this time, toward language. Is not human language, also, *vanitas vanitatum*?" (182). That is the end of Spitzer, and we saw what Ciriaco Morón Arroyo said about irony. I am repeating a quotation that you heard in a previous lecture. He says, "I agree with Spitzer's definition of Cervantean perspectivism." And then he quotes Spitzer, who says, "In terms of morals Cervantes is in no way a perspectivist."

That is the end of the Spitzer quotation within the Morón Arroyo quo- tation. In a note Morón Arroyo continues, in another quotation I am repeat- ing, "Perhaps we ought to point out here [this is Morón Arroyo] that perspec- tivism is inherent to Christian thought. Perspectivism in the sense of a form of modesty that recognizes the limits of all judgment and human knowl- edge is indeed Christian humility and intelligence in its strictest sense." And then he uses the Greek word for irony, *ironea*. So perspectivism, this partial view that creates this irony, Morón Arroyo underlines, is a very Christian perspective. I would add that the self-assurance of the Renaissance is being eroded and the ordered cosmos of the Middle Ages has long disappeared. These are the first of the grand themes: ambiguity and perspectivism.

The second of the grand themes is doubt because the self can impose its will on reality but only to a certain extent. The self is defined by the agonistic struggle to impose its will on reality. Captain Ahab in Melville's *Moby-Dick* is the most obvious modern example in fiction; he is an heir of Don Quixote, as Melville was a reader of Cervantes. Remember in this context of imposing our will on reality what I said about how we invent our beloveds when we are in love; that is part of this willful imposition of ourselves on reality. Why is doubt such an integral part of what we could call the aesthetics of the *Qui-*

xote? How can doubt be a positive value? The book gives substance to the sense of doubt brought about by the scientific discoveries and philosophical ideas of the period. The *Quixote* enacts doubts. It dramatizes them. It is the modern condition.

Recall what I mentioned about Copernicus and Galileo and the fact that humankind is no longer at the center of the world; the earth is no longer at the center of the universe, and this discovery has brought about a sense of doubt. There is doubt—continuing with this second grand theme— about the veracity of texts, the capacity of texts to convey the truth, including, most prominently, the Bible, or the Bible as interpreted by the Catholic Church. Such doubt was prevalent not only among Protestant thinkers but also among Catholic ones, like Erasmus of Rotterdam. The humanists, and Erasmus was one, were philologists. *Philologist* means, 'lover of language,' 'philo-logos,' lover of language, students of language, particularly classical languages like Latin, Greek, and Hebrew. Chairs for the study of these languages were created in Spain at the University of Alcalá, for instance, the town where Cervantes happens to have been born, by the way.

Humanists like Erasmus wanted to read scripture in the original Hebrew and Greek—Hebrew for the Old Testament, Greek for the New Testament—and challenge Saint Jerome's official Latin Bible; they wanted to do their own translations of the Bible. The Church did not like this at all, and the Erasmians in Spain were persecuted, but there is an underlying Erasmian subtext in most of Cervantes. Humanists like Erasmus wanted to say, "The reading of this word in Saint Jerome's Latin version of the Bible is wrong, it should be this instead," and changing that word changes the meaning of the text. So there was doubt about the sacred texts, doubt which spills over into doubt about texts in general and about language, and we certainly have echoes of this throughout Cervantes' work.

There is also ontological doubt; doubt about who one is, which is an encouragement to self-creation, to self-invention, to self-fashioning, as Stephen Greenblatt calls it in his book *Renaissance Self-Fashioning.* We have seen that in the *Quixote* many characters, not just Don Quixote, invent themselves: Ginés de Pasamonte, Marcela, Dorotea as Princess Micomicona, and others. Doubt leads to pondering—pondering comes from *pondus,* in Latin, 'weight'; so to ponder is to weigh the different possibilities, the diverse alternatives to being, to action. Self-doubt is the precondition of inventiveness, of the play of the imagination. It is the gateway to freedom, which is one of the main themes of the *Quixote,* as I have been pointing out continually. Doubt leads to vicarious lives lived through literature, as in the cases of Don Quixote and Marcela, for instance, and many others whom you will meet in Part II. This is, again, I underline, the freedom of the imagination. Why do we want to become others? In the age of myths we wanted to be gods; in the modern age we want to be heroes, just as Don Quixote wanted to be a chivalric hero and as people today want to be James Bond. Dissatisfaction with the world, a world that is unstable, leads to a desire to make it other and to make oneself other, and this is very much at the core of the *Quixote* from the outset.

The third of the grand themes I am reviewing as we conclude Part I is reading. The *Quixote* is a book about reading, and its protagonist is, first and foremost, a reader. But there are many readers in the book, like Marcela, Grisóstomo, Cardenio, and even the poor trooper who has trouble reading the order of arrest, as we saw in that hilarious scene. The *Quixote*, the book, encourages the reader to look for stories not told, or told indirectly by means of other stories, or imbedded in other stories. The *Quixote* is a book that is a lesson in reading, in interpreting, in the broad sense. There are so many scenes in which interpretations are challenged, in which interpretations by various characters clash. The pleasure of reading involves the discovery, the teasing out of these subtextual stories, as we saw when we talked about Cardenio's story and about Princess Micomicona's story. This is also a life lesson one can learn in the *Quixote*.

The fourth of the grand themes is that characters are relational, not static, that is, they develop in relation to each other. A given to us today, this was an innovation in the *Quixote*, an innovation developed from the picaresque, where there is character development in fiction for the first time. In *Celestina* (1499) there is some of that, but it begins to develop with the picaresque, *Lazarillo* (1554) and the *Guzmán de Alfarache* (1599). Characters influence each other. The mutual influence and transformation take place by virtue of dialogue, which posits that the self is relational and dependent on others. This is evident in one of the truly grand themes in the *Quixote*, first remarked upon by Salvador de Madariaga, which is the theme of the quixotization of Sancho and the sanchification of Don Quixote, meaning that Sancho is influenced by his master and Don Quixote by his squire. The most obvious modern example of this, to me, is a book and a film I mentioned earlier, Puig's *The Kiss of the Spider Woman*, in which, as I described, two fellows, one a political activist and the other a homosexual, are cell mates in jail in Argentina, and the whole story is about how the homosexual transforms the political activist by telling him the stories of movies he has memorized. It is a moving film with a very Quixotic structure to it. Don Fernando's transformation as well as that of Dorotea is a prime example of this evolution of characters. In addition, we have seen that characters can invent identities for themselves and have adventures in their new roles and within those new fictions, as in the case of Princess Micomicona; we will meet others who do the same thing in Part II.

The fifth of the grand themes of criticism—and this is mostly my own grand theme about the *Quixote*—is improvisation. I have talked several times about improvisation in the *Quixote*. My dictionary gives four meanings of *improvise*. "to prepare or provide offhand or hastily, extemporize; to compose verse, music, on the spur of the moment; to recite, sing extemporaneously; to compose, utter, or execute anything extemporaneously." The *Dictionary of the Spanish Academy* says tersely, "improvisar: hacer una cosa de pronto, sin estudio ni preparación alguna," 'to make or do something suddenly without study or preparation.' Improvisation has something to do with *bricoler,* a French concept that was popular during the heyday of structuralism and that means, according to my Robert, "Installer, aménager en amateur et avec ingeniosité. . . . Arranger, réparer tant bien que mal, de façon provisoire. . . . Arranger pour falsifier," 'To install something, to provide or arrange for something amateurishly and ingeniously. . . . To fix or repair something more or less in a provisional way. . . . To fix something up to falsify it or pass it off for something else.'

To improvise has, on the one hand, a positive side: it is a boast of skill to be able to do something without a model or plan; but it also has a negative side because the product of improvisation is usually shoddy, imperfect, fragile and provisional. We have seen that there is a great deal of implicit improvisation in Part I of the *Quixote* thematically, as it were, meaning that improvised things and actions are described. I gave Juan Palomeque's inn as an example of this because it is made up of patchwork, carried out over time haphazardly, but I also pointed out features of the novel itself that seem to betray their improvised construction. There are notorious Cervantine oversights, such as the disappearance of Sancho's donkey and several others.

For instance, I do not know if you noticed that Cervantes pulls out of his hat at the end the fact that the innkeeper, Juan Palomeque, was a policeman in the Holy Brotherhood, something that goes unmentioned during the earlier episode in the inn, when Palomeque snuffs out a candle to prevent a policeman from finding out what is going on in his establishment. How come, if he was a policeman himself? Are these lapses by Cervantes? or part of the aesthetics of the book? I would like to think it is part of the aesthetics of the book and that the air of improvisation is very much in line with the book's informal tone, with the fact that its origin is presumably a found manuscript whose discovery is episodic and whose redaction seems to be concomitant with the action and the reading, most notoriously, the prologue.

The prologue dramatizes the process of improvisation because it tells how it is being arduously written; the prologue sets the tone for the book, and it is also its defining epilogue, as I said earlier. It is an ode to improvisation, to imperfection, qualities to which the author resigns himself. Remember that Menéndez Pidal, in the piece you read, attributes improvisation to the Spanish character—he says this with resignation since he was a Spaniard himself; and E. C. Riley, a British Hispanist who loved Spain, admiringly compares the improvisation in the *Quixote* to bullfighting and to flamenco dancing, activities in which improvisation prevails. I believe that the 1605 prologue is a theoretical statement on the part of Cervantes, one which he proposes again in chapter 5 of the 1615 *Quixote*—the second part—when he has the translator apologize (you will get to that chapter) for transcribing a text in which Sancho does not sound like himself; he sounds too learned. This is a text that undoes itself as it is being read; it is also a critique of mimesis, of representation; it is an improvisation made from what there is and what the translator and transcriber passed on, resigned to its imperfections.

All of this is connected to the themes I mentioned before about doubt, self-doubt, and linguistic uncertainty. How can my poor self create something perfect and enduring in language, given what I have said about doubt, self-doubt, and the instability of language as conceived by the humanists? The whole thing also opens the question of temporality about this text that says, Well, it does not sound like Sancho, but I will transcribe it because it is my duty to do so. In what moment or at what moment does the text exist in relation to the originals on which it is based? One solution, perhaps the only solution, is to say that the text exists only at the moment of reading, of each reading, and that is a very modern, current conception of textuality that is already present in Cervantes.

So these are the grand themes in Part I that I wanted to review with you.

Now, we move to Part II, published in 1615: ten years, a whole decade, has elapsed. Cervantes had instant success with the *Quixote,* and he moved to Madrid in 1606. Publishers become interested in his work, and he brings out the *Exemplary Novels* in 1613 and *Ocho comedias y ocho entremeses, Eight Plays and Eight Interludes,* in 1615, the same year the second *Quixote* appears.

I have a page here that you have read, but I want to read it again, from Durán's book *Cervantes* and from the little biographical chapter I reproduced in
my *Casebook*, so that you have a synoptic view:

> In 1606 the Court settled again in Madrid [you have been fol-
> lowing in Elliott the migrations of the Spanish Court]: Cer-
> vantes and his family moved with it. Cervantes wanted to be in
> touch with other writers and was looking for new publishers; the
> women in his household, busy with fashion designing and sew-
> ing, were looking for customers. Miguel's last years in Madrid
> were relatively serene. He overcame through patience and wis-
> dom all of his adversities, the neglect of famous writers such as
> Lope de Vega—who seldom had a good word for his works—and
> the sadness of family crises; his daughter married but soon be-
> came the mistress of a wealthy middle-aged businessman; when
> Cervantes intervened in the interest of preventing scandal, she
> became estranged and never again visited him. Cervantes im-
> mersed himself in his work. It was harvest season for him: late
> in life, yet in full command of his talent, he produced in quick
> succession his *Exemplary Novels* (1613), the second part of *Don
> Quixote* (1615), and finally *Persiles and Sigismunda*, a novel in
> which his imagination and his love for adventure found an al-
> most limitless scope. (30)

Quoting Ángel del Río, a great Hispanist who was a professor at Columbia
University for many years and who in the forties published a superb history
of Spanish literature, Durán adds,

> Objectively, Cervantes' life was not a success story. He was sel-
> dom in full control: he was too poor; for many years he lacked
> public recognition. Yet, as Ángel del Río points out, "there is no
> reason to lament Cervantes' misfortunes nor the mediocrity of
> his daily life. He could thus, through an experience which is sel-
> dom obtained when the writer is successful and wealthy, know,
> observe and feel the beat of Spanish life in its greatness and its
> poverty, in its heroic fantasy and in the sad reality of an immi-
> nent decadence. He was to leave in his books the most faithful
> image of this life, reflected in multiple perspectives with bitter-
> sweet irony and penetrating humor." (31)

This is the moment when the decline of the Spanish empire had begun. To give you a clear vision of this, I want to read a text that presumably you have read in *Imperial Spain*. Elliott discusses how writers found sponsors for their work:

> At the same time, the moral and emotional involvement of the intellectuals in the tragic fate of their native land seems to have provided an additional stimulus, giving an extra degree of intensity to their imagination, and diverting it into rewardingly creative channels. This was especially true of Cervantes, whose life—from 1547 to 1616—spans the two ages of imperial triumph and imperial retreat. The crisis of the late sixteenth century cuts through the life of Cervantes as it cuts through the life of Spain, separating the days of heroism from the days of *desengaño* [this is a word we will be visiting again during the semester; it means 'to be undeceived']. Somehow Cervantes magically held the balance between optimism and pessimism, enthusiasm and irony, but he illustrates what was to be the most striking characteristic of seventeenth-century literature and artistic production—that deep cleavage between the two worlds of the spirit and the flesh, which co-exist and yet are forever separate. This constant dualism between the spirit and the flesh, the dream and the reality, belonged very much to seventeenth-century European civilization as a whole, but it seems to have attained an intensity in Spain that it rarely achieved elsewhere. It is apparent in the writings of Calderón and the portraits of Velázquez, and it prompted the bitter satires of Quevedo. "There are many things here that seem to exist and have their being, and yet they are nothing more than a name and an appearance," Quevedo wrote at the end of his life. . . . Was the reality of Spanish experience to be found in the heroic imperialism of Charles V or in the humiliating pacifism of Philip III? In the world of Don Quixote, or the world of Sancho Panza? Confused at once by its own past and its own present, the Castile of Philip III—the land of *arbitristas*—sought desperately for an answer. (319–20)

"Arbitristas"—from *arbitrio,* 'an opinion'—whom you will meet in the first chapters of Part II, were people who offered advice to the government on matters of the economy and also on military matters. Some of their advice

was really outlandish. These are the people who developed into today's econ-
omists, the ones who have brought us to the present crisis; this is what I
always think of when I think of the arbitristas. You will be meeting them,
as I said, at the beginning of Part II, when the characters discuss them and
discuss some of their advice, and Don Quixote himself acts as an arbitrista
by giving some advice on how to take care of the threat of the Turks, who are
descending on the Mediterranean again after their defeat at Lepanto. We are
not responsible for answering the question of what happened in Spain, why
it was different, but we are responsible for seeing the effects of this crisis as
reflected in Cervantes' work, and I want you to have a clear view of these two
ages of empire, one of triumph and one of defeat.

Now, the second part. Let us look at the various titles, the title page we
saw of the 1605 *Quixote,* the title page of the 1615 *Quixote,* and the title page
of the Avellaneda *Quixote.* He is known by his second last name, as some
people are, and you have to remember him because the two most important
things that have happened to Cervantes since the publication of 1605 is the
success of the *Quixote* and in 1614 the appearance of an apocryphal *Quixote*
published by Avellaneda. Here is the title page of the 1605 *Quixote,* the one
we have just finished; Part I, as it is known: *El ingenioso hidalgo don Quixote
de la Mancha* (see fig. 1). Remember we went over each one of those words
in one of the first classes.

Now, we go to the title page of the 1615 *Quixote,* and you see, *Segvnda
parte del ingenioso caballero don Qvixote de la Mancha* (fig. 12). There has
been a major change: he is no longer an hidalgo; now he is a *caballero,* a
'knight': *"Por Miguel de Cervantes Saavedra, autor de la primera parte,"* 'By
Miguel de Cervantes Saavedra, author of the first part.'

The name of Cervantes is emphasized because Avellaneda, in 1614, had
published an apocryphal *Quixote:* "*Segvndo tomo del ingenioso hidalgo don
Qvixote de la Mancha que contiene fu tercera falida* [it will be the 'third sally']
y es la quinta parte ['the fifth part' because, remember, the first part is divided in four, so this is the fifth part]." By "*Alonfo Fernandez de Avellaneda,
natural de la Villa de Tordefillas,* 'born in the village of Tordesillas'" (fig. 13).
Tordesillas is a little town near Valladolid, made famous by the Treaty of
Tordesillas, whereby the pope in 1494 divided up the New World between
Portugal and Spain. (Francis I of France complained in the sixteenth century
that he wanted to see in Adam's will where he had bequeathed all of these
lands to the Spanish and the Portuguese.)

Don Quixote is now a caballero, not just an hidalgo. Is this because
Cervantes felt his alleged deeds in the first part elevated him to knight?

Figure 12. Title page of the 1615 edition of Miguel de Cervantes, *El ingenioso cavallero don Qvixote de la Mancha*. General Collection, Beinecke Rare Book and Manuscript Library, Yale University.

Some believe the change was made by the printer, not by Cervantes, in part to distinguish this book from Avellaneda's, which still called him an hidalgo. Also, some have said that the printer felt—the *Quixote*, as you have learned, was immediately translated into several languages, English, French, and others—that *caballero*, 'knight', was easier to translate into other languages than *hidalgo*. Editors tend to make such changes in the interest of profits, but we do not know exactly why the change was made. The fact is that the title has been altered, and this is a good way of remembering that Part II is a new book.

The second part was finished in a hurry by Cervantes in large measure because of the publication in 1614 of Avellaneda's spurious second part. Second parts of *Lazarillo, Guzmán,* and *Celestina* had appeared, not to mention those of romances of chivalry, as we saw in the episode of the scrutiny of the books; there were whole cycles, second, third, fourth parts. Why? William Hinrichs has recently published a book about sequels, and he demonstrated

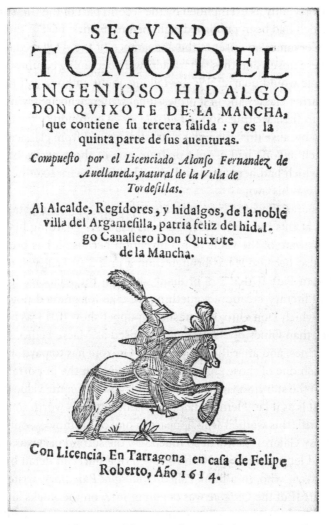

Figure 13. Title page of the 1614 edition of Alonso Fernández
de Avellaneda, *Segundo tomo del Ingenioso hidalgo don Qvixote
de la Mancha que contiene la tercera salida y es la quinta parte.*
SC6 C3375 F614f, Houghton Library, Harvard University.

that sequels pervaded in sixteenth-century Spain.[1] They were among the most popular of books and a whole poetics of the sequel emerged. It is not the same thing to write a book from scratch as to write a book that is the continuation of a previous book. Why did this happen? Well, it happened because with the advent of printing it was easier to produce books, to disseminate them, and to make a profit from them. So, second parts proliferated.

In writing a second part of the *Quixote,* Cervantes is following this trend, most recently as exemplified by the second part of the *Guzmán de Alfarache,* which had been published right before the first part of the *Quixote.* Why was Cervantes so upset at the appearance of the Avellaneda *Quixote*? Because these novels and these characters were becoming commodities over which people would quarrel. We are talking about authors, as I have mentioned in earlier classes, the first professional writers who are trying to make a living from their writing. So the *Quixote* was a commodity for Cervantes, particularly because this was not a character derived from classical mythology to which anyone had a right or from one of those cycles of chivalric romances which had been used and reused; this is a character he invented, so he felt it was his own.

The character would become a literary myth and then be taken up by others, but at this juncture Cervantes was jealously guarding his creation. He is quite aware of the value of his invention because it has brought him fame and also because it has brought him a profit. In fact, you will get to an episode in Part II that is a brilliant satire on the relationship between money and literary creation, something we take for granted now. It is the episode in which Don Quixote smashes a puppet show that was brought by none other than Ginés de Pasamonte disguised as Maese Pedro. He breaks all the figurines, and after the episode Don Quixote has to pay for each one of them, each one of those characters, depending on the importance of the character in the story. So you can see that it is a satire on the value of literary invention. It is as if Ian Fleming said, "My James Bond is worth so much and Pussy Galore" (this woman who appears in one of his movies, outrageously named Pussy Galore) "is worth so much." So the second part was written in a hurry, and let me show you in how much of a hurry in detail by quoting Henry Sullivan, who, in a book called *Grotesque Purgatory,* writes the following: "Part II of the *Quixote* was begun in 1612; on the stocks and well on its way by July 1613; about half-complete by 20 July 1614; then continued at breakneck speed in fall 1614 and finally completed by January or February 1615: a period of about two and a half years in all."[2] I will return to this topic by using a quote from Manuel Durán. How does Sullivan know this? From evidence and documents and statements by Cervantes and others about how the novel was developed. You will see that Part II is quite long. Now, one of the best critics of Avellaneda's *Quixote* was Stephen Gilman, a professor at Harvard for many years. He wrote an essay called "The Apocryphal Quixote" that is well worth reading, and in it he has a memorable phrase. Gilman says that Cervantes, rather than confront Avellaneda, which he does to a certain extent, "prefers to encompass Avellaneda in a web of irony."[3]

That is, Cervantes threw a web of irony over his rival. You will see how he does that because Avellaneda's greatest triumph—his book did not have much success—was to wind up as a character within *Don Quixote*'s fiction and having his characters incorporated into Cervantes' novel, to add to the game of mirrors that the *Quixote* already was. In fact, a critic—having enough time on their hands, critics and scholars will say almost anything—claimed in 1915 that the apocryphal *Quixote* had been written by Cervantes himself. That is absurd, but at some level it makes sense because if Avellaneda had not existed, Cervantes would have had to invent him in the way he uses him in Part II.

If you want to read the most outlandish take on all of this, you must read a story by the Argentine master Jorge Luis Borges, "Pierre Menard, Author of the *Quixote*," in which a French poet and minor scholar decides to write the *Quixote* again; not a different *Quixote*, but the same *Quixote*, word for word as Cervantes had written it.[4] It is a dizzying theoretical meditation on all of these games of authorship that Cervantes himself initiates in Part I and continues in Part II. In a sense, the appearance of Avellaneda is like a self-fulfilling prophecy. If there was a Cide Hamete Benengeli who was supposed to have been the real author of the *Quixote*—and is, of course, a fictional author—suddenly Cervantes finds himself with a real false author of the *Quixote;* so this is what Avellaneda's book adds to the *Quixote.* Avellaneda's book is tremendously boring. It is conceived within scholastic philosophy, the characters, instead of engaging in dialogue, have long monologues that are really obnoxious, Don Quixote is not in love with Dulcinea, he is the "unloving knight," Sancho is a bit pornographic. It is, in fact, a dull, dull book read only by those of us who are Cervantistas and cannot avoid reading it.

So much for Avellaneda. Now let us move on to Part II. You have a treat in store because, in my view, Part II is better than Part I, if that is possible, although scholars argue back and forth about this. But I think there is no question that Part II is a superior book. It is even much more complicated, and complicated by the fact that some characters in Part II have read Part I, adding to the game of mirrors. You will find this in the early chapters of Part II. I am going to read a few passages, again, from Durán's *Cervantes* because they serve as a good introduction to Part II. It is a kind of synthesis of what Durán thought about the *Quixote* at this point, so that you have some general ideas before embarking on reading Part II. Durán says, "The art of dialogue in Cervantes reaches its peak in the second half of his novel."[5] This is true: in the second part there is much more dialogue, and not just between Sancho and Don Quixote—those dialogues that we enjoy so much and of which there are more here—but among many different characters with different points of view and different ways of speaking. Again, Durán: "It is also in this second part when the interaction of the two main characters, the knight and his squire, reaches a climax. Sancho Panza becomes increasingly 'quixotized' and even at certain moments occupies the center of the stage, having become temporarily the novel's main character. It is an impressive trick: it is not done with mirrors—it is achieved through dialogue."[6] This is true as well. You will see that Sancho, in various chapters I am not going to anticipate and ruin for you, becomes the protagonist of the novel. Again, Durán: "Human memory, the memory of the squire and his master, ruminates upon the past. . . . Nothing that occurs in their travels is entirely finished; they will talk about what has happened to them and try to find a meaning to every obscure detail etched in their memory. Every possibility the future holds open will influence their present attitudes. Since the past keeps on echoing upon the present and the future keeps on working its magic upon the minds of the two characters, each moment of the present is made richer and more subtle by the interplay of past, present, and future."[7]

To this I might add that the presence of Part I, as a memory, is an important one in Part II, and a device of Part II is that many episodes are in some way a rewriting of episodes of Part I, a rewriting that is usually much more complicated and elaborate, but you can see the kernel of the episode from Part I in the episode in Part II. This raises philosophical issues about memory and about the repetition of the past that we will be talking about when we reach those episodes. The interaction between the individual and his environment is shown to be unique, it escapes logic and language because logic and language are systems of labels superimposed upon our experience, and Cervantes wants to free us from all labels by showing how much each individual is capable of interpreting his own facet of a multifaceted reality. The presence of reality in its variegated ways and the way of interpreting it become much more complicated in Part II because disguises proliferate and a lot more of the action takes place not in open air but indoors, where charades of various kinds can be organized. Now, the following quotation is a little long but takes us back to the composition of Part II and, I hope, will round out your knowledge of it as you approach reading it. Durán writes,

> The sense of unreality is heightened throughout Part II when Don Quixote and Sancho have to face their doubles, their reflection in the mirror. They meet people who have read Part I or have heard about it; they have to react to what these readers of their previous adventures think about them. Even worse: After II, 36 [which is when Cervantes finds out about the existence of Avellaneda's book], they have to fight off another image of themselves—the bogus image in the crooked mirror of Avellaneda's fake Second Part, the False Quixote. Towards the end of July, 1614, Cervantes was working on Chapter 36 of his second part; Avellaneda's book appeared in October of the same year. Cervantes reacted by writing thirty-eight chapters in seven months: a strenuous effort which may have exhausted what was left of a precarious health. The spurious second part was the work of an unknown author [Avellaneda is obviously a pseudonym, it's a pen name, we do not know who Avellaneda really was], but Cervantes' hard-won reputation was in danger until he could refute the piracy by issuing his own Part Two. He was also indignant at the lack of intelligence and sensitivity of his imitator. His anger is expressed through his main characters. Don Quixote and Sancho have to face their ugly ghosts: they must convince the readers of Avellaneda's book that *they* are real and Avellaneda's characters are intruders trying to usurp their personality, their selves, their reality. It is a situation only Cervantes or Pirandello could have devised.[8]

The allusion here is to Luigi Pirandello, a great Italian playwright of the twentieth century who wrote a famous play called *Six Characters in Search of an Author.* So Cervantes' characters are disputing other characters, their reality or fictionality. In a way, having read Part I yourselves, you are like some of the characters in Part II of the *Quixote,* and you are in a similar situation as you go through the second part.

CHAPTER 13

Renaissance (1605) and
Baroque (1615) *Quixotes*

Required Readings

Cervantes, *Don Quixote*, Part II, Prologue, chaps. 1–11,
pp. 483–557.
Elliott, *Imperial Spain*, 249–84.

I want to begin today by mentioning a virtual literary fact, a story that
does not happen; one that only exists in the "as if" of literature. It is make-
believe—literature is make-believe—but it is nevertheless suggestive of the
enigmatic and even prophetic powers of literature. In talking the last time
about Cervantes' reaction to the publication of Avellaneda's *Quixote,* which
he learned about when he was writing chapter 36 of his own second part,
I failed to mention a change he made in Don Quixote's plans in order to
distinguish his own book from that of the imposter. You may remember
that in mentioning the possibility of a third sally at the end of Part I there is
a reference to some jousts in Saragossa. And at the beginning of Cervantes'
Part II it is again said that Don Quixote will go to Saragossa to participate
in the tournament, which used to take place during the celebration of Saint
George's Day—Saint George is a saint who was a knight—on April 23. This
is where Don Quixote is headed as he sets forth for the third time. But it
so happens that Avellaneda had also taken the cue of the Saragossa jousts
from Part I and had his own Don Quixote actually go and participate in
the event. This was enough for Cervantes to change Don Quixote's destina-

182

tion in midnovel and have him divert to Barcelona without passing through Saragossa, which is what he does in the book: Avellaneda's Quixote goes to Saragossa, Don Quixote veers and goes to Barcelona in Cervantes' second part. This is all well and good, another instance of Cervantes' reaction to the apocryphal *Quixote*.

What Cervantes could not have known is that April 23, the day of those jousts, would be the date of his death, so he avoided, unknowingly of course, having the end of his book announce his own end. Now, this is all, needless to say, a fantasy on my part, but such implied coincidences make me wonder sometimes: is literature always an avoidance or a postponement of death? There is more to the telling of stories than the telling of stories, as Scheherazade knew when she told story after story, night after night, forestalling her own demise in *One Thousand and One Nights*. In some implicit way, perhaps only in my overheated imagination, this is what happens when Cervantes has his character swerve away from April 23. So much for that.

April 23, by the way, is a bad day for great writers. It is the date on which Shakespeare died, the same year as Cervantes. Not exactly the same day, though close enough, because England and Spain used different calendars, so there was a difference of two or three days, but April 23 is also the date of Shakespeare's death. There is something magical about April 23, so much so that Alejo Carpentier, the great Cuban writer, also died on April 23 centuries later. We should warn all writers not to take April 23 too seriously, but I am sure that some who wish to be as great as Cervantes and Shakespeare or Carpentier would take it and would rather just die on April 23 to be as great as they were. So perhaps this is just a mnemonic device, something to make you remember the date of Cervantes' death, to which we will return when we read his farewell in the prologue to the *Trials of Persiles and Sigismunda*.

Let us return now to the issue of the new features of Part II. I remarked on the discussion among Don Quixote, the priest, and the barber about Spain's political situation and the *arbitristas,* those who offered solutions to the problems at hand. I remarked that the discussion should be seen in the context of my commentary on the speech about arms and letters, when I said that by the sixteenth century government had become the object of intellectual reflection and mentioned Machiavelli's *The Prince* as a founding work of political science. I also told you that, during the sixteenth century, not a few books were written about the education of the prince in which guidelines were offered about how to prepare a young man for kingship. All of these preoccupations are in the background of this discussion among the

three characters. What the discussion also indicates—and this is very significant—is that the *Quixote,* Part II, is the first political novel because it deals
with and incorporates current events, such as the expulsion of the *moriscos.*

The moriscos were Arabs who had converted to Christianity and remained in Spain after the fall of Granada in 1492. There were large communities of Arabs in Spain, and many remained; they were, by decree and by
force, compelled to abandon not only their religion but their customs, and
they were ultimately expelled from Spain at the time Cervantes was writing
Part II of the *Quixote.* This polemical event is incorporated into the novel.
This is why I say that the *Quixote* Part II is the first political novel. In Part II
there is also a bitter satire of the aristocracy and their irresponsible ways,
in the figures of the Duke and Duchess, whom you will meet later. The satire
of the arbitristas is part of these political themes, as is Don Quixote's trying
to act like an arbitrista. Remember the outlandish idea he had on how to
fight off the Turks. It is part of the critique of the nobility, even if Don Quixote is a pathetic and impoverished hidalgo, but here he is trying to play the
role of the arbitrista. This is what the king should do, he argues.

Another new factor is that three or four of the initial chapters in Part II
take place indoors, in Don Quixote's house and Sancho's house; in contrast
to Part I, a great deal of Part II, as I noted, will take place indoors, reflecting
a more urban setting in the novel. We will have both the village of El Toboso
and the city of Barcelona. Inns will still play a role, but not as important a
role as Juan Palomeque's inn in Part I, and remember that with the holes in
the roof of that inn to be inside Palomeque's inn was almost to be outdoors.
Here, in Part II, there will be houses, mansions, and towns like El Toboso,
which is merely a village, and Barcelona, which is a great city. The novel, the
modern novel that develops from the *Quixote,* will be essentially an urban
genre dealing with cities—think of Balzac and Dickens—because in cities
there are more people engaged in playing many roles, a thicker social context. So we can see in this development a movement toward the city in the
novel. Although one could say that if the remote kernel of the novel, of the
modern novel, is *Celestina*—about which I have talked many times—that
work takes place in a city, presumably Salamanca, and although many of the
picaresques take place on the road, there are cities in *Lazarillo* and particularly in the *Guzmán de Alfarache.* Being indoors but also outdoors, much of
the action of Part II takes place at night, in the dark. We had night episodes
in Part I—the fulling hammers, the fracas at the inn, the episode with the
dead body—but most of it takes place outdoors on the road and in daylight.
Not so in Part II, in which the darkness will play an important role in several

episodes, and there are two that actually take place underground, in caves. Part II, as we will soon see, is more baroque, and the buildings and darkness contribute to it.

Another development in Part II is that it is being scripted and performed in the present, presumably as we read, not in the past by Cide Hamete Benengeli and his translators. It is being improvised on the go. In addition, as I already remarked, many characters have read Part I, which serves as the background, as a model, as it were, for Part II. We already had intimations of this in Part I; the novel being scripted and written as the novel takes place. In the episode of the dead body, when Sancho gives Don Quixote the moniker the Knight of the Sorry Face, the hidalgo remarks that the writer must have put the idea in Sancho's head, suggesting that the novel is being written as they perform it. But now we have the plans and preparations for the action being discussed by the characters, particularly by Sansón Carrasco. In Part II, Part I plays the role that the romances of chivalry play in Part I. Let me repeat that, because it is a bit convoluted: in Part II, Part I plays the role that the romances of chivalry played in Part I. It is the original that the characters who have read it want Don Quixote to reproduce and to act according to, so a new, larger mirror has been added to the play of mirrors already present in Part I. Don Quixote belongs to a previous fiction that the new characters who have read it want him to be true to. Everything now is part of Don Quixote's fiction.

Sansón Carrasco is the most important new character to emerge in Part II. He has a harsh-sounding name, Sansón Carrasco. He is a town boy, the son of Bartolomé Carrasco, and he has studied in Salamanca and come back with a bachelor's degree. He is another of several university graduates in the *Quixote*, the first being the priest, although the most memorable one so far is Grisóstomo. This is a reflection of the importance of universities in Spain during this period, particularly after the work of Cardinal Francisco Jiménez de Cisneros—about whom you have read in Elliott—who founded the University of Alcalá. There is a mild satire of intellectuals in the figure of Sansón Carrasco, as there is in that of the priest in Part I and throughout Part II. The priest was a graduate of a lesser university, not quite Salamanca. The start of the satire is that this new character is called Sansón but is quite small. He is not a giant like the Samson of the Bible.

Most important, he is a jokester, a prankster, an avid reader of romances of chivalry, and particularly of Part I of the *Quixote*, which he seems to know by heart. To judge by comments he makes, he was also a reader of Matteo Boiardo and Ariosto, so Sansón spent his time at Salamanca reading literature, not studying theology or the law, which is what he was supposed to be doing. He is the counterpart of the canon of Toledo in Part I but is not solemn and pedantic like the canon; he is quite the opposite. Sansón is a reader of Part I. He wants to reenact it, just like Don Quixote wanted to reenact and dramatize the romances of chivalry. His plan to cure Don Quixote is to defeat him within the fiction of his madness, like the priest and the barber in Part I, but in doing so he will become another Quixote, his double in a truer sense than all of the others in Part I. If Part I is held together by the overarching plot of the persecution and capture of Don Quixote by the Holy Brotherhood, the barber, and the priest, in Part II that function is played by Sansón's schemes to bring Don Quixote back within the fiction he has helped him create. That is, Sansón has helped create another fiction for Don Quixote that is really not a fiction; that is, that Don Quixote is a great knight-errant, already the object of a book. So he imbues Don Quixote with this idea: you are a great character already in a book, so you have to act accordingly.

In Part II, Sansón is the main author within the book. Cide Hamete Benengeli was a distant author, at least thrice removed by translators and transcribers. Sansón and others, like the duke's butler, whom you will meet soon enough, will be authors within the fiction we read and will script the action and watch it unfold, most of the time not like they intended it to. As author figures, they are—particularly Sansón—quite complex and modern; their intentions rarely match their results. Much of the fun, of the humor, in Part II is following the elaborate schemes of internal authors that go awry when the opposite of what they had planned actually happens, some of them spectacularly. This has much to say about authorship, about the creation of fiction, and about Cervantes' own creation of the fiction of the *Quixote*. I say that it is quite a modern conception of the author because this is the conception of authors we have in the modern period.

The whole of deconstruction, the famous literary movement that was mostly started here at Yale, had to do with deconstructing authors, showing how their intentions rarely, if ever, matched the results. But that's another story. So, in the hands of Sansón and other readers of Part I, the action in Part II is poised between the past, their remembrance of Part I, and the future; their scripts are based on it. It is like a balancing act between the past, Part I, and the future in the scripts they prepare. Hence it is like an action that unfolds in the present as it is being written, or just after following scripts whose development we, as readers, can more or less follow. Part II is a text in the making; we learn this quite early, in chapter 5, in the episode when Sancho goes home to convince his wife that he must accompany Don Quixote again. This is an episode I mentioned briefly at the end of my last lecture, but I want to revisit today. The question of translation and improvisation resurfaces here. Chapter 5, Part II begins with a disclaimer: "As the translator of the history begins this fifth chapter, he says that he considers it to be apocryphal, because Sancho Panza speaks here in a way that is quite different from what could be expected from his dull wits, and makes incisive comments that seem beyond his capabilities; the translator adds, however, that, concerned as he is to do his job properly, he has decided not to leave it untranslated, and so he continues" (II, 5, 514). Then the chapter proper begins. A little further on it is again reported that "it was because of this way of expressing himself and because of what Sancho says a little later that the translator of this history declared that he considered this chapter to be apocryphal" (II, 5, 517).

Let us reconstruct step by step what the comment by the translator at the beginning of chapter 5 suggests about the status of the text we read but keeping in mind that all of these games of authorship and textuality do not ultimately lead to a coherent system. We cannot really pin Cervantes down on the issue of authorship, and we cannot pin him down either on which is finally the text. The text exists supposedly in the original, in a form that seems to be apocryphal; that is, it is false, either a bogus addendum by somebody else or a falsifying rewriting of it. Did Cide Hamete write it this way? or was it falsified in some way so that Sancho appears talking like this? Then it is translated into the text we read by a reluctant translator who alludes to its falsehood but decides nevertheless to translate and transcribe it, but adding a note about its falsehood.

It is a text that is erased as it is being written and that should disappear as we read it. Moreover, there is a question of temporality: when does it exist and in what form? The answer is that it exists only at the moment of each reading. This is, I think, a model of how the entire Part II exists, poised, as I said, between the remembrances of Part I and the future actions scripted by the internal authors of Part II, actions that do not turn out to be quite like the script. Furthermore, the translator's admonition raises the issue of mimesis: which Sancho is the real one? is it the one he remembers from Part I? or the new Sancho, who has evolved, improving his speech and endowed with the desire for social advancement, not just for wealth? The translator's quip reveals that Sancho has changed, that he is not static. In fact, it reveals that reality in general is not static, and true mimesis has to be very much aware of the changing nature of things and people.

So there is an inherent provisional quality to the text we read and to the whole of Part II that, as I will suggest later, is part of its baroque nature. Here, Sancho is playing the role of Don Quixote, and his wife that of himself, as he used to be. This is hilarious, particularly when he corrects her mistakes as she misspeaks. Sancho is echoing Don Quixote's ideas, revealing that he has been not only quixoticized but also has acquired new values. All of this comes out in the discussion of their daughter's marriage, which they are looking at from differing points of view. The wife wanted her to marry her equal, and Sancho wanted her to marry somebody of higher status.

Sancho's social ambition is reflected in his intellectual improvement and swagger. In Part II of the *Quixote*, Sancho will play a more central role and prove himself to be capable of things that would not have been thought possible by the Sancho of Part I. The changes in Sancho, his elevation in status, have an ideological dimension as well as an aesthetic one. The poor and humble can learn and advance, and novelistic characters can move up and down the social ladder. This element of the *Quixote*, which is a political element, too, anticipates the Enlightenment and ideas that lead to concepts about social equality that will eventually become modern conceptions of democracy, but it also has a profoundly Christian background. We can recall Matthew's Gospel, chapter 5, the opening words of the Sermon on the Mount: "Blessed [these are the Beatitudes] are the poor in spirit for theirs is the Kingdom of Heaven; blessed are they that mourn for they shall be comforted; blessed are the meek for they shall inherit the earth."

If characters in novels evolve, they do so within a social context, so this is consonant with the political character of Part II; but this evolving also has much to do with the development and evolution of realism in literature, particularly in prose fiction. This brings me to Erich Auerbach. I gave you a handout that happens to be an obituary of Auerbach written by none other than René Wellek. Wellek was a great professor here at Yale for many years, the founder of the discipline of comparative literature in the United States. It just so happens that most of the professors and critics I will be mentioning in my lecture today were Yale professors. Yale has been at the forefront of literary studies for many, many years, and this is a reflection of it. I did not plan it this way, it just happens to be so. I will give you a thumbnail sketch of Auerbach and his theories.

Auerbach was the critic who put forth a theory about Christianity and the development of realism in his outstanding book *Mimesis: The Representation of Reality in Western Literature,* first published in the original German in Switzerland in 1946, a year after the end of World War II.[1] We will be talking about him next week, when you read his essay about the enchanted Dulcinea in the *Casebook,* an essay drawn from *Mimesis.* Auerbach—this is my thumbnail sketch of him—who was Jewish, born in Berlin, and trained in the German philological tradition, would eventually become, along with Leo Spitzer, whom you will also meet in the *Casebook,* one of its best known scholars. After participating as a combatant in World War I, Auerbach earned a doctorate in 1921, and in 1929 became a member of the philology faculty at the University of Marburg, publishing a well-received study titled *Dante: Poet of the Secular World,* a book that is still read today.

With the rise of Nazism, however, Auerbach was forced to vacate his position in 1934—he was thrown out because he was Jewish. Exiled from Nazi Germany, he took up residence in Istanbul, Turkey, where he wrote *Mimesis,* generally considered his masterwork and one of the best books of literary criticism of the twentieth century. He has said, in a moving statement, that he wrote such a general book because in Istanbul he did not have his books or the specialized journals he needed, so he just used the big works in Western literature. Thus it was these terrible circumstances that had the happy result of *Mimesis.* Auerbach moved to the United States in 1947, first teaching at Pennsylvania State University and then working at the Institute for Advanced Study in Princeton. In 1950 he was made Sterling Professor of Romance Languages at Yale, a position he held until his death, while still a professor here, in 1957. He died in Wallingford, Connecticut.

The main idea of *Mimesis,* a broad and profound one, is about the Christian mixture of the sublime and the low style in the New Testament leading up to the emergence of realism, the representation of everyday life and common people in serious literature. We take this for granted now, but it was not so until the New Testament. This was a break from the strict distinction between high and low styles in classical literature, in which the serious genres, like epic and tragedy, dealt with outstanding figures, including gods, and were written in a high rhetorical style where common speech had no place, whereas the minor genres, like comedy, dealt with low-class people who speak in vulgar speech and are invariably comical.

Auerbach derived his idea from Saint Augustine and the church fathers. The church fathers were those who, during the Middle Ages, wrote commentaries on scripture and expanded and deepened the Christian doctrine. They include major philosophers like Saint Thomas Aquinas, who wrote in the thirteenth century. There are Greek fathers and Latin fathers; I mean, there is a *patrologia,* that is, the writing of the fathers in Latin, and another one in Greek. Auerbach labels this Christian response to the classical separation of styles *sermo humilis,* 'humble sermon' or 'speech.' That separation of styles was derived from Aristotle and Roman rhetorical theory. The mixture of the transcendent and the low style is exemplified by Christ's passion, through which the quotidian drama of humankind, the daily drama of humans, assumes a deeper meaning: life does not end in the brief span of worldly existence, eternity is present in it as a message of hope. Seth Lerer writes about Auerbach, "Auerbach finds an apparently low or humble diction pressed into the service of transcendent spirituality. Again developing an argument of Augustine's—here on the power of the Christian word stripped of the trappings of classical eloquence—Auerbach sees the progress of late antique and medieval literature as moving inexorably toward the synthesis of the humble and the sublime."[2] One could say that the *Quixote* embodies such a synthesis of the humble and the sublime.

Lerer also acknowledges Auerbach's debt to Giambattista Vico, the great Italian philosopher of the eighteenth century. Vico found that the stories, the literature, the lore of a people, are a central part of their culture. His philosophy is compelling because his basic argument is that humans understand only that which was created by humans, not by gods. Therefore, he has the story of humankind begin not with Genesis but after the flood, when man remakes the world on his own. You will see all of this in action and understand Auerbach's essay on the enchanted Dulcinea much better with this background. The chapter by Auerbach on the *Quixote* is a highly polemical one; it was badly received by Hispanists and by Cervantes scholars. Through his study of the mixture of styles, Auerbach in the end comes up with the idea—which I think is very questionable—that the *Quixote* is mainly or essentially a comical book. But we will get to that after you have read Auerbach's essay on that hilarious chapter when Sancho tries to convince Don Quixote that one of the wenches who approach them on donkeys is Dulcinea. It is an episode that makes me laugh every time I reread it, no matter how many thousands of times. I laugh particularly when Don Quixote reports that the alleged Dulcinea smelled of raw garlic and that he was dismayed by this. That is part of realism that has to do with the humble and the comical.

I have been anticipating ideas about the Renaissance and the baroque, and it is time we begin a more focused discussion on these periods of Western art and literature. It is useful to be able to place a work like the *Quixote* within this period. It cannot be the goal of our readings; it enhances our enjoyment and understanding of a book such as this but does not explain it away. Now, first, to have a clear chronological notion, let us say that the

Renaissance covers from the fourteenth to the sixteenth century, and the baroque the seventeenth century and parts of the eighteenth.

The Renaissance, as we have seen, is the period when Western thought breaks away from medieval ideas and practices, which were centered on religious doctrine, and humanists attempt to revive the classical age, that is, Greek and Roman arts and ideas. It is a more secular period in which Neoplatonism is one of the principal trends of thought, basically the idea of perfection achieved through love and the possibility of achieving perfection by imitating the harmonious forms of classical art.

There is an inherent optimism in the Renaissance and in humanism in general because it was hoped that the revival of the classical past would revive the present and bring back a golden age, as we saw expressed in Don Quixote's speech. Also, there is confidence in human agency, in the ability to bring about perfection by the practice of classical norms. Utopia is one of the Renaissance ideas and ideals which gain concretion in Thomas More's famous book *Utopia*. The perfect society is obtainable through the application of rational norms. There can be a perfect ruler, as described by Machiavelli in *The Prince*, and a perfect courtier, as described by Castiglione in *The Book of the Courtier*, and even a perfect knight, as presented in the romances of chivalry. Nature and its representation can be harmonious and beautiful, perfect beauty is available in nature and attainable in art.

The baroque, on the other hand, is an age in which disappointment with these ideas and aspirations is expressed, and the perfect forms of the Renaissance are twisted and turned to generate a complicated, convoluted form of art that has often been seen as the blending of Renaissance forms with Gothic ones by looking back to the Middle Ages. Therefore, the baroque would be turning these Renaissance, neoclassical forms back to the Middle Ages and to the Gothic. Think of the Gothic as cathedrals, pointing upward, and think of classicism as buildings like those with a combination of perpendicular and horizontal lines. This is all overly simplified, but I want you to have clear ideas, which you can then elaborate on. Where there is light in the Renaissance, there is darkness, or at least chiaroscuro, a word I introduced you to before, in the baroque, a mixture of darkness and light.

The discussions of the priest and the barber with Don Quixote seem to center on the disappointments of the age. Part II is going to be redolent of baroque *desengaño,* a word I mentioned before that I am going to mention again today and discuss in some detail. When the games prove to be nothing more than that, games of illusions, Renaissance optimism gives way to baroque disillusionment. The commonplace then is that Part I of the *Quixote* belongs to the Renaissance and Part II to the baroque. Think of the two ages Elliott spoke about in that quotation I read to you from his book, one of imperial expansion and the other of imperial retreat. This is an oversimplification, but there is enough truth in it to merit consideration, so I will devote some time to the concept of baroque today.

What is understood by *baroque* in general? People have a general idea, a vague idea: "This is very baroque," they say. By that, they mean something very complicated, needlessly complicated. Webster's definition is good enough: "Irregular in shape like some pearls [actually the name baroque may come from the name of some irregular pearls]; artistically irregular, incongruous or fantastic; as a style of architectural and other decoration of the seventeenth and eighteenth century; tastelessly odd, bizarre and grotesque."

You do not want to be called baroque. Some of its features are excessive accumulation, difficulty, obscurity, and literally darkness, chiaroscuro. A good example is Gian Lorenzo Bernini's *The Ecstasy of Saint Teresa,* where one sees the effects of the spiritual or the physical which cannot express the sublime feeling of union with God (fig. 14). You can see that Saint Teresa is in ecstasy, and the folds of her clothing express this sublime feeling of union—clothing expressing mood by its folds, her body covered, except for the hand and the foot. This is certainly not a Renaissance statue; think of Michelangelo's *David.* This is not, because of its twists and folds; this is a Bernini statue, typical of the baroque.

Another good example is Antonio de Pereda's painting *The Cavalier's Dream,* where the ephemeral nature of the real is emphasized and the baroque emphasizes images of death and decay, so his dream turns into a theater, death, and books (fig. 15). This is a baroque dream that this cavalier is having. I wanted to show you those examples, but I am going to give you some more that are close at hand.

First let me comment on a few quotations on the baroque. The first one is from José Arrom, who was also a professor at Yale for many years:

> It is generally agreed today that in Europe the Baroque was an artistic climate created by the spiritual atmosphere of the Counter-Reformation. [Now you know what the Counter-Reformation is, having read Elliott, that movement in Spain that countered the Reformation in the rest of Europe.] This climate acted like an obscure force that pushed in the direction of what had prevailed before the eruption of the Renaissance in order to jump back to grounds that, because they had not been worked on, appeared to

Figure 14. Gian Lorenzo Bernini, *The Ecstasy of Saint Teresa*
(1647–52). Courtesy of Scala/Art Resource, NY.

be more solid. In this leap back, Europeans, constrained by the
landscape of their own history, fell into intellectual and artistic
currents that were aesthetically akin to the Gothic and intellectually to the Middle Ages.[3]

In Spain, the renewal of scholastic philosophy and the retrenchment brought
about by the Counter-Reformation, in general, signify this and lead toward
the baroque because of course there can be no return in history, and what
turns out is something completely new. The mixture, the uneasy mixture of
Renaissance forms with medieval ones, turns out to be the baroque.

Figure 15. Antonio de Pereda, *The Cavalier's Dream*
(1655). Courtesy of Album/Art Resource, NY.

The next quotation is from René Wellek, whom I mentioned above.
This one is a little denser because it has to do with the critical concept of
the baroque, but I want you to have an idea of it. Wellek traces the development of the term *baroque,* above all, its transfer from art history to literary
historiography. Baroque began as a term in art history. Wellek links the dissemination of the concept to the use that Oswald Spengler makes of it in
The Decline of the West, an influential book in the twentieth century. Wellek
thinks that the popularity of the baroque came about because critics saw in
it a form of expressionism, which was a kind of poetry in Germany at the
beginning of the twentieth century, in the 1920s, a convoluted, complicated
poetry; they saw that as a kind of return to the baroque.

Wellek distinguishes between those who want to turn baroque into a
typology; that is, that the whole of art history is a back and forth between
Renaissance and baroque; it is like others who have tried to turn all of literary history to an alternation of romanticism and the Enlightenment or romanticism and neoclassicism. Wellek is against all of those. The word that is
important here is a big one, *synesthesia.* What does synesthesia mean? Synesthesia means to express one sense through another. That is, when you say

something makes a blue sound, that is a synesthesia; or a shrill color, shrill is sound, and you apply it to color. That is synesthesia. It is a combination of sensations from various senses used one for the other. Wellek writes,

> For many other writers it will be possible to see an indubitable connection between the emblematic image and their belief in the pervasive parallelism between macrocosmos and microcosmos, in some vast system of correspondences which can be expressed only by sensuous symbolism. The prevalence of synaesthesia which in the Renaissance apparently occurs only under such traditional figures as the music of the spheres, but during the baroque boldly hears colors and sees sounds, is another indication of this belief in a multiple web of interrelations, correspondences in the universe.[4]

What this means is that in the baroque there is an attempt to reconstitute the kind of unified conception of the universe that was prevalent in the Middle Ages, that you see in Dante, and that you see in the Gothic cathedrals, all centered on the figure of the Christian God and on all the symbolism attendant to him; everything connected to God in a harmonious, satisfying whole where everything has a meaning and a place. In the baroque, writers and artists try to reconstruct this set of correspondences, but this is a world that is no longer centered. It is a world that is post-Copernican, and it is a world in which Galileo is producing his theories, so it is a decentered world. So the baroque is an effort, through synesthesia—that is, to express correspondences between colors, sounds, and so forth—to reconstruct that set of correspondences, that harmonious world that is no longer available, through art, and this is what gives the baroque such tension.

I have spoken about baroque elements in Part I, particularly the grotesque in characters like Maritornes, the play of illusion and reality, and the multiplicity of fictional levels, the chiaroscuro of the episodes in the inn, and the knight himself, who is a combination of things, a grotesque combination. But Part I still contains many elements of what could still be called Renaissance aesthetics. This is particularly so in characters such as Marcela and Dorotea, whose beauty reflects Neoplatonic ideals. The same is true of some of the settings, particularly the locus amoenus, which I have mentioned several times, where Dorotea is washing her feet, in an episode in which the classical background seems to be derived from Ovid. The rewriting of classical models is very much a Renaissance feature. Nature is present. Because so much of Part I takes place outdoors, nature appears to be plentiful and orderly, except when Rocinante gets a sudden and unexpected sexual urge and provokes a row.

There is also a kind of underlying sense of optimism and mirth in Part I, even when Don Quixote is returned home in a cage, which had something carnivalesque about it—remember that he gets home on a Sunday—and, after all, the various amorous conflicts are all resolved. Dorotea is betrothed to Don Fernando, and Luscinda to Cardenio, the captive is going to marry Zoraida, Luis and Clara will unite. Don Quixote's interventions have a positive effect in the end; the commonplace about this is that Renaissance aesthetics are based on an idea of order, symmetry, and perfection obtained by the imitation of classical models and the striving for humanly attainable goals: human agency, self-fashioning, straight angles, horizontal lines meeting vertical ones, ordered repetition in the columns. All of these are Renaissance features; the repetition of all of these stories is like those columns.

Part II, however, is going to be much more baroque. Much of it takes place inside of buildings, where it is generally darker. There is a chiaroscuro quality to it, and the chiaroscuro, as I have been saying, is typical of the baroque. There are more grotesque elements made up of the disparate, the contrasting, and the ugly. Here, the key figure, about which I will be speaking in other classes, is the monster. Part II is going to take place not in inns or in nature but in lavish country and urban houses. The baroque tends to be built up, to be complex.

In Part II we have not so much nature as architecture or what I like to call arch-texture, a texture that is intensified, therefore arch-texture. The multiplicity of fictional levels is going to increase by the fact that the characters now know and discuss Part I and by the appearance of Avellaneda's apocryphal *Quixote*. A central theme, a narrative device of Part II, is going to be desengaño, disillusionment, which could be the overarching design of the plot; one could say that the whole of Part II is leading to desengaño. This is how Part II is going to end, and desengaño is perhaps the most important element of the Spanish baroque.

CHAPTER 14

Deceiving and Undeceiving

Baroque *Desengaño*

Required Readings

Cervantes, *Don Quixote,* Part II, Prologue, chaps. 1–11, pp. 483–557.

Elliott, *Imperial Spain,* 249–84.

Something I will be charting as we move through the episodes that make up Part II is how they are reminiscent of others in Part I; how, in many cases, the episodes in Part II are rewritings of episodes in Part I. This is an issue that has to be not only stated but also pondered. What does this mean? Does it make a statement about there not being any possibility of something new and original, of memory impinging on the present so strongly that you cannot really move away from it? When I discuss these episodes I will try to link them to episodes in Part I, and I hope you'll do the same as you read because the book invites you to do so. From the very beginning, when Sansón Carrasco takes over as the internal author of Part II, you realize that what he wants Don Quixote to do is to reenact Part I, to be like he was in Part I and to do the things he did in Part I. In fact, many of the characters Don Quixote and Sancho meet in Part II want them to act the way they did in Part I. Such repetition can be seen as an overarching topic in my discussions of Part II, and I hope you will consider this element as you read and think about Part II.

I am going to begin today where I left off in the last class, talking about that all-important term *desengaño*. Desengaño, as I said, is perhaps the most important concept of the Spanish baroque. Remember, baroque is essentially the seventeenth century spilling over into the eighteenth, where it becomes rococo, if you want to be more precise. Desengaño means undeceiving, opening one's eyes to reality, awakening to the truth; these are all valid translations of the term. *Engaño*, in Spanish, means 'deceit,' to be fooled; *te engaño* means 'I fool you'; *engañarse* is 'to fool oneself.'

This concept is fundamental to Part II because the whole plot of the novel seems to be moving toward disillusionment. Let me give you some definitions of *desengaño* and comment on them so that we can have as clear an idea of this concept as possible. The first is from Otis Green's book *Spain and the Western Tradition*. Green was a prolific Hispanist at the University of Pennsylvania for many years, through the forties, fifties, and even sixties, and his book is a treasure of information about the Spanish literature and culture of the Golden Age. He writes, "This *desengaño* is related to the sort of awakening to the nature of reality that the Prodigal Son must have experienced: 'I will arise and go to my father.' This waking to true awareness is called *caer en la cuenta*: to have the scales fall from one's eyes, to see things as they are. Such a state of mind is desirable." I continue with Green: "Disillusionment comes to be viewed, even to be venerated, as a sort of wisdom— the wisdom of the Stoic *sapiens*, or wise man of antiquity, who was fully aware of what constituted the *summum bonum*, the supreme good, and was utterly unenticed by everything else."[1] You know who the Stoics were, so this wise, stoic man knew what the real good was and what was not valuable. Green continues, "*Caer en la cuenta*—to come to oneself—was the phrase most used in connection with the type of *desengaño* we are considering here. It signified a passing from ignorance to knowledge, an awakening from the falsity of one's dream."[2]

You can now see that there is a dialectic, as it were, between engaño and desengaño, deceit and undeceit, deceit and disillusionment, the synthesis of which is coming to realize what the truth is. The following is from Baltasar Gracián, a Jesuit who wrote about politics, wit, and rhetoric. He lived from 1601 to 1658 and wrote a famous allegorical novel. An allegorical novel is a novel in which the characters represent abstractions—reason, truth, and so forth. Gracián's novel is called *El Criticón, The Big Critic*. Here is a quotation from that book:

> The most monstrous of all is the placing of Deceit at the world's
> front gate and Disillusionment at the exit—a disastrous handicap
> sufficient to ruin our life entirely, since . . . to make a misstep at

the beginning of life causes one to lurch headlong with greater speed each day and end up in utter perdition. Who made such an arrangement, who ordained it? Now I am more convinced than ever that all is upside down in this world. Disillusionment should stand at the world's entrance and should place himself immediately at the shoulder of the neophyte, to free him from the dangers that lie in wait for him. But since the newcomer—by an opposite and contrary arrangement—makes his first encounter with Deceit (who at the beginning presents everything to him in perverted and reversed order), he heads for the left-hand road, and strides on to destruction.[3]

As you can see, this is highly allegorical. The left-hand road; the left is always the bad, the sinister; *sinistra* means 'left' in Latin, and this is why it has that connotation. The left road is the bad road. This is what he saying. Gracián was allegorical in his mode of thinking and expression. All of Don Quixote's illusions and those of the other characters in the novel are deceits, while desengaño is what they wind up achieving or what they reach; disillusionment is realizing that life is all vanity of vanities. This is why so much of what happens in Part II is staged. Deceit is manifest in the theatricality of so many events which are made up, constructed; deceit is the dream of books that Don Quixote dreams, it is the unbroken chain of texts masking reality and even of language also masking reality.

Don Quixote's dream of books, these illusions about the romances of chivalry and the knights of old, is a deceit, and disillusionment is coming to realize that it is that, that it is nothing but a deceit. The unbroken chain of texts exists because, in Don Quixote's mind, one text leads to another, leads to another, leads to another. It is a humanist dream. The humanists, who were philologists, lovers of language, students of the classics, thought in terms of texts leading to texts, leading to texts, without ever getting to reality, and of language as something that has its own reality. What the baroque does is undermine all of that and show that it is all a dream.

The best example of these patterns of deceit and disillusionment or of going from deceit to disillusionment is the play by Pedro Calderón de la Barca *Life Is a Dream.* This is one of the classics of Spanish literature. I am very fond of Calderón de la Barca and of *Life Is a Dream* because I wrote my doctoral dissertation about that play. In *Life Is a Dream,* Prince Segismundo has been kept in a tower since birth because an omen told his father, King Basilio, that Segismundo would be a ruthless tyrant if he ever became king.

So from the time he was a baby he has grown up in a tower, cared for by Clotaldo. To put him to the test, Basilio has Segismundo drugged and brought to the palace, where, when he awakens, he is treated like a king. Confused, Segismundo acts violently; he tries to rape a woman and throws a servant off a balcony, confirming the omen, in a way. So he is drugged again and brought back to the tower, where, upon awakening, he does not know if what happened in the palace was true or just a dream. Meanwhile, the people who have found out about Segismundo's existence, the people in the kingdom, revolt and come to get him to fight against his father. Segismundo hesitates because he does not know if this is another dream but decides to go with them and act prudently and justly this time. He realizes that even in dreams it is best to do good because, if life is a dream, the only true life is the life after death. He dethrones his father but does not kill him, and he marries the woman he should marry, not the one he had lusted after during his first day in the palace—he controls his desires.

The message is that life may well be like a dream in a Platonic sense, but even so, one must behave morally. As you can see, the plot of the play, which I have simplified, goes from deceit, the first visit to the palace, to disillusionment, when Segismundo awakens back in the tower, and wisdom, when he comes to know that life is like a dream, as is political power, the trappings of government, and everything else. The only thing, by the way, that he knows was true when he awakens in the tower is his love for this woman, the only continuity is the emotion of love, and that is a Neoplatonic element in the play. It is a more complicated play than I have just made it seem here. We will have occasion to revisit it because we will see a similar story when Sancho becomes a ruler later in the *Quixote.*

My suggestion here is that the plot of the *Quixote* as a whole follows a similar outline from deceit to disillusionment, from engaño to desengaño. We will have occasion to take this matter up again when we come to the end of the novel but keep it in mind also when you read the wonderful story "The Glass Graduate," *El licenciado vidriera,* which you will read for next week. Next week we have a big week: we have "The Glass Graduate," and also we are going to be doing two of the main essays in the *Casebook,* the ones by Spitzer and by Auerbach, about whom I spoke in the last class. So you should be prepared. "The Enchanted Dulcinea," an episode we are going to be discussing today, is the object of Auerbach's essay. This is so we can keep on a course of not going from deceit to disillusionment but to be wide-eyed about everything from the very beginning.

Let us begin today as we move to the episodes in the *Quixote* that include the discussion of Don Quixote and Sancho about knights-errant and saints. First, there is the exordium by Cide Hamete Benengeli and comments by the narrator about what the translator said or what the narrator said about Cide Hamete Benengeli, but the reader does not know where these comments appeared—we talked about that in the last class. They are not in the text, as it were, but in a sort of metatext or virtual text that is like a running commentary about the composition of the novel. This is one new feature in Part II that I mentioned before.

Sancho subjects Don Quixote to a rigorous cross-examination and gets him to say that saints are better than knights. Sancho has rhetorical skills, as does Sansón Carrasco, who earlier had used forensic rhetoric to ease Don Quixote's sally. Sansón may have acquired those skills in Salamanca, but where did Sancho learn them or anything else? Where did Sancho learn rhetoric or all of this culture he has in his mind? I think the intimation is that Sancho has learned a great deal not just from Don Quixote, which he does, as we have seen, but also from hearing sermons at church, which he mentions in his discussion with his wife.

The church is, on this level, part of popular culture or, better, a vehicle for the popularization of culture. Sancho may not know how to read, but he has a culture in his head that he has absorbed from the preachers. This is one way to explain the evolution of Sancho and his increased intellectual and rhetorical powers, although his relationship with Don Quixote is obviously the most important. The discussion per se, the theme, the topic of the discussion, is quite serious here, too, because it plays into religious debates of the time in Spain, whose background is the Reformation. The debates have to do with good works and with predestination and free will; Protestantism sided with predestination, Catholicism, or at least one element within Catholicism, the most important one, with free will. If you had free will you could, through good actions, gain access to heaven.

These are debates that to us, in this our secular age, seem vacuous, but they were not in the sixteenth and seventeenth centuries at all; they were of the utmost importance. Thus in this discussion the question is not only about arms versus letters, which is a set discussion piece—although there is a reminiscence of that here—but also about good actions for their own sake and good actions for the sake of glory. Sancho shows that the knight's actions seem to be of this second kind, actions to gain glory, and this feeds into the topic of desengaño and engaño. To perform actions for the sake of glory is to perform actions for the sake of deceit, of engaño.

Don Quixote counters by saying that there were knights who were saints. I suppose he refers to Saint George particularly, and he adds that not everyone can be a monk. Cervantes is, I think, pitting his relativistic, liberal take on life, which is not antireligious, against the religious zealots of the time. So the discussion has a contemporary relevancy that is political as well as religious, and this is connected to what I said in one of my earlier lectures about the fact that Part II is the first political novel. Religion and politics were intertwined in the Spain of the sixteenth and seventeenth centuries, with all of the caveats we have learned by reading Elliott. The discussion about this issue by the two characters is consonant with the political side of Part II.

Sancho also demonstrates, as he has before and as he will increasingly do, that he is endowed with natural reason, which can allow him to understand sufficiently the most difficult questions. Natural reason is a medieval concept that survives through the Renaissance and reaches the Enlightenment. It underscores God's gift of sufficient reason to every individual, no matter what her or his station in life, to understand the fundamental questions of life. This is an important topic in Part II.

One can see that because Sancho has been influenced by Don Quixote their arguments are like discussions the knight could be having within himself or with himself. What is the significance of their mutual influence? I think it is to propose a concept of the self as relational, not as individual or isolated. Not so much "I think, therefore I am" as "I relate to others, and my self emerges from that commerce or dialogue with them." This is what the *Quixote,* through the relationship between these two characters, seems to be suggesting. This is a profound philosophical statement, but it is also crucial in the development of modern fiction.

Think of Huck and Jim in *The Adventures of Huckleberry Finn,* of their dialogues and their influence on each other; think of Holmes and Dr. Watson, to give you an example from popular culture; and even of those Faulknerian characters that seem to overlap and blend into each other, to the point that you sometimes do not know who is really speaking in these Faulkner novels. You do not know because his characters' consciousnesses are blended and their individuality has been eroded. This is what I am suggesting is happening here between Don Quixote and Sancho, and why this debate about knights and saints is one that Don Quixote could have had within himself.

This discussion also brings up Don Quixote's knowledge of classical Rome and its architecture. Rome is the city par excellence in the Renaissance, and its architecture was the model for Renaissance architects. Remember that Cervantes spent quite a bit of time in Italy, so when he speaks of Rome he is speaking not only of things he has read about in books, but also things he has seen. This shows that Don Quixote is a humanist, that he has read beyond the romances of chivalry.

In Part II we are beginning to enlarge Don Quixote's library; we cannot reduce it to the romances of chivalry we found with the barber and priest in the scrutiny of the books; he had read other things. Don Quixote's knowledge of Rome also anticipates Part II's projection beyond Spain. I say "beyond Spain" because as Don Quixote and Sancho go to Barcelona they are moving to a part of Spain that is almost not Spain, Catalonia being, even today, a part of Spain that is independent in its culture and has, in fact, tried to become politically independent several times. Also, the battles you will see at the end of the book beyond the shores of Barcelona move beyond the borders of Spain, so this projection toward Italy is important in that respect.

This discussion also points out that architecture is an important issue in Part II. It is important because, as I mentioned before, a great deal of Part II takes place indoors, in houses and in mansions. In Part II we have less of those two places I mentioned in Part I: the *despoblado*, the unpopulated— remember that that is even a legal concept, that area where the law does not reach—and the *soledades*, which I did not emphasize but which you must have seen referred to many times. You are in the soledades when you are out in the wild. There is less out-of-doors in Part II and more shelter, more architecture, and this is why the discussion on Roman architecture is important, above all, in the context of humanism; Renaissance art copying Rome's architecture.

This emphasis on cities brings us to the entry into El Toboso. The third sally takes place at night. A day goes by, and then, after sunset, they enter the village of El Toboso. Taking place at night, this entrance anticipates much of the mood of Part II. Part I began at dawn. Don Quixote and Sancho want to arrive at El Toboso at night so as not to be noticed. It is a night that is called in the Spanish original "una noche entreclara," "a night that was not quite a dark one." I underline this because of the concept of chiaroscuro I mentioned before as something proper to the baroque. "Una noche entreclara." There is darkness and there are sounds: dogs barking, donkeys braying, swine grunting, cats meowing, a plough being dragged; there is an eeriness to this town that is augmented by these sounds. The farmhand they meet is singing a song about a great defeat, which adds to the omens, the bad omens. Sounds, as opposed to visual signs, appear before them. In Part I we had the fulling hammers, but in Part II there will be many more sounds, as you will see. The sounds here are scary by virtue of the fact that you cannot see their source, you can only hear them.

Seeing is going to be a different problem in Part II because of the increasing darkness. This is the first time Don Quixote and Sancho come into a town, and their arrival anticipates the entry into Barcelona, a city, a great city, toward the end of the novel. What is the significance of this? The novelistic genre, which develops from the *Quixote,* will be for the most part an urban genre, a genre often about cities, modern cities, and Don Quixote's influence on the history of the novel includes this urban part of the *Quixote,* particularly, as you will see, when you get to the Barcelona chapters. Here, El Toboso seems like a haunted city, one with blind alleys and peopled by strangers like the farmhand, who does not know anything about it because he is an outsider who cannot give them directions.

There are deep resonances, to me, of Spanish mysticism in this dark night of the soul, to echo Saint John of the Cross, the great Spanish mystical poet; it is the name of one of his great poems, "Noche oscura del alma." This episode of the *Quixote* evokes the depths of the soul in the darkness of night. Sancho is actually looking for a memory that is a lie: the story he made up about going to El Toboso. He is trying to remember something he knows does not exist, a made-up memory, while Don Quixote is looking for a nonexistent lady who is the object of his devotion. Both protagonists are searching for intangibles in the dark of night, as if it were within their troubled spirits. This is the impression that the dark El Toboso conveys. Right away we come across a line that has inspired much useless commentary. The line in Spanish reads, "Con la iglesia hemos dado, Sancho." "We have chanced upon the church, Sancho," our translation reads (II, 9, 540). Looking for Dulcinea, they have come upon the church.

Some modern readers have seen in that sentence a hidden meaning, that is, that Cervantes is decrying the interference of the church in all affairs. "Con la iglesia hemos dado, Sancho" has even become a standard phrase in Spanish to say that one has come up against some obstacle, particularly upon being denied something or other. I think that interpretation is because of the rhythm created by the way the sentence is written: not "Hemos dado con la iglesia, Sancho," but "Con la iglesia hemos dado, Sancho." It does not have anything to do with the church being an obstacle. This is why I said that the debate is useless, yet it has remained in the Spanish language as a ready-made phrase. I think what is significant here is that Dulcinea's castle has morphed into the church; that in looking in the dark for Dulcinea's castle they have found a church, in the gloom where things are difficult to identify. Sancho is scared because he knows that cemeteries are near churches, and he does not want to be in a cemetery at night. This could be a telling transformation, perhaps an indication that Don Quixote's love is a kind of religion or, more likely, given what will happen over and over again in Part II, is an intimation of death, of which there are many in this eerie chapter. This ghostly night in El Toboso, the first adventure in Part II, sets the tone for the rest of the novel.

Now to the chapter on the enchanted Dulcinea. It is notable not only because it inspired Auerbach's famous essay but also because it is a chapter that will play an important role later, in one of the most famous episodes of Part II and of the whole *Quixote,* the adventure of the Cave of Montesinos, where the enchanted Dulcinea will reappear.

First of all, it is one episode in which we notice, once again but very dramatically, an exchange of roles between Don Quixote and Sancho. The first time was when Sancho played the role of Don Quixote to his wife, who was playing Sancho's part in that hilarious dialogue that they had, but here the exchange of roles is much more dramatic. The first thing to notice is Sancho's Shakespearean monologue, which dramatizes his inner conflicts and reveals his apprehensions about Don Quixote. He does not quite know what to do; Sancho here is like a rustic Hamlet: "To be, or not to be." He weighs the various options he has and opts for trying to fool Don Quixote via the trick of turning a peasant woman into Dulcinea. Sancho is becoming a fuller character and increasingly important to the novel. He is one of the pranksters who fool Don Quixote. He will be, in this sense, like Sansón Carrasco and like the duke's butler, who will appear later. Also, Sancho is separated from his master here, as when he went to deliver the letter in Part I, but this separation prefigures several important episodes in Part II in which they are again separated and Sancho becomes the protagonist of his own part of the novel. But the most important thing about this Shakespearean monologue, as I call it, is that it exposes Sancho's inner world, his world of doubts.

Then there is the actual inversion of characters: Sancho is the one trying to convince his master that what they see is not really reality but something drawn from the chivalric romances, and he does a pretty good imitation of Don Quixote's own rhetoric in trying to convince him that this wench is Dulcinea. So reality, which Don Quixote perceives as it is, conspires, spontaneously or as arranged by someone, to appear as unreal, literary, artificial. Hence the episode depends on the memory of Part I and of similar episodes. Here, I think the incident in the background is that of the windmills. It was then that Sancho said, "What giants?" Here it is Don Quixote saying, "Where is Dulcinea? What do you mean, Dulcinea?"

The peasant lass cast as Dulcinea reacts to Sancho's rhetoric a little bit like the prostitutes in the first inn reacted to Don Quixote, though the prostitutes in the first inn were kinder to Don Quixote than these peasant women are to Sancho. They are upset because they think upper-class men are making fun of them. This is a truly hilarious event, one that makes me laugh every time I reread it, particularly the part about Dulcinea smelling of garlic. But there is also the issue of Dulcinea's bodily hair, specifically, in Don Quixote's interpretation, her pubic hair. Sancho says,

> "From her smell we'd at least have been able to work out what was hidden under that ugly outside although, to tell you the truth, I never did see her ugliness but only her beauty, which was boosted no end by a mole she had on the right side of her lip, a bit like a moustache, with seven or eight blond hairs like threads of gold growing out of it, more than a handsbreadth long."
>
> "According to the rules of correspondence between facial moles and bodily moles," said Don Quixote, "Dulcinea must have another mole on the thick of the thigh on the same side as the one on her face; but hairs of the length that you have indicated are very long indeed for moles."
>
> "Well, I can tell you," Sancho replied, "they were there all right, just as if she'd been born with them.
>
> "I believe you, my friend," replied Don Quixote, "because nature has given Dulcinea nothing that is not complete and perfect; and so, if she had a hundred moles like the one you have described, on her they would not be moles but moons—resplendent moons and shining stars." (II, 10, 550)

The description is remindful of Maritornes, but there is something specific about a hairy Dulcinea. Bodily hair, a lot of hair, was taken then as an indication of a heightened sexuality, of a strong sexual drive. There are other hints of bodily hair on Dulcinea and other women, moustaches and so forth. Look for them as you read the book, and, believe me, they are there, I have not invented them. These and other hints reveal a story behind the story here, which I have hinted at before.

What lurks beneath Don Quixote's courtly love style for Dulcinea is the sexual desire of an aristocrat (even if only a minor one) for a peasant lass, presumed to be of ardent sexuality, who promises to provide more satisfaction than the women of his class. There is a literary tradition behind this that reaches back to the Spanish ballads, but that is also quite alive in Cervantes' time. At least two of Don Juan's conquests—Don Juan is the notorious womanizer who first appeared in Tirso de Molina's play—were lower-class women: one a peasant and the other a fisherwoman.

The Dulcinea in this scene also underscores her physical prowess by the way she mounts her donkey. She takes a little run back to gather some momentum and leaps onto it from behind, riding it astride like a man. It is a highly suggestive and vulgar gesture she makes, one that I find absolutely hilarious. Sancho quips, "Our lady and mistress is nimbler than a hobby-hawk, and she could teach the best rider from Cordova or Mexico how to jump on to a horse Arab-style!" (II, 10, 549). Also, that she smells of raw garlic reveals her coarseness and also her proximity to food: food and sex go together. Now, I know that garlic does not sound very sexy to anybody anymore, but this is the intimation here. The whole transformation of Dulcinea will leave a deep imprint in the knight's subconscious, as we shall see in the episode of Montesinos's Cave.

But now Don Quixote and Sancho are about to meet theater on the road, this road that in Part II appears to be full not so much of real characters as of characters and objects playing roles or disguised as something other than what they are. They now meet the cart of the Parliament of Death, which is a cart carrying actors who have finished putting on a play in one town and are going to another nearby to repeat the performance; hence, they have not changed out of their costumes. The play they stage is a kind you have met before, though briefly, in the Grisóstomo and Marcela episode of Part I. In that episode, Grisóstomo was said to write *autos sacramentales*. These are religious plays performed on the day of Corpus Christi, the feast in honor of the Eucharist or communion, celebrated on a Thursday on the sixtieth day after Easter.

Therefore, it is coherent with the implicit chronology of the novel; the action is taking place in summer, so Corpus Christi, communion, the Eucharist, is celebrated in this feast every year, and part of the feast was the performance of those plays, which always deal with the topic of the Eucharist, the mystery of the Eucharist, the transformation of Christ's body and blood into wine and bread. They usually have plots drawn from scripture but some are from classical mythology. These autos were a medieval retention in every sense, and now think about what I said about the baroque going back to the Middle Ages, jumping back over the Renaissance; this is a medieval retention, the auto sacramental. They were one-act plays performed on carts. The actors are carrying themselves on the cart, and they are also carrying, with the cart, the stage because the way these autos were performed was, if you have a town square, the carts were put there and the performance took place on the carts. Elaborate props and scenery were created on them because these plays represented cosmic events, including the universe, sin, grace, Satan, and so forth. These would be represented as allegorical figures. Then, when the play was finished—this was a modest play with only one cart—the cart would move on to the next town.

The plays were simple enough that all of the people could understand them but sophisticated in versification, imagery, and theological content. Calderón de la Barca was the most famous author of autos sacramentales, but many other poets and playwrights wrote them, including Lope de Vega, the author of the play mentioned in this episode, *Las cortes de la Muerte,* which is a real one-act play by Lope de Vega translated here as *The Parliament of Death.* In the play, Man, with a capital *M*—remember, it is an allegorical play—is subjected to a trial after having been tempted by the Devil—this is why the Devil appears in this episode. Another figure is that of Madness, represented by the actor who spooks Rocinante with his bells and bladders. He is the one who comes onstage after Don Quixote and the Devil have had their dialogue. He has a stick—they did not have rubber balloons because there was no rubber to make them, so they made balloons out of the bladders of slain animals—with bladders and bells. He plays Madness. The most famous auto was one by Calderón called *The Great Theater of the World,* whose theme was that the world is a stage where man performs life, as if it were a play, before going on to the real life after death at the end of the play. The one performed by the players in this episode of the *Quixote,* who, by the way, were a real company of actors of the time, closely follows the lines of *The Great Theater of the World,* but the conceit here is that of a trial of Man. This is what is in the background of this scene. Theatricality is an important element in Part II because of what I mentioned; theatricality is part of the deceit that would lead to desengaño.

Death, who appears here as part of the ensemble of actors—Death was an allegorical figure that often appeared in these plays—is also important in Part II. This is another medieval retention, as is the Devil. Everyone is in costume in this scene, including Don Quixote. Reality is already a play, an illusion; there is no need for Don Quixote to misinterpret it. But notice the subtlety that the players then assume their roles in reality. Madness begins to play Madness in the reality of Don Quixote. The Devil plays a trick on Sancho, and the presence of Death, even in allegorical dress, is frightening. Reality is buried beneath a layer of various forms of representation. A man dressed as a literary character meets men and women dressed as literary characters. The Devil, who steals Sancho's donkey, parodies Don Quixote in his fall from Rocinante. Here is a madman facing an actor playing the role of Madness, as if reality were offering Don Quixote a mirror of his own deranged self. This is something that will happen over and over again in

Part II, and we will soon find another example, when Don Quixote meets the Knight of the Mirrors. Life is playacting, as Don Quixote says, using a word you are now familiar with. He says: "Y ahora digo que es menester tocar las apariencias con la mano para dar lugar al desengaño." Which I would render as, "And I say that you need to lay your hand on appearances in order to be undeceived."

Cervantes is punning here because in the Spanish of the seventeenth century *apariencias* also meant 'stage props.' When Calderón wrote the instructions for the carpenters to make scenery for the autos, he called them "Memoria de apariencias," or 'Account of Stage Props.' With this pun Cervantes is underlining the theatrical quality of this episode and of "reality." There are two important things to remember about this scene. First, that Don Quixote meets an image of his madness, something that will happen throughout Part II. It is kind of a point about madness for us readers, too: madness reflects madness. Second, we must remember the presence of death, which is a warning against the deceits offered by life. Death devalues all of the allures of life through its presence. We have met it before, in El Toboso when Don Quixote and Sancho bump up against the church with the cemetery nearby. Finally, notice the loop of this little story: this episode goes from deceit to disillusionment, from engaño to desengaño. If Micomicona and the process by which her story was concocted were like a representation of representation, the episode of the cart of the Parliament of Death is representation in motion, or actually, one could say, representation on wheels.

CHAPTER 15

Don Quixote's Doubles

Required Readings

Cervantes, *Don Quixote*, Part II, chaps. 12–21, pp. 557–630.
Cervantes, "The Glass Graduate." In *Exemplary Stories*, 106–30.
Auerbach, Erich. "The Enchanted Dulcinea." In *Casebook*,
35–61.
Elliott, *Imperial Spain*, 285–320.
Spitzer, Leo. "Linguistic Perspectivism in the *Don Quijote*." In
Casebook, 163–216.

I want to return briefly to *desengaño* because there may be some confusion caused by 'disillusionment,' the English word used to translate the term, which is an approximation, as all translations are. *Disillusionment* can mean disenchantment and disappointment, words that have a negative connotation, whereas *desengaño* does not quite have that connotation. At worst, it could mean 'resignation,' meaning, "I was resigned to finding out that such-and-such a person was not as good as I thought him or her to be." Remember the quotation from Otis Green that I read to you, in which desengaño was thought of as the summum bonum, the ultimate good desired by the Stoic wise man. Baroque desengaño is a positive condition at which the individual arrives after having shed the scales from his eyes and learned of the deceitfulness of appearances, of the mystifying allure of all he had taken to be valuable. "Everything that glitters is not gold" is what the individual learns, having gone through the process of engaño, that is, deceit, and desengaño, to put it in the simplest of terms. What I suggested, moreover, is that the plot of the *Quixote* and some of the stories embedded in Part II go through a similar unfolding from engaño to desengaño. We will be following this process in the episodes that we will be dealing with during the rest of the semester, some of which are the culminating episodes not only of Part II but of the entire book.

Let us first turn our attention to two critics whose essays you are reading this week in the *Casebook.* This is the high point of the *Casebook,* the two essays by Auerbach and Spitzer. We have discussed Auerbach's main thesis in *Mimesis,* his famous book, the thesis about the Christian mixture of the sublime and the low style in the New Testament, and how this led to the emergence and development of realism and eventually to the novel and to a book like the *Quixote.* This mixture of the sublime and low style, an idea Auerbach derives from Saint Augustine and the church fathers, the patristic tradition, was a break from the strict separation between high and low styles in the classical tradition.

This Christian response is to the classical division of styles, derived from Aristotle and from Roman rhetorical theory. The mixture of the transcendent and the low style was exemplified by Christ's passion, through which the drama of man's everyday life assumes the most profound meaning: life does not end in the brief span of worldly existence; eternity is present in the passion as a message of hope. Auerbach's application of this theory to the *Quixote* leads him to the belief that the *Quixote* is essentially a funny book, as you have read in the essay, "The Enchanted Dulcinea," an interpretation for which Auerbach was excoriated by Hispanists, particularly Spanish ones for whom the *Quixote* was a profound, transcendental book. Although many were motivated by a nationalistic interpretation of Cervantes, whom they saw as the highest example of Spanish genius, and his protagonist, as the very representative of the fatherland, they were not entirely wrong in their reactions.

What happened in Spain was that the *Quixote* was canonized, turned into a classic, in the eighteenth century, and then, by the early nineteenth century, during the romantic period, it was exalted as the highest point of Spanish genius and the highest representative of the Spanish language, a book in which the spirit of Spanishness was embedded. This highly nationalistic reading of the *Quixote* prevailed and still prevails in some quarters. The people who held this view of the *Quixote* were outraged by Auerbach's reading of the *Quixote* as essentially a funny book. They were not misguided in their reactions. By now it should be clear to you that a great deal of the *Quixote* is very deep and serious, both about life in general and about literature.

Auerbach's analysis, however, is revealing of how the low style, particularly in Sancho and other low-class characters, plays such a crucial role in the farcical episodes in the *Quixote*. Besides, in the modern period we are no longer familiar with this separation of styles, high and low styles or anything like that, and it is instructive to read Auerbach, who was steeped in it, even when, in my view, he goes astray. Auerbach's problem is that he cannot escape his own theoretical scheme, which equates seriousness only with tragedy. Don Quixote can be serious without being tragic, and in fact this is one of his most important lessons and most innovative qualities of the literature that emerges in the wake of the *Quixote*.

To say that Cervantes does not deal with the serious issues of his time is pure nonsense. To claim that the book is, above all, a farce is also nonsense. Besides, a novel's worth should not be gauged by how faithfully it represents reality, if such a thing can be gauged at all. Auerbach is wrong when he says that Don Quixote's idée fixe has no contact with reality and that it only causes confusion. On the contrary, his idée fixe serves, by contrast with reality, to clarify many things around him. But there are salvageable parts of Auerbach's essay, which is why I included it in the *Casebook*. Vladimir Nabokov, on the other hand, the great Russian novelist, has a horrible book on the *Quixote*, taken from a series of lectures he gave at Harvard.[1] The book is interesting only because Nabokov wrote it, but he says really outrageous things like there is no reflection of the Spain of Cervantes' time in the *Quixote*. What? Nabokov was a great writer but not a great critic.

I think the first salvageable thing in Auerbach's essay is his reaction against romantic criticism and the tendency to overinterpret, whatever that means, ultimately. Defining his position, Auerbach writes the following:

> For centuries—and especially since the romanticists—many things have been read into him [Cervantes] which he hardly foreboded, let alone intended. Such transforming and transcendent interpretations are often fertile. A book like *Don Quijote* disassociates itself from its author's intention and leads a life of its own. Don Quijote shows a new face to every age which enjoys him. Yet the historian [meaning himself]—whose task it is to define the place of a given work in historical continuity—must endeavor insofar as that is still possible, to attain a clear under-

standing of what the work meant to its author and his contemporaries. (58)

This is the dream of the philologists and the critics steeped in philology, namely, that they can actually get back to the meaning of the work in the period in which the author was writing and discern what his intentions were. We are not so sure anymore. Peter Russell, an English Hispanist of some note, in his book called *Don Quixote as a Funny Book,* follows Auerbach and is among those who styled themselves as the "hard school" of Cervantes criticism, based mostly in England, and whose hardness, in my view, is mostly of the brain. Just because Cervantes' contemporaries found the book funny or just because of what Cervantes said about the comic, it is impoverishing to see the *Quixote* in this light, particularly when the comic is not defined. If the comedic arises, as it does in the *Quixote,* from the toils of a mind out of sorts with the modern world, then it is a comedy of the highest form of seriousness. Comedy can be serious and profound, and it is so in the *Quixote.* Contemporaries often misread works written in their time, obviously, and authors' intentions are extremely difficult to ascertain. I will say more about that later.

Leo Spitzer was another great critic of the German philological school. He, too, escaped from Nazi Germany and preceded Auerbach in the chair at the University of Istanbul. Spitzer wound up at Johns Hopkins University, not at Yale, alas, like Auerbach. Spitzer was known to be irascible and belligerent in the defense of his points of view and wrote vicious reviews of books with which he disagreed. For example, Stephen Gilman's book on *Celestina* was shredded by Spitzer in an angry review. Spitzer was more thoroughly grounded in philology and linguistics than Auerbach. He was a philologist and a linguist, spoke many modern languages, and knew practically all of the classical ones. He was a very, very, very learned man and quite brilliant.

Spitzer believes that one can get at the core of a work of literature by starting from something marginal, on the periphery or surface, like a word, and pursuing it all the way to its center; he believed that a detail can, if properly analyzed, yield a comprehensive interpretation of the work. The geometric metaphors—periphery, circle, center—are a bit naïve here on my part. We use metaphors in writing theory and in writing criticism, and they appear naïve when we think about them. We learned to look for metaphors in criticism through the work of the great deconstructionist Paul de Man, who was a professor here at Yale whom I admired. So the geometric metaphors are facile, as is Spitzer's emphasis on discovering the personality of the author or his worldview, his *Weltanschauung*, to use the German word. He wants to get at the psychology of the author. These are approximations that Michel Foucault would argue limit the possible meanings of a work by reducing it to the alleged intention of its author.

If you say, "These were the author's intentions," you create a kind of fence around a work, and there can be no meanings beyond what you assume those intentions to be. But I believe that what Spitzer is trying to find is the "Cervantean," which to him is a point of confluence between form and content that makes for a coherent, overarching meaning. Since language is, after all, the primary material of a literary work, I believe Spitzer's work is a good lesson to critics who would leap to hasty interpretations without having a detailed knowledge of the text. That language is the primary material of a literary work might seem obvious, but it is a very complicated statement to make, because one could say that paint is the primary material of painting, and that does not get you very far. In the case of language it does; not as far as Spitzer would believe, but I think it does.

In the case of the *Quixote,* Spitzer accomplishes his task by meticulous work on polynomasia. You have these words in your *Casebook.* I know they are jawbreakers: polynomasia, multiple names; and polyetymology, multiple origins of words, meaning multiplicity of names and multiplicity of word origins that are present in the scenes he analyzes. Spitzer equates the multiplicity implicit in these words to the perspectivism inherent in the interplay of varied views in the novel by several characters—various characters and various different points of view—and this is reflected in the multiplicity of etymologies and in the multiplicity of names given to characters and to things.

The differences of opinion among the characters are evinced through the use of language. The key term in the novel is the portmanteau word Sancho uses to mediate the dispute about the barber's basin, the *baciyelmo,* or the 'basinelmet,' in English, by which he attempts to convey the conflicting points of view about the object. According to Webster's, a portmanteau word—James Joyce was famous for making them up—is a word that is a combination of two words in form and meaning, like the word *smog,* which is a combination of *smoke* and *fog.* Joyce uses them in funny ways: a passenger in Joyce is the *pas encore,* which in French means 'not yet.' Of course, a passenger is a *pas encore* because he has not gotten there yet; this is the kind of thing Joyce does. Baciyelmo, basinelmet, is a portmanteau word. Spitzer makes quite a bit out of that. But Spitzer argues that behind this multiplicity there is Cervantes, the creator of this whole artistic machine. He stands over all of the games of authorship and all of the ironies. That is, you can think of it as Cervantes; and then all of the polynomasia and all of the polyetymology are contained in this figure of Cervantes, the author, who is the author of all of the ironies and all of these games. Cervantes, Spitzer argues, is no relativist when it comes to morals—we saw this already—and perspectivism and irony are inherent in a Christian position, as Morón Arroyo argued, which is humble by definition, meaning I do not know enough and I will never know enough. Behind Cervantes, the creator, there is God, whom Cervantes never denies. So there will be God above Cervantes.

Spitzer provides a convincing historical scheme. During the Middle Ages there was a correspondence between words and things, names and characters, which is prevalent in the readings of scripture. In the Renaissance there is, on the other hand, a world of words, a word-world, to use my own portmanteau word. A world of words, one connecting or leading to the next by metonymy, and a book-world, a world made up of books, like Alonso Quixano's, who, as a result, becomes Don Quixote by inhabiting that book-world or that world of books. In the baroque there is a phantasmagoria of words that are like dreams and reveal the deceit of the world, including that of language. Here, in this world of desengaño, is where we find Cervantes, particularly the Cervantes of 1615. So Middle Ages, Renaissance, and baroque; correspondence of words to things, of words to words, and then of words that are deceitful and purveyors of engaño, leading to desengaño.

I am very interested in this because I think it is useful for us as readers and as students of literature, particularly the "Cervantean," according to Auerbach and Spitzer. The most interesting part of Auerbach's essay is precisely when he tries to define the Cervantean, *lo cervantino,* which can be compared with Spitzer's effort to come to a similar overall formulation. Theoreticians and critics can say there is no such thing as the Cervantean, yet there is. If you have read the *Quixote* and you know literary history, you know what belongs to the world of Cervantes. A great writer creates a world of his or her own; it is a set of plots, ideas, tropes that has some coherence and that can be identified. If you have read Marcel Proust, you know what I mean. You read one Proustian sentence, his long, flowing sentences, and you know immediately you are reading Proust. You read a sentence by Borges, with his refined irony, and you know you are reading Borges, or you read, "Many years later, as he faced the firing squad, Colonel Aureliano Buendía was to remember that distant afternoon when his grandfather took him to discover ice" and can tell at once that it is the beginning of *One Hundred Years of Solitude.*

In defining the Cervantean, Auerbach begins by giving up. He says, "The 'peculiarly Cervantean' cannot be described in words." But then he says, "First of all it is something spontaneously sensory: a vigorous capacity for the vivid visualization of very different people in very varied situations, for the vivid realization and expression of what thoughts enter their minds, what emotions fill their hearts, and what words come to their lips." These quotations from Auerbach were originally written in German, and German prose is very complicated, and it shows in the translation. Later he says, "And just as sensory is his [Cervantes'] capacity to think up or hit upon ever new combinations of people and events" (59).

I think Auerbach is right when he says that. He goes back to the idea of the mad gentleman running into people, and he says, "What attracted Cervantes was the possibility [this situation] offered for multifariousness and effects of perspective, the mixture of the fanciful and everyday elements in the subject, its malleability, elasticity, adaptability" (59–60). He finally proclaims the following:

> [The Cervantean] is an attitude—an attitude toward the world, and hence also toward the subject matter of his art—in which bravery and equanimity play a major part. Together with the delight he takes in the multifariousness of his sensory play there is in him a certain Southern [here meaning Southern European, not the American South] reticence and pride. This prevents him from taking the play very seriously. He looks at it; he shapes it; he finds it diverting; it is also intended to afford the reader refined intellectual diversion. (60)

He goes back over this: "The theme of the mad country gentleman who undertakes to revive knight-errantry gave Cervantes an opportunity to present the world as play, in that spirit of multiple perspective, non-judging and even non-questioning neutrality, which is a brave form of wisdom."[2] There is something, I think, also quite perceptive there. That is, that Cervantes is like a puppet master, like Master Pedro in the episode you are about to read, and he presents all of these many characters in action and stands back without passing judgment.

Spitzer, on the other hand, concludes with the following:

This means that, in our novel [the *Quixote*], things are represented not for what they are in themselves, but only as things
spoken about or thought about; and this involves breaking the
narrative presentation into two points of view. There can be no
certainty about the "unbroken" reality of events; the only unques-
tionable truth on which the reader may depend is the will of the
artist who chose to break up a multivalent reality into different
perspectives. In other words, perspectivism suggests an Archimedean principle [something on which the whole thing rests]
outside of the plot—and the Archimedes must be Cervantes
himself. (181)

One more quotation from Spitzer: "And we may see in Cervantes' two-fold
treatment of the problem of nicknames [polynomasia] another example of
his Baroque attitude (what is true, what is a dream?)—this time, toward
language. Is not human language, also, *vanitas vanitatum*?" (182). This is
Spitzer's synthesis, his conclusion after his thorough, brilliant analysis of
the novel.

In his glorification of the author, Spitzer does not take into account
Cervantes' errors; his famous oversights, which bespeak a flawed creator,
not godlike in any sense, hence pushing the whole issue of point of view to
the edge of the abyss of madness, since the final authority would be flawed.
Moreover, Cervantes plays so much with the author's lack of authority that
one has finally to take him at face value and agree that not even he has the
final authority over the book we read. I think Cervantes would have agreed
with this.

The same is true for Auerbach. My answer, as you will see in my essay
in the *Casebook,* is Ginés's cross-eyedness. Ginés is a figure of the author and
a figure of the modern author. He has pawned his book, he wants to make
money from it, he is from the low classes. He is cross-eyed, and this reveals
that there is perspectivism from within an assumed unified self. That is, that
this figure of the author here cannot be in possession of the truth because,
being cross-eyed, his view of reality is multiple and conflictive. Conflictive
because there are two eyes, not a single point of view: his two nonconverging eyes mean two separate visions. We will talk about that when we reach
the puppet play that Ginés de Pasamonte puts on later in Part II. So the author is multiple within himself, his eyes work independently of each other,
as it were; he is congenitally incapable of providing a single, cogent point
of view.

Now we turn to the assigned episodes in the *Quixote*. I will be looking into how much each resembles an episode in Part I, to what extent these episodes are rewritings of others that have already taken place in the first book. We will also see that a thread running through these episodes is the appearance of doubles of Don Quixote. The first is in the episode that is called, in your translation, "The Episode of the Brave Knight of the Spangles," but *espejo*, the original, really means 'mirrors.' So I say Knight of the Mirrors just to be consistent with the Spanish "Caballero de los espejos," 'Knight of the Mirrors.'

This episode brings to mind that of the fight of Don Quixote with the Basque in Part I, because you do have an actual combat. The most significant aspect of this incident is that in it Don Quixote meets his mirror image and defeats it. Sansón Carrasco has decided that the best way to subdue Don Quixote is to meet him at his own level, mostly by reenacting Part I in the way that Don Quixote has reenacted—and still reenacts—the romances of chivalry. Don Quixote will fight a copy of himself modeled after his own mad inventions, a copy rich in details. Notice that Dulcinea here is Casildea de Vandalia. Vandalia means Andalusia, land of Vandals; the Vandals were one of the Germanic peoples that invaded the peninsula with the collapse of the Roman Empire. Carrasco's getup as a knight-errant is quite something. He has outdone Don Quixote: "Don Quixote looked at his own adversary and found that his helmet was already in place with the visor down, so that he couldn't see his face, but he observed that he was a well-built man, not very tall. Over his armour he was wearing a surcoat or tabard of what seemed to be the finest cloth of gold, sprinkled with glittering spangles like little moons, which made him look extremely elegant and dashing; over his helmet fluttered many green, yellow and white plumes" (II, 14, 574).

The translation struggles with *lunas*, the word used for mirrors in the original, "muchas lunas de resplandecientes espejos," which contains that word, a most important suggestion in the passage. In Spanish, *la luna del espejo* is the reflecting part of the mirror. But *luna* also means 'moon,' and moon leads to lunacy, to madness. Sansón is the Knight of the Moons, the Knight of Lunacy, the Knight of Madness, which is quite appropriate because in trying to cure Don Quixote's madness, he is acting like a madman, like a lunatic. The moon is also the celestial body of reflected light, the same as the Knight of the Mirrors; Sansón, in this getup, is a reflection of Don Quixote. If Don Quixote came close enough to Sansón, he would be able to see himself reflected on the little mirrors. As in the episode of the Parliament of

Death, Don Quixote has met here a mirror image of his madness. It is more than just a reflection, that is, he is reflected in the Knight of the Moons who is acting like him, and he is also reflected in his armor, being reflected back from those little mirrors on Sansón's costume.

Sancho has also met his double in Tomé Cecial, whose false nose is a prodigious example of the grotesque, which is such a prevalent feature of Part II:

> But as soon as the light of day allowed objects to be seen and dis-
> tinguished, what first presented itself to Sancho Panza's gaze was
> the Squire of the Forest's nose, which was so large that almost
> all his body lay in its shadow. It is said to have been of vast size,
> hooked, and covered in warts, purple in colour like an aubergine,
> hanging down a couple of inches below his mouth; and its size,
> colour, warts and hook made the squire's face so ugly that when
> Sancho saw it his hands and feet began to tremble like a child
> with convulsions, and he resolved to take two hundred wallops
> before letting his anger be roused to make him fight the monster.
> (II, 14, 574)

Notice the exaggerated dimensions and utter hideousness of the nose, which, together with its artificiality, are characteristics that are new in Part II. Maritornes was naturally ugly, and though her physical deformities were extreme they were at least her own and likely to inspire not fear so much as repulsion. But here Sancho is moved to dread, which will happen often in Part II: fear is one of the emotions we encounter again and again in Part II.

Tomé Cecial's nose is connected to the aesthetics of the baroque, whose emblematic figure is the monster, a figure made up of disparate, conflicting elements, like the nose, and contrived to cause admiration. The monster is made to be shown, and this quality is embedded in the etymology of the word *monster*, or *monstrare*, in the Latin. Don Quixote has met in the Knight of the Mirrors an image of his madness; in Tomé Cecial, Sancho has met an image of his foolishness. Tomé is like a carnival figure of the fool, and his costume is reminiscent of those of the actors riding in the wagon of the Parliament of Death. His name is a pun: Tomé is a form of Tomás, Thomas; Cecial, at the time, meant a kind of trout. *Tomé*, being the past tense of *tomar*, also means 'to take' or 'to eat,' so if you step back and think about it, Tomé Cecial means 'I ate trout.' There are many names that mean something, and you may not catch on until you think about them.

Tomé is such a true reflection of Sancho's foolishness because he is Sancho's neighbor, his equal, a man with whom Sancho discourses on things proper to squires and whose gluttony and other habits he shares. The dialogue about the contingency of meaning and language, centering on *hijo de puta,* or 'whoreson,' is hilarious but bespeaks a very modern conception of language, as Spitzer mentions somewhere in his essay: that meaning in language is contingent, not fixed. Meaning is shifty, and this is consistent with the views of the Middle Ages, Renaissance, and baroque that we saw before—in the baroque, shiftiness in language is emphasized. In the dialogue of the squires there is also a critique of the upper classes, a frequent topic of Part II. They, particularly Sancho, do not accept the codes of chivalry that lead to such combats. Sancho seems to be saying that it is the upper classes that start wars, a far-reaching critique. This is part of the political element of the 1615 *Quixote,* but it also fits in with the thematics of desengaño because the accoutrements of the upper classes, their luxuries, are part of the deceits that are undone by desengaño. You will see this happening as we encounter the upper classes in the next few episodes.

What is the significance of all this doubling? Don Quixote meets a double, Sancho meets a double. I think that at the deepest level it means that the characters have met themselves, and each has struggled within himself to find meaning and identity, or identity within meaning, or a form of deep self-recognition, a troubled self-recognition. This is tied to the issue of self-reflexivity we have been discussing since the beginning. The Renaissance mind, the mind of the Renaissance—if I may use an abstraction—sallies forth in search of the real world, which it tries to interpret, control, and use; the baroque mind, in that sallying forth, finds mostly itself, its own inner workings.

This is parallel to Descartes's "Je pense, donc je suis," "Cogito, ergo sum," "I think, therefore I am," which is the ultimate truth Descartes (1596–1650) can find. He was roughly contemporary to Cervantes. The idea is both self-recognizable and disfigured in these images of the self, in need of further and further thought and reflection, with the emphasis on reflection, like in a mirror. It is appropriate, then, for these reasons, that the characters should meet distorted images of their own selves or twisted reflections of themselves in their adventures. Sansón Carrasco has fallen into his own trap, while Don Quixote and Sancho have an almost literal out-of-body experience seeing themselves outside of themselves and seeing themselves as they would look to others. This is especially troubling, I think, to Sancho, but also to Don Quixote, who, as the novel progresses, will find more such instances where reflections of this kind undermine his quest.

I move on to the episode of the lions, which is reminiscent of that of the galley slaves in Part I. The lions, like the prisoners, are prisoners, and they also belong to the king; they are also under the supervision of the Crown. Finding lions in the middle of Castile is not a common occurrence, so their appearance is another instance of the real conspiring to add to Don Quixote's madness by presenting him with beings and objects that are out of the ordinary. Like the players in the cart, lions are objects of amusements; they are being taken to the Court so they can be viewed by the people for display and entertainment. They are also fit for heroic action, and Don Quixote does act with great courage only to be mocked by the lion, which not only acts peacefully but turns his hindquarters to the knight; the ultimate insult. Heroism is no longer possible under these circumstances. It is a very cruel episode for Don Quixote, but together with the fight with the Knight of the Mirrors these are two victories for Don Quixote, victories which, in addition to his gaining the knowledge that he is now in a book, add to his inflated sense of importance and of accomplishment. The characters around him contribute to this delusion, but the lions are real and could have killed Don Quixote and the others. Jorge Luis Borges, whom I have quoted many times in this course, says that Don Quixote's courage is the one characteristic that is a constant from book 1 to book 2; and it is also a constant from Alonso Quixano to Don Quixote and back to Alonso Quixano at the end of the book.

So we come to the gentleman in green, the Knight of the Green Topcoat, Don Diego de Miranda, in whom Don Quixote meets another double but an inverted one, like a mirror image. Don Diego de Miranda appears to be the hidalgo Alonso Quixano would have been had he not read romances of chivalry, turned mad, and chosen to attempt to revive the age of chivalry. He is like the Knight of the Mirrors, another distorted reflection of Don Quixote, the one, I repeat, that he could have been. Don Diego is the image of what the French in the period called the *honnête homme*. He is reasonably well off, reads devotional books, hunts, and lives an honest, peaceful life at home. Don Quixote mocks him slightly in the episode of the lions when Don Diego prudently runs away and again as he takes his leave; Don Quixote says that he himself is not given to leisure, like Don Diego. Don Diego is a kind of pre-bourgeois character. He also has a son, Lorenzo de Miranda, who wants to be a poet.

We have once again the postprandial conversation, and again the discussion centers on the relative merits of arms and letters. This is a repetition of that earlier episode but now taking place in a well-appointed house, not in a dilapidated inn, and Don Quixote has interlocutors who are on his intellectual level. Lorenzo, who is quite a good poet, reminds us of Grisóstomo and Cardenio but does not take action as they did. Don Quixote reveals here that he knows a great deal about poetry, but the outcome of the exchange is, again, that chivalry surpasses poetry, that arms are superior to letters. This whole section seems to be an homage to Garcilaso de la Vega, the great Spanish poet of the sixteenth century whose name I have mentioned many times and who has become by this time the model of poet, courtier, and soldier. Garcilaso, who lived in the first half of the sixteenth century, died as a soldier in Charles V's army while attempting to scale the wall of a castle. The enemy dropped a rock on him. He lived for only thirty-six years, but his poetry changed the course of poetry in Spanish forever. Cervantes was quite devoted to him. The discussion turns to the issue of whether a poet can be made or is born. This is another example of Don Quixote's extensive readings besides merely books of chivalry. This is the library beyond the library that was expurgated by the priest, the barber, and the women at Don Quixote's house.

And then we come to the last episode I will be discussing today, which is a transition episode to Camacho's wedding. This is the incident involving the two swordsmen who argue about who is better and have a duel to prove it. One is very, very strong, and the other is an expert, a scientist of fencing. Since the advent of firearms, fencing had become a sport, not only a sport but even a science. Books written about it tried to explain fencing in geometric and mathematical terms, and Cervantes clearly liked to poke fun at this. However, it is the scientific swordsman who makes a fool out of his opponent, who is so strong that, in the end, when he is angry, he takes his sword and throws it so far away that it takes a long time to walk out where it landed and retrieve it.

The point of this throwaway adventure is that it shows that art triumphs over nature, that science triumphs over strength, and the triumph of art over nature is a baroque topic that appears time and time again in Part II. We are going to be discussing that in the next class when we talk about Camacho's wedding in relation to a painting by Velázquez called *Las hilanderas, The Spinners.*

But now we have to turn to our exemplary story, "The Glass Graduate," which I hope you have read. We have gone over the *Exemplary Novels* of 1613, how Cervantes published the book because publishers became interested in his work after the success of the 1605 *Quixote.* He also published them as a separate volume once he realized he could not use the stories in the way he had used them in Part I, for which he had been criticized. You have read his reply to these criticisms because they appear at the beginning of Part II. So Cervantes, who prided himself on being the first to ever write this kind of novella in the Spanish language, collected them in this wonderful book that would have given Cervantes a prominent place in the canon even if he had not written the *Quixote.*

"The Glass Graduate" is one of the better-known stories, famous for the strange kind of madness that afflicts the protagonist. He believes himself to be made of glass and lives in constant fear of being broken. The story is another example of Cervantes' profound interest in the workings of the human mind and in issues concerning knowledge and the ability to arrive at the truth. Tomás, the protagonist of the story, suffers from a very suggestive sort of paranoia; his illness has a Kafkaesque air to it. In Kafka's *The Metamorphosis* the protagonist becomes a bug; Tomás suffers a malaise that he experiences through fear of bodily harm, of physical fragility. It is a way of feeling different and vulnerable that can be extended to a general human condition, a form of alienation. I think this is the main reason the story is so compelling: the idea of this madness, that you feel yourself to be made of glass and therefore vulnerable, and you try to establish a distance between yourself and others, who might break you, and avoid everything. A tile falling from a roof might break you, and you take elaborate measures to protect your very fragile body.

The novella begins as if it were to be a compressed kind of a bildungs-roman—that is a German word meaning 'novel of education,' from *bildung,* 'education,' *roman,* 'novel'—but then it moves on to encompass Tomás's entire life. It is not, however, a biography, as it centers on only two or three periods of his life, most particularly on the one during his illness. The plot is circular, and circularity is expressed through Tomás's last name. At first his name is Rodaja, which means 'slice,' *una rodaja* is 'a slice,' not quite a circle, a fragment of a sphere, a thin one; then, when he recovers from his illness at the end and is in full command of his faculties, his last name becomes Rueda, which means 'wheel.' So he has been completed. We go back to Spitzer and his polynomasia. Now, during his illness he is known as Licenciado Vidriera, which is the name of the story in Spanish, which means "the Licentiate Glass Window." They call him "glass graduate" in the translation, but *vidriera* means 'glass window,' even a stained-glass window or a glass display case. So this is what his name is; again, we have to go back to Spitzer and names.

Except when he is ill there is something passive about Tomás: on the whole, things happen to him. He is lying under some trees when he is found by the young gentlemen who take him to Salamanca; he becomes their servant for eight years but also acquires an education. He shows a remarkable intelligence, though this is only reported, not dramatized, until he becomes ill; he is always on a second plane, as it were. As a soldier, he travels around trying to soak up as much experience and culture as possible. Tomás is then administered a poison by a spurned woman, a spurned woman who is no courtly damsel but a notorious whore who falls in love with him. The poisoned quince preserve, *membrillo,* that she gives him is redolent of sexual connotations; in Latin, in the classics, the membrillo, in the original Latin, was associated by way of resemblance with female sexual organs.

This is how she lures him into eating it, but there is no hint of what makes him attractive to her other than perhaps his fame as a brilliant scholar. It seems like a whim, that she falls in love with him. She disappears, and that is as far as the erotic theme goes in the story. When ill, Tomás displays a remarkable intelligence and wit, being not only insightful in his observations but making them with puns, wordplay, sharp witticisms, and clever circumlocutions. He is oracular and is consulted as an oracle by people. There is a correlation between his illness and his insightfulness, which seems to hinge on transparency since he believes himself to be made of glass. He challenges people to ask him questions that he will be able to answer because he was a man of glass rather than flesh: "For since glass was a fine and delicate substance his mind could function more quickly and efficiently in it than in a conventional body which was made of denser and earthier stuff" (113).

In other words, Tomás's mind makes the world around him transparent, just as his body is presumably transparent; transparency gives him access to the truth. But he is also said to be highly educated and intelligent, so his insightfulness, once he is ill, is like an expansion of these qualities. Or is it disconnected from it? It is not clear if it was the poison or the precarious condition in which he believes himself to be in that sharpens his wit. He is like the black man in the traditional story who can tell the emperor he is naked because he has nothing to lose. Tomás, because of his illness, has become a sort of freak; he has no reputation to protect, and so he pierces through all social convention and through hypocrisy and lies and tells the truth. In gauging the virtues and defects of each profession or trade, Tomás is following a traditional formula, a set piece that was a skit in comic theater:

having a fellow say jokingly that monks do this while cobblers do that, and so on. That is also behind this part of the story.

"The Glass Graduate" has much in common with the *Quixote* and seems to dramatize the repeated debate in the novel between arms and letters because Tomás is both a soldier and a student; a brilliant student at Salamanca, a law student. But whereas Don Quixote is mainly a reader of literature, of romances of chivalry above all, Tomás is a legal scholar whose mission is reaching the truth. His quest is more intellectual than literary, so in that sense he is not quite like Don Quixote; he is different, more philosophical, one could say. The ending seems to suggest, as throughout the *Quixote,* the preeminence of arms over letters: Tomás has to escape from Salamanca and go back to Flanders, and he has a career in the army in which he ends his life honorably. We will be looking at other *Exemplary Novels,* and you will be able to experience the variety of plots and narrative experiments the book contains, which, I think, is the reason these stories are called exemplary. They are like a collection of samples or examples of plots and stories.

CHAPTER 16

Present Varieties of Classical Myths

Ovid, Cervantes, and Velázquez

Required Readings

Cervantes, *Don Quixote*, Part II, chaps. 12–21, pp. 557–630.
Elliott, *Imperial Spain*, 285–320.

As we approach the episode of Camacho's wedding it should be readily apparent that the story was going to be a play. It has a beginning, a conflict or climax, and a resolution. Given that it has a happy ending it is safe to assume it was going to be a comedy. Actually, scholars have ferreted around and discovered evidence that, indeed, it was a play that Cervantes was planning to write. Cervantes, it seems, found in the *Quixote* a book in which he could sort of dump some of his work in progress.

The novelistic genre, as it is being developed in the *Quixote*, will be an inclusive kind of literary work with a loose format, not following the strict rules of literary genres derived from the classical tradition, in which these liberties were not available. The *Quixote* allows for this kind of incorporation of stories and of various texts. It is a feature that the novel will continue to have and that in the modern period will be exploited to its very limits. Notice also how this love story, Camacho's wedding, is neatly integrated into the plot of the novel, as opposed to the more tangential way in which such stories were inserted in Part I. Here, Don Quixote and Sancho are involved in the action, and Don Quixote plays a role in the outcome.

Given that this was going to be a play, there is a great deal of theatricality in the whole episode, which includes theater within the theater as the celebrations for the wedding unfold. Even nature has been artistically arranged, so much so that the outdoors has a roof. When the characters enter the meadow where the celebration of the wedding is going to take place it is noted that the trees have been arranged in such a way as to provide a canopy which the sun can barely penetrate to reach the grass. That is, nature is turned into architecture, as it were. The play within the play is a way of underlining that everything is theatrical; that there is no real action that is not already theater. That is, life is always theater in Part II, and this is part of the theme of desengaño I have been underlining for the past few lectures.

Notice also the abundance that prevails here and in Part II in general, in contrast with Part I. Whereas in Part I the characters ate frugally, now Sancho has so much food before him that he scarcely knows what to do with it. Compare this with the sparse meal Don Quixote had at that very first inn, when he ate fish because it was Friday. This clash of abundance contrasted with the starkest want is typical of the aesthetics of the baroque, and abundance ties in with the notion of sensuality, the sensuality of Cervantes' art that Auerbach spoke about in the essay you have all read and that he says is the hallmark of Cervantes' work. The sensual, the tangible, in all its abundance, turns into a simulacrum and reveals its opposite, which is quite literally death. This is the desengaño aspect. We have Sancho's speech about death being the devourer of all. As I said, the overarching plot and the plot within the work in these stories follow this pattern of engaño and desengaño.

Why are weddings so important in fiction? This includes film and the theater too. Surely there are many films you can remember that center on a wedding. Weddings mark a moment of social union and renewal, both of society and of nature. They are a transition marked by feasting, particularly by eating. In fiction, weddings tend to be conclusions: "They married and lived happily ever after" is a common traditional ending to stories. In wedding celebrations the world is consumed in a way that leads to the consummation of the marriage. The story of Camacho's wedding, like the myth of Pyramus and Thisbe on which it is based, is a conjunction of love and death, of Eros and Thanatos, or love that struggles against death for continuity and renewal. There are intimations of the death scene, the culminating death scene, which is really not a death scene but a contrived theatrical death scene. But there are intimations of that death scene in the calf that is impaled to be cooked, which the protagonists find when they arrive at the wedding celebration. One could also see in that impaled calf a scapegoat, which is typical of feasts and celebrations.

Camacho is rich and powerful, like Don Fernando in Part I. But Basilio's abilities and skills prevail over social and economic forces. His *industria*, his 'skillfulness,' wins the day, and there is much made of how many talents he has; he can play the guitar, he is an athlete, and we find out later that he is quite an actor also. Now, the episode is a prose epithalamium—a poem or song in praise of the bride or groom or both from the Greek *epi*, 'at,' and *thalamium*, 'nuptial chamber'—and a verse epithalamium is actually performed as part of the wedding celebration. This episode of a wedding with such celebrations is common in the literature of the period. The most prominent example is in the *Soledades*, the great poem by Luis de Góngora, the eminent Spanish baroque poet; it is from him that we get the English word *gongoristic* to describe something very baroque and complicated. He is famous for many poems, but the best known is the *Soledades*, and in the *Soledades* there is quite an elaborate wedding ceremony. It is like a spring ritual, a celebration of nature's replenishment—remember that Part II vaguely begins in spring.

But in the whole episode one wonders, is nature corrected by art or does nature prevail? I think the answer is obvious: art prevails, art corrects nature, and this is, again, one of the main themes in Part II of the *Quixote*. Don Quixote is on Basilio's side, not Camacho's, and in this the episode he is very remindful of Marcela's and Grisóstomo's in Part I, when Don Quixote is on Marcela's side. Perhaps this incident has the kind of ending that the Marcela–Grisóstomo episode should have had in Part I. There are also reminiscences of that episode in the attempted or faked suicide. In Part I, Grisóstomo, as we saw, had actually committed suicide.

The story is, as I noted, a version of the myth of Pyramus and Thisbe, which had been anticipated by Lorenzo de Miranda's sonnet during the conversation at Don Diego de Miranda's house, actually his father's house, and it is mentioned directly by one of the students who is traveling on the road to the wedding. It is also acted out in the *danza hablada*, the spoken dance, the epithalamium, during the wedding festivities. So the myth of Pyramus and Thisbe hangs heavily over this episode. John Sinnigen writes, "The occurrence of the ceremony in a *teatro* [theater-like environment] implies that the wedding is but one more *artificio*. Therefore, when Basilio appears, we become caught up with the spectators at the wedding. They—like the audience at the play—were '*suspensos esperando* [. . .]' [they were waiting in suspense to see what would happen]. The heralded star of the play has just stepped on stage, and everyone is anxious to see what he will do."[1] Sinnigen adds the following, comparing this episode, which is the only one on love in the second part, with the Cardenio tale of the first part:

> The final result of the action of Camacho's wedding is the confirmation of the propriety of romantic love and the rejection of the illegitimate claim on love by *interés*. The same conclusion was provided by Cardenio's tale. There are, however, important differences between the two stories. Cardenio's tale ends in a *venta* to which the hand of fate had led the two couples. The "Bodas de Camacho," however, ends in a *teatro* and the conclusion is brought about by Basilio's *industria*. The difference between these two endings reflects a significant difference between Part I and Part II. In Part I only Don Quijote and the priest (and very briefly the *ventero* in chapter II) acted as "authors" in the sense that they tried to impose fiction on reality. The role of art was of secondary concern to the other characters. In Part II, however, art and artifice are extremely important and a large number of characters (from Sancho Panza to the Duke and Duchess) act as "authors" by using fiction to impose their wills on other characters. In the "Bodas de Camacho" Basilio acts as "author" because he is not content to let fate decide the end of the story. Therefore he imposes his will on the other characters by using fiction to alter the course of the story away from its "natural" ending.[2]

Basilio is the author, but he is also the actor of the play he has made up. Another way to look at the episode is to see it as a modern version of the Pyramus and Thisbe myth, which is clearly in the background and looming, as I have just said, over the story. The Pyramus and Thisbe story in Ovid's *Metamorphoses* highlights the pagan theme of suicide, which Cervantes, in his Catholic environment, uses for dramatic effect but ultimately avoids. Ovid was a Roman poet of the last Augustan age. He is known for his *Ars Amatoria,* which someone called "the most immoral work written by a man of genius," a book on love. But the *Metamorphoses* is his most important work. It is a long narrative poem that recounts legends in which miraculous transformations of matter occur. In fact, the poem begins, "My intention is to tell of bodies changed into different forms."

And it begins with the change from chaos to cosmos and goes on to the moment when Julius Caesar is being transformed into a star. The Middle Ages took the *Metamorphoses* to be a kind of pagan bible, like an Old Testament. If the Old Testament tells the story of the universe, so does the *Metamorphoses,* using classical myths. Its influence in the Renaissance was tremendous, and even in the late Middle Ages. Ovid's poem was kind of a thesaurus of myths that artists—painters, sculptors, writers—used very often. In Spanish literature Ovid was very influential, as he was in English literature throughout the ages. He competes with Virgil in importance as a classical author to be followed.

There are deeper, more disturbing aspects of Camacho's wedding linking deflowering, blood, and the connection between life and death. I will discuss these in some detail. In the wedding, love appears as a mock death to promote life. Violence and love are complicit because violence is the subtext of love. The issue here is classical mythology contrasted with Christian doctrine. The question for artists of the Renaissance, who were deeply interested in the classical world but living in a Christian one, was what to do with the ancient gods.

The most common answer was allegory; the myths were seen as moral allegories, they told a moral tale. But in the case of Camacho's wedding, what Cervantes seems to be proposing is a modern reenactment of an ancient recurring dilemma concerning love, using for that the myth of Pyramus and Thisbe. Basilio's arts are used here to steer the story away from its pagan ending, suicide, to a victory of love and Christian marriage. The pagan ending is turned into theater, into representation, into art. Don Quixote has referred earlier to marriage as an irreparable accident, something that sounds very funny to us today; but he is using scholastic terminology to refer to it, and always in the context of these debates about marriage, which I will revisit today.

Basilio makes the accidental the result of choice, his own choice. The point is that skill and wiliness lead to a virtuous result here. The whole of the second part of the *Quixote* is an apology for art, for the artificial, for the constructed, for the contrived, for art helping nature attend to good ends, after going through the process of desengaño I have been underlining in the past few classes. It is a way of turning deceit, which would normally lead to disillusionment, into a positive force that leads to a happy ending. Basilio's skills overcome social and economic forces; his craftiness wins the day.

What I claim is that beneath all of that lies a kind of substory, a subtext. That story is a rewriting of the love stories of Part I that turn on unequal marriage and that involve the issue of secret marriages, which, as I said, were the hot topic of the day and were taken up by the Council of Trent. I spoke about these issues when talking about the episode in which Dorotea allows herself to be deflowered by Don Fernando. The difference here is the lurking presence of classical myth, more typical of the baroque. In Part I the stories about all of these young people seem to be drawn from contemporary legal archives, stories about conflicts involving social issues, estates, and legacies. Here, the source is much more imposing and ancient: the myth of Pyramus and Thisbe. But true to the political character of Part II, there is in addition a protracted discussion of the issue of marriage by the characters.

The issue of marriage was a political issue, not just a religious one; it is impossible to separate the two. Other echoes of Part I are Basilio's onset of madness when he hears of Quiteria's impending marriage, which recalls both Grisóstomo and Cardenio when they go insane—in the case of Cardenio mostly, as we do not see Grisóstomo actually act that out—and the issue of suicide, which evokes Grisóstomo. This is another case, I emphasize, of rewriting incidents from Part I; the rewritings here involve both the stories in Part I and classical myth, which is being rewritten. But there is a deeper take on marriage at the level of material transformations.

The story of Camacho's wedding is about the issue of marriage as a sacrament, a transformation of matter for transcendental purposes—that of creating a new human life—and how it is institutionalized through civil and canon law, that is, by society and religion. The law is based on prohibition: "Thou shall not," here, the ban instituted by Quiteria's parents once she and Basilio have reached sexual maturity, which is quite evident. If you read the story carefully, you'll see that their prohibition comes up when they have reached sexual maturity. She has begun to menstruate, and he is now capable of impregnating her. Her parents are reluctant to have her reproduce with an impecunious Basilio, who, for all of his skills, has no profitable ones.

As we saw when discussing the issue regarding Dorotea, clandestine marriages—lurking here in the background because we assume there had been one between Basilio and Quiteria—could lead to polygamy. I could say to any girl I was involved with, "Yes, yes, I will marry you," and then if my pledge took, as it were, I could be married to several such women. How can a vow hastily made in the heat of passion yoke partners for life in what Don Quixote calls, again using that scholastic terminology, "un accidente irreparable," meaning something that cannot be taken back? In the Catholic Church you cannot take it back. That is, how can such words, uttered in these circumstances, make a marriage? How can free will be so easily surrendered? The Council of Trent proclaimed that the church abhorred clandestine marriages and ordered the clergy not to celebrate weddings without published banns and the presence of witnesses. This decree was incorporated by Philip II into Spanish statutory law in 1564 and remained as the foundation of marriage in Spain until the nineteenth century.

The conflict is dealt with very subtly in this story. Basilio is proficient in canon law and civil law, and he puts his knowledge to good use in his trick to marry Quiteria. How does he do that? Well, he threatens to die without confession. I have to underline this because even if you are a Catholic this is very difficult to conceive of from a modern perspective. You want to die without confession? So what? Go ahead, be my guest! But by threatening to do that he is accusing them of sending him irrevocably to hell because suicide is a mortal sin, and if he dies without confession and commits suicide he is going to hell, no matter what. This is how he convinces everyone; he knows canon law and he knows civil law. So to die without confession if she will not give in would condemn him to eternal damnation. Quiteria and the others would have done more harm this way than by murdering him; murdering him would be nothing compared to eternal damnation. Then Basilio has both Quiteria and himself utter the words about free consent that would legitimize the marriage before church and society. I am sure you remember the episode in which he insists that the proper words, the legal words, be uttered, affirming consent. She later confirms her determination to dispel any doubt about her desires and make void any future attempts to dissolve the marriage; that is, she confirms afterward that it was not just in the heat of the moment that she assented. She ratifies that she wanted to marry Basilio.

All of these are very carefully constructed episodes that show Basilio's lawyerly skills. But, as I am suggesting, in this story Cervantes probes deeper into the question of marriage, going beyond legal issues. He goes back to marriage as a kind of transubstantiation, a transcendental metamorphosis of matter, a transformation of the flesh: the blending of bloods, literally, that makes the union indivisible, presumably. In looking at the episode with this background in mind, it appears that Cervantes is favoring the clandestine "I do" that Quiteria must have uttered, while at the same time having her and Basilio observe the rituals prescribed by the Council of Trent.

It seems to be a middle course: the sacramental nature of marriage lurks in the subtext of the story through the myth of Pyramus and Thisbe. It is a tragic story, one in which a cruel fate befalls the young lovers because of a misinterpretation, although it could also be read as an admonitory tale about the recklessness of youth. The myth goes back to the conjunction of love and death at the moment when love ripens and is about to become regenerative. Driven by desire, the young lovers are to meet at the tomb of Ninus, where they die, killed not by a lioness who bloodies Thisbe's veil but by their own hand. The bloody veil can be seen as an image of the hymen rent in the act of love, a bloody event. The renting of the hymen also recalls the onset of menstruation; that is, the beginning of the capacity for reproduction but also the recurrent death of a woman's ovum. The red of the tree's fruit is a symbol both of resurrection and of death, as it recalls menstruation in its recurring coloring. The myth reenacts a tragic human predicament symbolized by the spilling of blood at conception, birth, and death, leaving open the possibility that the law, here the parents' disapproval, can overcome or forestall the fatality of the situation. But the prohibition is also allied to death because it is instrumental in bringing about the tragic ending.

In Ovid the conflict appears to resolve itself in beauty, the gorgeous red fruit of the blooming tree. In Cervantes it goes further. In his story the myth of Pyramus and Thisbe is given in shards, fragments, within a faint outline, like a distant memory. It looks forward to Joyce, to his *Ulysses,* in which myth appears in fragments, more than backward to the Middle Ages and the Renaissance, when myths were more coherent. I am inclined to believe, however, that Cervantes had Ovid's text in front of him or that he had a prodigious memory. For instance, when Basilio feigns being near death, his eyes are part of the act: "[Basilio] was by now showing the whites of his eyes" (II, 21, 627). He is feigning that he is about to die, so he has his eyes turned into his head, which recalls the moment when Thisbe asks Pyramus to answer, whereupon—I am not going to read you the Latin because I will sound like a priest saying Mass—the translation reads, "At the name of Thisbe, Pyramus lifted his eyes, now heavy with death, and having looked upon her face, closed them again."[3] So the eyes are one of the shards of the myth that remains.

My argument follows what I would like to call an itinerary of blood. This begins with the calf on the spit, "pregnant" with suckling pigs, which Sancho sees when they arrive at the wedding and which foretells of the sacrificial victim, the groom, which it replaces. This also recalls the violence at weddings, Romeo and Juliet being the most famous example in Western literature. Violence and blood announce gestation and the spilling of more blood as the new human being, the most elemental purpose of marriage, is produced. The consumption of the animals, the wine, and the bread have obvious Christian symbolism, too.

To consume and to consummate go together in a wedding celebration. Guests consume the world around them, including the earth, through the wine. It is a form, again, of transubstantiation. Transubstantiation is the word for the Eucharist, when the bread and wine are transformed into the body of Christ. It is the transformation of one substance into another through actions that involve both pleasure and violence: hunting, butchering, squashing the grapes, and, of course, sex. Basilio's intervention postpones the blood Quiteria would have shed in Camacho's bed, substituting for it the fake blood he has concealed. This blood stains his garment; the proxy blood suspends the real blood that would seal the marriage. But I contend that there is another, hidden blood that forestalls the consummation of the intended marriage between Camacho and Quiteria.

You do not have to follow me on this or be persuaded if you do not want to. To put it bluntly, I think Quiteria is menstruating on her wedding day. The Spanish original says, "Venía la hermosa Quiteria algo descolorida y debía ser de la mala noche que siempre pasan las novias en componerse para el día venidero de sus bodas." Rutherford: "Quiteria the Fair was looking rather pale—it must have been from the sleepless night that any bride spends preparing for her wedding" (II, 21, 625).

Descolorida in Spanish does not just mean pale, but to have lost one's color because of an illness or a fright. And *componerse* means 'to dress up' but also 'to recover from an illness.' Why mention that she is pale? I believe the suggestion is that she is menstruating. Menstruation is fraught with all kinds of prohibitions and lore in all cultures; in ours, going back all the way to the Old Testament. Menstruation, in this case, would have been a providential blood that would have impeded the consummation of Camacho's marriage, postponing Quiteria's hymeneal blood and preserving it for Basilio's bed. Quiteria's menstruation, her *regla*, which is another word for menstruation in Spanish, means 'rule,' simply 'rule' would be a superior law inherent in the blood itself in determining the outcome of the conflict.

Marriage is seen as ordained by God, part of a divine plan that supersedes custom or law and overrides considerations of unequal social status. The process of marriage is embedded in blood itself, in the general transformation of matter according to divine grace. In the Bible, man and woman would become one flesh in marriage. In Ovid's pagan version there is no salvation possible; the lovers' fusion is only achieved as ashes in a funerary urn or in the beauty of a mulberry tree in bloom. In Cervantes a form of justice has been made, and there is every reason to believe that the commingling of bloods will lead to regeneration, to the birth of a new human being. This is a kind of conclusion we did not find in Part I, in which marriages are yet to occur, except in the tale about foolish curiosity where there is also a great deal of blood.

I think that in a deep sense Cervantes is true to Ovid and to the spirit of *Metamorphoses*—*meta,* 'movement,' *morphoses,* 'the change of form'—but has given it a Christian twist and translated it into the present. In Cervantes the myth is not retold with a didactic, satirical, or even aesthetic purpose. In fact, it is not so much retold as recycled. It is not an *Ovide Moralisé,* which was, from 1340, a book in French by Pierre Bersuire which influenced many writers, including Chaucer, and in which fifteen books or chapters of the *Metamorphoses* are turned into moral allegories. This is not what Cervantes does at all, either on the level of marriage as a social institution or that deeper level that I am claiming is told in this substory or subtext that I called the itinerary of blood.

In this use of myth Cervantes resembles Velázquez, so let's turn to Velázquez again, to *Los borrachos, The Drunkards* (fig. 16). I want to quote from the Spanish philosopher José Ortega y Gasset, whom I have mentioned before. He was the most important Spanish philosopher of the twentieth century, known in this country mostly for his book *The Revolution of the Masses,* but he should also be read for *The Dehumanization of Art,* which is about the

Figure 16. Diego Velázquez, *Los borrachos* (1629).
© Madrid, Museo Nacional del Prado.

avant-garde. Ortega y Gasset claimed that what Velázquez meant by mixing classical gods with unsavory or ordinary characters from everyday reality is that there are no gods and no transcendental meaning, if we take the gods to be the representation of the higher sense of things when seen in connection to each other. Velázquez, he says, is "an atheistic giant, a colossal impious man. With his brush he banishes the gods as if smacking them with a broom [I love this simile because you can think of the brush as a little broom]. In his *Bacanal* [which is this painting, known in Spanish as *Los borrachos*] there is not only no Bacchus but a rascal impersonating Bacchus."[4] *Bacanal* has nine figures, two of which seem to be dressed or, rather, undressed for a bacchanal, a feast in honor of Bacchus, the god of wine, celebrated in the spring and fall. Two guys are near naked, and the others are lusty peasants roughly clothed in contemporary dress. They have a casual, not a posed, air that characterized the naturalistic genre scenes called *bodegones* in Spain, which means simply 'still lifes.' This painting sought and achieved the effect of a casually chosen slice of life. But *Bacanal* is carefully composed around the light flesh of the bogus Bacchus at the center. Jonathan Brown, one of the great experts on Velázquez, writes, "Despite attempts to interpret this unconventional painting [*Bacanal*] as a parody of the Olympian gods or as a sermon on the evils of drink, it seems that Velázquez intended to represent Bacchus as a giver of the gift of wine, which freed man (temporarily) from the harsh, unforgiving struggle of daily life. . . . Deprived of the beneficent liquid, the beggar finds no respite from the hardships which, in sober moments, will be shared by all of the company."[5]

This marvelous painting hangs in the Prado Museum, and if you remember the words by Auerbach about the subtle plastic nature of Cervantes' art, of his depiction of things and of the sensuous quality of his work, you can see that there is, besides the connection I am trying to establish here, a kinship between Cervantes' art and that of Velázquez. You can imagine these characters in the painting appearing in episodes of the *Quixote*. Look at the face of stupor on this drunk; he has sort of a grin of stupidity and inebriation.

Las hilanderas, The Spinners, was painted around 1657 (fig. 17). It is thus a very late work, contemporaneous with *Las Meninas,* and nearly as complex and as ambitious. In it, Velázquez has combined two subjects, one from classical mythology and the other from his own time. It is a commonplace work scene, as you can see. There are, in fact, two stories from classical mythology combined in the picture: the fable of Arachne and the story of Jupiter's rape of Europa. In the foreground we have the activities of tapestry manufacturing as done in the factories under royal patronage in Madrid, and in the alcove, in the back, the classical tale of the weaver Arachne.

Figure 17. Diego Velázquez, *Las hilanderas* (c. 1657).
© Madrid, Museo Nacional del Prado.

The scene in the back of the painting takes place at Arachne's shop, where, as a great artist, she is visited by elegant ladies. The tapestry hanging on the back wall of the alcove, which is presumably Arachne's work, is the key to the relationship between the two scenes. It is a woven copy of Titian's *The Rape of Europa*. This is the actual painting by Titian, *The Rape of Europa*, which—back to the *Hilanderas*—we find in the back, in that tapestry. The rape of Europa is one of the most celebrated of Jupiter's erotic adventures with mortal women. Arachne has challenged Minerva, Jupiter's daughter and the patroness of weavers and goddess of wisdom, to a weaving contest. It was called a draw, but because Arachne's tapestry was judged to be the equal of Minerva's and, further, because it depicted such a scandalous act by her father, the goddess punished Arachne by turning her into a spider. This explains why Minerva is shown gesturing angrily. The story is also drawn from Ovid's *Metamorphoses*, book 6. Jonathan Brown believes that

> by inserting a quotation of this famous work [Titian's *The Rape of Europa*] into the composition, Velázquez implies his belief in the nobility and transcendental value of the art of painting. . . . In the *Fable of Arachne* [*The Spinners*], Velázquez seeks to reconcile

the artificial world of the myth with a palpable world of visual reality without sacrificing the decorum required by the one, or the
verisimilitude, by the other. . . . The contrast between the foreground, where sturdy women toil at burdensome tasks, and the
refined atmosphere of the artist's atelier [the scene in the back]
is perhaps Velázquez' way of implying his conviction about the
distinction between craft and art.[6]

At the time there was a raging dispute as to whether painters were artists
or mere artisans; this may seem strange to us, but it happened. Titian had
been a favorite painter of Charles V, in the previous century, and of Philip II,
so Velázquez's painting is in homage to him, and there is no doubt that by
inserting Titian's painting into his own Velázquez is putting himself on an
equal level. But there is a lot more to it, it seems to me. As in *Las Meninas*
there seems to be a revelation of the act of artistic creation, which in the
painting has to do with Minerva and Arachne but that, taking the whole
work into consideration, also has to do with Velázquez's own creation. Creation appears as a layered process that involves the real, either because art
is a reflection of reality or because art illuminates reality, but also because
reality unveils the artificiality of art.

In *The Spinners* we have paintings within paintings, and the presence
in the foreground—the present is the foreground—appears as a repetition
of the classical past. But it is a repetition that is also a comedown: can the
present-day spinners recall the myth of Arachne? It seems to me that what
Velázquez is doing, as Ortega y Gasset suggested about the *Bacanal,* is diminishing the gods, and also, by showing Minerva's studio within the weaving shop, he is showing the inner recesses of representation: it is backstage
tricks, as it were, as he displayed them in *Las Meninas.* The whole painting is
a desengaño. What we take to be gods are like today's spinners. The weaver's
shop is no different from Minerva's studio, as in both the deception of art is
used to deceive humans. We see the contemporary weavers in relation to the
classical fable, and we see at the center of Velázquez's painting a quotation
from a masterpiece. We are being given here, again, an infinitely receding
sequence, a play of mirrors within this workshop of representation, which is
like giving us a workshop of engaño; therefore, by giving us that workshop,
the painting is a desengaño.

The process is similar to what Cervantes does in the episode of Camacho's wedding and in the whole of the *Quixote* dealing with myth. The fable
of Pyramus and Thisbe takes place in fabulous Babylon; Camacho's wedding

takes place in an insignificant village in Spain. Basilio uses the artistry of the fable to deceive those in attendance, particularly Camacho and his friends, but also Don Quixote, Sancho, and even the reader, who does not know what is happening until the moment the trick is revealed to bring the story to a climax and eventual resolution. There is a mirroring of myth and present reality, and the elaboration of a deceit through artistry, acting, playing the role of the mythological Pyramus—Basilio playing that role, acting it out. The whole story is one of engaño and desengaño.

The backstage of representation is displayed, as in *Las Meninas*, and, as we shall see, in both the episode involving Maese Pedro—Ginés de Pasamonte as puppeteer—and, most revealingly, in the culminating episode in the whole of the *Quixote*, the one about the Cave of Montesinos, in which we are given the whole underpinning of Don Quixote's madness, his actual subconscious. Now, whereas in Part I Cervantes seems to be addressing the romances of chivalry and the picaresque as models and sources, in Part II he takes up the grand tradition of Homer, Ovid, Virgil, and Dante, particularly in episodes such as the Cave of Montesinos and the pageant in the forest that we will be seeing soon. This is very significant. It seems to me he now knows that he is in their league and that he has created a literary character that will endure like theirs and like the gods in classical mythology. He was right.

CHAPTER 17

Caves and Puppet Shows

Internal and External Representations

Required Readings

Cervantes, *Don Quixote,* Part II, chaps. 22–35, pp. 630–733.
Haley, George. "The Narrator in *Don Quijote:* Maese Pedro's
Puppet Show." In *Casebook,* 241–64.

Two of the most noteworthy episodes of Part II of the *Quixote* begin the
downward slope of the novel as it moves toward its conclusion. It is a protracted culmination and finale consistent with the slower, more deliberate
pace of Part II. One character from Part I, Ginés de Pasamonte, reappears
under the guise of the master puppeteer Maese Pedro, and there will be not
only repetitions of incidents from Part I but even repetitions of stories from
Part II within Part II. After the episodes I will discuss today, three major new
developments occur. First, Don Quixote will sometimes leave the center of
the action to be replaced by Sancho. Second, both Don Quixote and Sancho
will become objects of amusement for frivolous upper-class characters who
have read Part I. And third, the protagonist will be surrounded by many
more characters than before. The overarching theme of the novel continues
to be desengaño as most of the action is staged by internal authors. It is an
action that is highly theatrical, and the props or backstage of the skits are
revealed to the reader, either during the performance or right after.

The first of the two important events is the one about Don Quixote's
descent into Montesinos's Cave, a truly remarkable tour de force and one of

the most brilliant scenes in the Western literary tradition. Montesinos's Cave is one of the principal adventures of Part II and arguably of the entire work because it seems to engage the main literary topics and sources of the novel. It also provides a rare glimpse into the inner workings of Don Quixote's subconscious. It is as if we were looking behind the scenes of the *Quixote* or allowed to see its reverse side, as we see the reverse side of that painting within *Las Meninas* that Velázquez is working on. It is also as if we were allowed to dissect the protagonist while he is still alive. First, notice that this is an adventure that Don Quixote seeks, that he looks for, not one that is imposed on him by chance, like the encounters on the road, or prepared by other characters who are scripting his life.

As we have seen, Sansón Carrasco, from the very beginning, is trying to plan Don Quixote's life, and there will be several other internal authors doing that, but this is not the case at all here. This is an adventure Don Quixote wants to experience, and he tells the scholar, the cousin traveling with them, that he wants to do so and asks how to get to Montesinos's Cave. It is also an affair that is strictly Spanish and that seems to take Don Quixote into the depths of the Spanish soil: it is as if Cervantes is saying that these kinds of fabulous events also happen in Spain and in the present, although I will speak about the sources of the episode (descents into caves). But this is one based on a Spanish tradition. That is, people knew about Montesinos's Cave and talked about it—it actually exists—and Don Quixote wanted to go into it; he decided he had to have this adventure.

One way to see the episode as flowing from Camacho's wedding— which is the big episode preceding it—is through its connection with Ovid. The cousin or scholar who is their guide is writing, he says, a Spanish Ovid, and the explanation given about the rivers of Spain and their names is in the spirit of the *Metamorphoses*. This scholar is another satire of students and intellectuals, like the one we have seen in the case of Sansón Carrasco; this one is even more extreme. This is a really ridiculous scholar. He is trying to find out, for instance, who had the first cold in history. I said that in Part II Cervantes seems to be pointing at his sources: Homer, Virgil, Ovid, and, as we shall see, Dante. He seems to be claiming that his work is their worthy successor. I will speak about Virgil when we meet Altisidora, the character who is a version of Dido.

This descent into the cave has antecedents in the *Odyssey,* the *Aeneid,* and the *Divine Comedy,* although there are also sources in chivalric romances. This is an adventure on a higher literary level; it is going back not just to scenes in the chivalric romances but also to Homer, Virgil, and

Dante. There are also traditional stories in all cultures and in all literatures about people going into caves. If you have read your American literature you see that in the novels about Tom Sawyer and Huckleberry Finn there are episodes in which the characters go into caves. In the *Quixote* I think the sources are those I mentioned. Going down into the cave has deep psychological resonances having to do with Don Quixote's sexuality and, concomitantly, his fear of death. As he enters the cave he has to hack away at the brambles covering the entrance in actions that are symbolic or reminiscent of a deflowering, and the blackbirds that fly away in fright are clear intimations of death; they are bad omens. They have a kind of Hitchcock-like air. They remind me of that very frightening Hitchcock film *The Birds.*

What Don Quixote experiences in the cave is a dream, and this aligns it with dream literature. That it is a dream is made clear by his being asleep when he is pulled back up and from the story he tells about falling asleep when he sits down on the coiled-up rope inside the cave. Don Quixote says he wakes up from that sleep, but it is obvious that he awakens within the dream, that this is a dream within a dream, another mirror effect. The dream allows for the untrammeled emergence of Don Quixote's deepest fears in the form of stories related to his fantasies or drawn from his fantasies. It is as if he had been administered a drug, a truth serum, or as if he had relaxed on the psychoanalyst's couch and allowed himself to free associate.

The story of Durandarte and Belerma that Don Quixote tells is drawn from the Carolingian cycle. I mentioned the various cycles of the chivalric romances and the epics, and the Carolingian has to do with Charlemagne. This story is drawn from the Carolingian cycle and seems to have embedded in it not only the fear of death but also the fear of castration. All of the characters, except for Merlin, are from the ballads of the Arthurian and Carolingian cycle: King Arthur and Charlemagne. The characters are supposed to be dead, everyone is in mourning, and the procession is a mournful one, like a burial. Durandarte's body in the story has its heart removed and sent to Belerma as a symbol of his undying love; this is the original story. He asked to have his heart removed and sent to his beloved when he died. Here, his castrated cadaver, as it were, appears as the statue gracing his own tomb, unable to speak.

But the veracity of the story is compromised, or grotesquely legitimized, by Montesinos's explanation that he has had to salt the heart so that it will not rot and begin to smell. This destroys the fantasy. I mean, if this great hero has his heart sent to his beloved, one never thinks that this heart will be subject to the laws of nature; this is a fantasy world, but here that fantasy is destroyed and the story—the verisimilitude of the story, in other words—can be guaranteed by the fact that they have to salt it so that it will not rot. Natural laws threaten the story's verisimilitude but are invoked to protect its veracity. A beef-jerky heart is not the same as the heart that symbolizes love, courage, and masculinity. The heart has all of those symbolic connotations. If you think of the heart as being made of beef jerky all of those resonances are destroyed or become grotesque.

Although time is flexible within the cave its effects on flesh are active. I say that the time is flexible because, how long was Don Quixote in the cave? The scholar and Sancho say an hour, at most; he says three days! And then there is the issue of how long ago these stories occurred; hundreds of years ago, one presumes, yet these characters are still there. So time within the story is malleable, as time tends to be in dreams. We know now from modern studies of dreams that stories that seem to take a long time actually take a few seconds in a dream and that there is this compression that Freud talks about; how a dream compresses stories into a very short time. This is intimated here in that Don Quixote says he has been there for three days while his companions say only an hour. But the effect of time on dead flesh is evident; it rots. Now, this detail of the effect of time on flesh reveals Don Quixote's doubts about the legitimacy of chivalric legends. Remember that this is a story he himself is telling, so if the story comes up in his subconscious it is because he has doubts about the genuineness of the chivalric legends. These legends violate natural law, hence they are fantastic, as other characters have been telling Don Quixote all along, and all of this seems to have had an impact on him.

Don Quixote has been recognized as a great knight, a constant that began with Sansón Carrasco's revelation of the existence of Part I, and this is something that will happen over and over again in Part II. But in this case he is recognized by characters whose own existence is very, very doubtful and that he himself will doubt from now on by anxiously asking others, like Master Pedro's monkey, if what happened in the cave was real. Also, by insisting that Sancho believe that what he says about the cave was real and by striking deals with him—"I'll believe that if you believe the Cave of Montesinos"—it shows he is not so sure about its veracity. So the recognition by these characters of his being a great knight is hardly an assurance. I am underlining these doubts that the stories reveal about his own fantasies, but the most disturbing part is the appearance of Dulcinea in the guise of the ugly wench that Sancho tried to make him believe was his lady. We know from Freud's great book *The Interpretation of Dreams,* which was published in 1900, that these are the remains of the day; how a dream picks up elements from the previous day and incorporates them into stories.

The appearance of this rustic convinces Sancho that Don Quixote is insane because he was the author of that charade, but it also shows to what extent that incident of the three peasant women has shaken Don Quixote's beliefs and reached deep into the sources of his desires for Dulcinea and of his invention of Dulcinea. This peasant Dulcinea who smells of raw garlic, as you remember, just as she smelled of sweat in Sancho's earlier story about her, is, I think, close to Don Quixote's own real desire for Aldonza Lorenzo, the original Dulcinea. It seems to be the repressed desire for a vulgar, physically strong, sexually vigorous younger woman who is the very opposite, in fact, the correlative opposite, of his idealization of her. The more vulgar this woman of his desires is, the more idealized she will become in his fantasy.

Also, there is the risible part of the story when Dulcinea asks for a loan—the last thing you imagine is that Dulcinea will ask Don Quixote for a loan—which is going to be backed up, by the way; the guarantee is an intimate, inner garment of Dulcinea's, a very elaborate underskirt. I mean, these details are highly sexualized. But Don Quixote is short two *reales:* she wants six, but he has only four. This is a clear sign of his deeply repressed fear of sexual inadequacy—it could not be clearer; you do not have to be Freud— which this story may conceal, the source of his heroic fantasies. He is old, he feels sexually inadequate, so he wants to imagine himself as a young, vigorous knight who can go into combat and seduce maidens.

Sancho's concoction of the enchanted Dulcinea has dug deep into Don Quixote's dread and into the source of his fantasies. In this topsy-turvy world of the cave there are also eerie images of death. I already mentioned the blackbirds at the mouth of the cave. Durandarte's cadaver posing as a statue on its own sarcophagus is the eeriest of them all and the uncanniest: it is an inversion. The statue on a sarcophagus presumably represents the body of the dead person within it. I am sure you have been to European cathedrals where you find all of these sarcophagi, and you see on top the recumbent statue of the person within it; they usually have their hands one on top of the other, and they have their swords near them. I find that eerie enough to begin with, but in any case, here the cadaver is the statue; nature has replaced art or has become art. Instead of having a representation you have literally the cadaver on top of the sarcophagus.

Don't forget that we are dealing here with death and are also in the realm of temporality; remember that Durandarte's heart was salted so it would not smell. How can the cadaver replace the statue and not rot like its heart? Art has been taken over by death, too; this is what the intimation is. Nothing, not even art, is immune from death in this world of the cave. There may be a ghoulish pun embedded here: *sarcophagus* comes from the Greek *sarcos*, 'flesh,' and *phagein*, 'to eat.' The sarcophagus literally eats flesh, the flesh of the dead body it contains, but here the dead body has escaped to become its own statue. This is a very baroque image. We will be discussing another sarcophagus in the course of the next few chapters.

The stories and images inside Montesinos's Cave highlight the central topic of Part II: desengaño. Desengaño, as we have seen, can mean the destruction of all illusions. When Don Quixote comes to, after emerging from the cave, he declares the following, in what is a classic expression of desengaño: "God forgive you, friends [he tells the scholar and Sancho], for taking me away from the most delicious and delightful life and sights that any man had ever lived or seen. Now indeed I have understood that all pleasures of this life pass away like a shadow or a dream, wither like the flowers of the field. O hapless Montesinos! O sore wounded Durandarte! O unfortunate Belerma! O weeping Guadiana, and you, luckless daughter of Ruidera, showing in your waters the tears shed by your lovely eyes!" (II, 22, 637). Don Quixote says a bit later, "I awoke and found myself in the middle of the most beautiful, pleasant, delightful meadow that nature could create or the liveliest human mind imagine" (II, 23, 638). This is the locus amoenus of Renaissance pastoral literature I have mentioned before—you remember the locus amoenus into which Rocinante wanders and falls in love with the mares. It is a topic of Renaissance literature as the most pleasant of places, and this is where Don Quixote lands and presumably where he has his dream. Desengaño, as I have been saying, means to peel away the illusion, the delusion. It is a form of self-analysis, of recognition comparable to the one achieved today through psychoanalysis. Don Quixote seems to have dived into his subconscious. Is this a *regressus ad uterum,* an atavistic return to the womb? I mean, is it an attempt to get back into the mother's womb, seeking solace and refuge? Don Quixote's descent, as we have seen, makes him look harshly upon himself. It does not completely shake his beliefs or dispel his madness, but it is a serious blow, and from now on he will act saner. How can it have been pleasurable, however? It can be so only if one thinks that once in the cave he was at least in the living presence of his fictions—this would have been pleasurable—and that the disillusionment became repressed, as he experienced it. When he found all of these elements that threatened his fantasies, Don Quixote repressed them immediately, as we tend to repress unpleasant experiences. He was not aware, as we readers are, that what he experienced threatened his beliefs. So he comes back with doubts about himself and his mission but not conscious doubts.

Everything seems to converge in the scene of Montesinos's Cave: Don Quixote's belief in the authenticity of the romances of chivalry and the reality of what he sees when he sees windmills, for instance, are questioned. The topics of the courtly love tradition, which had filtered into the romances of chivalry, tumble through literalization by being exposed to the laws of nature. I have alluded several times to Durandarte's salted heart. Belerma, for her part, may have looked under the weather because she had her menstrual period, though not really, it is explained, because the problem was actually that she was menopausal. Real time and, with it, periodic bodily functions, age and aging, and decay have crept into the world of chivalric fiction contained in the cave. There is no harsher way to dispel the idealization of a Renaissance beauty than to imagine her menstruating or going through menopause, meaning that she has already aged; imagine Botticelli's Venus with those problems. It is grotesque! It is brilliant, however, to subject these idealizations to temporality. Why would Dulcinea need a loan? It is said, in passing, that need or necessity is everywhere; the world of magic is invaded by needs and physical laws, and what ensues are grotesque images.

There are many literary antecedents to the Cave of Montesinos episode, and I have already mentioned Homer, Virgil, and Dante, but the originality of the episode lies not so much in the descent into the cave as in the revelation of Don Quixote's subconscious. This is Cervantes' way of showing us the knight's mind from within, unencumbered by reason. As such, it seems to be a better device than the soliloquy in Shakespeare or in Calderón, which are parallel devices to show what a character's thoughts are: "To be, or not to be," and so forth, and in Calderón, "¡Ay, mísero de mí!" This is from *Life Is a Dream*. It is also more modern and acceptable, this device in Cervantes, to contemporary readers, it seems to me, because no one goes around delivering soliloquies that are perfectly structured rhetorically.

But telling a dream is a common activity, not only to psychoanalysts; you tell your dreams to relatives and friends. In the episode there is a grotesque combination of fantasy and not just reality but the possible, all having to do with the decay of human flesh. But as I have suggested, is this not also a tale of castration fear? These are the repressed figures in Don Quixote's mind. Peter Dunn, who was a very good British Hispanist who taught for many years at Wesleyan University, wrote the following in a very perceptive article on this episode. Dunn wrote this article in Spanish, and I am translating him into English. This is what he said: "What is observed, in the cave of Montesinos episode, is quixoticism from the inside. He looks at himself in the mirror of his madness where comedy and spectator merge and the enchanter and the enchanted coalesce. Far from offering us an image of eternity, Montesinos' cave constitutes a frozen temporality. Don Quixote will have to return to his own bed, and dream the dream of death so Alonso Quixano can awaken, purged of his dreams and ready to contemplate himself without theater in the mirror of eternity."[1] This is anticipating the death of Alonso Quixano at the end of the book. Anthony Cascardi, an American Hispanist, links the episode to the dream argument in Descartes and makes quite a few valuable observations about Don Quixote as a whole, particularly about the entire debate concerning the relationship between reality and fantasy. He says,

> I see his engagement as with problems of skepticism and episte-
> mology, and more specifically with the use of fiction as a mode
> of knowledge of the world. His response to skepticism and to
> its complement, epistemology, is to reject epistemology while re-
> maining anti-skeptical; but this is only another way of saying that
> his purpose is to affirm the role of fiction in our relationship to
> the world (which, it might further be said, is an affirmation of the
> role of fiction in the task of philosophy). Cervantes shows that
> we relate to the world, including the "world" of our own experi-
> ences, in ways other than what the epistemologist calls "knowl-
> edge," and that all we know of the world cannot be characterized
> in terms of *certainty*. Cervantes' will to include the imagination
> and dreams within the range of valid human experience—within
> what we call the "world" in the broad sense—free of the caveats
> of reason, points this up.[2]

Cascardi tends to be a little too philosophical. What he means, in short, is that stories, literature, are a form of knowledge and a method of approaching knowledge of the world and of ourselves and a way to understand both the world and the workings of our own minds. Psychoanalysis knows this, and this is why Freud availed himself of figures like the Oedipus myth to name mental processes. Freud acknowledged that his sources in the development and invention of psychoanalysis—he was really the inventor of it—were literary and that he learned more from literature than from the nineteenth-century science that preceded him. The point is that these stories in Montesinos's Cave show that stories are valid ways of approaching knowledge, knowledge of the world and knowledge of our own minds. And this is what this episode, I think, suggests brilliantly, independently, and also within the structure of the novel.

Moving on now to the second important episode I want to discuss today, Master Pedro's puppet show. The reappearance of Ginés de Pasamonte establishes a concrete continuity with Part I. Other than Sancho, the women of Don Quixote's house, the priest, and the barber, Ginés is the only character from Part I who comes back in Part II. If, before, Ginés was a rogue picaresque author, a Mateo Alemán (the author of *Guzmán de Alfarache*), now, as Master Pedro, he is a miniature playwright, a Lope de Vega in miniature (Lope de Vega, Cervantes' rival, the great Spanish playwright). As both Alemán and Lope, Ginés stands for the modern author, who is not an aristocrat or a cleric and has to earn a living from his craft. Lope liked to put the "de Vega" in his last name to pretend he was aristocratic, and he made up fables about his family's nobility. But as his enemies mercilessly reminded him, he was not really an aristocrat.

Ginés also stands for Cervantes himself, and the whole episode is like a laboratory for fiction, to carry out experiments about it as Cervantes tends to do. We have seen that Ginés is wily; he does not respect literary tradition or rules, and he shows up the limitations imposed by the medium of literature. Like the imagined friend of the 1605 prologue—remember the imagined friend whom Cervantes says comes to visit him and helps him write that prologue?—this modern author does not have a conventional or a deep classical education and has to rely on compendia and books of familiar quotations for his erudition. Lope was known for this, getting his information here and there while pretending he had read widely. He did read a great deal but not in the way humanists had read, and he made it up, just as the friend tells Cervantes to do in the prologue: to just go and get this book and that and then simply make a list of sources in alphabetical order. That is the way these modern authors operate.

Ginés now has his left eye covered. It is presumably the one that made him cross-eyed because he knows that this is a distinctive trait that is dangerous for him to display. He can be spotted, described, and nabbed by the Holy Brotherhood, so he has to disguise himself; this is why he has to cover it. The left eye is his signature, his body signature, which is that he is cross-eyed, like having a prominent scar or something like it. Remember the description of Don Quixote that the Holy Brotherhood officer reads when he is about to arrest him toward the end of Part I. A description of Ginés would probably begin by saying, he is cross-eyed. So he has to cover that eye to be safe. Ginés is a fugitive from justice. He is one of the galley slaves Don Quixote set free, so whatever other crimes he committed to make him be a galley slave, he has also fled from the authorities. Hence, I quote: "I almost forgot to say that this Master Pedro had his left eye and almost half his left cheek covered with a patch of green taffeta, indicating that something was wrong with that part of his face" (II, 25, 657).

But being one-eyed, as it were, even if it is faked, suggests fresh restrictions that impinge on Ginés's art because of his limited perception of reality. I am glossing over my article in the *Casebook* that you have read, I hope, by now. This deformity also makes him look furtive, dangerous, sneaky, and also aesthetically interesting, like the characters in Part I and those in Velázquez's paintings. He is no Renaissance idealized model of a man, although it is said several times that he is gallant and good-looking, but he is cross-eyed.

Ginés lacks depth perception, which is very suggestive with regard to the show he will stage at the inn. Ironically, by eliminating one eye Ginés is overcoming the problem of nonconverging sight lines; it is a radical way of doing so, but now he lacks perspective. Biocular sight can lead potentially to double vision. Because of this, there are in some cultures deities that overcome this condition by having a pineal eye, which is an eye in the middle of the forehead that serves to mediate between the other two. So, Ginés is eliminating one eye in order to have only one and therefore only one vision, whereas before, being cross-eyed, his sight lines did not meet. But now, having only one eye, as we know, he loses depth.

The whole scene of the puppet theater is yet another critique of Lope de Vega and a protracted experiment on mimesis like that of Princess Micomicona, and not just in literary terms but also in pictorial terms. As a critic of Lope, Cervantes again harps on the carelessness with which Lope used history to write his plays. Remember the episode with the canon of Toledo in which there was a protracted discussion and critique of Lope for just grabbing historical elements pell-mell without being very faithful to facts. When Don Quixote protests in the middle of the show that it is wrong to have Moors ringing bells instead of beating kettledrums, Master Pedro answers with what contemporaries were sure not to miss as an allusion to Lope de Vega: "Don't worry about trivialities, Don Quixote sir—you can't make anything without making mistakes. Aren't thousands of plays performed all the time full of thousands of blunders and absurdities, and despite that they have a good run and are greeted not only with applause but with admiration too? You carry on, my lad, and let them say what they like—so long as I fill my money bags it doesn't matter if I make more blunders than there are atoms in the sun" (II, 26, 666). This is as clear a dig at Lope de Vega as could be made, and remember that Avellaneda may have been a follower and a defender of Lope de Vega, which is why he wrote in the prologue to his *Quixote* such insulting comments about Cervantes.

As a laboratory of mimesis, the show Master Pedro and his assistant put on is of a conceptual complexity worthy of the Velázquez of *Las Meninas* and *The Spinners*. To begin with, the performance of the puppets is not enough in itself, as Master Pedro's figures and props require a supplemental oral commentary or narrative voiceover executed by his assistant. Ginés needs the additional narrative by the *trujamán,* which was the word of the period for such a prompter. But the visual and verbal representations do not harmonize properly, and both Don Quixote and Ginés have to admonish the boy, who is the author's offset or compensatory voice. It is like a voiceover in a film, but it is as if the voiceover and the film images did not quite mesh.

The author's invention, which is Ginés's, is expressed in two ways, visually and orally at the same time, in the hope they will complement each other. But they do not mesh satisfactorily, as if there were an inherent flaw in the recital that reflects the awkwardness of the theatrical routine. It is very clumsy to represent stories with these material objects, puppets, that stand in for human beings, so what we have here is a flawed combination of the oral and the visual trying to produce a performance, a satisfactory production. It attempts to generate mimesis, representation; in fact, it is a critique of mimesis and representation. Don Quixote's correction of the boy is made in the language of geometry as applied to painting: "'Come, boy,' exclaimed Don Quixote, 'proceed with your story in a straight line, and don't go wandering round bends or up side-roads; for to reach the truth about something like that, proof upon proof is needed'" (II, 26, 664).

What could seem like a mere rhetorical flourish on the part of the knight is, on the contrary, of surprising propriety in the context of the episode because the whole effect of the puppet show depends on a visual trompe l'oeil—this is a French term for visual trick. *Trompe l'oeil* is used in English; *trampantojo,* an old word in Spanish, is the same. The puppet show is a visual trick based on perspective, exactly the way a painting is organized according to geometrical rules that produce the effect of mass, depth, and distance. Master Pedro himself, by the way, agrees with Don Quixote, and his admonition to the boy also appeals to the language of geometry and painting: "'Look here, my lad, I don't want any flourishes, just do as the gentleman says, that'll be the wisest course'" (II, 26, 664).

"Flourishes" is "dibujos," or 'drawings,' in the original. Don Quixote's and Ginés's words say more than they know, a common occurrence in Cervantes, as we have seen many times. The puppet show's effect, its verisimilitude, is based on a question of proportions and perspective and has a great deal to do with the straight line that Don Quixote demands that the boy narrator follow, without much success. It is a metaphor to apply a straight line to how a story, a narrative, unfolds. The narrative straight line and the straight line that can be drawn from the spectators to the show are related. That is, the straight line from the spectators to the show as they look at it, and I am relating that to the straight line in the story that Don Quixote refers to when he admonishes the boy. If the spectators look directly at the theater to engage in its fantasy, they have to disregard that at such a short distance human figures, horses, and buildings should appear so small, as if they were much further away.

Perspective has to be assumed as if different geometric relations between the public and the tiny actors obtained, as if the geometric physical relations between the spectators and the show were different than they are because they are so close. The narrator goes "round bends or up side-roads," as Don Quixote calls them, to achieve the illusion of simultaneous action taking place and to hold the spectators' attention and approval in the same way that a stage play in a theater has to abuse the rules of geometry to stage the action in what is presumably a greater space; but it is compressed on the stage, and the proportion between the various elements—the actors and the horses and all of that—is not followed. Ginés cannot vary the figures' dimensions as they come closer or further away from the public; the dimensions are a given that cannot be changed. This whole ensemble of virtual lines, like those in Velázquez's paintings, holds up the fiction and its props at the same time in front of the audience.

The audience here is aware both of the fiction and of the props that are there to make up the fiction, as in Velázquez's paintings. To sustain the illusion the narrator avails himself figuratively not only of the geometric figures but also of the rhetoric of visions, repeating the anaphora—anaphora is a rhetorical figure in which you repeat a word or a turn of phrase, as when an orator repeats something like, "Let us not forget . . . , let us not forget. . . ." That is an anaphora, and the language of visions in medieval literature used this figure. The boy says, "Observe . . . ," "Look . . . ," and so forth. What he is really telling them with all of these repetitions is, "Don't actually see what is really happening. Overlook it to be able to accept the fiction."

Within the very illusion of a show we have a kind of mirror duplication of the problem of perspective and vanishing point. Remember that I talked about the vanishing point in *Las Meninas* regarding the gentleman who is at the back, who is literally leaving and vanishing, so there would seem to be a pun in the painting. This becomes literal in the puppet show when Melisendra and Don Gaiferos, riding the same horse, gallop away desperately, running from the Moors toward "la línea de Francia," toward the line dividing France from Spain, the border. So if they are on the horse, here, they are moving toward the back of the stage and toward a vanishing point, there; so this geometric design here is literalizing the vanishing point in the fiction.

All of these tricks manage to confuse Don Quixote, who predictably lunges toward the action to participate in it, caught in a net of rhetorical and geometrical figures that have blinded him, not letting him see the difference in size between his own body and those of his enemies. He has lost the sense of proportion, and this is what encourages him, in addition to his madness, of course, to join in the action.

I think Cervantes projects himself in Ginés/Master Pedro as author of modern fictions, as he did in the galley slaves episode in Part I. Do not overlook the fact that Cervantes was also maimed, just as Ginés is cross-eyed. Cervantes had a lesion on his left arm, an injury suffered at the Battle of Lepanto that disabled him. Ginés/Master Pedro is struggling with the difficulties of authorship, as it were, by adjusting his ability to perceive reality and hence to represent it. Making himself one-eyed, Master Pedro manages to prevent the problems created by his cross-eyedness. Remember that with two eyes, let alone two crossed eyes, there are two visions, which may or may not coincide but certainly will not if he is cross-eyed. This is the cause of his not being able to foresee an ending to his autobiography—remember? You could project that as a problem of vision, too, if autobiography goes this way and life that way, and your vision does not allow for a coincidence of the two; that infinitely receding end of the fiction, or infinitely to the end of his life, could be seen as part of his problems with his eyes.

Having only one eye, however, Master Pedro would be able to look straight through only one visual axis, but this is not a happy solution either. To compensate for his loss of one half of the visual field he must look sideways: if he has his eye covered he has to look sideways, askew with his head. He cannot achieve a harmonious vision, and he makes himself more awkward and interesting, hence he cannot represent reality properly. Having only one eye, Master Pedro cannot create a perspective that will correspond to reason, to follow Alberti's treatise on painting. His reading of literary tradition is also askew, like the tilt of his head. We also know that because he has only one eye he would also lose his depth perception, which would disastrously affect his capacity to create perspective. His rewriting of the Melisendra and Gaiferos story is fraught with errors, like Lope de Vega's plays, and Don Quixote tries to correct them, as we saw.

Only that ideal reader Alonso Quixano, who instead of writing romances of chivalry tried to act one out, can see straight in the lucid nights spent in his library and perceive fictions that are harmonious and very similar within themselves and to himself. Don Quixote, in the darkness of Juan Palomeque's inn, slashes the wineskins and thereby makes the various fictional levels converge and resolves the conflictive stories. It is the ability to fuse all of those nonconverging levels of fiction that makes Cervantes such a great modern author, one whose fictions will not destroy themselves from within, as Ginés's does here. Cervantes' is a happy cross-eyedness because the various lines do not fuse in his imaginative world yet cohere in some way. To him, the origin of vision is always already a double vision, with irony being congenital to it and with representation depending on it.

I like to see this episode of Master Pedro's puppet show as an allegory of the whole of the *Quixote,* with Cervantes the author hidden inside there but outside his fiction, which he controls through strings with a voice projected by an agent, Cide Hamete Benengeli or his translators, whom he cannot quite control either. The story itself, like that of Melisendra and Gaiferos, is drawn from literary sources but distorted and rearranged as needed, and the public, we, the readers, are drawn into this fiction but are not completely aware, as we are of the artifice of the whole construct. I am moved, romantic that I am, by Cervantes' identification with Ginés, the fugitive from justice, roaming through Spain struggling to make a living with this fiction-making contraption.

Cervantes wraps up this take on modern literature and its labors in the brilliant scene that closes the episode of Master Pedro's puppet show, the one in which, aided by Sancho and the innkeeper, Don Quixote compensates the puppeteer for the figurines he has smashed. The value of each broken piece depends on his or her relative importance in the fiction, not on its material value based on the stuff of which it is made, plus the workmanship.

Charlemagne is worth a great deal because of who he is in the story, for instance. The real and the fictional worlds cut through each other here. Real money is being paid in restitution for damages, but the amount of the compensation is figured on fictional values. What I mean is, a figurine of a slave or a peasant or a servant would not, even if it is beautiful and big, cost as much as that of the king. What Cervantes seems to be underlining here is the value of fictional characters as the creations of their author. How much would a Don Quixote or a Sancho be worth to Cervantes? How much a Hamlet to Shakespeare? How much would it take to compensate García Márquez for Colonel Aureliano Buendía or Borges for Pierre Menard?

These are fictional entities, but now they have a real monetary value in a world in which literature is becoming a commodity, without ceasing to be, at the same time, one of the great expressions of the human spirit. This scene is reminiscent of the one that occurs toward the end of Part I, when restitutions are made to the barber whose basin has been taken, to the innkeeper for expenses and damages, and marriage vows are exchanged to make up for Don Fernando's dishonest behavior toward Dorotea. It is a miniaturized scene of restitutions, a small-scale repetition of that scene in Part I. To me, it is as if Cervantes were boasting of how many ways he can rewrite episodes in Part II, and in that he is certainly a master puppeteer himself.

CHAPTER 18

Don Quixote and Sancho in the Hands of Frivolous Aristocrats

Required Readings

Cervantes, *Don Quixote*, Part II, chaps. 22–35, pp. 630–733.
Cervantes Saavedra, Miguel de. *The Exemplary Novels of Miguel de Cervantes Saavedra*, 469–84. Trans. Walter K. Kelly. London: Henry G. Bohn, 1855.

I said at the start of the last lecture that after the episodes I would be discussing then, namely, the Cave of Montesinos and Maese Pedro's puppet show, three significant new developments take place in the *Quixote*. I want to go over them again now. The first is that Don Quixote will sometimes not be the center of the action, which will focus instead on Sancho. The second is that both protagonists become the objects of amusement of aristocratic, frivolous characters that have read Part I and want them to behave according to it. The third is that Don Quixote and Sancho will be surrounded by many more characters than before. The overarching theme of the novel continues to be desengaño, and most of the episodes are staged by authors within the fiction, which is highly theatrical, and the backstage of the pranks, the stage machinery, as it were, is revealed to the reader either during their performance or right after.

The episode of the enchanted boat was needed to get our protagonists across the Ebro River. In Part I the territory Don Quixote and Sancho covered was not very specific in geographic terms. Seville is mentioned as the destination of the prostitutes at the first inn, and it is also mentioned as the destination of Andrés, when he reappears. The Sierra Morena is the setting for Don Quixote's penance and the place where Cardenio is hiding in shame and in madness. This relative vagueness is consistent with the narrator's refusal to mention the village where Alonso Quixano lives and to which Don Quixote returns.

In Part II, however, geography becomes much more precise, starting with El Toboso, our protagonist's first stop, which is a real village in Castile, and continuing with their original destination, Saragossa, where Don Quixote wants to participate in jousts celebrated on Saint George's Day, April 23. A stream figures in the episode of the fulling hammers, but now Don Quixote and Sancho are on their way to Saragossa and have to get across the Ebro, one of the major rivers of Spain. Castile is not only landlocked but has very little water in general, and this is reflected in the novel. It only rains once in Part I, as we have seen.

The second part adds geographic concreteness to its realistic portrayal of Spanish life. This is not new with Cervantes. He derives it from the picaresque. In *Lazarillo de Tormes,* Tormes is a real river; it is the river that goes through Salamanca, as a matter of fact. And in the *Guzmán de Alfarache,* the geography is quite precise, both in Spain and in Italy. So Cervantes has derived this specificity from the picaresque, but the episode of the enchanted boat also serves to highlight—comically, of course—the difference between Don Quixote's obsolete Ptolemaic notions of geography and the new Copernican conception of the universe, which is being expanded as a field of knowledge even as Cervantes writes. The Copernican universe is infinite, while the Ptolemaic universe is limited.

Galileo was making important discoveries in favor of Copernicanism in the early decades of the seventeenth century—he was in Spain for a while—and developing instruments of observation like the telescope. But Don Quixote still adheres to Ptolemaic ideas and calculations, as he demonstrates in his hilarious exchange with Sancho when he asks his squire to check to see if he has any lice on his body. It was common lore that when one crossed the equator all such vermin carried on one's body would perish, as if by magic. Sancho discovers that his fleas or lice are still very much alive, and he underscores the plural in saying he has a few. Like chivalry, Ptolemaic geography is a medieval retention struggling to survive in a world which, after the discovery and settlement of the New World, was wholly untenable except to the likes of Don Quixote and Sancho, who does not care either way. It does not make any difference to Sancho. Ptolemy, in fact, was revived in the Renaissance as part of the rediscovery of the classical world, ironically, just as Copernicus was rendering his theories obsolete.

The crossing of the Ebro is significant also because our characters are moving beyond landlocked Castile toward coastal regions of Spain that are in touch with other cultures and languages. In the second part we will reach such regions as Barcelona, where Catalan is spoken, not Spanish. The river incident is a rewriting—I am always talking about the episodes of Part II being rewritings of episodes of Part I—of the windmills adventure in Part I because of the wheels in the river; it has similar results, except that Don Quixote and Sancho, again, have to make restitutions for damages, and, like all crossings, this one is a transition.

We can be amused by the efforts the translators make to render it into English, especially the puns that are involved in Don Quixote's and Sancho's exchange about cosmography, which are a little bit obscene in the Spanish. After Sancho wonders how far they have traveled, Don Quixote says, "'Mucho,' replicó Don Quijote, 'porque de trescientos sesenta grados que contiene el globo del agua y de la tierra según el cómputo de Ptolomeo, que fue el mayor cosmógrafo que se sabe, la mitad habremos caminado llegando a la línea que he dicho.' 'Por Dios,' dijo Sancho, 'que vuesa merced me trae por testigo de lo que dice a una gentil persona, puto y gafo, con la añadidura de meón, o meo, o no sé cómo.'"

The ugly word in Spanish for saying 'to urinate' is *mear*, the equivalent in English of 'to piss,' and in the name Ptolemy in Spanish, Ptolomeo, there seems to be included the first person singular of the indicative of the word *mear, yo meo,* and this is what Sancho hears in Ptolomeo's name. And *cómputo*, 'computation,' to him sounds like *puto*, which is the masculine of *puta*, 'whore,' and means 'homosexual.' So what Don Quixote has told Sancho lacks all weight when his authority has to do with a person who is a homosexual who pisses a lot. This is what Sancho hears. The effort by Jarvis is not very good: "'By the lord,' quoth Sancho, 'your worship has brought a very pretty fellow, that same Tolmy with his amputation to vouch the truth of what you say.'" He is trying to get 'computation' and 'amputation' to get the pun; not very funny. Smollett, also from the eighteenth century, tries to get it this way: "'For God!' cried Sancho, 'your worship has brought a set of rare witnesses to prove the truth of what you say. Copulation and Kiss-me-Gaffer, with the addition of Tool-i'-me, or some such name.'" This is actually better because it catches the spirit of the obscenity of what Sancho is saying. Rutherford writes, "'Good God,' said Sancho, 'that's a fine character you've dredged up as a witness, with his sexy butts and his tomfoolery, and what's more a great pornographer, or whatever it was you said'" (II, 29, 684). The point is that Cervantes is making fun of the whole Ptolemaic system, which by this time is obsolete, but Don Quixote is invoking it as his authority to tell where it is they are going as they ride in the boat.

When Don Quixote and Sancho arrive at the house of the Duke and Duchess they enter a realm of games and frivolity they have not known before. These are irresponsible aristocrats that belong to the leisure class; in fact, the house in which the action takes place is not even their regular house, it is a summer home for recreation. Don Quixote first meets the Duchess, who is out falcon hunting, all decked out for the occasion and surrounded by an entourage. Hunting with falcons was very ceremonial; people went out with servants, and the falcons, the hawks, were trained to catch the prey. I do not believe there was much real exercise involved, as the hawks did all the work, but this is part of the recreation of these aristocrats. The Duke and Duchess are devoted to pleasure, one source of which is obviously reading, for they know Part I of the *Quixote* quite well. They are idle readers, like the one Cervantes addressed in the first words of the prologue of Part I.

Don Quixote and Sancho are like toys to the Duke and Duchess or, better, they are like literary characters, which, in fact, is exactly what they are. I mean, Don Quixote and Sancho have fallen into the hands of these people who are devoted readers of Part I, and, wow!, here we have the "real" Don Quixote and Sancho at our own home, and so they try to make the best of it. Everything in the Duke's and Duchess's home is like fiction, except that fiction can be harsh and cruel. The truth of their fiction is that reality, too, is like fiction, and that both reality and fiction can hurt you. Actually, at the Duke's summer home reality is always reality plus the props to create the fiction; it is not reality by itself but reality improved by or changed by the props. This is the harshness of desengaño. Not only that being deluded can be hurtful, and to be undeluded also can be hurtful, but that the physical process may indeed involve injury. Peter E. Russell, a distinguished British Hispanist whom I have quoted before, says, "The Duke and Duchess are remarkably unfeeling aristocratic pranksters; some of their jokes involve causing physical harm to their two guests."[1] You will see that Don Quixote is scratched by cats, and he and Sancho fall from Clavileño, the wooden horse. Russell adds, "Social satire directed at various levels of society is more prominent in these chapters than anywhere else in the book."[2] This is true: social satire is very important in these chapters.

In addition—this is a detail I hope you pick up on—the Duke's and Duchess's expensive pleasures are underwritten by the peasant whose son does not want to marry Dueña Rodriguez's daughter, which is the reason no pressure is put on him by his master to make good on his promise. This young man has pledged to marry Dueña Rodriguez's daughter because he has impregnated her, and she complains that no influence is exerted on him because his father, who is a rich peasant within the realm controlled by the Duke and Duchess, lends them money at opportune moments, that is, when the Duke and Duchess are in dire economic straits.

This is a highly significant detail. These are not only idle upper classes, but upper classes in hock who finance their high living with loans. Since you are readers of Elliott's *Imperial Spain,* you will no doubt see that it is easy to draw an analogy between the behavior of these aristocrats and the policies of the Spanish Crown, which lived off the shipments of precious metals from the New World and off loans from the Fuggers, the German bankers who financed the expensive pleasures of the Hapsburgs at their court, for instance, the building of the Buen Retiro palace, which you can still see in Madrid. Velázquez paints these Hapsburgs hunting and engaging in these kinds of pleasures, too. Most of this rich life was underwritten by loans from German bankers, so this is all part of the political side of the 1615 *Quixote,* which, as I mentioned before, is the first political novel. In this context, Sancho's social aspirations do not appear to be that outlandish, in the sense that Cervantes is showing how the social order and its hierarchies are crumbling because the upper classes are so corrupt. This is evident in the fact that a mere peasant is financing these aristocrats' frivolous lifestyle.

This is kind of a topsy-turvy world which bespeaks the crumbling of the social order. What Cervantes is dramatizing here is that a new order is in the making in which class mobility (up or down) may very well be possible. We see characters like the butler in the household of the Duke and Duchess, who has enormous power over his masters, and we see Sancho elevated finally, even if fictionally, to the position of governor of an island. So the second part of the *Quixote* reveals a social order that is not as stable as it used to be, that is shaking, and Cervantes is giving us very precise financial details about the transformation through this satire: the kind of financial details you expect to find only in nineteenth-century novels, such as Balzac's, in which the monetary dealings of the characters play a central role. But here in Cervantes we have these details already, such as the fact that the Duke gets loans from this peasant.

Fiction, as performed at the Duke's house, is mirthful and playful but also cruel and uncaring. Fiction is also both ephemeral and substantial, like the props that hold it up. With the Duke and Duchess, Don Quixote and

Sancho temporarily realize their dreams: Don Quixote is treated like a great knight, and Sancho is finally made governor of an island. When Don Quixote entered the Duke's and Duchess's palatial summer home, they had already prompted their help to treat Don Quixote as a great personage and have all kinds of things ready to secure his comfort. But these fabrications quickly disappear. It is, again, desengaño: the truth of fiction is that it illuminates the fictional quality of real life or the ephemeral quality of real life, if you like. An American Hispanist, Ruth El Saffar, who died very young, tragically, and was a significant Cervantes scholar, wrote, "All of Part II is based on the mistaken assumption, on the part of the would-be all-controlling char-acter-authors, that they can deal with a fictional character and maintain at the same time a distance which allows them never to slip into that fictional world with which they plan to entertain themselves. Like Sansón, they are trapped from two directions: they are controlled to some extent from within their play by the very characters whom they intend to manipulate, and from without by an author of whom they are unaware, by whose will and whose hand all they do is contrived."[3] As we have seen already in the case of Sansón Carrasco, this controlling author falls into his own trap. He loses to Don Quixote in the combat they have, and we will see, time and again, that the butler, who is a very clever fellow and organizes all of these elaborate pranks, does not succeed with them. Eventually they come tumbling down. Sansón Carrasco is the principal internal author, as I said and as we have seen from the very beginning, bent on recreating the fiction of Part I, but now, at the Duke's house, the Duke's butler will compete with Sansón quite favorably. He is the originator of complicated pranks like the island where Sancho will be governor and like the pageant in the forest, but none turn out quite as he planned them, and he gets caught in them.

This butler, by the way, if you think about the pageant in the forest, was not only clever in creating these pranks, but he was also a poet; he must have written the lines that Merlin delivers in the pageant. The significance of all of this, apart from its baroque character, is that Cervantes is speculating, as usual, about his own position vis-à-vis his fiction, this fiction that seems to be always getting away from him; this is what the presence of these internal authors, who are beset by problems of distance and control, reveals. It is the same kind of situation in which Maese Pedro finds himself with his puppet theater.

One of the early events that occurs at the Duke's and Duchess's house is the debate Don Quixote has with the ecclesiastic. This is a criticism of the church, not of religion, and may also be a commentary on Spanish politics and the role the clergy is allowed to play in them. Here is another instance of the social and political criticism that appears in the novel. Don Quixote intimates that the ecclesiastic is a leech living at the expense of the Duke and Duchess, who in turn live off of the rich peasant who loans them money. Don Quixote tells the priest that he speaks without authority because he lacks experience and accuses him of acting aggressively because he is protected by his investiture, meaning that Don Quixote cannot challenge him to a duel because he is an ecclesiastic and therefore takes advantage of that protection to be able to act with haughtiness.

But notice that there is some truth to what the ecclesiastic says to the Duke and Duchess about how they are dealing with Don Quixote, encouraging him to go on with his insanity about being a knight-errant. There are no uniformly negative characters in Cervantes, and even this very unpleasant priest is right in some of the things he says. He ruins the whole dinner and is very unpleasant, but some of the things he says are quite true. Perspectivism, as we have been seeing throughout the semester, means that no one is in possession of the entire truth; that is, the truth is made up of the various points of view of the characters, and the truth may be spoken by the most unlikely of people, even those who are not very pleasant. This is a constant in Cervantes. Notice that the debate with the ecclesiastic is what we could call a preprandial speech; it is a speech before dinner, which is ruined, anyway, by the dispute. It is another rewriting of the arms and letters speech because Don Quixote always seems to be able to return to that topic, as he did at the house of Diego de Miranda when he expounded on the virtues of poetry and of the military.

We move on now to episodes that are quite independent and that seem to build not on Part I but on previous episodes of Part II. It is fiction issuing from fiction, like a telescope that you are pulling out from within itself. These are very important episodes, not quite on the level of the Cave of Montesinos but very important, very memorable incidents that make a coherent unit, although there will be a return to the Duke's and Duchess's house when Don Quixote is on his way back home.

To begin with the hunt, here we have again this effect of the infinitely receding sequences. The hunt and the elaborate pageant in the forest are games within games, plays within plays. What is the hunt? The hunt is a mock war. Aristocrats no longer participate in wars, so they now engage in mock wars, specifically in hunting. We saw that both Don Quixote and Don Diego de Miranda are hunters. The hunting of the boar involves strategies that are akin to those of a battle, demanding horsemanship as well as the playing of drums and various horns and trumpets; many of the ceremonial aspects of war are reproduced in hunting. War has become a sport, and sports, modern sports, too, are mock wars. Think for a moment of American football. The metaphor of war is very crass in American football: I invade your territory whereas the other team defends its territory, and so there is a dividing line, which is like the frontier between two countries at war, and all of the terminology is derived from the military.

As at Camacho's wedding the pageant in the forest begins with a killed animal, as if a scapegoat is needed both to start the action and to provide food for the feast, at which it will be consumed. Feasts, ceremonies, and parties seem to demand a scapegoat of some sort. It does not have to be a goat; it can be a turkey at Thanksgiving or a pig in many celebrations throughout the Caribbean, but it seems to be an atavistic need of the human race to have these propitiatory victims. New traditions of this kind have emerged in Spain, where some towns have started a practice whereby at their big feast they take a goat up the church steeple and throw it off. Gross. But what I am underlining is that at the beginning of the pageant the killing of this boar has an atavistic and ritualistic air to it.

This pageant in the forest is one of the most baroque episodes in the whole of the *Quixote*. The episode gathers elements of the Cave of Montesinos and the wagon of the Parliament of Death; it is a kind of synthesis of the two. This is what I meant by episodes that are derived from episodes, but it is also a version or, more accurately, a perversion of a certain moment in Dante's *Purgatorio* XXIX, a parody. Cervantes' sources are not just the romances of chivalry but Ovid, Virgil, Homer, and Dante, no less.

In Dante's *Purgatorio* XXIX the pilgrim-poet experiences a moment of anagnorisis, of self-discovery. The pilgrim is now left by Virgil, who has guided him up to this point but who will not be able to enter Paradise because he is a pagan. So the pilgrim must proceed on his own to meet Beatrice. Virgil dwells in limbo, at the entrance of Hell, where he is lodged with other worthies of the pagan world, neither punished nor rewarded. This is a marvelous invention of Dante: limbo, where he puts all of these great figures of antiquity who could not have been Christian because they lived before Christ and therefore cannot enter Paradise. They are put in limbo, where they are together in a palace, neither happy nor sad, with a kind of faint smile, a mysterious smile on their faces, discussing their works with each other. It is a kind of a perpetual seminar. . . . Not bad.

That is where Virgil dwells, the place from which he departed to accompany the pilgrim up to but not quite into Paradise. The whole object of the journey was to meet Beatrice. The pilgrim moves on to the end of *Purgatorio* to be met by her. I will get to the solemn procession that meets him, on which the procession in Cervantes is based, but first let me tell you that the meeting with Beatrice is, to me, one of the funniest moments in all of Western literature. The pilgrim-poet has gone through Hell and most of Purgatory to meet her, and the first thing Beatrice does when they meet is to reproach him for having been interested in other women after her death. I find this delicious, very funny, and a great lesson: no good deed shall go unpunished.

But what ensues in Dante is an elaborate procession as Beatrice appears: at the front march seven luminaries, the seven gifts of the Holy Ghost, followed by the twenty elders of the Apocalypse. Canticles announce the impending arrival of Beatrice, four mystic animals appear, the four gospels, and a cart pulled by a griffin; the four cardinal virtues follow and then the three theological virtues with Saint Peter and Saint Paul, four doctors of the Church, and Saint John. The procession stops before the pilgrim-poet, and the triumphant Beatrice, symbol of theology, makes her appearance. This is the background of the pageant that the Duke's butler has organized with the help of other servants, including the beautiful (male) page playing the role of Dulcinea.

One must pause to ponder—at least I pause to ponder—the distance between the universe created by Dante in the *Divine Comedy* and that created by Cervantes in the *Quixote*. Cervantes' pageant in the forest is quite a bold parody, verging on the irreverent. What is the difference between Dante's and Cervantes' worlds? In my view, it is the progressive crumbling of the certainties of the medieval world, the cosmology grounded on the Ptolemaic system that has been shattered by the discovery of the New World and the Copernican revolution and the Protestant Reformation. The minutely ordered, symbolic universe of Christian doctrine apparent in medieval cathedrals and in the *Divine Comedy* is no longer available. The fusion of Neoplatonic love and its courtly derivatives, which could coalesce in the figure of Beatrice uniting worldly love with divine love and faith, has been torn asunder, so that what Don Quixote finds in this brilliant scene is not a Beatrice but a transvestite Dulcinea no less, who reveals to him perhaps the depths of his madness and the true nature of his desire. Javier Herrero, whom I have quoted several times in the course of the semester, says the following: "It is a remarkable twist of Cervantes' irony that the incarnated Dulcinea is a lie of the duke's built on a previous lie of Sancho. To top it all, Dulcinea is really a man, a page of the duke's that the butler has selected to play this role because

of his beauty. Such is the ontological status of the earthly Dulcinea, a labyrinth of lies built upon lies of contradictory appearances."[4]

Think about the radical difference between Beatrice and this Dulcinea.
There is an enormous difference between the sublime image of Beatrice,
who incarnates theology in the *Divine Comedy,* and this outlandish figure
of the Duke's page, who is very beautiful, playing the role of Dulcinea. This
is the evolution of the ideal woman from Dante to Cervantes, which goes
through Laura in Petrarch, Isabel Freyre in Garcilaso, and winds up in this
brilliant figure of the transvestite Dulcinea that we have here in this pageant
in the forest. Here Cervantes reaches levels of penetration into the evolution
of the Western mind that are really uncanny. We have not really gone much
beyond him, if at all.

The pageant in the forest is bristling with baroque elements; it is, as
I said, the most baroque scene in the entire novel. First, it takes place in a
chiaroscuro atmosphere, a darkness that is half illuminated by torches. It is a
fabrication, a construction, an assemblage of disparate elements: theatrical,
self-conscious, humorous. It is play and it is a play; the carts carrying the
costumed players are like those used to represent autos sacramentales. As
in much of the second part, these are complicated *burlas,* 'pranks,' based on
literary allusions, like the Cave of Montesinos episode, which drew from the
classical tradition and the romances of chivalry—remember the descent into
Hades in Homer and Virgil and the ones in the romances of chivalry.

In this pageant in the forest we have, as in Montesinos's Cave, literary
figures, like Merlin and the Devil, representing themselves. You would think
that a literary figure represents presumably a real person, but these literary
figures are representing literary figures; there are several layers of fictionality here. It is literally a Dantesque world with clear allusions, as I have
mentioned, to *Purgatorio.* Baroque art is what we call in Spanish *efectista;*
it aims at generating reactions from the audience because of its outrageous
dimensions or its exaggerated qualities: that is the essence of the baroque.
The reader is treated to the effects of this art and shown the reactions of the
spectators and participants, like Sancho, who faints, and also its impact even
on those who are responsible for the whole charade. The Duke and Duchess
are caught within their own fiction and are scared. The most jarring effect in
this episode is caused by sound:

> With this, the night darkened and lights and more lights began to
> flit about the wood, much as the gaseous exhalations of the earth
> flit about the sky and look to us like shooting stars. At the same
> time a dreadful din was heard, like that made by the solid wheels

of ox-carts, from which relentless creaking and groaning it's said that wolves and bears flee, if there are any in the vicinity. To this great tempest of sound was added another that was greater still, because it truly seemed that in the four corners of the wood four separate battles were being fought at the same time: on one side the harsh racket of fearsome artillery rang out, on another countless muskets were being fired, not far away the shouts of the combatants could be heard and in the distance the Moorish war-cries were being repeated. In short, the bugles, the horns, the clarions, the trumpets, the drums, the artillery, the muskets and, above all, the fearsome creaking of the ox-carts made together such a chaotic and horrendous clangour that Don Quixote had to summon up all his courage to endure it. (II, 34, 725)

The "son confuso," 'confused sound,' causes "pasmo," 'astonishment,' "suspenso," 'suspense,' "admiración," 'admiration,' and "espanto," 'fright.' I am quoting words from the original. The key here is the shrill disharmony; the sounds are "ronco," 'hoarse,' and "espantoso," 'frightening.' The voices, "horrísona," 'horrible'; the devil is sounding a "desaforado cuerno," an 'outrageous horn.' There are visual effects, too. The devils are ugly: those "feos demonios," and Merlin, as the figure of death, is terrifying. The whole scene is cast in this clash of sounds and sights artificially created for effect. Even in the translation I just read you can hear that Cervantes has created this effect stylistically, with harsh-sounding words and onomatopoeias, that is, words that sound like what they represent.

In addition to all of this baroque atmosphere, Dulcinea is a transvestite. Dulcinea is a man disguised as a beautiful woman, more precisely, a beautiful young man disguised as a beautiful young woman; it is underlined that the page is beautiful. This is the most outrageous of the transformations Dulcinea undergoes, even worse than her appearing as a peasant wench smelling of garlic: it makes her femininity something artificial that, with the proper disguise, can be forged. The transvestite is a common baroque figure in Spanish literature because in the baroque even gender can be constructed, fabricated. From the ideal beauty drawn from the Neoplatonic and the courtly love tradition from which Don Quixote invents Dulcinea, to the grotesque peasant of Sancho's lie, to this baroque construction, there is an increase in the level of fabrication, of artificiality.

I guess we do invent the objects of our desires; this is what the novel keeps telling us. You have to be careful that you do not invent the object of your desire and it turns out to be a transvestite, unless you are into that sort of thing. I have seen some who can fool anybody. I wrote a book on a Cuban writer called Severo Sarduy whose chief figure is a transvestite; he lived in Paris, and I visited a few places with him that are not in the tour guide-books and where you would find transvestites that could really fool anybody. The grotesqueness is augmented in the *Quixote* and made even funnier by the feature that exposes Dulcinea's true gender, which is . . . her voice! Rutherford is too literal by writing that Dulcinea spoke, "with virile assurance and in not very feminine tones" (II, 35, p. 730). In the original it says that Dulcinea's voice was not very "*adamada*," from 'dama,' lady, 'adamada.' The voice was not very lady-like. Dulcinea's voice is masculine. She has this voice and when she delivers the speech the contrast is that she is beautiful, because the page is beautiful and dressed like a beautiful woman, but suddenly what emerges from her is the hoarse voice of a male. She has too much testosterone and this contrast, this clash, is what is important here.

This episode reminds me of a movie that is perhaps too old for you to have seen, but it is such a classic that you may have seen it: *Some Like It Hot,* with Marilyn Monroe. It is a wonderful movie. The man played by Jack Lemmon, who is in drag, responds to a marriage proposal by an old suitor by saying, "But I'm not even a woman!," and the suitor replies, "Nobody's perfect." I guess this Dulcinea is not perfect; I mean, first of all, she is a man. She may be beautiful, but she has a voice that is simply not very feminine. This entire elaborate prank is concocted to disenchant Dulcinea, to bring her out of the state in which Sancho's lie has put her. Hence the need, within this grotesque fiction, for Sancho to punish himself by giving himself three thousand lashes on his buttocks.

The prank has a logic of its own which operates at the level of the lies, which are fictions in their own right. At that level Sancho is the culprit, so he must pay the price. But why lashes on his butt and not his back? Traditionally, prisoners are punished by having a number of lashes administered to their bare backs, but here it is to Sancho's bare bottom. This adds to the humor of the whole charade because Sancho wants to protect his butt. It is an allusion to Sancho's being so dependent on his digestive system, as it were. He has already defecated twice in the novel—remember, in Part I, in the fulling hammers, and then when he takes that concoction Don Quixote gives him and has a terrible bout of diarrhea—so defecation and the rear end are very much a part of Sancho. Sancho's ample rear represents his fleshy character; it is his signature as much as his belly is in the last name, Panza.

A finale on the Duke and Duchess: Joaquín Casalduero, a Spanish Hispanist from the forties, says that at the Duke's house Don Quixote for the first time feels like a real knight-errant, but that this is not enough for him. This is Casalduero in my translation: "Man's inner reality seeks to be confirmed in society, which when it gratifies the man of action grants him a personality; but any social confirmation of what is spiritual is always a parody. Don Quixote, a spiritual man, sees his own image as a knight-errant, which he has heretofore always contemplated in the purity of action. It is an image of his external self: the honor, the social status, the fame that society can grant the man of the spirit are nothing but a burlesque image of him, a distortion of his inner life."[5] Casalduero posits that any manifestation of one's inner life in the world outside has necessarily to be burlesque, that it cannot match its essence in the purity of thought and desire. Perhaps Don Quixote is making this discovery as he is subjected to pranks, like those he suffers at the hands of the Duke and Duchess and their minions.

I want to end with a few words about "The Pretended Aunt." This is a novella that appeared in a bundle of manuscripts that included some of Cervantes' stories like "Rinconete and Cortadillo," but it was not signed. As might be expected, the debate has raged over the centuries as to whether it was written by Cervantes or not. In favor of considering the story to be by Cervantes, I would say that Esperanza is an independent young woman who shapes her future by dint of her will and courage; she rebels and winds up married to a well-to-do young man; she erases her past as a whore and becomes respectable and married. In this, she is like other Cervantes characters, including Marcela, Dorotea, and Zoraida. Also, the story has a Cervantine ending in that it concludes with an unequal marriage similar to those in the *Quixote.*

Against the story being by Cervantes is the strong, too strong, influence of *Celestina,* above all in the salacious episodes and details about "repairing" virgins. There is nothing quite as dirty as that in any text by Cervantes, including "The Deceitful Marriage" and "The Dialogue of the Dogs," stories you will be reading toward the end of the course. It could be that "The Pretended Aunt" is an early Cervantes story, before he was Cervantes; it could also be a Cervantes imitator who wrote it. What do you think?

CHAPTER 19

Bearded Ladies and Flying Horses

The Duke's House of Tricks

Required Readings

Cervantes, *Don Quixote,* Part II, chaps. 36–53, pp. 734–850.
Elliott, *Imperial Spain,* 321–60.

I have been insisting in my last few lectures on how Cervantes rewrites episodes from Part I in Part II, and I want to begin today with some general statements on this theme and offer a few other general statements as we approach the end of the *Quixote.* First, I want to make clear that not all episodes in Part II are modeled after others in Part I. There is no antecedent, really, for the Cave of Montesinos adventure, which is the highlight of Part II and perhaps of the whole book; neither is there really an antecedent for the Clavileño flight. So there are a number of important episodes in Part II that are not modeled on episodes from Part I. You will also get to see, as I mentioned, episodes in Part II that repeat or rewrite episodes within Part II itself, which is very interesting.

Second, I want to emphasize that the rewritings are expansions of those episodes in Part I; they are like blowups, one could say, of episodes in Part I in that they tend to have more characters and the actions are outrageous in comparison to those of their antecedents. For instance, there is something of the fight with the Basque in Don Quixote's encounter with Sansón Carrasco disguised as the Knight of the Mirrors, but the second episode is richer. In the first, they are both mounted and armed, and Don Quixote wins. The same thing occurs in the second episode, but now his opponent is playing the role of a knight. His outfit reflects Don Quixote, literally and metaphorically, and the whole setup is carefully prepared to resemble a contest between two knights. None of this is present in the earlier episode. Such expansion or enlargement is consonant with the increasingly baroque aesthetics of Part II, and each instance of a rewriting is like one more proof of the baroque aesthetics. Cervantes has not remained the same in the ten years that have elapsed between Parts I and II, and the old Cervantes is his own measure of development, as it were.

In the episodes I will be discussing today and in subsequent lectures, this process of expansion is itself expanded, reaching the limits of representation, which is, again, also a characteristic of the baroque. I also want to insist on something that I have only hinted at in previous lectures and that you may have noticed on your own: the increasing presence of Virgil and his *Aeneid* as we move toward the end of the second part of the *Quixote*. I will be more specific about this when we meet Altisidora, who is a parody of Dido. I want to mention this because the Virgilian background may suggest something important about how Cervantes conceived Don Quixote in Part II. Aeneas is known for his prudence, for his sense of duty from the very beginning, when he carries Anchises on his back as they leave a burning Troy and when he repeatedly fends off temptations, Dido being the most memorable, so that he can fulfill his destiny, which will be nothing less than the founding of Rome.

Aeneas has the greatest excuse for leaving a woman in all of Western literature: I have to go found Rome! Don Quixote cannot aspire to such a grand design, but Cervantes has given him a different though no less serious one, and one that is consonant with the age in which he lives, which is no longer the heroic age of Virgil's characters: that mission is to conquer himself. This is going to be Don Quixote's task. The evolution of the mad Don Quixote toward sanity and self-knowledge is the modern equivalent of Aeneas's prudence and his task of founding the great city. This, it seems to me, is the overall suggestion in these repeated allusions, direct and indirect, to Virgil. Before, I spoke of Homer, Ovid, and Dante and about how Cervantes' field of allusions and sources had moved up from the romances of chivalry to the core of the Western tradition, though without abandoning, to be sure, the romances of chivalry. I also want to emphasize (I have already mentioned it) that in these episodes that are rewritings and in the major episodes in Part II there is a strong presence of death, one way or another. Sometimes, as in the pageant in the forest, it is the very figure of Death as an allegorical figure. This is, again, and I will be emphasizing it today in discussing one of the episodes, very much a part of the baroque.

Before I move on to some of the truly outrageous adventures I want to discuss today, let me say something about Sancho's letter to his wife and about the exchange of letters that takes place in this part of the novel. Cervantes, who anticipated so many things in the *Quixote,* is anticipating epistolary fiction in Sancho's letter and in these exchanges of letters between Teresa and the Duchess.

The epistolary novel is one in which the whole text consists of an exchange of letters among the characters. As a genre, it became very popular in the eighteenth century in the works of authors such as Samuel Richardson, with his immensely successful novels *Pamela* (1740) and *Clarissa* (1749). In France, there was the *Lettres persanes* by Montesquieu, followed by *Julie, ou la nouvelle Héloïse* by Jean-Jacques Rousseau and Choderlos de Laclos's *Le Liaisons Dangereuses.* In Germany, there is Goethe's *The Sorrows of Young Werther* and Friedrich Hölderlin's *Hyperion.* What Cervantes is anticipating here would become a very popular genre in the next century. The exchange of letters in the *Quixote* also reflects a society in which writing is becoming a crucial component of life.

If you have been reading your Elliott, you will have learned that sixteenth-century Spain was a society obsessed with documents, mostly legal documents, which is a class to which some letters belong. In the *Quixote* the letters also represent writing within writing; the epistles are documents not processed into the fiction but presented raw, as it were, meaning, it does not say that Sancho wrote to Teresa saying this, that, and the other thing; no, the document appears in the novel presumably as it was dictated by Sancho. Modern fiction will expand on this device. I am thinking here of James Joyce, of John Dos Passos, of Julio Cortázar, and other writers whose books contain documents such as these letters, unabsorbed into the text of the fiction.

Sancho's letter, if we want to look for an antecedent in Part I, is an echo of the one that Don Quixote wrote to Dulcinea and that Sancho forgot to take with him and tried to memorize. Those episodes in which he tries to retell it are very funny. What is humorous in Part II is that both Sancho and his wife are illiterate, so this is a letter sent by a character who cannot write and received by a character who cannot read. The whole issue of the production of the letter and the Duchess overseeing it and all of that is part of the humor here, just as the production of the letter for Dulcinea was also part of the humor in that episode.

Now, on to these outrageous episodes I want to discuss today, and I am sure when I mention what they are you will see why I use that adjective. The first is the episode involving the afflicted matron, known as Countess Trifaldi and Trifaldín of the White Beard, her squire. This is one of the wildest inventions of the Duke's butler and one of the strangest in the whole *Quixote*. It has no possible antecedent in Part I. The butler is described as follows: "The Duke had a butler, a wag with a ready wit, who'd played the part of Merlin, made all the arrangements for the recent adventure, written the poem and persuaded a page to play Dulcinea. And with the help of his master and mistress the butler prepared another adventure, the strangest and funniest and most ingenious adventure imaginable" (II, 36, 734).

The butler is another internal author, like Sansón Carrasco, and Master Pedro. In fact, Sansón Carrasco is another author who scripts adventures for Don Quixote, something Maese Pedro does not do, although he is another one of the authors within the *Quixote*. So the butler not only organizes the whole pageant but also writes the verses, as the quotation says, and plays the role of Merlin and then that of Trifaldín. He is as versatile as Ginés de Pasamonte—even more so. He is a poet. Internal authors in the second part, like the butler and Sansón Carrasco, get to put their creations into action, and, as you have seen, the results are not exactly what they planned; but they do get to put them into action. The staging of the butler's arrival as Trifaldín is theatrical and baroque in the extreme. Again, the intention is to astonish both with the elaborateness of the props and with their fearful appearance and sounds or noises. So they astonish with the act of creation. What I mean is, the creator of these baroque pranks is boasting of his ability and also astonishing his audience through the very nature, size, and noise of his appearance. Here is the arrival of this character:

> As they all sat there in amazement, they saw two men come into the garden dressed in clothes of mourning so full and so long that they brushed the ground; these two men were beating large drums, also draped in black. By their side came the fife-player, all in black like the other two. These three were followed by a gigantic personage, blanketed rather than dressed in a pitch-black cassock, the skirts of which were similarly vast. Over his cassock his body was crossed diagonally by a broad sword-strap, also black, from which hung an enormous scimitar with a black cross-guard, in a black scabbard. His face was covered by a transparent black veil, through which it was possible to glimpse a long, long beard,

as white as snow. He paced along to the sound of the drums with ponderous solemnity. In short, his size, his gait, his blackness and his escort could have astonished and indeed did astonish all those who saw him and didn't know him. He came, slow and stately, to kneel before the Duke, who rose to his feet with all the others to greet him. But the Duke would by no means allow him to speak until he had also risen. The prodigious apparition did so, and once he was on his feet he lifted the veil from his face and revealed the most horrendous, longest, whitest and thickest beard the human eyes had ever gazed upon, and then he wrenched and wrested from his broad and swelling breast a solemn, sonorous voice as he fixed his eyes upon the Duke. (II, 36, 737)

Notice the preponderance of black, and notice that, as in the pageant in the forest, there are many superlatives. Everything is the largest, the whitest, the most horrible; the intention is to cause admiration and fear in the spectators. Sancho dives into the Duchess's skirts the moment he sees this apparition, as he does whenever he is afraid at the Duke's and Duchess's house; he fainted in her arms in the pageant in the forest. And notice also the figure of the monster. I have spoken about the figure of the monster before, which is made up not only of the most outrageous features but also of contrasting ones, like the black dress and the white beard. The monster is a baroque figure. It does not have to be ugly, just composed of clashing features. In Calderón de la Barca, the playwright I have mentioned several times, there are beautiful monsters, namely, beautiful women dressed as men.

Do not confuse this figure of the monster with the romantic Frankenstein, who is ugly, repulsive, a death-warmed-over type. These baroque monsters are not like that. The important thing in the monster is the clash of opposites (the clashes between the two genders in the case of the Calderonian figures); we saw that clash in the figure of the Dulcinea of the pageant in the forest. Such figures are the opposite of Renaissance harmony, but they are, however, announced in the figure of Dorotea in Part I, who cross dresses. And, as in the Cave of Montesinos and the pageant in the forest, we have a procession, a parade of freaks, and the sound of drums, which mark the pace of the whole ensemble. In these theatrical shows the characters do not walk, they march. In the Cave of Montesinos all of these eerie kinds of women are marching in a procession. And in the pageant in the forest we have a huge procession, a parade, so there is no natural motion such as

Figure 18. Gustave Doré, *Duennas with Beards*. General Collection,
Beinecke Rare Book and Manuscript Library, Yale University.

walking; it is marching to the beat of the drums and the sounds of the various instruments.

The most remarkable thing here is the punishment the *dueñas* have
suffered (fig. 18). The predicament of the dueñas is once again a question of
cross-dressing or of cross-gendering. Their mock affliction seems to be an
excess of testosterone that provokes a wild growth of facial hair. Remember
that they suddenly, within this fiction—boom!—have beards. It is described
in minute detail, how the hairs are supposed to come out of the pores. This is
Cervantes at his wildest. This is a hilarious condition and part of the mockery
of the ladies-in-waiting of the whole episode. Sancho's diatribe against them
perhaps reflects an attitude of the times. Dueña Rodríguez, from whom we
will hear more later, mounts a spirited defense of them. Defining the dueña,
Sebastián de Covarrubias says the following: "In the old Castilian languages
it meant an old, widowed lady. Now, it generally means those who serve
wearing long gowns that look like nuns' habits to distinguish them from
virgins. And in the palaces 'honored dueñas' are principal ladies who are
widowed, and the queens and princesses keep them near" (my translation).[1]
Webster's defines lady-in-waiting as "A lady of rank who is a member of the
royal household and in attendance of a queen or princess."

I suppose there is a sexual connotation to this category of women because they are unattached and presumably available but not young, unmarried, and virginal. Why so many widows? People died at a younger age in the sixteenth and seventeenth centuries, and since men generally live a shorter life than women, even today, there are bound to be a lot of widows around, and what do you do with all these widows? Where do they fit in society? I guess some might go to a nunnery. "Get thee to a nunnery," remember Shakespeare, but others are in palaces; they are of rank. They are a bit like segundones, the female counterpart of the segundones, but they cannot quite go out and start a career at sea or in church, so they are involved in providing or facilitating sexual encounters; they tend to be go-betweens, as happens in the story concocted by the butler.

There are all kinds of jokes about widows throughout all traditions, and this is why they are given, in jest, a strong masculine trait, a beard, the opposite of the role they are supposed to play, which is very feminine. So the last thing you would expect them to have is a beard. But also, as you remember from my explanation of Dulcinea's hair, hair signified a certain kind of sexuality. In the case of the enchanted Dulcinea, hair meant—remember the wench that had the mole on her face with some hairs sticking out of it, who Don Quixote said must have another one on her thigh with hair—sexual proclivity, being sexually hot. These women are to be seen as amorously active, but only in a sexual way. That is, they are not to be loved and idealized but only to be seen as sexual beings, and this is the reason for the joke of having them grow hair.

We move now to the story about the Countess Trifaldi, whom we encountered in Spitzer's article. Recall the long discussion by Spitzer about "Tri-faldi," *tres faldas,* and all of that and how these names are made up by Cervantes. The story about Countess Trifaldi is very much like that of Princess Micomicona in Part I, except that it is madly exaggerated. In the Micomicona story there was a fantastic geography with outrageously made-up names; it is a meta-metafiction, concocted by the characters of the main fiction. Here, in contrast to Part I, the process is much more premeditated and complicated and is played out as in a theater, not out on the road. If you remember, the priest and Dorotea make up the story of Micomicona on the go, and that is why she makes mistakes.

The butler has taken his time to compose this one. It is a very well wrought story. Maguncia and Archipiela are the deceased parents. These are funny names. Maguncia is the German town of Mainz, and it sounds very strange to the Spanish ear: Maguncia, Mainz, in Germany; and the second refers to archipelago, a series of islands. These names are geographic in origin because the story is something of a geographic fable. Kandy is, like "el reino Micomicón," another made-up kingdom. But of all of these names the funniest is Antonomasia, the young woman, because it is the name that takes the name of names. It is a rhetorical figure that names that which is the quintessence of something, a Hercules, for a strong man, is an antonomasia; a Hitler, for an evil man, is an antonomasia: "From the Greek, to call by another name the use of an epithet or title, instead of the proper name of a person as when [I am quoting Webster] when his honor is used for a judge or when, instead of Aristotle, we say 'The Philosopher'; the use of a proper name, instead of a common noun as when an eminent orator is called Demosthenes." It is something like saying par excellence, the quintessence of something.

Why is she called Antonomasia? She is given the name of a linguistic or rhetorical term because she is made up of words: she is a fiction within the fiction made up by the butler, so she is not to have the name of a real person because she is made up of words. This is what the name is underlining. Also, she is so named because she and her story are quintessential, archetypal, commonplace. Joaquín Casalduero, whom I have mentioned before several times, says in his *Sentido y forma del Quixote* (in my translation): "Don Quixote in his purity launches forth to disenchant, to save the lovers and the *dueñas* to make them recover their original form. He fights for the whole of humanity, which is why the story is filled with a sense of the real. Without alluding to anyone in particular because all are involved. The name of the seduced young woman is Antonomasia. What he means is that Antonomasia's name suggests that Don Quixote fights for all seduced and punished young ladies."[2]

This is the sense of her name, the prototypical one. But, also, since the issue here is, one more time, marriage, unequal marriage, freedom, social status, I think Cervantes, via this name, is perhaps poking fun at himself for repeating the same story under various guises throughout the *Quixote*. He is saying, well, this Antonomasia is the prototype of all the women in the stories about marriage—Dorotea, Marcela, Zoraida—that I have been telling and am telling again, so I am making fun of myself by giving her this very funny name. He may also be casting a resigned and ironic glance at human nature for always repeating itself: young women will always be seduced by charming young men, and trouble will ensue. The name Antonomasia suggests this too.

If in Part I we learned to look for the story behind the story, in Part II we learn how a story is made. The way the butler appears and the way the story is told and presented and represented is a way of showing the inner workings of the story. This is another way we can establish a contrast between the two parts. In Part I we were looking for the story behind the story of what Cardenio said. Here, we are shown the stage props, the machinery, the stage machinery through which the story is being made. Part of it is the name of this character, Antonomasia. To sum up the story made up by the butler: Maguncia and Archipiela are the parents of Princess Antonomasia, who is impregnated by Don Clavijo, a Don Juan type, with the connivance of Dueña Trifaldi. Notice that Clavijo is a phallic name. A *clavija* is a peg in a string instrument. Now they have a little mechanism with a screw-type thing, but the old clavijas, the old pegs, were simply stuck in by pressure into the wood, and hence the name Clavijo is a very phallic name; another joke on the part of Cervantes. Now, Dueña Trifaldi is a Celestina type who arranges for their encounters, but she herself falls in love with the young man, which gives the story an original twist, a kind of sophisticated twist. This older woman has fallen in love with Clavijo, a very charming guy who plays the guitar. It is as if she vicariously had the affair with Clavijo through Antonomasia; so there is an erotic sophistication involved in the story. The butler is a very clever author.

Don Clavijo does marry Antonomasia, as he had promised, but the queen dies of grief because of the disparity in social class between them. He is merely a knight; he has the "don," so he is a knight, but Antonomasia is the princess, so Malambruno, a giant and the queen's first cousin, who is the Pandafilando of this story, turns them into the ornament atop a sarcophagus. If Pandafilando, remember, was a pan-philanderer, one who had many affairs with women, Malambruno is a bad man: from *mal,* 'evil' or 'bad,' and *hombre,* 'man,' or *hombruno,* 'manly.' He is a bad man, Malambruno. It is also a comical name. In any case, this is the gist of the story:

> Sitting on top of a wooden horse on the Queen's grave we saw the giant Malambruno, Magnuncia's cousin, who besides being a cruel man was an enchanter, and to avenge his cousin's death and punish Don Clavijo for his audacity, and indignant at Antonomasia's brazenness, he used his magic arts to put them both under a spell there on top of the grave itself—she was turned into a brass monkey, and he into a fearsome crocodile of some unknown metal, while between the two of them stands a column, also of metal, with an inscription in Syriac which, translated into Kandian and now into Spanish states:

> These two foolhardy lovers will not regain their original form until the brave man of La Mancha engages with me in single combat; for his mighty courage alone the Fates reserve this unparalleled adventure. (II, 39, 748–49)

Notice the baroque suffusing of love with death. The lover's likeness will lie on the tomb of the dead mother—do not overlook that. The butler, the author of the story, is learned as well as clever, as we found in the pageant of the forest with all of its Dante allusions. Here he has contrived a truly baroque image in the sarcophagus. American tombs tend to be very simple. There is a headstone and then the tomb is just the grass covering the body or the casket; there is something very beautiful about it. Dust will become dust, and so forth and so on. But in the European tradition, in the Continental tradition, tombs tend to be much more elaborate, ornate, and made of stone or hard substances. They are like little buildings; there is a whole architecture of tombs. What is a sarcophagus? Remember the etymology I gave you when discussing the Cave of Montesinos episode, *sarcos* in Greek, 'flesh,' and *phagein*, 'to eat,' so the sarcophagus eats the flesh of the dead body.

Sarcophagi were common among the ancient Greeks and Romans. It was a limestone coffin or tomb often inscribed and elaborately ornamented. The point of the sarcophagus in this story is the display and the ornamentation, which are the baroque elements, as in the figure of the monster. In Montesinos's Cave the ornament on Durandarte's sarcophagus was his own cadaver. The statue was made of flesh; it was an inversion, with nature playing the role of art. Here we have a much more elaborate kind of ornamentation. How do we interpret the figures of the monkey and the crocodile? There are monkeys in Cervantes, as we saw in Micomicona and also the monkey that Maese Pedro had with him. As I said when mentioning those episodes, they allude to mimesis, to representation, because monkeys like to imitate humans. Here the ensemble could allude to lust, the crocodile eats the monkey, as it were, but both animals, the monkey and the crocodile, are supposed to be demonic and symbolic of dissimulation, of fakery. This is why they grace the tomb of these lovers, I think.

The story of Antonomasia and Don Clavijo is one of consummation and pregnancy. I think the pregnancy is part of the baroque grotesquerie of the episode, as is the interested intervention of the dueña. What I mean is that there is something grotesque about the go-between, the older woman, falling in love with the young man, and the same kind of grotesqueness is involved in the pregnancy. You will find these contrasts in the poetry of

Altisidora, for instance, when she appears and sings a song; there will be sublime lines followed by very vulgar ones. And this is, I think, the effect here of the pregnancy. Pregnancy would be unthinkable in the stories of Part I involving Dorotea, Marcela, Luscinda, or Zoraida, although consummation did take place with Dorotea. But pregnancy literalizes lust as the facilitator of reproduction, removing all idealizations about love. It underscores love's functional biological drive. Pregnancy is not very sublime, except when thought of as the creation of life. It is not part of the courtly love tradition. It is unthinkable to imagine Beatrice, Dante's beloved, pregnant. There will be another pregnancy later, involving Dueña Rodriguez's daughter. At this stage in the *Quixote* we are well beyond the idealized love of Grisóstomo and Marcela and of Don Quixote and Dulcinea.

So now we come to the end of this adventure, the end of this very well wrought story the butler has composed, whose inner workings we are observing as we read. We move now to the episode of Clavileño. Clavileño has become such an ingrained name in the Spanish tradition that there was a very famous literary journal in the fifties in Spain called *Clavileño*. Now, this story brings to a close the story of the bearded dueñas and the disenchantment of Antonomasia and Clavijo. The chapter begins with a mock tirade of self-praise on the part of Cervantes about his narrative techniques and characters:

> All those who enjoy histories like this one should really and truly be grateful to its first author, Cide Hamete, for his meticulousness in telling us about all its most minute particularities, never neglecting to bring every little detail, however trivial, clearly to light. He depicts characters' thoughts, reveals their fancies, answers unspoken questions, clears up doubts, brings arguments to their proper conclusion: in short he reveals every last atom of information that the most curious reader could ever want to know. O celebrated author! O happy Don Quixote! O famous Dulcinea! O funny Sancho Panza! May all of you together and each of you in your own right live on for ever, for the pleasure and entertainment of everyone in the world! (II, 40, 750)

This is very funny. Cervantes is praising himself, and he is praising himself by itemizing, as it were, the props of his own fiction, of his own art. What Cervantes is doing is dismissing Aristotelian injunctions concerning the writing of history in this passage. According to the Philosopher, to use an antonomasia to refer to Aristotle, history should concern itself not with minutiae, but only with that which is relevant to grand narratives that have to do with major historical figures. History should not deal with characters of the ilk Cervantes is dealing with, nor should it dwell on their thoughts, except when expressed in highly rhetorical speeches that are presumed to display their personalities.

Aristotle's history is very much contrary to modern conceptions of history—and Cervantes is already aware of them—because we do want details about characters, whether important or nonimportant characters, in history; we feel that in the details one may find the truth. But this desire does not hold in the Renaissance conception of history. What I have just read to you is the core of the Renaissance poetics of history, but in this mock history Cervantes is writing it is precisely the particular details as well as the thoughts and imaginings of the characters that are of interest. The element of this Renaissance poetics of history remotest from us is the question of the speeches. There were no recording devices at the time, so when you hear a king deliver an oration, it is all made up by the historian, whose art involved the creation of such speeches on the part of these historical characters, speeches that would reveal their personality. It was a way of delving into their psychology.

I know this is completely contrary to our notions of how to write history, but this is why Cervantes is underlining it here. He is interested in the details, and he is interested in the imaginings and the thoughts of characters that are not that important but are the characters that will fill the novelistic genre he is in the process of creating. In other words, this tirade shows that Cervantes is increasingly aware that he is creating a new kind of writing, which is derived from both history and genres, old and knew, such as the epic, the picaresque, and the romances of chivalry. The tirade, by the way, is presumed to be uttered by the second author or translator, who frequently comments on Cide Hamete's work, a historian—remember—who is a Moor, given to prevarications. So all of these folds and layers of irony are still present. But this passage is important because of what I said before: stories in Part II display how they are being made up.

I move now to Clavileño: first, the name of the horse. It is derived from *clavo*, which means a 'nail,' but there is also an echo of *clavija*, the word I mentioned before in reference to Don Clavijo because the clavija itself is derived from clavo, meaning something that is stuck into something, and this alludes to the steering peg, to steer this horse, and to *leño*, which means 'wood,' which is what the horse is made of. But leño or leña is a kind of wood used for firewood, for burning. The more noble wood used by woodworkers to make furniture or cabinets is called *madera*. This is an unwieldy word, but at the same time Cervantes is underlining that the wood of which Clavileño is made is not of the noblest kind.

There is something demeaning about leño. I kept thinking what a good rendering into English might be. I thought the horse could be called Firewood or he could be called—what I think would be the best—Woody. I think if we were to translate everything in the book, Clavileño would be called Woody, as in Woody Woodpecker. But Rutherford wisely sticks to Clavileño.

The adventure of Clavileño is derived from several similar ones in romances of chivalry, so the parody of romances of chivalry is carried out now not so much by Don Quixote and his actions but by the Duke's servants, particularly the butler. He is not only learned and clever, as I have been emphasizing, but also a reader of romances of chivalry, and of the first *Quixote* as well. The motif of the flying horse has a long tradition, including Pegasus in Greek mythology, but the figure traveled far in time and space after the Indian and Persian versions (fig. 19). He appears in the Arabic story "The

Figure 19. Gustave Doré, *The Flight of Clavileño.* General Collection, Beinecke Rare Book and Manuscript Library, Yale University.

Ebony Horse" in *The Thousand and One Nights*. From there, it was disseminated to France and Spain. I will not give you the titles of romances in which it appears, but it does appear fairly frequently. So Clavileño reveals the butler's knowledge of such romances of chivalry.

One of the interesting features of the flight is the all-encompassing view from above that the characters presumably have, which is typical of the baroque; the baroque effort at all-inclusiveness, which is now available given the knowledge that the earth is round and complete within itself. The episode has a great deal to do with contemporary discoveries about the infinite dimensions of the cosmos, about which I have spoken before, and the inability of Ptolemaic and Aristotelian cosmologies to represent such a cosmos. Don Quixote and Sancho believe themselves to be traveling through the spheres, as described in the old cosmology, and the pranksters encourage this by having a fire next to their beards. Thus they figure they are going through the sphere of fire, and Sancho claims he took a stroll among the constellations as they are described in the old cosmology. A corollary of the new discoveries is that the world is one and the same everywhere. Sancho had introduced the topic a few pages before when, upon hearing the story of Antonomasia and Clavijo in Kandy, he says, "So there are policemen, poets and seguidillas in Kandy, too—I swear it makes me think the world's the same all over" (II, 38, 747).

Sancho thinks the world is the same everywhere, and this is what the view from above suggests. Clavileño's flight in the *Quixote* is the correlative opposite of the Cave of Montesinos descent. Appropriately, given his increasing importance, it is now Sancho who tells a story like the one Don Quixote told after emerging from the cave. He speaks of a celestial flight drawn from similar flights of the spirit that are available in Cicero, *Somnium Scipionis*, in Boethius, *The Consolation of Philosophy*, and even in Fray Luis de León's "Still Night," or "Noche Serena." Fray Luis de León is another great poet of the sixteenth century who is somewhere in the background here. As in other adventures, in this second part Don Quixote shows real courage before what appears to be actual danger, and so does Sancho; but they have played, again, the role of objects of others' amusement. The Clavileño episode is another prank, another "burla" at the expense of Don Quixote and Sancho conceived and executed by the Duke's minions, particularly the butler.

All of these pranks are a critique of mimesis in that they are literary or theatrical acts of representation which are presented as pitiable attempts, ultimately given up in favor of humor. These are attempts at literary representations of mimesis that wound up being funny. I think they encapsulate

Cervantes' own effort in the *Quixote*. They are dramatizations of his plight, an answer to the problem of trying to represent reality, coming up with a funny version of it.

But there is something else too, something perhaps even more important, in these pranks and in the Clavileño one in particular. While it is true that Don Quixote and Sancho are made fun of and that they endure hardship and danger when the whole contraption blows up, it is they who show courage and determination, and it is they who do fly in their imaginations, while the pranksters remain earthbound, some, like the Duke and Duchess, astonished and even frightened by the machinery they had constructed. I think this sums up Cervantes' attitude toward the protagonist. He may very well be ridiculous in his efforts, but his efforts have a certain nobleness that others lack. Just as he emerges physically unscathed from the explosion and fall, so his dignity too remains untouched. In brief, Clavileño does afford Don Quixote a flight at once heroic and inspired. As in the episode of the lions, he has demonstrated his courage, even if the context is not a heroic one.

CHAPTER 20

King for a Day

Sancho's Barataria

Required Readings

Cervantes, *Don Quixote,* Part II, chaps. 36–53, pp. 734–850.
Elliott, *Imperial Spain,* 321–60.

What is the significance of the real date on Sancho's letter, one wonders? I do not have a ready answer for that, but, remember, it does have the real date. It is the date when Cervantes is writing this part of the *Quixote.* It may be a way of emphasizing that the novel is dealing with current history and situating the novel's chronology in a specific way. This is why the letter is given a date. It did not have to have a date, but I think that that is the reason for it. That is the best answer I can give to the question of why the letter has that date on it, and what the significance of it is. But this is the kind of detail I want you to look for. Remember my mantra: details, details, details. Literature is made of specific, concrete details, not of abstractions, like philosophy, and this is why it is important to notice and to remember the details and to base your interpretations on them.

As we move closer to the end the *Quixote* I would like to make some general comments and revisit some of the themes I touched on earlier as a way of summing up our reading of this great classic we have been enjoying all semester. In the last lecture I talked about the increasing presence of Virgil and of his *Aeneid* and suggested that Cervantes is hinting at the weighty responsibility his protagonist is assuming, which is quite different from that of the classical hero but no less important: to conquer himself, to come to grips with and control his madness and to assimilate his newly won realization of the vanity of his dreams and the futility of his quest. His task is to bring himself into harmony with the world in which he lives, full of imperfections and disappointments and to assume a resigned attitude toward it and prepare for his impending death. At the beginning of the semester I quoted György Lukács, the Hungarian critic, to the effect that the *Quixote* was the epic of a world abandoned by God. Don Quixote's epic task within the novel is to cope with such a world, to conquer such a world, as it were. His is a very modern condition in that sense but not necessarily a despairing one. This, I think, is what the novel shows as the hero begins his return home.

Don Quixote's change is gradual. It began with Dulcinea's supposed enchantment by Sancho, the shock of seeing this peasant woman as Dulcinea; and it peaked, I believe, during the descent into the Cave of Montesinos. I think he will display or is already displaying a deepened kind of wisdom, nowhere more memorably than in the counsel he gives Sancho as his squire is preparing to take over the government of the island of Barataria. Don Quixote takes Sancho aside and tells him not to gloat about his good fortune but to thank God that this has happened to him without his really even trying, evincing, somewhat, a little bit of envy. He takes Sancho aside to counsel him.

This passage of the *Quixote* is one of the more anthologized ones in the Spanish-speaking world. I know a judge in Puerto Rico who has these pages framed in gold in his office, and he shows them proudly to anyone who happens to be near. It is wonderful advice that Don Quixote gives Sancho. Don Quixote's wisdom has obvious philosophical and literary sources, and there are also clearly critical statements that refer to the current situation in Spain and its empire, particularly the bit regarding the corruption of people in power and in government. These are barbs aimed at the Spanish bureaucracy. Don Quixote's advice has bookish roots, but it sounds deeply felt and as if it were grounded in experience. This is the knowledge of a mature man, and Don Quixote is more than a mature man; he is an old man by the standards of the age, so he is in a position to counsel Sancho, who is younger and his squire.

The counterparts to Don Quixote's wisdom are Sancho's proverbs, which express a folksy kind of astuteness and knowledge of humankind, and, as we have seen, Sancho can spew proverbs at the drop of a hat. Proverbs have been taken to be the accumulated wisdom of the ages, stored in the common memory of humankind, and they were of great interest to Renaissance thinkers. Renaissance thinkers were keenly attracted by language and the knowledge it contained, both as a system of communications, that is, language as grammar, and also for the contents of the lore it stored; not only in Latin, Greek, and Hebrew but also in the vernacular languages in which they were immersed.

In the end, Sancho's wisdom is not going to be different from that of Don Quixote. It is certainly not inferior, and in practice it proves to be quite effective. Don Quixote's advice extends to Sancho's appearance—his mode of dress, the length of his fingernails, and the clothes he should wear on different occasions—and to how to have his wife behave so that she will not show she is just a peasant. That is the funny part of the advice. But Sancho's knowledge, Sancho's wisdom, is up to the task. His acumen is sufficient for him to deal with the challenges of government, as it is for him to face the challenges of his own life. Sancho is endowed with natural reason.

This is a medieval concept that courses through the Renaissance and reaches the Enlightenment, where it will be instrumental in the elaboration of modern ideas about democracy that we all share today. It is, ultimately, as I have said several times, a common Christian doctrine, namely, that we are all endowed by God with enough intelligence to succeed in the world no matter what our station in life or level of education. But at the end of the Barataria episode, which turns out unsuccessfully through no fault of his own, Sancho rues that he was not born to be a governor. He accepts the social order, which was based, in spite of what I have just said about natural reason, strictly on the notion that a person's social station was determined by God and that it was best, as Sancho says, to stick to what you are and to the condition into which you were born.

Barataria is a conflictive moment in the *Quixote*. The fact is that Sancho has done very well as governor, and only the pranks of the Duke and his minions rob him of his real achievements; real achievements in this fictional world in which he accomplished them, one must remember. Now, in connection with this, recall Auerbach's theory about the birth of realism and the *sermo humilis*, that is, the common speech of Christianity. You can see that all of this is connected, but the contradiction is that within society, which is a society that is crumbling, as I have been saying, these social distinctions are significant. They are crumbling because the cleverest fellow in this whole episode is the butler, who, after all, is a servant, and also Sancho does very well as a governor. So this is the overall theme of today's class: the social structures are crumbling in Don Quixote's world.

As for the island of Barataria, I want to talk about the name. In the original, Sancho refers to the island as an *ínsula*. By this time the word for 'island' in Spanish was already the current word, which is *isla*, from the Latin *insula*. When you had two consonants like *n* and *s* together, the tendency in the Romance languages is for the second one to absorb the first one, so from *ínsula* you get *isla*, and in French you get *île*.

Sancho repeats "ínsula," unaware that it is an archaic word for island which Don Quixote uses because he has learned it by reading the romances of chivalry. Completely lost in the translation is that Don Quixote, whenever the issue of chivalry or of Dulcinea arises, lapses into a kind of archaic Spanish. He will say, for instance, *fermosa* for *hermosa*, which was by then the current Spanish word for 'beautiful.' *Hermosa,* if you want a little more philology, comes from the Latin *forma, formosa,* 'shapely.' That is how Formosa got its name. Philology is fascinating. So, whenever Don Quixote talks about chivalric topics, he uses *fablar* for *hablar,* using the archaic *f* of the Latin, which by the sixteenth century had become a silent *h.* Sancho uses "ínsula"; he wants to rule an "ínsula," an island, and he uses the archaic word. Thus, "ínsula Barataria." Because Don Quixote and Sancho use this archaic word in the *Quixote,* it has currency in Spanish now, and there is even a famous journal in Madrid called *Ínsula.*

Barataria comes from *barato,* meaning 'cheap.' So this would be "cheap-island." Because of its low cost and its shoddy, fragile construction, the island is like an improvised stage set on which to perform the play that the butler has prepared. It is cheap also in the sense that it is not real. I think a better translation for Barataria, if we were going to translate everything, would be something like Chintzy Island. Sancho does not see through the name and realize that it is not a very promising name for the kingdom he will be ruling, Cheap Island. He does not know exactly what *Barataria* means.

What are the sources of the butler's invention? The practice of making someone king for a day was common in carnival celebrations throughout Europe ever since the Middle Ages and, further back, in saturnalias. The humor of the practice lay in seeing how a low-class dolt would act out his role as a king or to have someone play the role of someone from the lower classes trying to act like a king. It was a skit, part of the carnival practice, to make somebody a king for the day. This involved, in saturnalias and in these kinds of carnivals, an inversion of roles. In the 1940s and 1950s there was a radio and television show called *Queen for a Day,* in which a common housewife was crowned queen for the day in the show, and she got to rule over people and to have anything she wanted. The practice extends to cultures beyond the Western tradition. Besides, making a stranger king and then deposing him is so prevalent that James Frazer devoted many pages of his classic *The Golden Bough* to the practice. The idea was to punish the ruler for the perquisites he enjoyed while being king and for not having been able to solve problems, such as droughts and other natural catastrophes.

The butler is basing his elaborate prank on a traditional routine, though he does take it to an extreme. This is not just king for a day but for several days; this expansion, this exaggeration, is consistent with the baroque character of Part II. The point is that the whole thing is supposed to be a joke at Sancho's expense, part of the merriment at the Duke's and Duchess's palace. It is also part of the merriment for the participants in this whole charade; they are acting it out as if this were a carnival. There are other traditional elements in the episode, traditional acts, traditional scenes, for instance, the one in which Sancho passes judgment on several cases that come up before him.

Hence this is a traditional episode that goes back even to the Bible—King Solomon—and also to folk traditions, the traditions of riddles that rulers or wise men are supposed to solve. The tradition of oracles goes back at least to the Greeks. Sancho solves several complicated cases, every one of them coming from folk tradition, but it is humorous at the same time. For instance, Sancho solves a case involving an alleged rape. A man is accused of having raped a woman; the man is the lowest of the low. He is a hog herder, a pig keeper. Remember in Part I when the keeper of pigs arrives and even the mention of the word *puerco* in Spanish has to be followed by "excuse me." The pig keeper is supposed to have forced himself on this woman, and Sancho has to decide who is telling the truth. He asks if the man gave her a bag of money, and when she is leaving Sancho tells him to take it from her. She fights like an animal so as not to give up the money, and Sancho says, "Well, if you had defended yourself like that there would have been no rape."

Then Sancho is presented with a very complicated case about Clara Perlerina, *Clara,* 'clear,' *Perlerina* derived from 'pearl,' 'clear pearl.' She is quite a pearl. Remember, this is the young woman in this completely made-up story within the made-up story, the usual receding sequence in Cervantes, who is half beautiful and half horrible:

> "What I was saying," said the farmer, "is that this son of mine who's going to be a BA fell in love with a girl in the same village called Clara Perlerina, the daughter of Andrés Perlerino, a farmer of great wealth; and this surname Perlerino isn't inherited

from their ancestors, but comes from the fact that everyone in the
family's paralytic, and people call them the Perlerinos to make it
sound better, although if truth is to be told that girl is just like a
pearl of orient, and looked at from the right-hand side she's like
a flower of the field—not so much from the left, because the eye's
missing on that side, it popped out when she had the smallpox;
and although she's got these big pock-marks all over her face, her
admirers say they aren't pock-marks at all but graves where her
lovers' souls are buried. She's such a clean girl that to avoid dirty-
ing her face her nostrils are as you might say rolled up, and look
just as if they were running away from her mouth, and yet she's
a real good-looker, because she's got a big mouth and if it wasn't
for the missing ten or a dozen teeth it could stand out among the
very best mouths there are. I won't say anything about her lips."
(II, 47, 802)

Sancho sees through it all as something made up and refuses to grant the
request to intercede in favor of the marriage. But Clara is very interesting
because of the figure of the monster, as I have mentioned, who is made up
of contrasting features, of opposing features. In the case of Trifaldín it was
the black robe and the white beard, black and white, and here it is extreme
beauty on one half and on the other, this horrendous face, pockmarked and
lacking an eye; the two very opposites clashing in one figure. This is in reference to the baroqueness of Part II but also to show Sancho's sharp wit
in seeing this as a prank they are trying to play on him within the prank
he is already enduring. If you compare Clara to Maritornes, you see that
Maritornes is not that symmetrical. Maritornes is ugly from top to bottom,
whereas here we have a perfect symmetry, as it were. You have to keep in
mind that this is all made up by the butler, who is the author of this whole
charade. Now, the gist of the episode is given by the butler himself, when
he says, "'There is so much in what you say, my lord Governor,' said the
butler, 'that I am astounded to see that a man as untaught as you are, being, I believe, totally illiterate, can make so many observations full of wise
maxims and good counsel, so different from what those who sent us here
and we who have come here had been given to expect from your mind. In
this world every day brings a new surprise; jests turn into earnest, and jest-
ers find the tables turned upon them'" (II, 49, 814). It is good to remember
here the quotation, and I am going to repeat it, from that American Hispanist Ruth El Saffar, which is very appropriate at this point. She wrote, "All of

Part II is based on the mistaken assumption, on the part of the would-be all-controlling character-authors, that they can deal with a fictional character and maintain at the same time a distance which allows them never to slip into that fictional world with which they plan to entertain themselves. Like Sansón, they are trapped from two directions: they are controlled to some extent from within their play by the very characters whom they intend to manipulate, and from without by an author of whom they are unaware, by whose will and whose hand all they do is contrived."[1]

This is the case of the butler here, who is himself acknowledging that things have not turned out quite the way he had planned them, that he and the Duke and Duchess had originally planned it merely to have fun at the expense of Sancho. But Sancho turns out to be, against all expectations, quite a good governor, and so the tables are turned. This is another of these inversions that happen regularly in Part II of the *Quixote*. It is also good to notice that the butler is aware both of his construction of this whole episode and of its collapse.

In a larger sense Barataria has to do with the breakdown of aristocratic authority and the emergence of the common man as potential ruler. Sancho proves to be surprisingly wise, and in spite of all the pranks he and his master endure. As in the case of Clavileño, the episode we discussed in the last class, his dignity remains untouched, and the mockers are the ones who are mocked. Sancho became a good governor; this is the ironic result, a counterintuitive resolution that thwarts the designs of the Duke and Duchess and undermines the authorial intentions of the butler, who obviously wanted Sancho to provide humor by acting stupid. All this is, in part, something I have not mentioned before but that is easy to figure out: these are misreadings of Part I by characters in Part II. They assume the characters are going to act in a certain way on the basis of how they have interpreted Part I, and they have interpreted Part I with Sancho as a buffoon, as a comic character, which is how Avellaneda misinterpreted Sancho. So keep in mind that these are misreadings by the butler and the Duke and Duchess, who all expect Don Quixote and Sancho to act in a given way determined by their interpretation of Part I.

Besides the folkloric sources of Barataria I have mentioned, its background is literary and philosophical. Barataria is a self-contained society, presumably well run. This is the humanistic theme of Utopia, going back to Thomas More, the author of *Utopia*, published in 1516; and also to Tommaso Campanella, 1568–1639, who published *City of the Sun* in 1602, which was also a utopia. This is the idea that a perfect society can be established on this earth following a rational, human design. The concept goes back to Plato's *Republic* and to all of the treatises that begin to appear in the Renaissance about the art of government, including Machiavelli's *The Prince.*

The Prince is also in the background here because Sancho is trying to act like the perfect ruler. What does this all mean? Utopias, by the way, are the origin of modern political systems or of the idea that through a political system you can create or improve a society to make it like a utopia. In the eighteenth century particularly these ideas will become a reality, and they have become, as we know, nightmares in the twentieth century. Some of these utopias have turned out to be quite the opposite, to the point that you had to have walls to keep the people inside of them. What is the relevance of utopia in this episode of the *Quixote?* Is it a parody of these notions of utopia? Barataria is a mock utopia, with a fake king, and it all ends in a great catastrophe. Is it a parody showing the futility of such attempts? It could be. I think the episode is important enough and given enough relevance in the book to invite interpretations of this kind.

Barataria, being an island, reflects three other things. First, the idea of self-containment and self-sufficiency, of roundness, as it were, and at one point it is referred to as being *redonda*, 'round.' The island is round, and islands tend to be self-contained because they are surrounded by water. Third, I think Barataria also reflects the recently discovered islands of the Caribbean—recently as in late fifteenth century, early sixteenth century— where, in Hispaniola and in Cuba, the Spaniards attempted to create socie- ties almost from the ground up, and also the wished-for but never reached islands of the classical tradition. The unreachable islands were called ante- islands, and this is where the name Antilles comes from, those before-islands; these were fugitive islands, that is, islands that you saw in the distance and were supposed to reach, but, like the oasis in the desert, as you came closer they got further and further away from you, suggesting that these were is- lands you wanted to arrive at and where perhaps you would find utopia or an oasis. On this level, the island has that quality of elusiveness that one would associate with Atlantis. So, you can see the depth of this episode in the *Qui- xote* by dint of the many sources, ideas, and books that lie behind it.

Freud mentions Barataria in *Totem and Taboo,* and his take on this episode is very instructive. Remember, I mentioned earlier that Freud was a devoted reader of Cervantes, and as an adolescent had created a Cervantes club with several friends to read Cervantes and discuss his works. As you will see, Freud interprets this episode by reducing it to his own system; thinkers tend to do that. Freud examines the suffering a king must undergo to pay for his exalted position in the traditions I have already mentioned—remember Frazer. For Freud, this is played out chiefly in the amusing scene in which Sancho is denied food. Freud is drawing an analogy between certain neuroses and the behavior of primitives, focusing on the ambivalent attitude toward kings and its analog in the relationships of children to their fathers. He says,

> Here the importance of a particular person is extraordinarily heightened and his omnipotence is raised to the improbable in order to make it easier to attribute to him the responsibility for everything painful which happens to a patient. Savages really do not act differently towards their rulers when they ascribe to them power over rain and shine, wind and weather, and then dethrone or kill them because nature has disappointed their expectation of a good hunt or a ripe harvest.[2]

You can see in this the figure of the father, the omnipotent father, and remember all of the theories Freud had about the Oedipal complex. He goes on:

> Thus, also the taboo ceremonial of kings is nominally an expression of the highest veneration [because the relation to the father is an ambiguous one, of veneration and hostility] and a means of guarding them; actually it is the punishment for their elevation, the revenge which their subjects take upon them. The experiences which Cervantes makes Sancho Panza undergo as governor on his island have evidently made him recognize this interpretation of courtly ceremonial as the only correct one. It is very possible that this point would be corroborated if we could induce kings and rulers of to-day to express themselves on this point.[3]

Here, Freud is being ironic: let us ask kings and rulers today if they want to undergo this kind of process. Then, he goes on to make the unavoidable comparison with the Christian myth:

> Why the emotional attitude towards rulers should contain such a strong unconscious share of hostility is a very interesting problem.... We have already referred to the infantile father-complex; we may add that an investigation of the early history of kingship

would bring the decisive explanations. Frazer has an impressive discussion of the theory that the first kings were strangers who, after a short reign, were destined to be sacrificed at solemn festivals as representatives of their deity; but Frazer himself does not consider his facts altogether convincing. Christian myths are said to have been still influenced by the after-effects of this evolution of kings.[4]

He means the idea of the slaying of Jesus Christ, presumed King of the Jews. But you can see how this illuminates what is going on in Barataria with Sancho Panza, how Freud's take on this helps us understand the mechanisms at work in the episode. This is part of the traditional background of Barataria, but there is also the nightmare of finally getting what you crave and not being able to quite get your hands on it. You know, those wish-fulfillment dreams, where you have that cake—let us put it in those terms and not give it an erotic twist—that pie or something you want and you are about to get and you do not quite get; but also the disappointment of achieving things. Things achieved are never quite as we imagined or desired them to be. They say be careful what you wish for because you may get it, and once you get it, it may turn out not to be what you expected.

This is the strong element of desengaño of these episodes on the island. The scene that so fascinated Freud involves Pedro Recio de Agüero—that is a name we might want to unpack also—the doctor, the very funny doctor, who keeps saying, "No, no, no, you can't eat that; that's the worst thing you can eat! No, no, no, you cannot eat that." *Recio* means 'hard.' *Me llevas recio*, 'you're treating me hard,' you say in Spanish; *de Agüero* can be a last name, but *agüero* means 'omen.' *Mal agüero*, 'a bad omen'; and he is a "natural de Tirteafuera." That is the name of the town he comes from; it means, 'keep you out.'

When I was a kid and an adult wanted to get rid of me he would say, "Go see so-and-so and ask her to give you some *tenteallá*, 'keep you there.'" Tirteafuera is more or less like that. This is quite a remarkable character, this doctor. This is a very Molière-like scene. In Molière there is always this uproarious criticism of doctors, who are always going around with a huge syringe trying to give an enema to somebody, or whenever the situation is difficult they begin declining Latin nouns and verbs, because the idea is to know Latin well in order to be able to read the sources because medicine was at this point still very scholastic, based on written sources more than on experience. Part of the baroque is the clash between the scholastic, traditional knowledge that does not stand up to actual experience, and this is why the critique of medicine is so important and so relevant. It is not just funny, though this scene is very, very funny, but also significant because it reflects a condition of the time.

The end of Sancho's government is catastrophic. It is an episode, as in the fall from the wooden horse when it explodes, in which he might have been injured. Barataria is like a laboratory experiment in fiction, in fiction making. How does one create a fictional world coherent within itself? All fiction, all novels and stories, are the creation of a coherent world within it-self, one that is round, as it were, like an island. The fiction obviously gets out of hand for the butler, and he cannot quite stand outside of it, like a puppe-teer. This is parallel to Master Pedro and his puppet show. Perfection in this fictional world cannot quite be achieved, and this is similar to Cervantes' situation vis-à-vis the *Quixote*.

One way I imagine it is that this is a world of fiction the butler has cre-ated and is trying to control, but once he is inside it he does not have the all-encompassing perspective to do so, and he has all of the problems the char-acters he has created have. This is where the irony comes in. This effort to create a self-contained, coherent fiction anticipates . . . what? Macondo! The fictional village in *One Hundred Years of Solitude*. Or Comala, the fictional village in the novel *Pedro Páramo* by Juan Rulfo, the great Mexican writer. So there is not such a great distance between the idea of Utopia and the idea of creating a fictional world. All this is behind the island of Barataria.

I'll talk about Altisidora in the next class, this mock Dido I hope you are reading about, and also about Dueña Rodríguez. Dueña Rodríguez is the one whose daughter is impregnated and whose boyfriend refuses to marry her, and they do not put pressure on him because he is the son of the peas-ant who lends money to the Duke and Duchess. Dueña Rodríguez is an interesting character; she is the one who reveals the physical defects of the Duchess and of Altisidora. What physical defects do these women have? The Duchess, the beautiful huntress, apparently has sores on her legs from which some fluid flows, and Altisidora has bad breath. Dueña Rodríguez says, with great resentment, that the beautiful Altisidora, who sings so beautifully, has "un aliento cansado," 'a tired breath.' These are defects we did not find in the idealized women of Part I, and so this trait of Dueña Rodríguez's and the things she reveals are full of import.

But I want to finish by talking about Don Quixote and Sancho because I came across two recent articles on the two of them as a pair that I want to summarize for you. One is by Antonio Carreño Rodríguez. Carreño talks about the influence of Don Quixote and Sancho on modern comedy pairs, such as Abbott and Costello and Oliver and Hardy, and even takes it all the way up to characters in *Seinfeld,* a show I confess I have never seen in my life. But Carreño has a picture here of characters from that show, which apparently evinces a decided influence from Don Quixote and Sancho. He also gives the folkloric background of these pairs, going back to the Middle Ages, and then projects forward to the present. I mean, Abbott and Costello, one is fat, the straight man, and the other—you can see immediately, the moment I mentioned it, yes! This is Don Quixote and Sancho in film.[5]

The other article is by my friend Edwin Williamson, who is a distinguished Oxford Hispanist, and it has to do with what he terms the power struggle between Don Quixote and Sancho, which is resolved ultimately in favor of the squire because Don Quixote has to beg him to give himself the lashes necessary to disenchant Dulcinea. Williamson mentions four episodes: the fulling hammers, when Don Quixote hits Sancho over the head; the enchanted Dulcinea, when there is an inversion of roles, and Sancho is now the one creating the chivalric kind of reality out of normal, everyday life; Merlin's prophecy, when Sancho must give himself the lashes on his behind to disenchant Dulcinea, which then makes Don Quixote dependent on Sancho; and finally, an episode you may not have read yet, in chapter 60, the fight between the two of them when Don Quixote tries to force Sancho to lash himself and takes his clothes off to give him the lashes, and Sancho wrestles Don Quixote to the ground and puts his knee on his chest and says he will do no such thing. Williamson gives an appropriately political reading to this power struggle, one with which I agree. I think he is unduly harsh about the end, where, he says, Sancho is being totally cynical, even at Don Quixote's deathbed. I think Williamson went a little bit too far there, but I want to read you his conclusion because it is very much in tune with what I have been saying about Barataria and the rise of the common man to a position in government:

> Cervantes, moreover, was not unaware of the wider political dimension of the power-struggle that he had first adumbrated as far back as the Fulling Mills episode in Part One. In the final crisis, when the knight has been forced to the ground by his squire, Sancho's defiant assertion, "Ayúdome a mí, que soy mi señor" [I help myself because I am my own master], inevitably carries political resonances, for it implies a conscious rejection of the traditional basis of authority and status, and portends the

emergence of a different world, a world that Cervantes himself must have imagined with disquiet, if not with dread. Thus, at the heart of the *Quixote* there is an intriguing irony: Cervantes may well have started out on his adventure of writing with the purely literary aim of discrediting the "máquina mal fundada destos caballerescos libros" [the chivalric romances], but by a series of logical steps arising from the interaction of master and servant he was led to undermine the principal hierarchy that was the cornerstone of the ideology of his day.[6]

CHAPTER 21

Borders and Ends

Moriscos and Bandits

Required Readings

Cervantes, *Don Quixote,* Part II, chaps. 54–70, pp. 850–960.
Elliott, *Imperial Spain,* 361–86.

There are three issues I want to bring up as I begin today: improvisation; the international dimension the fiction of the *Quixote* acquires; and the influence of art or of literature on reality. As he moved to the conclusion of the *Quixote,* the question of how to bring the novel to a close must have loomed large in Cervantes' mind. The plot of the *Quixote* is repetitive more than sequential, with the protagonist's vague quest to revive the age of chivalry and, concretely, to participate in the jousts in Saragossa as goals. But there is no obvious or compelling aim to the characters' wanderings. One could, on the other hand, argue with Williamson, the critic I mentioned in the last lecture, that the disenchantment of Dulcinea is the main purpose of Don Quixote and Sancho, as set by Merlin's prophecy.

Yet this is no clear mission whose accomplishment would bring the novel to an end. What if Dulcinea is disenchanted? how could she be disenchanted? what would that mean? would she and Don Quixote then marry? which Dulcinea would he wed? Marriage is not mentioned by the protagonist, nor is marriage normally a desired end to courtly love. Love itself is the purpose of courtly love: the love of love. It is obvious that the only end possible would be the death of Don Quixote, making his life the shape of the fiction, though which life would still be the question. Is it the life of Alonso Quixano, the hidalgo who went mad and became Don Quixote, but about whose early life and family we know next to nothing? or is it the life invented by Don Quixote, the would-be knight-errant? Would that be the life that comes to an end, to close the novel? Improvisation, I have been saying all along, seems to rule the plot of the *Quixote;* the serendipitous actions provoked by chance encounters on the road and by characters that pop up in the second part who want to script the knight's life, or at least the adventures of the knight's life.

What role will improvisation play in the ending of the novel? In the final chapters of the *Quixote* there is a confluence of actual geography with current historical events, such as the expulsion of the moriscos, brigandage in Catalonia, and the Turkish and Huguenot menaces. These events return us to the beginning of Part II and the discussion at Don Quixote's house about some of them, particularly the Turkish threat. This is a form of closure, too, this return to those discussions in the beginning of Part II. The novel acquires an international projection announced by Don Quixote, the priest, and Sansón Carrasco talking about the Turkish threat in the early chapters, as if Don Quixote were going to try to resolve that problem.

But notice the concurrence of various real geographical settings. I spoke of the Ebro River, and now we have Barcelona, redolent with historical actions. So we have seen the Ebro River; now we have Barcelona, and we will see historical events involving that city. None of the historical circumstances that appear in the *Quixote*—by historical I mean contemporaneous historical incidents—is more current and pressing than the expulsion of the moriscos, which is taking place as Cervantes is writing Part II.

The topic of the expulsion centers on the character of Ricote and his family. He is one of the principal new characters in Part II. The international reach of the novel allows Cervantes to introduce fresh kinds of characters who are different from those mainly Castilian ones he has presented so far. Though, as we know, not all are exclusively Castilian; some are Basque, others are Galicians and Asturians. That is the second of the broad topics I want to touch on today. The third is the one about art influencing reality. In several of the episodes I will be discussing, particularly the one involving Tosilos but also in others, there seems to be a decided influence of art on reality and a coalescence of the two, by which one could say that reality, or the real, is improved by art, as we have already seen in other episodes. But we have some today where that seems to be the main topic.

To begin with Ricote, one could say that this story is a rewriting of the captive's tale from Part I, with Ricota, Ricote's daughter—whose name is really Ana Félix—being Zoraida and Pedro Gregorio, her suitor, the captive. But at the same time these two episodes are very different. The one involving Ricote is much richer, although the captive's episode is quite elaborate, as we saw. In these last few chapters of the *Quixote* Cervantes appears to be offering many possible variations of narrative fiction or some of the narrative modes available to him at that moment. Ricote and his family provide the opportunity for a mini *novela morisca,* or 'moorish novel.' A novela morisca is a tale about the love between a Christian young man and a Moorish young woman, with all of the predictable obstacles and conflicts. The best known novela morisca is named after its protagonists, *Ozmín y Daraja,* and is embedded in the *Guzmán de Alfarache.* The other fictional mode in this kind of smorgasbord of narratives is the Byzantine romance. The Byzantine romances entailed drawn-out adventures over vast geographical areas, lovers seeking to find each other and suffering abductions, shipwrecks, and being lost in strange lands only to find when they finally reunite that, unbeknownst to them, they are brother and sister and cannot marry. This is a kind of romance written at the time, very convoluted, hence Byzantine. Cervantes was writing just such a romance as he raced to finish the *Quixote.* It is called *Los trabajos de Persiles y Sigismunda, The Trials of Persiles and Sigismunda.* We will be revisiting this book when we talk about its prologue. Cervantes thought that book would be the culmination of his lifework. But he was wrong. A very interesting idea—one that I do not know if criticism has taken up—would be to study the influence of the writing of *The Trials of Persiles and Sigismunda* on Part II of the *Quixote,* as these were books that Cervantes worked on at the same time.

Toward the end of his life, because of his diminishing health, Cervantes was rushing to finish both the *Quixote* and *The Trials of Persiles and Sigismunda,* and it would be interesting to see how much one influences the other. But in the Ricote story, the influence of the Byzantine romance in the novel is obvious. Ana's and Pedro's abduction by the Turks and their sea journey and rescue are like a small-scale Byzantine romance played out in sight of the port of Barcelona. This is like a Byzantine romance in a nutshell; they are abducted by the Turks, they are taken away, they finally meet, and there is no ending to it because she is a morisca and hence forbidden to come back to Spain. A comical tidbit in this story is that Ana, eager to protect Pedro, a very beautiful young man, from their abductors, dresses him up as a woman to make him *less* attractive to the Turkish captors. This is a comic dig at the Turks, whose alleged homosexual proclivities were notorious and are even mentioned in good old Sebastián de Covarrubias's *Tesoro;*

in the entry on the Turks there is a not-so-veiled allusion to this practice that Cervantes is alluding to in, I think, a very comical way. It is a kind of transvestitism to the second power.

Why Cervantes wanted to provide this mixed bag of narrative possibilities here at the end is a mystery to me. One reason—other than its constituting simply a boast of artistic mastery—may be that he is consciously seeking variety in his work, and he is aware and has been since Part I that for all of the possibilities of his newly found hero, Don Quixote's adventures could become monotonous, and so he decided to include this technical extravaganza as a kind of overture. This accumulation of narratives is also a form of closure by accumulation, one could say.

But let's get back to Ricote. First, consider the name: Ricote; *rico* means 'rich' in Spanish; being rich, one is *rico*. *Ric-ote* is an augmentative ending, an ending that increases something. *Ricote* means he is very rich, which he is, though some critics claim that his name derives from his being from the Valley of Ricote, a valley with that name. I don't buy that. I think it's a little bit too tangential. It is obvious he is Ricote because he is very rich, and we know that because he talks about the treasure he has buried before leaving Spain. In Ricote, Cervantes is passing judgment on a contemporary event, one that is taking place as he writes the book.

The moriscos were expelled in 1609, the date of the Edict of Expulsion, but the whole process lasted several years, years during which Cervantes was writing Part II of the *Quixote*. If you read your Elliott you will know that a long debate preceded the expulsion, as many people were against it, mostly for economic reasons. The moriscos were an integral part of the economy of several regions of Spain and had some clout in the government. Their expulsion caused ruin in some areas of Spain, as did the expulsion of the Jews in 1492, which had also brought about all kinds of dire consequences in the country. There is a confluence, a coalescence of the text, of the fiction, with current history that we have not seen before in Part I or even Part II, or in any other fiction anywhere. A possible exception is the *Guzmán de Alfarache*, but there it is not explicit, and the events mentioned are not as dramatic and as present in the moment as the expulsion of the moriscos.

The story will remain unresolved—the lovers have to petition Madrid to have Ana Félix pardoned for returning to the peninsula. She faces the possibility of being sent back to Morocco or even of being executed. The fact that the story is unfinished leads me to think that Cervantes is considering here how closure can be brought about in a tale that blends with ongoing time, with current events. How can you bring closure to a story that deals with something that is in the process of happening? How can fictional time offer closure to something that is taking place in real time? If you do that, closure would be a way of fictionalizing what is real by giving it an artistic shape. This is a theoretical issue that I am sure was on Cervantes' mind, and if you remember, in Part I the very last of the love stories is also left unfinished. I will take this up again as I consider the ending of the *Quixote*.

But what is the significance of all this business of current events in terms of Cervantes' opinion about the expulsion of the moriscos? This has been, as you can imagine, a hotly debated issue, with presentism playing a heavy role in the debate. Presentism is a way of alluding to a form of criticism, be it of literature or an interpretation of history, that favors the present. You interpret the past in terms of the present; or you project the present onto the past. The issue is whether one can ever completely avoid doing this, but there are some critics and some historians who practice presentism to the point where it is obvious that it is not right. A great deal of presentism has played a role in the debate about whether Cervantes really favored the expulsion of the moriscos or not. All of this is colored by the many twentieth-century discussions about minorities and their rights. Some critics want to make Cervantes into a contemporary and have him espouse the views of a modern liberal thinker, a crass anachronism.

Cervantes is obviously appalled at the expulsion of those moriscos who were clearly a part of the fabric of Spain, particularly those who had truly converted to Christianity. But I think he tries to give a balanced view of the whole conflict, being worried about the presence of an internal enemy within the state, given the international situation. It is possible, and this has been mentioned, that he was also concerned about himself personally if he expressed an opinion blatantly opposed to that of the Crown. But think about this: Morocco is directly across the Strait of Gibraltar from Spain, barely a few miles away.

Morocco was in the hands of enemies of Spain who were of the same race and religion as the moriscos. In other words, as opposed to the Jews, who had been expelled in 1492, the moriscos had an international projection, a potential international connection. They could be allied with foreign enemies and become a fifth column within Spain. A fifth column is what you call a group of individuals who are against a government but live within the nation ruled by that government. Through their presence, the moriscos, as in the story of the captive in Part I, threaten one of the central myths of the constitution of modern Spain after the unification of the country under Ferdinand and Isabella: the story of the Reconquest, meaning the recovery of Spanish territory from Moorish control, which culminated with the fall of Granada in 1492.

What I mean by this is that the moriscos, by their very presence, recalled the presence of the Moors in Spain until 1492. The Reconquista had become a central patriotic myth holding Spain together. The moriscos were expelled in 1609 in order to stoke people's fears that the Reconquest could be undone and hence that the whole country would collapse. This was a ridiculous notion, but governments do tend to motivate the populace via such fears, particularly totalitarian governments. Hitler did that; in Cuba, Fidel Castro has been announcing an impending Yankee invasion for fifty years—it has never come—to keep the people aroused; and this is what was happening in the Spain of this moment: the moriscos might somehow unleash a counter-Reconquest and bring the whole country down.

In terms of our protagonists, Don Quixote and Sancho, the most relevant thing is that we observe Sancho making a difficult and delicate moral decision with respect to Ricote. That decision is whether to help him—Sancho is in need, and Ricote offers him a very substantial material reward—or to be loyal to the king by obeying his edicts. Sancho's memories, by the way, play a part in the episode. He recalls that he cried when Ricote's family left his town, and he reveals that Ana Félix has Pedro Gregorio, a mayorazgo, as her suitor. Pedro Gregorio is not only a Christian young man but also a very well-to-do Christian young man. Sancho chooses a middle ground: he will not help Ricote dig up the treasure, but he will keep silent about Ricote's illegal return to Spain and his plan to take the money out of the country, which was also a punishable offense. There were heavy sanctions against taking money out of the country because, with the expulsion, as always happens when certain people are expelled from a country and take their riches with them, it affects the economy negatively. So there were laws against the moriscos taking their wealth with them, too. Ricote is guilty of two crimes: having returned and also of planning to take money out of the country. Sancho makes a difficult choice because he himself is taking a risk; if it is learned he has not reported Ricote's return, he could be held responsible.

Ricote himself is a complex character and one of the few figures not mocked in any way in the book. By complex, I mean he is caught in conflicting dilemmas, and he is able to weigh different solutions. He is comparable to Hajji Murad, Zoraida's father in Part I, but here the conflict is expanded because Ricote's wife has converted to Christianity, and his daughter was born into Christianity, but he himself has not quite converted. He is in a highly difficult situation. Ricote says he is not against the Edict of Expulsion;

he understands the reasons of state behind it but laments that even those moriscos who have joined the mainstream of society, having even converted to Christianity, are paying for the actions of those who are seditious and with whom he does not agree. In the marvelous postprandial exchange he and Sancho have after he and the German beggars get drunk on wine and sated with food, Sancho confesses his travails as governor and his unsuitability for the position, and Ricote, who is clearly better educated than Sancho and can tell that the whole thing had to be a hoax, does not press the matter. In this, Ricote displays a deep human understanding and forbearance for the shortcomings of another human being: Sancho's ignorance. It is a very fine touch by Cervantes.

There is a certain neighborly complicity by which the figures of Sancho and Ricote are filled out. The squire is growing intellectually and spiritually as the novel progresses, and Ricote, as I said, is a complex, well-rounded character who goes through a very dramatic process here. My friend the distinguished Puerto Rican scholar Luce López-Baralt, a professor at the University of Puerto Rico, has written eloquently—she is an Arabist—about the moriscos and the literature they produced; learning about it may help us understand Ricote's plight better, as depicted by Cervantes in the *Quixote*. I am referring to an article by López-Baralt entitled "What Image Did the Moriscos Have of Themselves?" She writes,

> If we were to symbolize the fundamental image that the Span-
> ish *moriscos* had of themselves, I believe that the epithet used
> by Mancebo [a morisco she's writing about] would be the most
> appropriate: "criers" or "weepers." . . . When the *moriscos* being
> deposed [by the authorities] cry, they are not rewriting elegant
> passages from their literature, but rather they are determined to
> preserve for posterity a faithful image of themselves and of how
> they reacted before the historical crisis that was coming upon
> them. . . . [Then she adds,] And this is precisely what *morisco*
> literature is about. It constitutes a literary monument in the col-
> lective effort to defend, at all costs, Islamic identity mortally
> wounded in the Spain of the Golden Age. It was an enormous
> effort, as has been studied in detail, since the fundamental ele-
> ments of Islamic culture—language, proper names, distinctive
> dress, religious ceremonies, even the *zambra* dance—had been
> strictly forbidden by numerous official decrees issued through-
> out the sixteenth century.

She adds, finally,

> But these very same *moriscos,* divided in the deepest recesses
> of their being, found themselves facing a new dilemma when
> Philip III decreed the Edict of Expulsion against them in 1609.
> They had not been allowed to become bona fide Spaniards in
> their country of origin, but they did not have time to become au-
> thentic Muslims during the first decades of their exile in Barbary,
> either. The *morisco* community thus went through two different
> processes of assimilation. Their Islamic identity had been torn
> from them forcibly in the Spain of the sixteenth and seventeenth
> centuries and, when they were finally immersed in the process
> of assimilating themselves to "official" Spanishness, they found
> themselves forced by circumstances to begin another process—
> now the opposite one—of cultural assimilation.[1]

In other words, when the moriscos went back to their countries of "origin"
(what countries of origin? they were from Spain) they found they were not
accepted in the Muslim communities where they thought they would be
welcomed and where they thought they would be able to blend into the
mainstream. However, they were exiles again, among their "own" people;
they were in a no-man's-land, culturally speaking. This is the drama that
Ricote and his family are living out and that Cervantes is dramatizing.

In short, what Cervantes accomplishes in the episodes involving Ricote
is to provide a vision of the effects on the people that are directly affected by
the actions that ensue from political decisions made out of concern for the
nation as a whole. The novel is neither a treatise on political philosophy nor
a commentary on government policies; it is a medium through which the
particular can be perceived in the lives of concrete people.

More broadly speaking, the issue is how nations and states define themselves negatively, as that which they are not, and try to wage wars against real
or perceived enemies and cleanse their own population of potential internal
enemies that may be accomplices of external ones. This seems to be a constant in human history, and one can see its manifestations in the Bible and in
classical literature. The modern history of abuses provoked by these tenden-
cies is long and shameful, from the expulsion of the Jews from Spain in 1492
to the extermination of millions of them by the Nazi regime in Germany. In
the Spain we are studying, it was not only moriscos who did not fit within
the homogenous body of the nation: also included were gypsies, conversos,

and people in regions such as Catalonia and Galicia, who were out of sorts with the Castilian-driven state.

Cervantes' *Quixote* is the first substantial work of fiction that deals with this conflict, and the Ricote story is the most dramatic episode. From the point of view of literature, the thing to keep in mind is that the conflict involving the expulsion of the moriscos is seen in its particulars, not in general terms, and that its poignancy derives from the believability of the characters, especially Ricote, and also in the tenderness, the neighborly solidarity, he and Sancho display. These are human qualities and emotions that are beyond political policies, and from now on novels will always be about them, these particulars, not the general themes. So much for Ricote and Ana Félix for the time being. Now let us fall into the pit with Sancho.

I assume you have read this wonderful chapter in which Sancho falls into a pit, which is a symmetrical—correlative—episode to the Montesinos's Cave adventure of his master Don Quixote. There is an internal parallel by means of which Cervantes parodies himself within Part II. I told you there are episodes in Part II that are repetitions of episodes within Part II. This episode is a parody of the Montesinos's Cave story, which was itself a parody of several chivalric episodes as well as of episodes in Homer, Virgil, and Plato. This lifts Sancho to a kind of equality with his master; it is a funny equality but nevertheless an equality.

Sancho falls into the pit after losing his island: think fall of Troy, Aeneas's descent. There is a kind of pattern here. I have a series of quotations I want to gloss from an excellent article written jointly by Raymond McCurdy and Alfred Rodríguez. They write, "As an internal parallel the series of actions that we study [meaning the fall into the pit] have exceptional characteristics. It is, in the first place, the most prominent example of the deliberate parallelism that largely structures the *Quixote,* the parallel in which the obvious resemblance that strikes one is descent, fall, common subterranean stay [they are talking about the Cave of Montesinos parallelism]." They quote Juan Marasso, who says, " 'We notice the correspondence, the striking parallelism of cycles in Part II: enchantment of Dulcinea [like the loss of Troy], descent to Montesinos' Cave [the infernal descent of Aeneas], Sancho Panza loses his island [loss of Troy], falls into a deep and very dark pit [infernal descent].' "[2] So you can see that McCurdy and Rodríguez have noticed these parallelisms. They add, "The parallel that we're studying by offering a curious parody of a parody becomes a mirror that reflects Cervantes' entire creative process [because this is a parody of a parody, a parody of Cervantes himself]. Cervantes produces with a Sancho Panzean adventure—at least for

the reader who picks up on all of the hints strewn by the novelist—an innovative, and at the same time snide re-parody, double parody. By doing this,
the great novelist purposely touches on the aesthetic limits of his own artistic procedure, for it would appear to be the limit of parodic creation, a limit
insurmountable and innovative, a self-parody that is, moreover, a parody of
a parody."[3] This is reaching deep into that series of repeated images that is
the *Quixote.* Now, we also notice, leaving McCurdy and Rodríguez, that this
episode involves a desengaño which makes Sancho even more reflective: he
no longer yearns for the island. Rather, he values his service and attachment
to Don Quixote more than that and yearns for the human intimacy of their
relationship.

Don Quixote finds Sancho because he has gone out to practice for his
joust, the encounter he is supposed to have. By chance he hears Sancho's
laments. The combat the knight is practicing for is going to be the one to
restore Dueña Rodríguez's daughter's honor by having the young man who
promised to marry her go ahead and marry her. Here we arrive at the third
topic I mentioned at the beginning of class, an instance of art influencing
life. The prank organized by the Duke and his minions brings about the possible marriage of the young woman to the young man who plays the role of
her estranged fiancé because it is no longer the real fiancé who is involved
but someone who is playing the estranged fiancé.

This adventure will turn out like the love conflicts of Part I that Don
Quixote solves, except that here fiction is turning into reality, whereas in the
Dorotea, Don Fernando, Pandafilando affair the giant is only symbolically
slain. Fiction and reality are no longer separate in Part II. They are part and
parcel of each other. Fiction does not simply reflect reality, it affects it. In
other words, reality is nature improved by art. In the episode, we have, again,
a marriage in which social mobility is involved. Dueña Rodríguez's daughter
was going to marry up economically because the young man was of a higher
social class, but the groom's proxy, Tosilos, is a mere servant, a lackey.

The daughter concludes that it is better to marry low than not at all and
accepts Tosilos in a gesture of pragmatism that is completely at odds with
all of the notions of idealized love we have here. I find this to be very funny.
The fight is about to begin, and this proxy groom looks at the woman and,
wow!, he falls in love with her on the spot and says, I do not want to fight, I
surrender, I will marry her. And in the end she says, okay, I will marry him,
better him than nobody. So the fiction becomes reality.

There is an echo here of Camacho's wedding, so in a sense this episode is a repetition of an episode in Part II, like Sancho's fall and the Cave

of Montesinos adventure. But the point is that fiction has improved reality, and this is a theme that is repeated in the next two episodes I will discuss very briefly. They are very significant. The first and most commented on is when Don Quixote and Sancho find images of chivalric saints covered with sheets on the road. This episode is remindful of the one toward the end of Part I in which the penitents carry an image of the virgin—remember, in the procession—and Don Quixote takes her to be a lady in distress. Here, as in the case of the actors in the Parliament of Death episode, Don Quixote makes no mistakes.

Actually, he makes quite an erudite commentary of the image of Saint George. Don Quixote knows these are representations. Critics have seen in this episode a reflection of the debates involving Erasmians and Protestant objections to images and other devout representations. Having read Elliott, you know there was a debate about whether there should be religious images in the churches or not. The faction in favor of religious images won in Spain, but there was controversy about it. The point is that reality, here, appears to have turned into art; what he finds on the road are already representations of these saints, artistic images of the saints.

The second episode, which I find most charming, is that in which Don Quixote is caught in a green net placed among the trees to capture birds. The net was put up by some young ladies playing at being shepherdesses and getting ready to perform an eclogue by Garcilaso, that poet I have mentioned so many times. They have learned the lines, the young woman says, and Don Quixote vows to stand in the middle of the road and defend them for however long it takes. So reality again appears as art: young women dressed as shepherdesses about to stage an eclogue by the great Garcilaso. Notice that Garcilaso's poetry has become a part of common discourse; it has improved common everyday discourse. These young ladies want to represent his poetry.

I'll conclude by talking about Roque Guinart. Roque Guinart was a Catalan bandit who really existed, and, like the moriscos, he gives the novel an international dimension. Brigandage was common in Catalonia, where there were gangs of bandits like Guinart's that the Crown felt it had to put down, not only because they were outlaws but also because they could become accomplices of the French Huguenots. Catalonia is right next to France and in some ways is more French than Spanish. Certainly more French than Castilian. The Catalans have been very secessionist, like the Basques. The Catalans believe that they have their own culture and that they should have their own nation. Bandits like Roque Guinart could be in cahoots with the

French Huguenots—Huguenots were the French Protestants with a Calvinist background, who believed they could attain salvation without the intervention of the Church. They believed in reading and interpreting scripture directly, typically the things the Catholic Church rejected radically. So Huguenots were dangerous.

Furthermore, Spain and France had been at odds throughout the sixteenth century, so the French were no friends of the Spaniards, and thus the Spanish Crown feared these Catalan bandits because they could be agents of the French Huguenots. Remember what I said about states defining themselves negatively, as what they are not? What the Spanish Crown was not was Protestant, for sure, and not French and not Muslim. But Roque Guinart is a compelling, attractive figure. Cervantes was fascinated by the autonomous world of the bandit and by his chivalry. A bandit like Roque invents himself on the margins of the law. There is something romantic avant la lettre in Roque; he anticipates the bandit figures who are heroes in nineteenth-century novels, like Jean Valjean and all of the others.

Guinart is a kind of Catalan Robin Hood who robs the rich and helps those in need. He is lawless, except within the very strict laws of his band. You saw how strict they are. One of his associates questions the division of the booty, and Roque beheads him. In this respect Roque is like Monipodio and his brotherhood in "Rinconete y Cortadillo": his band is an anti-Utopia, a counter society, a self-enclosed world built from within. Is goodness possible within an outlaw society? Goodness always appears to be possible in Cervantes. Remember Maritornes, who is good to others. She is kind to Sancho and also reliable within the practices of her profession, perhaps not a bad trade, even if her profession is being a prostitute. Is Guinart a new exemplar of the heroic that Cervantes can never stop dreaming about? Is he an exemplary man of arms as opposed to a man of letters? Is Guinart Don Quixote's counterpart? Is he not a modern knight-errant of sorts? Is this not what makes him attractive to Don Quixote?

Notice that Don Quixote and Roque Guinart treat each other with respect. Don Quixote knows about the existence of Guinart, and Guinart seems to have read or heard about Part I of the *Quixote* because he has heard of Don Quixote. So there is a kind of self-recognition between them parallel to the one we find in the episode with Cardenio, when Don Quixote finds Cardenio and they have that meeting where they looked at each other and had an uncanny feeling of knowing each other. Here, when Don Quixote meets Roque Guinart, we have the same kind of mutual recognition: I know you because I know myself, as it were.

So that is Roque Guinart, who makes possible Don Quixote's entry into Barcelona because he has influence with important people in the city. Don Quixote gets a kind of safe conduct from the bandit to enter the great city of Barcelona. I cannot conclude without mentioning an episode within the episodes of Roque Guinart, and it is that of Claudia Jerónima. In Claudia Jerónima we have yet another love story with a lady in distress because her lover, Don Vicente, seems to be hesitant to marry her owing to a class disparity. Claudia Jerónima takes drastic action by killing her fiancé, Don Vicente, who is a potential Don Fernando. In his death throes, he swears he has been the victim of false rumors and has not been unfaithful to Claudia Jerónima. Too late: Claudia Jerónima took care of him.

This is one of the Cervantean women characters who wants to take her destiny into her own hands; she goes a little too far, here. Perhaps the episode is a reprise of Camacho's wedding, because of the death scene, but with a different and tragic ending. Here, uncharacteristically, tragedy occurs before marriage, which is unusual. Tragedies in Golden Age Spanish literature tend to happen after marriage, and we do not know if it is just another instance of Cervantes taking episodes from Part I or even within Part II and taking them one step further. In the next class I will be talking about our protagonists' arrival in Barcelona and about Avellaneda's spurious *Quixote*, which by now has appeared and which Cervantes knows about. It resurfaces in the scene of their visit to the printing shop. I will also talk about Don Quixote's final defeat. But I want you to pay special attention to Altisidora's dream; Altisidora is this very active young lady with an active imagination and proclivity to acting, and she has a marvelous dream in one of the episodes, when Don Quixote and Sancho go back to the Duke's and Duchess's palace. Her dream is an episode in which the whole issue of books will resurface.

CHAPTER 22

Dancing and Defeat in Barcelona

Don Quixote Heads Home

Required Readings

Cervantes, *Don Quixote,* Part II, chaps. 54–70, pp. 850–960.
Elliott, *Imperial Spain,* 361–86.

To me, the most evocative moment in the *Quixote,* as we reach the beautiful city of Barcelona, is the appearance of the sea. The sea suggests the infinite, as we approach the end, and also death: "Death's dateless night," to quote Shakespeare's sonnet 30. Castile is landlocked, and so Spain is defining its borders as the novel reaches its end and defines its own limits. Don Quixote and Sancho most probably have never seen the sea, but Cervantes certainly had, as we know, and he boasts of it in these last chapters of the *Quixote.* There are all these details about life aboard ships and about the galley slaves in which he uses very precise maritime terminology. But Sancho and Don Quixote are unlikely to have ever seen the sea. We are not told if they had, but one, I think, should assume they had not. The novel, which as a genre began with the *Quixote,* will be an urban genre, meaning it will deal mostly with cities; the settings will nearly always be cities. Yet, Barcelona is the only city that appears in the *Quixote,* though Part II began with a visit to El Toboso, a village.

Is Don Quixote being like Aeneas, who went from Troy to Rome? Obviously not; as I said earlier, such heroic and historically defining acts are no longer available to Don Quixote. Besides, El Toboso is a mere village in

Spain, and it endured no war, like Troy, and Barcelona is not the culmination of a journey and the harbinger of an empire to come, like the Roman, which the *Aeneid* announces and celebrates. It is significant that, in contrast to the history of the novel, which is mainly urban, this is the only urban setting in *Don Quixote*. But it is urban with a vengeance, with its collective festive celebrations and private parties, which are very much city activities. I am thinking here of *Le temps retrouvé,* the last volume in Marcel Proust's *À la recherche du temps perdu, Remembrance of Things Past.* There are quite a few parties in that novel.

The first thing that Don Quixote and Sancho suffer in Barcelona is public shame, when street urchins goad Rocinante into throwing Don Quixote. The city will mean public display, and there are a lot of people around. It is also extremely significant that Don Quixote and Sancho arrive on the eve of San Juan; that is to say, they arrive during carnival time or carnival-like time. It is as if they had arrived at a costume ball already costumed because they are literary characters playing themselves. In fact, by the time Cervantes is writing this, 1614 probably, Don Quixote and Sancho had already appeared in a carnival. Two men dressed as Don Quixote and Sancho paraded in a carnival in a town near Lima, Peru, in 1609. So Don Quixote and Sancho were already figures that people could dress up like at carnival, and here they are entering into a carnival atmosphere. Barcelona will be a stage for various festivals and theater-like representations. The city is carnival, it is theater, it means acting out roles; it is the opposite of nature, it is art. Here we have literary genres compressed and staged, like the Byzantine romance and the novela morisca I described earlier.

The Byzantine romance is also called a Greek romance. The mini Greek romance in the *Quixote* is the one which winds up Ricote's, Ana's, and Gaspar's story. Cervantes has compressed all of the elements of the Byzantine romance into this adventure: abductions, sea voyages, maritime battles, characters in costume. The episode is also a reprise of the captive's tale, with a good ending, however, promised to the Muslim father. I repeat what I said in the last lecture: at this time Cervantes is working on his own Byzantine romance, *The Trials of Persiles and Sigismunda,* so it is not surprising he should include elements of the genre in this part of the *Quixote.* The new novelistic genre Cervantes is creating is a compendium of narrative genres. To me, as I've said, the most amusing moment of this mini Byzantine romance is when the beautiful Gaspar Gregorio is dressed up as a woman so as to be *less* attractive to his Turkish captors. As I said, this is a baroque kind of transvestitism; transvestitism turned around.

The story of Gaspar Gregorio and Ana is not concluded; it has no closure. The reason may be that this is the only love story with a social and political connection to reality, the whole business of the expulsion of the moriscos and their return to Spain being against the law. This is not just a story but part of ongoing history. The novel the *Quixote*, like its protagonist, is coming closer to reality, not to the demands of fiction or of madness. Perhaps closure other than death is available only in those realms, not in real life. That is, closure is perhaps available solely in fiction, where it has rounded, completed forms, whereas ongoing time cannot have closure. Perhaps closure is possible, then, only in fiction or within Don Quixote's madness. I continue to worry about the ending of the novel, about the impending finish of the novel, which must have vexed Cervantes a great deal as he moved forward.

Is Cervantes offering us a falsified Spain with these well-to-do citizens of Barcelona and government officials who are so lenient with the moriscos and the renegades? or is it the Spain that Cervantes would like to see? We will never know, but on the whole there is tolerance shown here, even by the government officials who are breaking the law in being so lax. Further activities in Barcelona take place at the house of Antonio Moreno. His house is now the setting for the action, but for the time being we have left the house of the Duke and Duchess. In Antonio Moreno's house we have a display of the pleasures of the bourgeoisie. This is not quite a bourgeoisie, it is higher than the bourgeoisie; it announces the emergence of the bourgeoisie as a class. So the events here are not as elaborate or ornate as the ones at the Duke's and Duchess's palace.

At the party at Moreno's house Don Quixote displays social skills, such as dancing, that we did not know or imagine he possessed. They bespeak of a past in the protagonist's life that Cervantes chose not to fill out. Where did Don Quixote learn to dance? where did he dance before? (Just as we learned in the episode of the boat that he knows how to swim; how did he ever learn how to swim?) We are not given any details about this part of Don Quixote's past; we can only imagine it. He acts, here, like an accomplished courtesan. When he is at Moreno's house, Don Quixote is the object of entertainment, as he was at the Duke's and Duchess's house, but not of cruel pranks. These bored Catalan bourgeois are having a ball when suddenly a literary character pops up among them; it is a godsend to them. Imagine, you are having a party, and James Bond shows up. Wow! Everybody is excited. All of this is the stuff of a Woody Allen movie.

The talking head caper is reminiscent of the Maese Pedro episode and his monkey, who could divine what is happening to people. The whole prank centers on making literal a rhetorical figure, prosopopeia, *prosopopeya* in Spanish. The definition of *prosopopeia* is as follows: "A figure in rhetoric in which things are represented as persons or by which things inanimate are spoken of as animated beings, or by which an absent person is introduced as speaking or a deceased person is represented as alive and present, a kind of personification." You have prosopopeia when a ventriloquist makes a puppet speak, projecting his voice and pretending it is not his. Here, as on other occasions, Cervantes is hinting at the disconnect between language and signification. It is a staging of pure voice without a source. He is also playfully presenting the inner world of man as being made up of wood and tin because the talking bust is made of wood made to look like stone or marble, and the whole device through which the student, who is the assistant in this case, speaks is made of tin. So here, in addition to prosopopeia there is a hint that Cervantes is playfully suggesting that the inside of a human is just like this piece of wood with a tin tube through which the voice emerges. It is one of the episodes in the *Quixote* that has all kinds of philosophical suggestions, always in a light tone.

The most meaningful episode in Barcelona is the visit to the printing shop. This is the acme of self-reflexivity. It is as if, jokingly, Don Quixote were visiting his true origin in the most material sense. Don Quixote, a character who emerged from books, is at the place where books are literally made; it is a kind of reductio ad absurdum because literature cannot be reduced to the material status of paper, ink, and glue: what you make a book with. But Cervantes is delving into the most basic building blocks of his craft, aware that the machinery of bookmaking cannot be its real origin, but he is playing with that idea. This adventure must be seen in relation to the scrutiny of the books and to Altisidora's dream, which I will come to. All these events deal with the question of the book. The visit to the printing shop, I repeat, is the last frontier of self-reflexivity. It is a visit to the origin of all reflections and representations. Here is a fictional character observing the printing of a book about himself, but, to add to the confusion, the book is an apocryphal one. It is Avellaneda's book. The sign the boys hang on Don Quixote also demotes him to language, a label; he is abased to letters. Cervantes is taking the question of the book to the very limits.

Avellaneda's spurious *Quixote* came to the attention of Cervantes when he was at about chapter 36 or 37. The moment he learned about it, he changed Don Quixote's destination to Barcelona, away from Saragossa. Avellaneda's book allows Cervantes to add yet another dimension to his play of illusion. Later, he will borrow a character from the false *Quixote* and make him swear he had never seen Don Quixote and Sancho. The legal document he makes him sign is a satire of Spain's legalistic bureaucracy. Can you imagine? A legal document that a fictional character is making another one sign stating that he, the one giving him the document, is the real one. It is a parody of those legal documents at the origin of the constitution of the picaresque, for instance, but there is a great deal more here. This is a metafictional realm where characters from two novels can actually meet and talk to each other. The play of illusion, the blurring of the border between fantasy and fiction, is emphasized by the various layers of fiction involved and by the brilliant move by which Cervantes, in not allowing Don Quixote to go to Saragossa, intends to correct history. Of course, it is a history that is a fiction to begin with.

There is no position one can take outside the world of fiction in the *Quixote* because the fiction is manmade; it is all that we can know. In a way—I have mentioned this before—this principle anticipates the philosophy of the great eighteenth-century Italian philosopher Giambattista Vico. *The New Science* is the name of his wonderful book. One of Vico's main ideas was that humankind can only understand what humankind has made; therefore, he begins his history of humanity not with Genesis, where it was God's creation, but after the flood, when it is humans who remake the world. What I am saying is that this world of fiction is human-made, and it is all that we can understand. So the modern self that emerges from this vision is a very light and fragile one, like Hamlet's, or like the one proposed by Milan Kundera in *The Unbearable Lightness of Being*. It is a modern self devoid of certainties because the feeling this *mise en abîme,* this infinitely receding sequence, provokes is that if anything envelopes our world, if anything contains our world, it may be yet another fiction.

This is a Cervantean Borgesian predicament in which we find ourselves and from which we cannot escape in the *Quixote*. It is what we saw in *Las Meninas*, when we visited Velázquez's studio, and by watching we became a part of the fiction of the painting. The visit to the printing shop is like the visit to that studio of Velázquez's; this is the shop where fiction is made. The only way out of this predicament is by an act of will, like the one Don Quixote performs at the end, when he spurns all of the seductions and all of the consolations his comrades offer him as he nears death. His is an act of faith and of will, not an intellectual decision.

Moreover, Avellaneda and his *Quixote* may also represent a misreading of Cervantes' *Quixote* by the society of his time. Avellaneda's *Quixote* presents a character that is essentially ridiculous and funny and a Sancho who is a glutton and a drunk, so it is the vision of the *Quixote* as essentially a funny book, a misreading that has been repeated in recent times by the so-called hard school of critics of Cervantes in England, about whom I said that the only hard thing involved is their brain arteries. In a way, Cervantes preempts all of them by doing what he does with Avellaneda's *Quixote*, but the misreading is interesting in itself.

If Avellaneda's book stands for that misreading, I have quotations from two critics, one of whom you have heard before, who will help clarify that potential misreading and also situate it historically. George Mariscal wrote a book on Avellaneda's *Quixote* in which he underscores the misreading by pointing out that in Avellaneda's book Don Quixote is actually chained and sent to jail. Mariscal writes, "Physical imprisonment in the original text [meaning in the Cervantes' *Quixote* of 1605], with the exception of the open cage in the final chapters, is displaced by images designed to represent the inescapable, complex, and often tenuous mediations between material conditions and the subject (ropes, strings, nets, and so on). In Avellaneda's novel, on the other hand, he whose behavior is judged to be a product of unorthodox subject positions must be held forcibly in place so that he can be refunctioned by state violence and the shame produced by exchanges with the community [the subject here meaning Don Quixote]."[1] He goes on: "The condemnation of Don Quixote by the subordinate classes underscores the extent to which Cervantes's character is refigured as other by Avellaneda and attests to the success enjoyed by the Spanish elites (in this case, with Avellaneda as spokesman) in their drive for ideological homogeneity."[2] As you can see, Mariscal is equating Avellaneda's imprisonment of Don Quixote with the mainstream ideology of the Spanish of the times. He goes on: "Avellaneda imprisons his protagonist because he is mad [meaning the protagonist, not Avellaneda], but his more pressing ambition is to refunction the alternative forms of subjectivity which Cervantes's first novel had figured forth. Cervantes's representation of a radically autonomous individual runs head on not only into the traditional constraints of shame and revenge but finally into the twin powers of early Spanish absolutism (with Avellaneda as their literary spokesman), which work to suppress it."[3]

So Avellaneda is working to suppress these forms of subjectivity that are present in the *Quixote*. Finally: "The refusal to subject himself to any of the hegemonic forces at work in his society underscores the strong motif of wandering which has been noted by critics ranging from Lukács to Foucault. Moving along the margins of the dominant culture, Cervantes's Don Quixote is not the romantic rebel many traditional critics have wanted him to be; nonetheless, he works to clear a space in which modern forms of subjectivity would later appear."[4] Mariscal is not aware that the individual alternative forms of subjectivity that he talks about are bourgeois in origin and destiny, if we are going to see them from the Marxist point of view that he, I presume, is looking at them from. Moreover, he works, I think, with a utopian vision of the liberated self that Cervantes would have never been naïve enough to accept. But what he says is very suggestive about the source of Avellaneda's concept of the character he has taken from Cervantes.

Manuel Durán, the other critic, whom you have encountered many times, writes,

> Gilman has demonstrated the coincidence between Avellaneda's attitude and that of post-Tridentine morals, which were ascetic and orthodox. Avellaneda would then be the representative of all, the people's voice, but this does not explain why Avellaneda shows himself to be so favorable to the *moriscos*. His likely Aragonese origin is not sufficient enough proof. In any case, if one accepts that Avellaneda's book is a kind of negative collective response by Spanish society of the time to the freedom and inner independence with which Cervantes had endowed his characters, we will then understand why Cervantes did not have immediate and direct successors in Spain, and the reason why the modern novel invented in Spain by Cervantes would have to wait until the middle of the nineteenth century to be able to return to its birthplace. Official Spain in contrast to the nearly underground Spain found in a path that goes from Rojas to the mystics and to Cervantes did not believe in individual autonomy and freedom.[5]

What Durán means here is that there is an official Spain, orthodox and becoming increasingly so in the sixteenth century, but that there is also an underground Spain that goes from Rojas, the author of *Celestina*, through the mystics, Saint John of the Cross, and others who were looked upon with great suspicion by the Inquisition, to Cervantes, and this is a counter-official Spain. Avellaneda represents orthodox Spain, which suppresses that other Spain, and that is why he gives us his erroneous version of the *Quixote*. Cervantes' relatively mild response to Avellaneda is in line with his ironic stance.

There is a great deal of humor in what Cervantes does to Avellaneda, and we will see it immediately, when we get to Altisidora's dream vision.

An ironist like Cervantes can never be so sure of himself as to be virulent in controversy and in debate. One of Cervantes' most admired traits is his restraint and self-mockery, and it shows in his answer to Avellaneda. If you remember the 1605 prologue, you remember this self-mocking Cervantes who does not know what to do about writing the prologue, and all of these authorial games by which he distances himself from his creation. Only someone with that attitude could do to Avellaneda what he did, according to Gilman, that is, throw a "net of irony" over him to contain him. He did say a few nasty things in the prologue of the 1615 *Quixote*, but Avellaneda had said terrible things about Cervantes, even mocking him because of his maimed hand.

We come now to what I think is the culminating event in Barcelona, which is Don Quixote's defeat at the hands of the Knight of the White Moon. The Knight of the White Moon is the latest reincarnation of Sansón Carrasco, who we learn has been pursuing his neighbor since his failure as the Knight of the Mirrors. Sansón looked for Don Quixote in Saragossa and did not find him, and now he is in cahoots with the Duke and Duchess, who tell him where Don Quixote has gone. The rules are carefully agreed on before combat, as in the earlier encounter, and Don Quixote is defeated fair and square within those rules. He speaks as if he is already dead from within his armor as he lies on the ground: "Don Quixote, battered and stunned, did not raise the visor but spoke as from inside a grave, in a feeble, faltering voice" (II, 44, 928).

Poor Don Quixote! If Don Quixote had been killed, it would have been a plausible ending to the novel, but even his merely being defeated could have ended it too. Why does it not? It does not because he has not yet given up his persona as knight-errant. Hence the process of his coming to himself is not yet finished, and that is his most important task, the one comparable to the heroic mission Aeneas accomplishes in Virgil's *Aeneid*. The profound suggestion of Don Quixote's defeat at the hands of the Knight of the White Moon is that, given that this knight is like the Knight of the Mirrors, a reflection of Don Quixote himself, it may be that Don Quixote is being defeated by a projection of his own inner world. If in Part I Don Quixote's body is imprisoned in the cage, here it is as if his spirit were the one being defeated by a projection of itself. It is as if Don Quixote were conquered by his own reflection, by something within his own self. This is what is profound about this scene. It is easy to establish that the Knight of the White Moon is not only an image of Don Quixote—remember that *luna* means the reflecting part of the mirror, *la luna del espejo*, but also that *lunatic* refers to Don Quixote's madness. The moon is a celestial body of reflected light, so Sansón is in a way reflecting Don Quixote's light or a vision of Don Quixote's spirit.

I am intrigued by the name of this knight, which seems to be redundant. I mean, the moon is always white, so why white moon? The doubly white moon seems to cancel itself out in its repeated whiteness; this brings to mind the white pearl on the white forehead at the end of Dante's *Paradiso*; the white pearl on Beatrice's forehead cannot be seen because it is white on white. Don Quixote is fighting, as it were, against his own nothingness, that light being what I mentioned before in alluding to Hamlet and to Kundera, this nothingness, which is this white on white, which disappears onto itself because white can also mean absence, and in that sense the Knight of the White Moon can also be an image of death. Is there any significance in the fact that Don Quixote is defeated near the sea? To me, the sea is an image of death. It is an image of the infinite, of the eternal, of death. There seems to be a correspondence between the white of the knight and the sea.

Don Quixote now imagines living his life as a shepherd, an image drawn from the pastoral romances. Cervantes, in a way, is adding the pastoral to what I have called a smorgasbord of narrative modes, but only as a project by Don Quixote. This would be another novel parallel to the *Quixote* in which the pastoral romances would play the role of the chivalric ones. Remember that we have had a mini Byzantine romance and a mini novela morisca, and if you remember Don Quixote says,

> This is the meadow where we came across those charming shepherdesses and gallant shepherds who were reviving and imitating the pastoral Arcadia, an original and intelligent idea that I should like us to imitate in our turn, Sancho, if you are agreeable, and turn ourselves into shepherds, at least for the time during which I am obliged to withdraw from the world. I shall buy some sheep, and all the other requisites for pastoral practice, I shall call myself "the shepherd Quixotiz" and you will be "the shepherd Panzino," and we'll wander around the hills, the woods and the meadows, singing here, lamenting there, drinking the liquid crystals of the springs or of the pure streams of the mighty rivers. The evergreen oaks will give us their sweet fruit with generous hands. (II, 47, 940–41)

This is a description of Arcadia, a pastoral utopia. This meta-novel he imagines is a funny one; in it Don Quixote and Sancho would be shepherds along with the priest and Sansón, and all of them would take pastoral names derived from their real names and give names to their ladies. Sancho says he is going to call his wife Teresona, with the augmentative, because apparently she is fat like him. This is the world of Garcilaso's eclogues, brought to Don Quixote's mind, as he mentions it, by the episode of the young women who are preparing to stage one of the eclogues, which has been anticipated by all of the references to the poet in Part II. It is also a circling back to Cervantes' first book, *La Galatea,* of which he always said he would write a second part but never did. In this new novel there would be a world of love without violence, an ideal Neoplatonic universe. The same clash between a fallen present and an unrevivable ideal past that appears in the *Quixote* is alive in this projected novel, not to mention that all the potential characters are too old to be pastoral lovers, and one, the priest, can be no lover at all. So it is kind of a grotesque pastoral romance in the making, as the *Quixote* is in some ways also a grotesque chivalric romance.

This is followed by the episode in which they are run over by a herd of pigs. Critics have found that Cervantes tinkered around with where to place this episode, but the important thing is that there seems to be no end to the humiliations Don Quixote is enduring toward the end of the book, because, remember, there is nothing lower than a pig or a swineherd.

Now our heroes are returned forcibly to the Duke's and Duchess's house. The Duke and Duchess are not satisfied with all of the pranks they have played on Don Quixote and Sancho and prepare yet another elaborate one for them when they hear of the knight's defeat and return to his village. Here Cervantes inserts a statement by Cide Hamete to underline the questionable state of mind of these frivolous aristocrats: "And Cide Hamete says even more: he considers that the perpetrators of the hoax were as mad as the victims, and that the Duke and Duchess, going to such lengths to make fun of the two fools, were within a hairsbreadth of looking like fools themselves" (II, 70, 956).

This is a world where there has been a contamination of madness from character to character. The skit with the dead Altisidora is full of literary allusions. The staging is elaborate: there are bleachers for the audience, an elevated place for the Duke and Duchess, and blazing torches to turn the night into day. Sancho is costumed in a shroud of flames and a bonnet with devils on it, which seem like Dantesque allusions, and the lines recited during the skit, or at least one of the octaves, are directly taken from Garcilaso's poetry. The farce is a representation of the death of the beloved in the courtly love tradition and in Renaissance poetry. The famous deaths portrayed are those of Beatrice (Dante), Laura (Petrarch), and Isabel Freyre (Garcilaso).

Deaths marked the poetry of these major poets, dividing their works into a before and after: before the death of Laura, after the death of Laura, before the death of Isabel Freyre, after her death, and so forth. A high point in the history of Western poetry is being staged here: a staging of the interplay of Eros and Thanatos, of love and death, but in a baroque farce involving the protagonists and, it seems, a whole household in attendance. This prank is as elaborate as the pageant in the forest.

Sancho's body is again the object or, better, the vehicle for expiation, and the dueñas are his executioners; they are going to slap him around and pinch him and stick pins in his butt, which will allow Altisidora to be revived. Why? Sancho has been cast in the role of the fool who must suffer all of the physical shenanigans, meaning the fool drawn from the carnival tradition. This reading of his figure is parallel to the one Avellaneda made, turning him into a farcical glutton and drunk; the reading the Duke and Duchess and their minions have of Sancho—because, remember, they had read Part I—is parallel to Avellaneda's. This is why he is made to endure these humiliations.

The flames on Don Quixote's dress and the lighting of the courtyard seem to be an allusion to Dido, who, after killing herself when abandoned by Aeneas, was burned in a funeral pyre. Don Quixote's return and impending departure are like those of Aeneas, and Altisidora is playing the role of Dido. In her anger, the insults she hurls at Don Quixote, which are very colorful and actually accurate, picture him as being very ugly—she says he looks like a camel. But all of these truths play into the fiction because it sounds like she is saying them out of spite because he is leaving her; so even these truths are absorbed into the fiction. The whole episode is thick with literary references and literary staging. It is a staging of great literature and a reducing of it to play.

The most remarkable passage in the whole sequence of incidents involving Altisidora is her infernal vision. Sancho is curious to learn what Altisidora saw when she was dead, what the afterlife was like. He wants to know particularly about hell; he wants to know what it is like. Notice that Altisidora's infernal voyage is like Don Quixote's descent into the Cave of Montesinos and Sancho's fall into the pit. Her reply to Sancho, which she must have made up on the spot, like Dorotea did the story of Princess Micomicona in Part I, is a truly brilliant boast of imaginative skill on her part and, of course, Cervantes':

"To tell you the honest truth," Altisidora replied, "I can't have died completely, because I didn't go right into hell: if I had, I couldn't ever have gotten out again, however much I wanted to. The fact is that I reached the gate, where about a dozen devils were playing pelota, all stripped down to doublet and hose, with broad, floppy collars trimmed in Flanders lace, and ruffles of the same material serving as cuffs, and displaying four inches of arm to add length to their hands, in which they were holding rackets of fire; and what most amazed me was that instead of balls they were serving books, full of wind and stuffing, an extraordinary, unheard-of thing. But this didn't astonish me as much as seeing that, although it's natural for winners at games to be happy and the losers to be glum, in that game they were all grumbling quarrelling and cursing each other."

"That's no wonder," Sancho retorted, "because devils, whether they're playing games or not, can never be happy, win or lose."

"Yes, that must be it," Altisidora replied, "but there's something else that amazes me, or rather that amazed me when I was there, which is that there wasn't one ball that could withstand the first volley or was in any condition to be served again, and so books old and new came in quick succession, an extraordinary sight. One of them, brand-new and well bound, was given such a thump that its guts poured out and its leaves flew all over the place. One devil said to another:

" 'Go and see what book that is.'

"And the other devil replied:

" 'It's the second part of the history of Don Quixote de la Mancha, not written by Cide Hamete, its first author, but by some Aragonese person who says he comes from Tordesillas.'

" 'Remove it,' replied the other devil, 'and consign it to the depths of hell; I never want to see it again.'

" 'Is it as bad as all that?' the other one asked.

" 'It's so bad,' replied the first devil, 'that if I'd tried my very hardest to write a worse one the task would have been beyond me.'

"They continued their game, serving and returning other books." (II, 70, 957–58)

There is a lot of Dante in this episode, but the story of devils playing a form of "pelota" with the souls or the heads of the dead is a traditional gruesome story. But Cervantes has embroidered it by making them use books instead of heads or souls for balls. The attack on Avellaneda is very funny, but the commentary on books goes beyond the apocryphal *Quixote*. This episode reflects a change in the appraisal of books by the beginning of the seventeenth century in the West. Their value has diminished. It seems to follow an elementary economic law: with the advent of the printing press, the number of books increased dramatically, and then the value of each decreased—this is basic economics—but it is more complicated than that. Philosophy has moved toward knowledge as a result of experience, not because of something acquired from authoritative sources in books.

In Spain, Neo-Scholasticism, a revival of the medieval philosophy of the church fathers which relied on syllogism and the opinion of authoritative sources, had become the ideology of the state. Neo-Scholasticism, or whatever you want to call it, was the ideology of the Spanish Crown. Logic argumentation and authorities supplied the foundations of knowledge. We have seen something of this, and I mentioned it in regard to the satire of doctors in the person of the doctor Pedro Recio Tirteafuera, who says to Sancho, "You cannot eat this, you cannot eat that"; the knowledge of medicine at the time was based mostly on books, not on experience. The ability to read many books did not bring one closer to wisdom but to an inordinate, perhaps infinite, enlargement of the library and perhaps to Don Quixote's madness. I believe this idea is implicit in the marvelous passage about Altisidora's infernal visitation. As customary, Cervantes deals with very complicated issues in such an unaffected, spontaneous, and amusing way that it seems almost like a miracle, but Neo-Scholasticism is what lies behind this episode about books being whacked with flaming rackets.

CHAPTER 23

The Meaning of the End

Don Quixote's Death

Required Readings

Cervantes, *Don Quixote*, Part II, chaps. 71–74, pp. 961–82.
Cervantes, Miguel de. "Self-Portraits: Introduced by Roberto González Echevarría." In *Casebook*, 265–71.

As we approach the end of the semester we also, naturally, approach the end of the *Quixote*, and I'll move on to a brief consideration of other works by Cervantes as well as to reactions to his works by two major writers, Kafka and Borges. Today, I will talk about the end of the great novel, and next class I will devote to those other works and also to Cervantes' death, but before that I want to address two topics that have fallen by the wayside: humor and Cervantes' self-portraits, following my little essay in the *Casebook*.

Other than the slapstick humor we find occasionally in the *Quixote*—in the episodes at the inn in Part I, for instance, as well as some of the scatological instances, such as when Sancho defecates in the fulling hammers episode—Cervantes' humor is broad, more encompassing, and sophisticated, and it is laced with irony. By irony I mean there is a benign detachment, a discreet perspective from which humanity is being seen in contrast to the mad hero. Don Quixote's madness allows the narrator and the reader to appreciate everyone's folly. No one is safe. Not the priest, not the Duke, not university graduates like Sansón Carrasco, and not even the narrator himself. Sancho's wisdom is another measure by which to judge other characters, those who are presumably better educated. He is not just the wise fool, the funny fellow who stumbles on truths by chance, but the possessor of natural reason, which allows him to be right when others, who are well-read, are wrong.

I believe the critic who best encapsulated Cervantes' humor was the late Lowry Nelson, whom I quoted in the first lecture. He writes the following in the introduction to his *Cervantes, A Collection of Critical Essays*:

> As depicters of the human condition both Shakespeare and Cervantes belong to the select company of those I would call universal ironists as distinct from tendentious ironists. Universal ironists contemplate the world with a kind of gentle resignation and compassion in full knowledge of both the grandeurs and miseries of human life: among them I would number Chaucer, Chekhov, Kafka, and [Italo] Svevo. Tendentious ironists view the world from a programmatic stance connoting accusation, bitter protest, and meliorist reformation of human ills [meliorist, meaning to make better]: among them I would include Flaubert, Ibsen, Hardy, and Mann. The distinction is only approximate but nonetheless significant. Neither attitude is qualitatively superior or justifiable, though it is perhaps the universal ironist who can view mankind with greater tolerance and understanding; it is he who can encompass a broader span of human types and human experiences; it is he who can best present the inviolability and unique essence of the particular and the individual. It is precisely this ability in Shakespeare and Cervantes to create particularized essence that leads us, their readers, to draw the general conclusion, to see the individual as representative. Hence the seeming plenitude of humanity we find in such odd and peculiar figures as Don Quijote and Sancho Panza, not to mention Sansón Carrasco, the Curate, Marcela, Ginés de Pasamonte, and others.[1]

"Particularized essence" here means that individual objects, and especially characters, are full within themselves; they are round, as it were. This is why details are so important in the *Quixote*. By "plenitude of humanity" Nelson means the foibles, weaknesses, and also the grandeur of these figures, as he says; their mistakes, their bumps against the real are funny and counterbalance their virtues. Irony resides in the fulcrum, where the two are added to each other, without canceling each other. With respect to Shakespeare, though, I agree with Nelson. I want to reiterate what I have said in previous classes. There is a level of despair in Shakespeare's plays that is never reached in Cervantes. Cervantes has a gentler perspective on the human condition and a more optimistic one. I am thinking of *Hamlet* and also of *King Lear.* So much for humor.

As for the self-portraits, I included those texts in my *Casebook* because the Oxford format called for an interview with the author in question, and since Cervantes was not available I thought it would be best to include self-portraits, which would make a good substitute. I toyed with the idea of inventing an interview with Cervantes, but I did not think I could get it past the editors at the very staid and serious Oxford University Press. The things I would like you to remember from my little prologue to the self-portraits are these: that individualism led to portraiture in the Renaissance, an individualism that was aided and abetted by wealth; also, that the development of perspective—think of Alberti—allowed for a more realistic, particularized kind of portrait, showing details of the face and body, not all necessarily flattering although those who paid for the portraits wanted to be flattered; in addition, that the first self-portrait by a painter that we know of was that by Albrecht Dürer, in which he shows his piercing eyes and fine hand, the instrument of his craft; finally, that this self-portrait announces and anticipates the one by Velázquez in *Las Meninas,* where the artist appears in a prominent position, full of energy and self-assurance in the act of painting.

Then there are the concomitant self-portraits by Cervantes, which are characteristically self-deprecating. In one, he talks about the changing color of his hair; in another, he talks about his missing teeth; so he is self-deprecating, particularly with regard to the effects of time on his body. I would add that we should see those self-portraits in relation to the 1605 prologue to the *Quixote* and Cervantes' self-presentation as author. It is certainly different from that of Velázquez, who is much more self-assured and self-promoting obviously, but perhaps this is the effect of the different mediums they are using, painting and literature, but most likely it is a difference in their personalities.

Now, on to Don Quixote's return home. The novel's plot, with its repeated returns home, suggests that life consists of going off and coming back, a compressed *Iliad* and *Odyssey* together, and is made up of a series of apparent repetitions, reencounters, and reprises. Both parts end with a return home after a sally; actually, there are three returns. It seems as if the *Quixote,* the whole novel, is suggesting that in fiction there are two basic plots: one going out and the other coming back; one the *Iliad* and the other the *Odyssey,* as I just said. That is too simplistic, perhaps, but that seems to be the implication in the combined two parts of the *Quixote.* What do these repetitions reveal? what do we learn from them? Perhaps that to live is to live again, and that life includes the remembrance of life, as Proust would discover and exploit almost three centuries later in his great novel *À la recherche du temps perdu, Remembrance of Things Past.*

That is why we approach the end by returning to the beginning. In the process, Cervantes has once again underlined that reality has become fictionalized in Part II, independent of Don Quixote, and that his own hero belongs to the great fictions of the ages, to the great characters of all time. I have been mentioning this, and I will repeat it now when I comment on a particular passage. Cervantes also, in this return—I will go over it—underscores the nature of Don Quixote's victory, which I mentioned with regard to Aeneas in the *Aeneid.* As he returns home, Don Quixote encounters a character from the apocryphal *Quixote,* Don Álvaro de Tarfe. It is as if his memories had a life outside of himself in literature. Cervantes is again poking fun at Avellaneda, but the way he does so is full of other suggestions, as I mentioned in a previous class, and I referred to the work of Stephen Gilman.

The first and clearest suggestion is that Don Quixote lives in a world of fiction that intersects that of Avellaneda's fiction. It is the ultimate proof that in Part II reality has become fictionalized without the help of Don Quixote's fantasy; it is out there, already fictionalized. Characters from two fictional books meet, and one asks the other to sign a notarized document to testify that the book in which he appeared was false and that he is now the real one. This is enormously funny at a very sophisticated level. The document is crucial, as legality would be the ultimate way of guaranteeing that a fiction is real.

We come now to the last inn, which Don Quixote does not confuse with a castle anymore. At the last inn where Don Quixote and Sancho lodge on their way back, their room contains representations of Helen of Troy and of Dido. The passage, I believe, is one more example of Cervantes' awareness of the importance of his creations:

> He was lodged in a ground-floor room where in place of leather
> hangings here were old painted cloths of the sort common in vil-
> lages. On one of them some clumsy hand had painted the rape
> of Helen, at the moment when the audacious guest carried her
> off from Menelaus, and on another was the story of Dido and

Aeneas, she on a high tower, apparently signaling with half a sheet to the fugitive guest who was escaping across the sea in a frigate or a brigantine. Don Quixote noted that Helen wasn't too sorry to be stolen away, because she was laughing to herself on the sly, but the lovely Dido was shedding tears the size of walnuts. As he looked at the paintings he said:

"These two ladies were most unfortunate not to have been born in the present age, and I am even more unfortunate not to have been born in theirs: had I confronted these gentlemen, neither would Troy have been burned nor Carthage destroyed, because by my simply killing Paris all those calamities would have been avoided."

"I bet," said Sancho, "that before long there won't be a single eating-house or roadside inn or hostelry or barber's shop where there isn't a painting of the story of our deeds. But I'd like it to be done by a better artist than the one who painted these." (II, 71, 964–65)

Anyone who has been to Spain, especially to Madrid's Barajas airport, knows that Sancho has won the wager, for there are hundreds of painted and sculpted figurines of Don Quixote and Sancho of every kind for sale, including mouse pads for computers. In fact, the statues of Don Quixote and Sancho grace the Plaza de España in Madrid (fig. 20). If you have been to Madrid, you have surely seen them. Such has been the identification of the *Quixote* with Spain, Spanish culture, and the Spanish language that, as we shall see a bit later, some modern Spanish writers, like Miguel de Unamuno, have even spoken of the religion of Quixotism, "religión del quijotismo."

Cervantes knew his protagonist would be counted among those of classical times; a heady assumption for an artist of the sixteenth and seventeenth centuries whose reverence for classical art was immense. I do not know if he could have foreseen that there would be a statue of his protagonists in Madrid. It is a realization, that is, of the importance of his characters, particularly of Don Quixote, based on the accomplishment of his hero, which, as I have been saying, is quite different from those of the likes of Aeneas. Don Quixote returns a conqueror of himself, says Sancho as they enter their village: "Open your eyes, my longed-for village, and see your son Sancho Panza returning, not very rich but very well lashed. Open your arms, too, to welcome your son Don Quixote, who has been conquered by another's arm but comes here as the conqueror of himself; and that, he's told me, is the

Figure 20. Statue of Don Quixote and Sancho in the Plaza
de España in Madrid. Photo by Matthew S. Tanico.

best conquering you can wish for" (II, 72, 970). This is Don Quixote's greatest triumph. What does this mean? At the most literal level, it means he has
accepted his defeat at the hands of the Knight of the White Moon gracefully
and is willing to abide by the rules agreed upon before combat. In that way
he has conquered himself, but it may also mean what I have suggested, that
the Knight of the White Moon is a reflection of Don Quixote himself, hence,
that he has been vanquished by his own projection, by himself. I think that
more broadly speaking it means that Don Quixote has come to know himself

better and to accept himself for what he is; that he has vanquished the madness within him, or is about to. As we heard in the quotation about Helen and Dido, this has not been quite accomplished yet; he talks about defeating Paris. But we have also seen that, since the Cave of Montesinos episode, Don Quixote has been dealing differently with reality and with himself, so his return is a triumphant one, according to Sancho. There is also an echo here of the Greek "know thyself"; that Don Quixote has vanquished himself because he has come to really know himself.

So we finally come to the end. We should begin by pondering why ends or endings are so important. Let me summarize what Frank Kermode says in his beautiful book *The Sense of an Ending,* from 1967, about which I spoke earlier when dealing with the end of Part I. All of us in the modern era think we live in a world of crisis; that is, at the end of an epoch and the beginning of the next. Hence, we are keenly concerned with the sense of what we perceive as the impending end, the sense that that end can give to the past and to the future. The fictions we create reflect this anxiety and are designed to show "the concord of the middest," which is what Kermode calls our condition, men and women in the middest, in the middle; this middest that we inhabit, which presupposes beginnings and ends. These fictions, in which there is this relationship between beginning and end, Kermode calls "fictions of concord."[2] There seems to be, according to him, a human need to relate beginnings to ends, even if we are not religious believers or believers in secular versions of Providence, like Marxism. *Providence,* from *providere,* means 'foresight,' but mostly *providence* means the care of a benevolent God who guides our lives and our steps. Apocalypse is one of the fictions of concord; it ends, transforms everything, and is concordant. *Apocalypse* is from the Greek 'to uncover,' which means revelation, hence the book of Revelation, the last book of the New Testament. Prophecy is another form; it tells us the shape of the future; it connects the present with that end and beyond. We are born in the middle, and, according to Kermode, "to make sense of our span we need effective concords with origins and ends, such as give meanings to lives and to poems."[3]

Millenarianism, the end is near—you have seen all these cartoons of guys holding a cardboard sign saying "The end is near, repent," and so forth—millenarianism has to do with a thousand years, with something lasting a thousand years, like those who believed that the end of the world would come in the year 1000, and some even in 2000. Back in 2000 there were all kinds of prophecies. Of course, all of these people who prophesied are quick to recalculate. If the end does not happen, they recalculate. They always recalculate. The year 2000 came and went, and many people were waiting for all kinds of catastrophes to happen. *Chiliasm* is another word you should remember. *Chiliastic,* from the Greek for 'one thousand,' is the belief that Christ will rise in one thousand years. So we have beginning, man or woman in the middest, and end. This is how Kermode explains it all in a very charming way:

> Let us take a very simple example, the ticking of a clock. We ask what it *says:* and we agree that it says *tick-tock.* [This is in English. In Spanish it goes *tic-tac.*] By this fiction we humanize it, make it talk our language. Of course, it is we who provide the fictional difference between the two sounds: *tick* is our word for a physical beginning, *tock* our word for an end. We say they differ. What enables them to be different is a special kind of middle. We can perceive a duration only when it is organized. It can be shown by experiment that subjects who listen to rhythmic structures, such as *tick-tock,* repeated identically, 'can reproduce the intervals within the structure accurately, but they cannot grasp spontaneously the interval between the rhythmic groups,' that is, between *tock* and *tick,* even when this remains constant. The first interval is organized and limited ["tick-tock"], and the second is not. According to Paul Fraisse [I don't know who this is] the *tock-tick* gap is analogous to the role of the 'ground' in spatial perception [that is, blurry and undifferentiated]; each is characterized by a lack of form, against which the illusory organizations of shape and rhythm are perceived in the spatial or temporal object. The fact that we call the second of the two related sounds *tock* is evidence that we use fictions to enable the end to confer organization and form on the temporal structure. The interval between the two sounds, between *tick* and *tock* is now charged with significant duration. The clock's *tick-tock* I take to be the model for what we call a plot, an organization that humanizes time by giving it form; and the interval between *tock* and *tick* represents purely successive, disorganized time of the sort that we need to humanize.[4]

So, the end is meaning; the end provides meaning, and this is why it is so necessary. Kermode goes on: "Men in the middest make considerable imaginative investments in coherent patterns which, by the provision of an end, make possible a satisfying consonance with origins and with the middle."[5]

The plots of our poems, plays, and novels reflect that need for significant endings. So what is the significance of Don Quixote's ending? or is it significant? In the next to the last chapter Sancho discards the omens that Don Quixote sees in various things and events as they come into the village, omens which will connect the end of the novel with a future beyond it; they are prophetic. "*Malum signum, malum signum!* [this is Latin: 'bad sign, bad sign'] Hare flees; greyhounds chase: Dulcinea appears not!" says Don Quixote (II, 73, 971). Remember the hare that is running and that Sancho actually catches because it is so tired. In the Spanish Don Quixote says, "Liebre huye; galgos la siguen: ¡Dulcinea no parece!" Rutherford provided some syntax, which the Spanish does not have. Don Quixote has abandoned syntax and appears to speak in tongues, as if he were having a vision or a revelation, which is what he is trying to find in this bad omen, this *malum signum* he sees. The incident shows that in his subconscious he is still in the world of dreams and of literature where these concords occur. The prophetic would extend that world for closing and ending. But Sancho dismisses these omens in a very wise way, appealing to Christian doctrine. It is as if Cervantes himself were wavering about how to end the novel.

But what is the meaning of the end Cervantes does give the novel? There are in the *Quixote* three forms of potential closure. First, Don Quixote is defeated; second, he regains his sanity; third, he dies. One could say that this scheme points to a tripartite conception of reality or of the worlds in which Don Quixote lives, each form of closure corresponding to each of the three. I have made a crass representation of these three worlds as concentric circles (fig. 21). First, the fictional world of chivalry: Don Quixote is defeated. This is the realm of books. Second, present-day reality: Don Quixote returns to being Alonso Quixano. Third, Don Quixote dies and presumably reaches the true reality, that is, the afterlife. Hence, life itself was like a fiction in that it was ephemeral and made up of things of dubious substance. It is a self-contained fiction of concord, to recall Kermode. A possible fourth form of closure, at a metafictional level, would be the defeat of Avellaneda's apocryphal *Quixote*. But let us go over the three primary ones in more detail.

First, the fictional world of chivalry. Don Quixote is defeated by the Knight of the White Moon, hence his quest comes to an end within his madness and within the fiction of chivalric romances. But as I said earlier, there are signs that the Knight of the White Moon is like a reflection of Don Quixote himself or of his madness and, more profoundly, of nothingness, that very fragile being, his very fragile self. This is why the knight is white, almost transparent, a ghost of Don Quixote. So this defeat within the world of

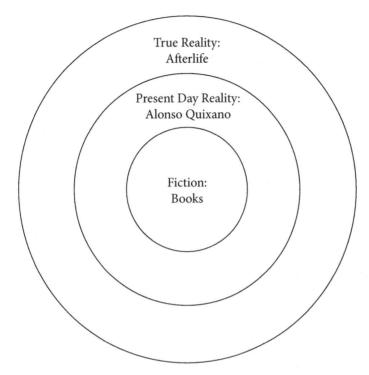

Figure 21. Levels of fiction.

books announces or prefigures his regaining his sanity and even announces his death, as white suggests a void, hence death. Then, there is present-day reality: Alonso Quixano regains his sanity. It is like a conversion story. The conversion story is typically one in which the old man dies and the new one is reborn. So there is a death and a resurrection involved.

Don Quixote sleeps and awakens changed, as if he had undergone a mystical experience, similar to the sleep and awakening after the Cave of Montesinos episode which prefigured this one. How can he know he has now awakened to his true self in the real world? Don Quixote had the memory of who he had been, but if his life as Don Quixote is now complete and his life as Alonso Quixano is about to be complete, what differentiates the two? This is the conundrum of Segismundo in Calderón's *Life Is a Dream*, that play I have recounted to you in which the young prince is drugged, taken to the palace, commits all kinds of crimes, is drugged again, taken back to the tower, and awakens, and he cannot tell if what he experienced in the palace was a dream or if he is now dreaming in the tower; he cannot tell.

So Segismundo's answer in Calderón's play is to cut through the ambiguity and will himself to be good because life may be a dream, but it may also be a rehearsal for a life that is more enduring.

Now, the afterlife, that outer circle. I do not know if you have taken notice of this, but Don Quixote dies unmarried and without succession, which is evident in the scene with the notary when he is dictating his testament because he has to leave everything to his niece and to friends. There is no one else. Again, it is very much like Segismundo's awakening to the dreamlike quality of life itself. It is as if all of life were like a dream, his madness was a dream within that dream, and death is the only access to a true permanent life. Hence, it is not only his madness that is like a dream, but also everything else. His madness is a dream within a dream. Only death can put an end to the play of reflections, and in a way this is why Alonso Quixano has to die. Don Quixote's death is the last in a series of mock deaths that have appeared throughout the book and prefigured this one; one appears at the end of Part I, when he is knocked unconscious; then there is the Cave of Montesinos, when he awakens as if he had been dead.

So, Don Quixote's death is the last in a series of mock deaths. One has to take into account that the death of Don Quixote, at least within the plot of the novel, is also a kind of return. Don Quixote returns home to the *heimlich,* to use Freud's word, to the familiar, to the place where he was Alonso Quixano, where he was sane. This makes the entire series of episodes that make up the whole book, his madness, all the more like a bubble or a dream. It is like the Barataria episodes are to Sancho, another dream. Repetitions of this kind lead one to consider the fiction in between as something one could dispense with. Do the events within that bubble occur in some sort of concert with one another? or are they themselves just a series of repetitions? Is there a successive sense to the novel's plot? Is there a sequential quality to the novel, a temporality in the *Quixote* that leads to that end? For instance, we have been able to more or less follow the months, and perhaps even the days, during which the adventures take place; but is there a sense of temporality, of chronology, of inevitability?

We know he has to return at some point to the village, as he did before, and once he is defeated we know that his madness is now on the wane. There is a sense of inevitability in the transience of his madness, of this invention of self, and of his very life. In addition, a close reading of the last chapter does not reveal anything about the death of Cide Hamete Benengeli, for instance. When did Cide Hamete Benengeli die? There is no possibility for total closure in the *Quixote*. I think Cervantes plays with it ironically; he knows that no matter how many times he says Don Quixote is dead and that Cide Hamete is hanging up his pen, any writer can still come up with a new *Quixote*, as Juan Montalvo did, an Ecuadorian writer, who published a wonderful book called *Chapters of the Quixote that Cervantes Forgot*. It is a pastiche, meaning it imitates Cervantes' style. So Cervantes knows there can be no closure. (I'll talk about that when we take up "Pierre Menard," the story by Borges, in our next class.) The *Quixote* is not a book that has a plot in the Aristotelian sense, with a beginning, a middle, and an end, all tied together tightly in a sequence of events leading to a finish. It is the life of Don Quixote that gives it form, as in the picaresque the life of the pícaro gives form to the narrative. We can think here, again, of what Ginés de Pasamonte said jokingly about not finishing his book because his life is unfinished, poking fun at autobiography as a literary convention.

The book has to end with Don Quixote's death; death is a form of closure that everyone understands; it gives life shape, as Francisco de Quevedo, the great seventeenth-century poet, said. He has a poem about death in which he ends by saying that death will organize his life, will give it meaning. So death provides an end toward which everything will seem to have been pointing. Aristotelian plots are artificial. They say "tick-tock" and will make sense if you believe there is a tight concert to the world and to history or if you believe in Providence. In this sense, Cervantes is showing that the novel is a form that cannot be bound by these artificial shapes of art, like the epic and like tragedy, but by the shape of life as everyone understands it.

This is profoundly so when we take into account that Cervantes' own death is near as he writes about Don Quixote's death. This is also the reason there is, for instance, no closure to the story of Ana Félix, Ricote's daughter. One may ask also, why is there so little about Don Quixote's birth and youth? One could say that the only life of Don Quixote that is worth knowing is his life as the mad knight, that everything else is of little consequence. So it is the life that Don Quixote gave himself that is important in the conception, execution, and structure of the book; but it is a life, not a completed action in the Aristotelian sense. Why not end the book, then, by making him sane? A sane Don Quixote would close the plot of Don Quixote's metalife, his life as art and literature. One answer would be to say that only by making him die can Cervantes blur the distinction between our daily lives and the invented lives of literature; both have endings with significance. So Don Quixote's death as Don Quixote and his rebirth as Alonso Quixano are not enough to close the book; Alonso Quixano also had to die, but only if the theme of the book is—as I believe it is—the unreality of worldly life and our hope for a real life after death.

I am going to mention what some major authors said about the shape of the *Quixote*, since we can now look at it as a whole, and I will then get to the author I mentioned before, Miguel de Unamuno. Unamuno was a philosopher and also a writer, a novelist, a poet, a thinker in general. He was the president of the University of Salamanca, what we would call today a public intellectual. He was a Basque, born in Bilbao in 1864, and he died in Salamanca in 1936, just at the beginning of the Spanish Civil War. You may have heard the titles of some of his books, *Del sentimiento trágico de la vida, On the Tragic Sense of Life*, a book I recommend you read, *La agonía de cristianismo, The Agony of Christianity*, and a very, very well known novel called *Niebla, Mist*, from 1914. In 1905 Unamuno published *Vida de Don Quijote y Sancho, The Life of Don Quixote and Sancho*, which is a commentary, chapter by chapter, on the *Quixote*, a very sui generis kind of commentary.

Unamuno liked to be outrageous. For instance, he says he believes, or feigns to believe, in the real existence of Don Quixote and Sancho, claiming that Cervantes, a mediocre writer, by a stroke of luck got to write the story written about the pair by one Cide Hamete Benengeli. This is his conceit. He riles against Cervantes. To Unamuno, there is no assurance that Don Quixote will find a life after death, stressing that, perhaps, this life is all there is and that it is like God's dream; so he hopes God will go on dreaming us, he says, humorously, because if he stops dreaming, we will all disappear along with the universe. God gave us the desire to be immortal, like him, and created a symbol of it in Don Quixote, who does what he does because he wants to be immortal, and so Unamuno mourns Don Quixote's passing and riles against Cervantes for trivializing his death, and he affirms that at least Don Quixote passed on his madness to Sancho. You remember in the last scene, where Sancho says to Don Quixote, "Don't die, please, let us go on now!" And so it is Sancho who will carry on with the madness. Unamuno goes on to say that Antonia Quijana, the niece, does marry a sensible, boring man who never heard of chivalric romances, so therefore she inherits her uncle's estate and forces her husband to live a humdrum life devoid of adventure.

Dulcinea, or Aldonza Lorenzo, on the other hand, does understand her elevation to ideal lady, and she leads men to heroic action; that is, the ideal of such a lady leads men to ideal action, meaning to take risks. She and Sancho keep alive, according to Unamuno, the religion of Don Quixote, which is on the wane in Spain as he writes his book in 1905. To him, this defeat signals the end of *quijotismo,* this having been defeated by the upstart American nation, and he longs for a return of the Quixotic spirit to Spain, one that rebels against commonplace reality and abhors mediocrity and submissiveness. Unamuno belonged to the so-called Generation of '98, a group of writers who all wrote about the miseries of Spain at the turn of the century, particularly complaining about the defeat at the hands of the United States in the Spanish–American War of 1898.

Jorge Luis Borges wrote a marvelous essay about the last chapter of the *Quixote.* He points out, as I have mentioned before, that the one quality

Figure 22. Pablo Picasso, *Don Quixote* (1955). © 2013 Estate of Pablo Picasso /Artists Rights Society (ARS), New York. Photo credit: Erich Lessing/Art Resource, NY.

uniting Don Quixote and Alonso Quixano is courage; Alonso Quixano faces death with courage and serenity. So this is the one quality they have in common, even if one is sane and the other is mad. Borges writes, "Cervantes, without a doubt, could have imagined a more astonishing episode [to bring about Don Quixote's return to sanity], but chose something more convincing and more mysterious: the obscure process of sleep. What happens to us as we sleep, from what mysterious world do we return when we awaken?"[6] This is what Borges picks up on with those six hours of sleep, six hours of sleep are like death, so that Don Quixote dies and is resurrected as Alonso Quixano. Borges remarks on what he calls the "lateral and casual way" in which Don Quixote dies at the end of a sentence. If you have followed the ending, there is a sentence that ends, "By which I mean to say he died"; "Quiero decir que . . . murió." Borges writes, "It is the last of many cruelties that Cervantes has visited upon his hero. Perhaps this cruelty is a form of modesty, and Cervantes and Don Quixote understand each other well and forgive each other."[7] Borges claims that the whole book was written for this last scene of death.

I am going to finish with Pablo Picasso's *Quixote* (fig. 22). Picasso was a Spanish painter, although he lived in France most of his life. But he was a Spanish painter born in Málaga in 1881, and he died in 1973. I left Picasso for last. I think Picasso's *Quixote* is so schematic because he considers him an archetype, and archetypes are schematic by nature. Notice the skeletal Rocinante made up of lines, the plump Sancho, and the donkey's ears. I think the donkey's ears are its signature. In Spanish *burro* means 'donkey,' and it also means someone who is dumb. You have pointed ears like that, and it says you are a donkey. So this is why the donkey's ears are so prominent. Picasso has injected some humor into his painting, which I think is quite appropriate. The windmills in the background are Don Quixote's own signature, and the bright sun beating down on him is Castile's hot sun, which is present through much of the novel. But what is not so evident, it seems to me, until you look for a while, is that Don Quixote's figure is like a question mark. So I leave you with that question mark of Picasso's.

CHAPTER 24

Cervantes' Death and Legacy

Required Readings

Cervantes, *Don Quixote,* Part II, chaps. 71–74, 961–82.

Cervantes, "The Deceitful Marriage." In *Exemplary Stories,* 237–49.

Cervantes, "The Dialogue of the Dogs." In *Exemplary Stories,* 250–305.

Miguel de Cervantes died in Madrid on April 23, 1616. In the last five years of his life Cervantes published the *Exemplary Novels,* in 1613; *The Voyage to Parnassus,* in 1614, which is a long poem in which he passes judgment on the poets of the period; Part II of the *Quixote,* which appeared in 1615; and also in 1615 his volume of theater, called *Eight Plays and Eight New Interludes Never Before Performed.* In 1617 *The Trials of Persiles and Sigismunda* was published posthumously. Let me repeat a quotation from the biographical essay by Manuel Durán that opens the *Casebook:* "[Cervantes] died in Madrid on April 23, 1616, at peace with himself and with the world, having received the last sacraments, and was buried in the convent of the Trinitarian nuns. He died without bitterness or regrets since he had been fully conscious of his merit, indeed of his genius, and was aware that his literary creations would endure: a writer cannot hope for a greater source of consolation" (31). Later reconstructions of that convent building led to the disappearance of Cervantes' bones. Durán adds, in a quotation that I have also used before and that contains a statement by Ángel del Río:

337

Objectively, Cervantes' life was not a success story. He was sel-
dom in full control: he was too poor; for many years he lacked
public recognition. Yet, as Ángel del Río points out, "There is no
reason to lament Cervantes' misfortunes nor the mediocrity of
his daily life. He could thus, through an experience which is sel-
dom obtained when the writer is successful and wealthy, know,
observe and feel the beat of Spanish life in its greatness and its
poverty, in its heroic fantasy and in the sad reality of an immi-
nent decadence. He was to leave in his books the most faithful
image of this life, reflected in multiple perspectives with bitter-
sweet irony and penetrating humor." (31)

In his time Cervantes never attained the recognition of Lope de Vega, whom
Cervantes criticized and admired at the same time. But Cervantes was a
greater writer than Lope; history has confirmed this fact. Though Lope de-
serves a prominent place in the Western canon, he is not at the same level
as Cervantes. Lope never created a figure of universal appeal like Don Quixote, even though he created thousands of characters and wrote hundreds of
plays, perhaps a thousand, many of them masterpieces, including *Fuenteove-
juna* and *El caballero de Olmedo*. This is all true. But he was not Cervantes.

Ironically, though, in his lifetime Lope was tremendously successful.
His story is really a successful one: he became rich, he had a great following, and his name was even synonymous with being of good quality. He
lorded it over the Spanish literary landscape in the early seventeenth century. Lope fought in the Spanish Armada, he had many women, mistresses,
wives, ten or fifteen children, some of them legitimate, and at the end of his
life he became a priest and impregnated one of his mistresses. A life worthy
of a novel or a movie. In the meantime, Cervantes was chugging along in
Madrid, within blocks of Lope's house, creating a work that was ultimately
superior to Lope's.

One question to ask, as we draw a balance, is whether Cervantes would
have deserved such recognition had he written everything but the *Quixote*.
Would we have such high regard for him if he had published all of his work
minus the *Quixote*? The answer has to be no, though not by far. He would
have been acknowledged as an important writer of short novels on the basis of the *Exemplary Novels*. He was also the author of a mediocre pastoral
romance, *La Galatea,* and some good plays and brilliant *entremeses,* comic
one-act interludes. Remember that he mentions *La Galatea* in the episode
of the scrutiny of the books, but he himself had some critical things to say

about that pastoral romance, and toward the end of his life, in the very last year, he was still thinking of writing a second part. But *La Galatea* was a mediocre work with flashes of brilliance that announced the *Quixote* but that are important only because of that, not in themselves.

Cervantes was also the author of that very uneven and very ambitious Byzantine romance *The Trials of Persiles and Sigismunda*. This is a very odd work, as Byzantine romances tend to be, and Cervantes was deluded into thinking it was going to be the culmination of his work. Well, he was wrong. Authors are often wrong about the worth of what they write, and Cervantes certainly was wrong about this. The book is missing most of the qualities we admire in the *Quixote:* it lacks a central figure as compelling as the mad knight; except for some episodes in Spain where there is a somewhat realistic cast; the geography is strange and abstract; it begins in the snow and ice-bound regions of the North Pole and ends in Rome; the dialogues are stilted, not like the ones in the *Quixote,* where Sancho speaks in his very folksy way; and it is a very digressive novel. Because Cervantes was the author of the *Quixote,* it has some moments that we see as being brilliant and some odd and interesting features. For instance, the characters carry around a banner depicting their adventures so that whenever somebody asks them where they have been they just unfurl it and there it is. The *Persiles* is important because it was written by the author of the *Quixote.*

As a playwright, Cervantes was a master of the entremeses I have mentioned, which have many characteristics in common with the *Quixote,* particularly the funny parts of the *Quixote.* But his full-length plays were stiff and neoclassical because he followed the rules of the *preceptistas,* those who had read Aristotle's *Poetics.* You remember the discussions among the characters of Part I, especially those involving the canon of Toledo, about the plays being written at the time, where Cervantes, through his characters, is criticizing Lope for not following those rules. Cervantes did follow the rules, for the most part, and his plays turned out to be duds. Some are okay, but they are not that good. It is one of those ironies of literary history that Cervantes was so wildly imaginative and daring in prose fiction yet timid and conservative when it came to the theater.

The high point of Cervantes' production other than the *Quixote* was the *Exemplary Novels. Novela,* the word we use in Spanish for 'novel' today, did not exist in Cervantes' time. Novela was *nouvelle,* that is, a short novel or a long short story, like the ones we have read: "Rinconete and Cortadillo," "The Glass Graduate," and the ones in Part I of the *Quixote.* Some of the *Novelas ejemplares* are true masterpieces of the genre and can stand next to the greatest stories by Cervantes' Italian predecessors Giovanni Boccaccio, whom I have mentioned many times, and Matteo Bandello, whom I have also mentioned before. Now, I mentioned them when we discussed some of these novels, mainly "The Glass Graduate" and "Rinconete and Cortadillo." Today, I am going to speak about "The Deceitful Marriage" and "The Dialogue of the Dogs," two connected novels that wind up the volume of the *Exemplary Novels*.

As we approach these two novels we have to return to the picaresque. Let me summarize again why the picaresque was so important in the development of prose fiction. In the picaresque there is for the first time, except for *Celestina*—although *Celestina* was a dialogue in and of itself—a dramatic dialogue, not a narrative. It was not a story with a narrator but the representation of everyday life and common people, with an emphasis on poor people engaged in the struggle for existence in a setting that is contemporaneous with the author and the reader; both the author and the reader recognize the setting as being their own. It is the present. There is no fancy, faraway geography, as in the romances of chivalry and the Byzantine romances; there is no remote time, like the magical time of fantastic stories; the picaresque novels take place in the here and now.

The protagonist is no hero by conventional literary standards. On the contrary, he or she—there are feminine picaresques, and I will be talking about one today—is a minor criminal in trouble with the law, and, in fact, the central conceit of novels like *Lazarillo de Tormes* and *Guzmán de Alfarache* is that the text is a confession or deposition addressed by the accused delinquent to a figure in authority. So the picaresque is an indictment of society written in the form of the legal documents used by the authorities to enmesh the pícaro in the net of the law. We saw how Don Quixote and Sancho themselves are fugitives from justice and are finally apprehended by that funny police officer of the Holy Brotherhood who cannot read very well. The picaresque makes it possible for the novel to depict contemporary society and common social types, such as the ones appearing and acquiring relevance in the sixteenth and seventeenth centuries, as this is the beginning of a leveling of society that is moving toward the eighteenth and nineteenth century and of political revolutions that you are very familiar with.

These kinds of characters begin to appear in paintings as well as in novels, if you remember the paintings by Velázquez that we have looked at during the semester. Rafael Salillas, whom I have mentioned before, was a brilliant Spanish criminologist of the late nineteenth and early twentieth century. He claimed that the picaresque was the origin of the social sciences, specifically of sociology and criminology. That is, sociology and criminology find their source in these kinds of picaresque novels that depict the lower strata of society in great detail. He includes Cervantes' work among those works he places at the origin of the social sciences. So it is, to me, very suggestive that Cervantes chose to wind up his volume of *Exemplary Novels* with these two novellas in the picaresque style. Not picaresque per se because Cervantes never wrote a picaresque novel in the strict sense, but novels with a picaresque ambience and cast of characters.

The volume consists of a prologue and twelve stories. Remember, I talked about that number because if "The Pretended Aunt" was by Cervantes, maybe he did not include it because he wanted to avoid the number thirteen. But in any case, there are twelve stories, and these two, "The Deceitful Marriage" and "The Dialogue of the Dogs," are the final ones. The order of stories in such a volume is always meaningful, so to me it is significant that the volume should end with these interlocking stories.

As we saw with Roque Guinart, the Catalan bandit, with Ginés de Pasamonte, the galley slave, and then later the master puppeteer, and Monipodio in "Rinconete and Cortadillo," Cervantes often paints a sympathetic portrait of criminal types. At least, he never paints one that is one-sidedly negative, and he seems to have a liking for these characters. One reason may be that, like Don Quixote, who is also a delinquent, as we know, they represent original ways of life, different from mainstream society and hence more interesting and appealing from a literary point of view. If you are good, you are not interesting to literature, for the most part.

So these criminals are interesting because they are criminals. We saw the same tendency in Velázquez, who paints dwarves and near criminals because they are different. Also, criminal life—and this would go back to Salillas—could represent the origins of societal norms or how societal norms develop, norms that emerge out of the clash of instincts, desires, and laws, and this is why the criminals are attractive. The penchant for criminal types found in the picaresque and in Cervantes is something that will become a staple of the novel; the nineteenth-century novel is peopled by criminals of all kinds, appealing criminals like Jean Valjean in *Les Misérables*.

I move now to these two stories, "The Deceitful Marriage," or "El casamiento engañoso," and "The Dialogue of the Dogs," or "El coloquio de los perros." Notice that these two stories, one embedded in the other, as it were, follow the narrative device called the framed tale, that is, the tale within the tale. It is a device that goes back to the origins of storytelling, in the *Thousand and One Nights,* for instance. This allows Cervantes to finish his volume of stories with one of his cherished infinitely receding sequences.

The volume is open-ended, but it is open-ended unto itself; there could be more and more and more stories if you dug deeper into these stories. There could be yet another story, and, indeed, there is one that is virtual or postponed in the second story, "The Dialogue of the Dogs," because the life story of one of the dogs, named Scipio, is not told. When I wrote an essay on this many years ago I called it "The Life of Scipio," suggesting that my essay was like the telling of this life that was not told in the story.

In "The Deceitful Marriage" marriage is deconstructed, as it were, both as a social institution and as a narrative tool. We should read the story against the backdrop of all the tales about marriage we have read in the *Quixote* and also in the context of "The Pretended Aunt." In fact, "The Deceitful Marriage" is the one story by Cervantes that comes closest in salaciousness to "The Pretended Aunt," whose authorship is contested. That is, it is the dirtiest of Cervantes' stories if "The Pretended Aunt" is not by Cervantes. I am sure you will agree with me, and you will agree even more once you hear my reading of it. Estefanía, the protagonist, is a self-possessed female, a female protagonist like others in Cervantes, including Dorotea, Marcela, and Zoraida. She charts her own course and follows it with cunning and with courage. She is a prostitute, but she is an enterprising, female, Cervantean protagonist. She dupes ensign Campuzano, luring him with her beauty and pretended wealth—we could call it that—mainly, her house, which is not hers.

Notice the detail. I have told you often to look for details in Cervantes. How does she lure the ensign? She has beautiful hands, and that is the first thing the ensign notices when he sees her. Cervantes has a fetish for hands and feet; remember Dorotea? But Estefanía has beautiful hands. She traps the ensign into marrying her, but then it turns out she was not the owner of the house. The true proprietors come back, and she scampers away with the jewels with which he thought he had fooled her—he thought he had fooled her because he boasts that the jewels are counterfeit. It turns out, however, that she had the last laugh because she had infected him with syphilis, a kind of delayed action counterblow by which she wins again. It is clear that what Estefanía did was her modus operandi, and that the ensign was neither her first nor her last victim. The so-called cousin who is present at the wedding was obviously her pimp. Well, not obviously because Cervantes does not make things that obvious, but it is there. Who was this guy? Well, this guy was her pimp, and this is a routine they use to ensnare fools like the ensign Campuzano. He thinks he is going to have a good time and is going to fool her because he is making plans to take off and go back to war once he has had enough of a good time.

What is of interest to me in the story is how Cervantes has manipulated literary conventions. The story begins with a marriage, virtually; that is, it begins where stories normally end and works backward, to undo a union that never took place legitimately. It is a marriage into which they enter presumably without pretense or illusions. She tells him she is no virgin, that she has had her life, and he does not care. He is not a wealthy aristocrat by any means, and they know it. So they enter into marriage under no illusions, but the marriage is based on the worst forms of deceit. It also ends with an inversion that should have been a beginning: the man is fooled, and the woman flees. In traditional stories, it is the opposite: the woman is fooled, and the man flees.

Marriage is normally how stories end. They bring closure to the action, the restoration of order, and the continuation of the species. Here, however, Cervantes has inverted the formula: the story begins with a marriage. As we have seen, and as I have said many times—and don't take it as a warning—everything that happens before marriage is the stuff of comedy in Cervantes, everything that happens after marriage is the stuff of tragedy. But here, surely because the marriage is phony, what follows is comical, and worse. The marriage, by the way, would have been annulled under Spanish law, and even under church canon law had the ensign sued Estefanía for misrepresenting herself: she was not the owner of the house. But he could not sue her because he, too, had misrepresented his wealth; the jewels were counterfeit, and he had plans to quit the premises as soon as he could.

The emblem of all of these deceits is the house, which should have, on the contrary and conventionally, provided the foundation of the marriage. It is in the house that they spend a brief period of matrimonial bliss. This is the engaño part that precedes the desengaño. Legally and traditionally the house is the concrete site of marriage, and in Spanish the word for marriage, a word that is in the title of the story, is *casamiento*. *Casa* means 'house' in Spanish.

The plot of "The Deceitful Marriage" is very, very disturbing because it leads to total disorder, to a dissolution of the social pact, the social contract altogether. This is why I find it such a troubling and powerful story. Husband and wife—though they are not really husband and wife—disappear, never to be heard from again: Estefanía vanishes, she has to vanish like the galley slaves because the authorities are probably after her, and Campuzano winds up in the hospital with a venereal disease from which most of those infected never recovered. It is as if the story, with this formal play of inversions, is hinting not at tragedy but at something perhaps worse, if that is possible: the disappearance of all bonds, the unraveling of the fabric that holds human society together.

This is what is hinted at in this extremely disquieting story. Indeed, what follows is the story of the ensign Campuzano in the hospital and the hallucination that leads him to write the next story, "The Dialogue of the Dogs." It is ironic, in a way that I find bitterer than is normal in Cervantes, that what leads to literary creation here is not just a disease, but the disease of love, syphilis, which was called at the time in Spanish, el mal francés, 'the French disease.' The love madness of courtly love poets is literalized here; love madness is also a love disease. It literalizes a venereal illness. "The Dialogue of the Dogs" is like Estefanía's and Campuzano's child, the product of their deceitful marriage. I find this to be a very alarming suggestion.

As for "The Dialogue of the Dogs," let me begin by considering the names of the dogs, the heroic Scipio, Cipión in Spanish, and the picaresque Berganza. Historically, there were two Scipios, the one who took and destroyed Carthage, and his son, who destroyed the Spanish town of Numancia, an event on which Cervantes may have based his most successful play. So Cervantes knew much about Scipio. Berganza is derived from bergante, a slightly old-fashioned word now. Bergante is a 'rogue,' a 'rascal,' whereas Scipio is a heroic name, the name of a military commander. The two dogs make up a pair, like Don Quixote and Sancho, if you think about it, the sort of picaresque Berganza and the military Scipio. Scipio's life is the one not told. It would have been a mock-heroic dog's life, I suppose. Ensign Campuzano's predicament linking illness and creativity is a spoof, as I have said, of the sick lover-poet able to compose poetry because of his condition. This will become a romantic trope in the nineteenth century, but here this illness is dramatically and literally an illness of love of the lowest kind. Remember that the only cure at the time, other than some potions, was to let the patient sweat it out in the hospital. Some survived, but not very many. Notice also the ironic name of the hospital. It is Hospital de la Resurrección, and it is through a kind of resurrection that ensign Campuzano comes out of the hospital after he has sweated out his syphilis, or at least some of it.

Cervantes skirts the supernatural in the story with the idea that dogs can talk. The supernatural never appears in Cervantes' works, but he leaves open here the possibility that the story of the talking dogs is merely a hallucination on the part of Campuzano, who is ill, and in his illness and fever he imagines this. It can also be a literary ruse on the part of the ensign; I mean, it is the character within the story that is making this up, Cervantes would say. He wants to leave the origin of his literary creation in an ambiguous state. To me it is very suggestive—I do not know if you found it so—that he falls asleep while his lawyer friend, called Graduate Peralta in your translation (*licenciado Peralta,* which means a 'lawyer'), is reading his story. It is also very significant that the reader is a lawyer, someone trained to read texts and ascertain their truthfulness. This is another ironic reading scene.

On one level, it is as if the text belonged to the realm of dreams, the fact that the author is sleeping, and it is as if the reader is tapping directly into his dreams as he is sleeping. This occurs to me because the author is asleep while his text is being read. On another level, it is as if there is a necessary gap between the creator and the text for the reader to judge it independently. That is, he is asleep, he is no longer in control of the text, the text is now in the hands of the reader, and it is for the reader to determine whether it is true or not; this is why he is asleep. Of course, this is also a way of having the creator do something while the other one reads. The other way would have been to have him go to the market or go for a walk, but I think this is much more suggestive, the fact that he falls asleep. I like to think of it as the reader tapping directly into his subconscious as he sleeps.

Peralta, in a way, is a stand-in for us, the readers. He offers a literary judgment at the end, pronouncing the story good, though hardly believable, and encouraging his friend to go ahead and write the next life. Notice, in the context of my discussion of the ending of the *Quixote* in the last lecture, that life here is the shape of the story: a life, the life of Berganza, and the next life is going to be the life of Cipión, Scipio. It is also following in the autobiographical shape of the picaresque that we saw when we discussed the figure of Ginés de Pasamonte, who has written his life in prison. There is more than a hint, too, that the story the ensign tells or writes through the dog is an encoded autobiography—that it is about his own life. This is a picaresque autobiography in which the pícaro pretends to be a dog. It is a very ingenious and original turn on Cervantes' part. Why is it autobiographical? Particularly because when he takes the manuscript from his pocket he takes it out of his *seno. Seno* means 'bosom'; he is taking it out of his heart in a way, so this suggests to me that this is ensign Campuzano's story but deflected into the life of this dog.

It is quite interesting that literature issues out of these tawdry living conditions and figures. Literary creation emerges here, as it did in the case of Ginés de Pasamonte, who wrote his life while he was in prison, and also in the case of Cervantes himself, whose life, if not quite as tawdry, sometimes was like that when he was a prisoner, a captive in Algiers, and the couple of times when he was jailed in Spain for irregularities in his accounts when he was collecting for the Spanish Armada. So I think this is Cervantes' take on the origins of modern literature; it originates in these conditions and out of figures like these.

The point is that Cervantes is showing the virtual workings of the literary imagination, which takes the real and the tawdry or the seedy life of the ensign and deflects it into the life of the dog, which has a slightly classical form because of the fables where animals speak, which are mentioned in the text. The uncertain origin of the dogs, who might be the transformed sons of that witch, in that marvelous scene with the witches that I am sure you remember and that allude or harken back to *Celestina,* or they could have been simply dogs born, where? In the slaughterhouse of Seville. Seville is the capital of picaresque life, and the slaughterhouse seems to be the capital within the capital of picaresque life. But Cervantes is also leaving the origin of the story in an air of indeterminacy, like Don Quixote's origins. I think the significance of the ending of the story, again, back to the infinitely receding sequences, is that it brings about no closure at all to the volume.

I'll make a little digression here before we come to the end of the lecture to discuss Kafka's parable. Kafka (1883–1924), is the Czech author who wrote, in German, such masterpieces as *The Metamorphosis* (1915), *The Trial* (1925), and *The Castle* (1926), in which he presented a world ruled by arbitrary and mysterious bureaucratic laws, by which the characters, impelled by obscure forces, seem to abide. He never published his work, which he ordered to be destroyed upon his death, an instruction that fortunately was not followed. I think the following brief text—it is just a paragraph long— shows to what extent Kafka connected with the core of Cervantes' literary imagination, with Cervantes' notion and feel for literary creativity. The text is entitled "The Truth about Sancho Panza," and it reads in its entirety,

> Without making any boast of it Sancho Panza succeeded in the course of years, by devouring a great number of romances of chivalry and adventure in the evening and night hours, in so diverting from him his demon, whom he later called Don Quixote, that his demon thereupon set out in perfect freedom on the maddest exploits, which, however, for the lack of preordained object, which should have been Sancho Panza himself, harmed

nobody. A free man, Sancho Panza philosophically followed Don
Quixote on his crusades, perhaps out of a sense of responsibility,
and had of them a great and edifying entertainment to the end
of his days.[1]

Kafka is turning Cervantes' fiction upside down, but within the spirit of Cervantes, by making Sancho the inventor of Don Quixote and following him
around afterward. The whole fiction comes out of Sancho's demon, that is,
the demon of a common man, like those both Kafka and Cervantes like to
invent—"The Glass Graduate," for example, is another common man—and
also, like other authors in Cervantes, Sancho's creation gets out of hand and
acquires a life of its own. I think this is Kafka's reading of Cervantes. I think
it is a very profound reading even if it is, or perhaps especially because it is,
so brief.

I also wish to bring up the Borges story "Pierre Menard, Author of the
Quixote," one of his most famous pieces. Pierre Menard is this French minor
poet who decides to rewrite the Quixote; not just rewrite the Quixote but
rewrite it word for word, as Cervantes had written it, the idea being that it
is much more difficult to write the Quixote in seventeenth-century Spanish,
especially by a Frenchman, than it was for Cervantes to write in his own
time and his own language. It is a big literary joke on the part of Borges,
but at the same time Borges is unsettling the romantic notion of the link
between creator and work. But Borges shows he cannot completely unsettle
that notion because Pierre Menard dies of the effort it takes him to carry out
this task, which he could naturally never finish.[2]

The task he sets for himself is an impossible one. Borges was also re-
acting, in 1939 when he wrote the story, to what he considered to be proto-
fascist readings of the Quixote by Spanish scholars and writers. Remember,
the Spanish Civil War has just ended, and the Franco regime was promoting
Hispanidad, Spanishness. Borges is trying to show that Cervantes' great creation does not belong to any single language or any single national tradition,
but that it can, potentially, be written or rewritten by anyone. Also, he is
underlining something he himself said with Cervantean self-deprecation,
that once you write something that is good, it does not belong to you anymore, it belongs to the literary tradition. Borges's story implies that Cervantes' creation has escaped him because it now belongs to the language of
literature, not to him.

Let's finish by talking a bit about Cervantes' death, going back to the
beginning of today's class. I think Cervantes identified with the death of

Don Quixote and Alonso Quixano because he feels that life as fiction has to come to an end, and a form of truth must be reached on the brink of death. It is a form of truth which, ironically, literature has prepared him for through the understanding of desengaño. Cervantes seems to be saying that he, like Don Quixote, is renouncing a life of make-believe. So what is the sense of the novel's ending? Perhaps it is the feeling of sadness, of regret, that the book, the madness, the entertainment, and the fun have to come to an end, like everything else. It is not so much sense as in meaning, as sense as in feeling, not *sentido* as *significado,* but *sentido* as *sentimiento.* It is in this sense that Unamuno uses the word *sentimiento* in the *The Tragic Sense of Life.*

This is the sense of the ending of the *Quixote,* it is a sense of sadness redolent with potential meanings, but these are meanings we cannot understand all together. In the prologue to the *Persiles,* which is Cervantes' farewell, he presents himself as a man resigned to his impending death and content with his accomplishments, going back to what Durán said in the quotation I cited at the very beginning of my lecture today. The dedication to *Persiles*—the dedication, not the prologue, although they must have been contemporary to each other—was dated April 19, 1616, that is, four days before Cervantes' death. He says he was given extreme unction, the last rites in the Catholic Church, and then he writes the following. I am going to quote it in Spanish and then in English because I am going to say something about the rhythm of the prose. So I need the original:

> Sucedió, pues, lector amantísimo, que viniendo otros dos amigos y yo del famoso lugar de Esquivias, por mil causas famoso, una por sus ilustres linajes y otra por sus ilustrísimos vinos, sentí que a mis espaldas venía picando con gran prisa uno que, al parecer, traía deseo de alcanzarnos, y aun lo mostró dándonos voces, que no picásemos tanto. Esperámosle, y llegó sobre una borrica un estudiante pardal, porque todo venía vestido de pardo, antiparras, zapato redondo y espada con contera, valona bruñida y con trenzas iguales; verdad es no traía más de dos, porque se le venía a un lado la valona por momentos, y él traía sumo trabajo y cuenta de enderezarla.
>
> Llegando a nosotros dijo:
>
> –¿Vuesas mercedes van a alcanzar algún oficio o prebenda a la corte, pues allá está su Illustrísima de Toledo y su Majestad, ni más ni menos, según la priesa con que caminan, que en verdad

que a mi burra se le ha cantado el víctor de caminante más de una vez?

A lo cual respondió uno de mis compañeros:

–El rocín del señor Miguel de Cervantes tiene la culpa desto, porque es algo pasilargo.

Apenas hubo oído el estudiante el nombre de Cervantes, cuando, apeándose de su cabalgadura, cayéndosele aquí el cojín y allí el portamanteo, que con toda esta autoridad caminaba, arremetió a mí, y acudiendo asirme de la mano izquierda, dijo:

–¡Sí, sí; éste es el manco sano, el famoso todo, el escritor alegre, y finalmente el regocijo de las musas!

Yo, que en tan poco espacio vi el grande encomio de mis alabanzas, parecióme ser descortesía no corresponder a ellas. Y así, abrazándole por el cuello, donde le eché a perder de todo punto la valona, le dije:

–Ése es un error donde han caído muchos aficionados ignorantes. Yo, señor, soy Cervantes, pero no el regocijo de las musas, ni ninguna de las demás baratijas que ha dicho. Vuesa merced vuelva a cobrar su burra, y suba, y caminemos en buena conversación lo poco que nos falta de camino.

Hízolo así el comedido estudiante, tuvimos algún tanto más las riendas, y con paso asentado seguimos nuestro camino, en el cual se trató de mi enfermedad, y el buen estudiante me desahució al momento, diciendo:

–Esta enfermedad es de hidropesía, que no la sanará toda el agua del mar Océano que dulcemente se bebiese. Vuesa merced, señor Cervantes, ponga tasa al beber, no olvidándose de comer, que con esto sanará sin otra medicina alguna.

–Esto me han dicho muchos-respondí yo-, pero así puedo dejar de beber a todo mi beneplácito, como si para sólo eso hubiese nacido. Mi vida se va acabando, y, al paso de las efemérides de mis pulsos, que, a más tardar, acabarán su carrera este domingo, acabaré yo la de mi vida. En fuerte punto ha llegado vuesa merced a conocerme, pues no me queda espacio para mostrarme agradecido a la voluntad que vuesa merced me ha mostrado.

En esto llegamos a la puente de Toledo, y yo entré por ella [they are going into Madrid], y él se apartó al entrar por la de Segovia. Lo que se dirá de mi suceso, tendrá la fama cuidado, mis amigos gana de decilla, y yo mayor gana de escuchalla.

Tornéle a abrazar, volvióseme a ofrecer, picó a su burra, y
dejóme tan mal dispuesto como él iba caballero en su burra, a
quien había dado gran ocasión a mi pluma para escribir donaires; pero no son todos los tiempos unos. Tiempo vendrá, quizá,
donde, anudando este roto hilo, diga lo que aquí me falta, y lo
que sé convenía. ¡Adiós, gracias; adiós, donaires; adiós, regoci-
jados amigos; que yo me voy muriendo, y deseando veros presto
contentos en la otra vida![3]

In English:

It so happened, dearest reader, as two friends and I were coming from the famous town of Esquivias, famous for a thousand
reasons, one of them being its illustrious families and another its
even more illustrious wines, that I perceived someone behind me
spurring his mount on in a great hurry. He apparently wanted to
overtake us and soon made that clear by calling out for us not to
spur on so urgently. We waited for him, and on a she-ass up came
a drab student, drab because he came dressed all in rustic brown
with leggings, round-toed shoes, a sword in a chaped scabbard,
and a starch laced collar with its matching ties; the fact of the
matter is that he only had two of these ties to hold it on, so every
other minute the collar kept falling over to one side and he was at
great pains to keep it straight.

Catching up to us he said, "You, sirs, must be on your way
to court to obtain some office or benefice—for his Most illustrious Grace of Toledo and His Majesty themselves are doubtless
there—judging by the hurry with which you're traveling, since
even my ass, which has been praised more than once for her
speed, couldn't catch you." To this one of my companions replied,
"It's the fault of Señor Miguel de Cervantes' nag, which is somewhat long-stepping."

Scarcely had the student heard the name Cervantes when
he dismounted from his pack animal, sending his saddlebags
flying in one direction and his valise in another—he traveled
so completely outfitted—and rushed up to me, seizing my left
hand and saying, "Yes, yes, this is the complete cripple, the completely famous and comic writer, and lastly, the delight of the
muses!"

I, who in so short a space of time saw such great compliments in my praise, felt it would have been discourteous not to respond to them. And so, embracing him around the neck, whereby I destroyed his collar all together, I said to him: "That is an error into which many of my uninformed admirers have fallen. I, sir, am Cervantes, but not the delight of the muses or any other foolish things that you mentioned. Round up your ass, mount up, and let's pass the brief remainder of our journey in pleasant conversation."

The obliging student did just that, we reined in slightly, and then resumed our trip at a more leisurely pace. As we traveled we talked about my illness and the good student immediately diagnosed me a hopeless case, saying: "This sickness is dropsy, incurable even if you were to drink all of the waters of the Ocean Sea made sweet. Señor Cervantes, sir, you should limit your drinking and don't forget to eat, for thereby you will recover without any other medicine."

"That's what many have told me," I replied, "but I just can't give up the pleasure of drinking all I want, for it almost seems I was born to it. My life's race is slowing at the rate of my pulse, and by this Sunday at the latest it will complete its course and with it my life. You, sir, have made my acquaintance at a difficult moment, for there isn't enough time left to express my gratitude for the goodwill you've shown me."

At this point, we arrived at the Toledo bridge where I crossed into the city and he rode off to enter by the Segovia road. As to what may be said of this incident, fame will take care to report it, my friends will take pleasure in telling it, and I even more pleasure in hearing it. Once again we embraced each other, he spurred his mount and left me just as ill at ease as he was in trying to be a gentleman on that ass. He had afforded my pen a great opportunity to be witty, but you can't always make of one moment what you can of another. A time may come, perhaps, when I shall tie up this broken thread and say what I failed to here and what would have been fitting. Goodbye, humor; goodbye, wit; goodbye, merry friends; for I am dying and hope to see you soon, happy in the life to come![4]

Here we find the same Cervantes of the *Quixote* prologues.

There are five points I want to make. One, the prologue is a dialogue, as was the prologue in Part I and throughout Cervantes' work, instead of an expository piece in the first person. He needs to create another person to tell the story of his own self. Why? Do these dialogues reflect those going on in his mind? They do reflect his ironic stance before his own sense of self and before his own sense of the truth, because this is the perspectivism we have seen throughout. Two, here, as so many times in the *Quixote*, we have another student, complete with funny details about his clothing. Students are seekers of knowledge, readers who are of great interest to Cervantes. The details, like all details in Cervantes, are revealing of character, of personality. This is a very economical way of talking about this guy's personality, by showing his vanity through the clothes he is wearing. Three, the scene takes place on the road, a symbol of time and of life, as in the *Quixote*. Four—and I think this is the subtlest and this is why I wanted you to hear it in Spanish—the rhythm of the prose and of the story itself seems to echo that of the trotting horses; the trotting of the horses and the various paces that the horses follow are marking time, and time, its fleetingness, is the theme of the piece. Life's race and life's journey coalesce as death approaches and is marked by the trotting of the horses and by the rhythm of the prose. Five, Cervantes deals ironically with his late fame, which comes when he is near death. It is untimely because by now it is of little consolation or benefit to him. So we have here the same self-deprecating Cervantes we have learned to love. It is in that same spirit that I ask of him, wherever he happens to be, and that I ask of you, forgiveness for my own shortcomings in commenting on his work. Thank you very much.

Notes

CHAPTER 1
Introduction

1. Ian Watt, *Myths of Modern Individuality: Faust, Don Quixote, Don Juan, Robinson Crusoe* (New York: Cambridge University Press, 1996).
2. Roberto González Echevarría, "Introduction," in *The Ingenious Hidalgo Don Quixote de la Mancha,* by Miguel de Cervantes Saavedra, trans. John Rutherford (New York: Penguin Books, 2001), vii.
3. Sebastián de Covarrubias Horozco, *Tesoro de la lengua castellana o española,* ed. Ignacio Arellano and Rafael Zafra, 1099 (Madrid: Editorial Iberoamericana, 2006). My translation.
4. Ibid., 898.
5. György Lukács, *The Theory of the Novel: A Historico-Philosophical Essay on the Forms of Great Epic Literature,* trans. Anna Bostock (1920; reprint Cambridge: MIT Press, 1971), 88.
6. Lowry Nelson, "Introduction," in *Cervantes: A Collection of Critical Essays,* ed. Lowry Nelson, 4 (Englewood Cliffs, N.J. : Prentice-Hall, 1969).

CHAPTER 2
Chivalric Romances and Picaresque Novels

1. Chris Baldick, *The Concise Oxford Dictionary of Literary Terms* (New York: Oxford University Press, 1990), 191.
2. Fernando de Rojas, *Celestina,* trans. Margaret Sayers Peden, ed. and intro. Roberto González Echevarría (New Haven: Yale University Press, 2009).
3. Jane Kramer, "Me Myself, and I," *New Yorker,* 7 September 2009, 34–41.

CHAPTER 3
Don Quixote and Sancho on the Road

1. Stephen Greenblatt, *Renaissance Self-Fashioning* (Chicago: University of Chicago Press, 1980).

CHAPTER 4
Literature and Life

1. Charles Singleton, "The Poet's Number at the Center," *Modern Language Notes* 80 (1965): 1–10.

CHAPTER 5
Ugliness and Improvisation

1. Karl Ludwig Selig, "Don Quijote, I/16: The 'Escaramuza' at the Inn, and/or Structure within a Structure," *Teaching Language Through Literature* 20 (1980): 4.
2. Thomas A. Lathrop, "Contradictions in the Quijote Explained," in *Jewish Culture and the Hispanic World*, ed. Samuel G. Armistead and Mishael M. Caspi, 297–301 (Newark, Del.: Juan de la Cuesta, 2001).

CHAPTER 6
Modern Authors

1. Wallace Stevens, "Sunday Morning," in *Harmonium* (New York: Alfred A. Knopf, 1923), 103.
2. Wallace Stevens, "Man Carrying Thing," in *The Collected Poems of Wallace Stevens* (New York: Alfred A. Knopf, 1954), 350–51.
3. Anthony Grafton, *New Worlds, Ancient Texts: The Power of Tradition and the Shock of Discovery* (Cambridge: Harvard University Press, 1992), 1.
4. Ibid.

CHAPTER 7
Love and the Law

1. See Roberto González Echevarría, "The Prisoner of Sex (Quijote, I, 22)," in *Love and the Law in Cervantes* (New Haven: Yale University Press, 2005), 1–16.

CHAPTER 8
Memory and Narrative

1. Edward Dudley, "The Wild Man Goes Baroque," in *The Wild Man Within: An Image in Western Thought from the Renaissance to Romanticism*, ed. Edward Dudley and Maximillian E. Novak, 117 (Pittsburgh: University of Pittsburgh Press, 1972).
2. Ibid., 122.
3. Ibid., 128.
4. Ibid., 132.
5. Ibid., 136–37.
6. Frederick de Armas, *Cervantes, Raphael and the Classics* (New York: Cambridge University Press, 1998); Frederick de Armas, ed., *Writing for the Eyes in the Spanish Golden Age* (Lewisburg, Penn.: Bucknell University Press, 2004).
7. Javier Herrero, "Sierra Morena as Labyrinth: From Wilderness to Christian Knighthood," *Forum for Modern Language Studies* 17.1 (1981): 60.
8. Javier Herrero, "The Beheading of the Giant: An Obscene Metaphor in Don Quijote," *Revista Hispánica Moderna* 39.4 (1976): 144–45.

CHAPTER 9
Love Stories Resolved

1. David Quint, *Cervantes's Novel of Modern Times* (Princeton: Princeton University Press, 2003).
2. René Girard, *Deceit, Desire and the Novel,* trans. Yvonne Freccero (Baltimore: Johns Hopkins University Press, 1965), 52.
3. Nicolás Wey Gómez, "The Jealous and the Curious: Freud, Paranoia and Homosexuality in Cervantine Poetics," in *Cervantes and His Postmodern Constituencies,* ed. Anne J. Cruz and Carroll B. Johnson, 170–98 (New York: Garland, 1999).
4. Javier Herrero, "The Beheading of the Giant: An Obscene Metaphor in Don Quijote," *Revista Hispánica Moderna* 39.4 (1976): 148–49.
5. Javier Herrero, "Sierra Morena as Labyrinth: From Wilderness to Christian Knighthood," *Forum for Modern Language Studies* 17.1 (1981): 64–65.
6. Ibid.
7. Ibid., 55.

CHAPTER 10
Fugitives from Justice Caught

1. Américo Castro, *El pensamiento de Cervantes,* ed. Julio Rodríguez-Puértolas (1925; reprint Barcelona: Noguer, 1972), 218. My translation.
2. Ibid., 219.
3. Mikhail Bakhtin, *Rabelais and His World,* trans. Hélène Iswolsky (1964; reprint Bloomington: Indiana University Press, 1984), 281.
4. Ciriaco Morón Arroyo, "La historia del cautivo y el sentido del *Quijote,*" *Iberoromania* 18 (1983): 104. All quotations from Morón Arroyo are my translations.
5. Ibid., 100.
6. Ibid.
7. Ibid., 103.
8. Ibid., 92.
9. Ibid., 96.

CHAPTER 11
The Senses of Endings

1. Peter Russell, *Cervantes* (New York: Oxford University Press, 1985), 51.

CHAPTER 12
On to Part II

1. William H. Hinrichs, *The Invention of the Sequel: Expanding Prose Fiction in Early Modern Spain* (Rochester: Tamesis, 2011).
2. Henry W. Sullivan, *Grotesque Purgatory: A Study of Cervantes's* Don Quixote, Part II (University Park: Pennsylvania State University Press, 1996), 17.
3. Stephen Gilman, "The Apocryphal 'Quixote,'" in *Cervantes Across the Centuries,* ed. Ángel Flores and M. J. Benardete, 247 (New York: Dryden Press, 1947).

4. Jorge Luis Borges, "Pierre Menard, Author of the *Quixote*," in *Collected Fictions*, trans. Andrew Hurley (New York: Viking, 1998), 88–95.
5. Manuel Durán, *Cervantes* (New York: Twayne, 1974), 106.
6. Ibid., 107.
7. Ibid., 110.
8. Ibid., 129.

CHAPTER 13
Renaissance (1605) and Baroque (1615) *Quixotes*

1. Erich Auerbach, *Mimesis: The Representation of Reality in Western Literature*, trans. Willard R. Trask (Princeton: Princeton University Press, 1953).
2. Seth Lerer, "Erich Auerbach," in *The Johns Hopkins Guide to Literary Criticism*, ed. Michael Groden and Martin Kreiswirth, 56 (Baltimore: Johns Hopkins University Press, 1994).
3. José Juan Arrom, *Esquema generacional de las letras hispanoamericanas*, 2d ed. (Bogotá: Instituto Caro y Cuervo, 1977), 66. My translation.
4. René Wellek, *Concepts of Criticism*, ed. Stephen Nichols (New Haven: Yale University Press, 1963), 109–10.

CHAPTER 14
Deceiving and Undeceiving

1. Otis H. Green, *Spain and the Western Tradition: The Castilian Mind in Literature from El Cid to Calderón* (Madison: University of Wisconsin Press, 1966), 4:44.
2. Ibid., 4:49.
3. Quoted in ibid.

CHAPTER 15
Don Quixote's Doubles

1. Vladimir Nabokov, *Lectures on Don Quixote*, ed. Fredson Bowers (New York: Harcourt Brace Jovanovich, 1983).
2. Erich Auerbach, *Mimesis: The Representation of Reality in Western Literature*, trans. Willard R. Trask (Princeton: Princeton University Press, 2003), 357.

CHAPTER 16
Present Varieties of Classical Myths

1. John Sinnigen, "Themes and Structures in the 'Bodas de Camacho,'" *Modern Language Notes* 84.2 (1969): 165.
2. Ibid., 167–68.
3. Ovid, *Metamorphoses*, trans. Frank Justus Miller (Cambridge: Harvard University Press, 1977), 1:189.
4. José Ortega y Gasset, "Tres cuadros del vino (Tiziano, Poussin y Velázquez)," in *Obras completas* (Madrid: Alianza Editorial-Revista del Occidente, 1983), 2:58. My translation.

5. Jonathan Brown, *Velázquez: Painter and Courtier* (New Haven: Yale University Press, 1986), 66.
6. Ibid., 253.

CHAPTER 17
Caves and Puppet Shows

1. Peter Dunn, "La Cueva de Montesinos por fuera y por dentro: estructura épica, fisonomía," in *Modern Language Notes* 88.2 (1973): 202. My translation.
2. Anthony J. Cascardi, "Cervantes and Descartes on the Dream Argument," *Cervantes* 4.2 (1984): 121–22.

CHAPTER 18
Don Quixote and Sancho in the Hands of Frivolous Aristocrats

1. Peter Russell, *Cervantes* (New York: Oxford University Press, 1985), 64–65.
2. Ibid., 66.
3. Ruth El Saffar, *Distance and Control in* Don Quixote: *A Study in Narrative Technique* (Chapel Hill: University of North Carolina Department of Romance Languages, 1974), 92–93.
4. Javier Herrero, *Who Was Dulcinea?* (New Orleans: Graduate School of Tulane University, 1985), 17–18.
5. Joaquín Casalduero, *Sentido y forma del Quijote (1605–1615)* (Madrid: Ediciones Ínsula, 1949), 294. My translation.

CHAPTER 19
Bearded Ladies and Flying Horses

1. Sebastián de Covarrubias Horozco, *Tesoro de la lengua castellana o española,* ed. Ignacio Arellano and Rafael Zafra, 734 (Madrid: Editorial Iberoamericana, 2006). My translation.
2. Joaquín Casalduero, *Sentido y forma del Quijote (1605–1615)* (Madrid: Ediciones Ínsula, 1949), 307. My translation.

CHAPTER 20
King for a Day

1. Ruth El Saffar, *Distance and Control in* Don Quixote: *A Study in Narrative Technique* (Chapel Hill: University of North Carolina Department of Romance Languages, 1974), 92–93.
2. Sigmund Freud, *Totem and Taboo: Resemblances Between the Psychic Lives of Savages and Neurotics,* trans. A. A. Brill (New York: Vintage Books, 1946), 67.
3. Ibid., 69.
4. Ibid.
5. Antonio Carreño Rodríguez, "Costello + Panza = Costanza: Paradigmatic Pairs in Don Quixote and American Popular Culture," *Journal of Popular Film and Television* 37.2 (2009): 80–89.
6. Edwin Williamson, "The Power Struggle Between Don Quixote and Sancho: Four Crises in the Development of Narrative," *Bulletin of Spanish Studies* 84.7 (2007): 857–58.

CHAPTER 21
Borders and Ends

1. Luce López-Baralt, "¿Qué imagen tenían los moriscos de sí mismos?," in *Actes du VIIIe Symposium International d'Etudes Morisques sur: Images des Morisques dans la Litterature et les Arts,* ed. Abdeljelil Temimi (Zaghouan: Fondation Temimi pour la Recherche Scienifique et l'Information, 1999), 151–52, my translation.
2. Raymond R. McCurdy and Alfred Rodríguez, "Algo más sobre la visitación subterránea de Sancho Panza," *Crítica hispánica* 3.2 (1981): 143. My translation.
3. Ibid., 145–46. My translation.

CHAPTER 22
Dancing and Defeat in Barcelona

1. George Mariscal, *Contradictory Subjects: Quevedo, Cervantes, and Seventeenth-Century Spanish Culture* (Ithaca: Cornell University Press, 1991), 162.
2. Ibid.
3. Ibid., 172.
4. Ibid., 174.
5. Manuel Durán, "El Quijote de Avellaneda," in *Suma Cervantina,* ed. J. B. Avalle-Arce and E. C. Riley (London: Tamesis, 1973), 376. My translation.

CHAPTER 23
The Meaning of the End

1. Lowry Nelson, "Introduction," in *Cervantes: A Collection of Critical Essays,* ed. Lowry Nelson, 10 (Englewood Cliffs, N.J. : Prentice-Hall, 1969).
2. Frank Kermode, *The Sense of an Ending: Studies in the Theory of Fiction* (New York: Oxford University Press, 1967), 59.
3. Ibid., 7.
4. Ibid., 44–45.
5. Ibid., 17.
6. Jorge Luis Borges, "Análisis del último capítulo del *Quijote*," *Revista de la Universidad de Buenos Aires,* quinta época, vol. 1 (1956): 30. My translation.
7. Ibid., 36. My translation.

CHAPTER 24
Cervantes' Death and Legacy

1. Franz Kafka, *Parables and Paradoxes: In German and English* (New York: Schocken Books, 1971), 179.
2. Jorge Luis Borges, "Pierre Menard, Author of the *Quixote*," in *Collected Fictions,* trans. Andrew Hurley (New York: Viking, 1998), 88–95.
3. Miguel de Cervantes, *Los trabajos de Persiles y Sigismunda,* ed. Juan Bautista Avalle-Arce (Madrid: Clásicos Castalia, 1986), 47–49.
4. Miguel de Cervantes, *The Trials of Persiles and Sigismunda, a Northern Story,* trans. Celia Richmond Weller and Clark A. Colahan (Los Angeles: University of California Press, 1989), 15–16.

Index

Printed and bound by CPI Group (UK) Ltd, Croydon, CR0 4YY

13/04/2025

14656468-0001